Henry Baur
Huffman 007

EMPEROR WU ZHAO
AND HER
PANTHEON
OF
DEVIS,
DIVINITIES,
AND
DYNASTIC MOTHERS

Sheng Yen Series in Chinese Buddhist Studies

The Sheng Yen Series in Chinese Buddhist Studies
Chün-fang Yü, series editor

Following the endowment of the Sheng Yen Professorship in Chinese Buddhist Studies, the Sheng Yen Education Foundation and the Chung Hua Institute of Buddhist Studies in Taiwan jointly endowed a publication series, the Sheng Yen Series in Chinese Studies, at Columbia University Press. Its purpose is to publish monographs containing new scholarship and English translations of classical texts in Chinese Buddhism.

Scholars of Chinese Buddhism have traditionally approached the subject through philology, philosophy, and history. In recent decades, however, they have increasingly adopted an interdisciplinary approach, drawing on anthropology, archaeology, art history, religious studies, and gender studies, among other disciplines. This series aims to provide a home for such pioneering studies in the field of Chinese Buddhism.

Michael J. Walsh, *Sacred Economies:*
Buddhist Business and Religiosity in Medieval China

Koichi Shinohara, *Spells, Images, and Maṇḍalas:*
Tracing the Evolution of Esoteric Buddhist Rituals

Beverley Foulks McGuire, *Living Karma:*
The Religious Practices of Ouyi Zhixu (1599–1655)

Paul Copp, *The Body Incantatory:*
Spells and the Ritual Imagination in Medieval Chinese Buddhism

EMPEROR
WU ZHAO

AND HER
PANTHEON
OF
DEVIS, DIVINITIES,
AND
DYNASTIC MOTHERS

N. HARRY
ROTHSCHILD

Columbia University Press
New York

Columbia University Press
Publishers Since 1893
New York   Chichester, West Sussex
cup.columbia.edu
Copyright © 2015 Columbia University Press
All rights reserved

Library of Congress Cataloging-in-Publication Data
Rothschild, N. Harry, author.
Emperor Wu Zhao and her pantheon of devis, divinities, and dynastic
mothers / N. Harry Rothschild.
pages cm. — (Sheng Yen series in Chinese Buddhist studies)
Includes bibliographical references and index.
ISBN 978-0-231-16938-7 (cloth : alk. paper) — ISBN 978-0-231-53918-0 (electronic)
1. Religion and politics—China—History. 2. Wu hou, Empress of China, 624-705.
3. Goddesses, Chinese—History. 4. Ancestor worship—China—History. 5. Buddhism
and state—China—History. I. Title.

BL1803.R68 2015
299.5'112114—dc23

2014028256

Columbia University Press books are printed on
permanent and durable acid-free paper.
This book is printed on paper with recycled content.
Printed in the United States of America
c 10 9 8 7 6 5 4 3 2 1

COVER IMAGE: Heroes and Heroines of Chinese History, including
Empress Wu, Chinese School / Private Collection / Peter Newark
Historical Pictures / Bridgeman Images

COVER DESIGN: Milenda Nan Ok Lee

References to websites (URLs) were accurate at the time of writing.
Neither the author nor Columbia University Press is responsible for URLs
that may have expired or changed since the manuscript was prepared.

For my father, Michael

Contents

Illustrations xi

Dynasties and Rulers Through the Mid-Tang xiii

Wu Zhao's Titles at Different Stages of Her Career xvii

Reign Eras from 655 to 705 xix

Acknowledgments xxi

Introduction:
Wu Zhao and Her Pantheon of Female Political Ancestors 1

PART I
GODDESSES OF ANTIQUITY 23

ONE
Wu Zhao as the Late Seventh-Century Avatar of
Primordial Goddess Nüwa 25

TWO
Sanctifying Luoyang: The Luo River Goddess and Wu Zhao 43

THREE

First Ladies of Sericulture: Wu Zhao and Leizu   60

PART II

DYNASTIC MOTHERS, EXEMPLARY MOTHERS   75

FOUR

The Mother of Qi and Wu Zhao:
Connecting to Antiquity, Elevating Mount Song   79

FIVE

Ur-Mothers Birthing the Zhou Line: Jiang Yuan and Wu Zhao   95

SIX

Wenmu and Wu Zhao: Two Mothers of Zhou   109

SEVEN

Four Exemplary Women in Wu Zhao's *Regulations for Ministers*   124

PART III

DRAWING ON THE NUMINOUS ENERGIES OF
FEMALE DAOIST DIVINITIES   145

EIGHT

The Queen Mother of the West and Wu Zhao   149

NINE

The Mother of Laozi and Wu Zhao:
From One Grand Dowager to Another   167

TEN

Rejected from the Pantheon:
The Ill-Timed Rise of the Cult of Wei Huacun   179

PART IV
BUDDHIST DEVIS AND GODDESSES 191

ELEVEN
Dharma Echoes of Mother Māyā in Wu Zhao 195

TWELVE
Bodhisattva with a Female Body: Wu Zhao and Devi Jingguang 209

Conclusions 227

Appendix: Wu Zhao's Pantheon of Female Political Ancestors 237
Glossary of Chinese Places, Names, and Terms 239
Notes 247
Bibliography 311
Index 339

Illustrations

I.1. Wu Zetian, from *Portraits and Eulogies of the Ancients*   4

1.1. Fuxi and Nüwa from a Tang tomb in Xinjiang   27

1.2. Wu Zhao as a Buddhist goddess in Huangze Temple (Guangyuan)   39

2.1. Reproduction of Gu Kaizhi's *Goddess of the Luo River*   45

3.1. Altar of the First Sericulturist   64

3.2. Leizu, surrounded by other lesser silk deities   67

4.1. Woman of Tushan and Yu the Great   80

5.1. Jiang Yuan instructs the young Lord of Millet   100

6.1. Mother Wen and King Wen   111

6.2. Dancing girl from a mural in Li Ji's tomb   117

7.1. Lady Ji of Lu   131

7.2. Mother of Mencius   134

7.3. Mother of General Zifa of Chu   139

7.4. Mother of General Kuo of Zhao   140

8.1. A Korean painting of the Queen Mother of the West   162

11.1. The supernal elephant visits Māyā   196

12.1. Apsara from Dunhuang   216

C.1. Wu Zhao and her pantheon of female political ancestors   232

Dynasties and Rulers Through the Mid-Tang

Limited to emperors and empresses included in this work.

Three Sovereigns (Sanhuang 三皇)
   Fuxi 伏羲/Nüwa 女媧, Suiren 燧人, Shennong 神農
Five Emperors (Wudi 五帝)
   Huangdi (Yellow Emperor 黃帝), Zhuanxu 顓頊, Di Ku 帝嚳, Yao 堯, and
   Shun 舜 (also known as Yu 虞) (Shaohao 少昊 is sometimes included
   in their company)

XIA 夏 (2200–1766 B.C.)

Yu 禹 the Great
Qi 啟

SHANG 商 (1766–1045 B.C.)

Cheng Tang 成湯 (Tang 湯)
Di Yi 帝乙
Wu Ding 武丁
Zhou (last ruler) 紂

ZHOU 周 (1045–221 B.C.)

King Wen 文王
King Wu 武王
King Cheng 成王
King Mu 穆王

DYNASTIES AND RULERS THROUGH THE MID-TANG

SPRING AND AUTUMN ERA 春秋時代 (771–481 B.C.)

King Ping 平王 (r. 770–719 B.C.)
King Ling 靈王 (r. 571–545 B.C.)

WARRING STATES 戰國時代 (481–221 B.C.)

QIN 秦 (221–206 B.C.)

Qin Shihuang 秦始皇 (r. 221–210 B.C.)

WESTERN HAN 西漢 (206 B.C. TO A.D. 220)

Gaozu 高祖 (r. 206–195 B.C.) and Empress Lü 呂后 (regent, 195–180 B.C.)
Jingdi 景帝 (r. 157–141 B.C.)
Wudi 武帝 (r. 141–86 B.C.)
Chengdi 成帝 (r. 37–7 B.C.)

XIN 新 (A.D. 8–23)

Wang Mang 王莽 (r. A.D. 8–23)

EASTERN HAN 東漢 (24–220)

Mingdi 明帝 (r. 58–75) and Empress Ma 馬后
Han Andi 安帝 (r. 106–125) Huandi 桓帝 (r. 147–167)

CAO WEI 曹魏 (220–265)

Wendi 文帝 (r. 220–226), Cao Pi 曹丕 and Empress Zhen 甄后
Mingdi 明帝 (r. 226–239), Cao Rui 曹叡

JIN DYNASTY 晉 (265–420), WESTERN JIN 西晉 (265–316)

Wudi 武帝 (r. 265–290) and Empress Yang 杨皇后 (238–274)
Yuandi 晉元帝 (r. 318–323)
Mingdi 明帝 (r. 323–325)
Mudi 穆帝 (r. 344–361), under regent–dowager empress Chu Suanzi 褚蒜子

DYNASTIES AND RULERS THROUGH THE MID-TANG

SOUTHERN (420-589) AND NORTHERN (386-581) DYNASTIES 南北朝

NORTHERN WEI 北魏, TOBA WEI (386-534)

Taiwu 太武 (r.423–452)
Wenchengdi 文成帝 (r.452–465)
Feng taihou 馮太后, dowager empress Feng (442–490)
Hu taihou 胡太后, dowager empress Hu (d. 528)

NORTHERN QI 北齊 (550-577)

Wenxuandi 文宣帝 (r. 550–559) and Empress Li Zu'e 李祖娥
Feidi 廢帝 (r. 559–560)
Wuchengdi 武成帝 (r. 561–565)
Gao Wei 高緯 (r. 565–577)

NORTHERN ZHOU 北周 (557-581)

Yuwen Yu 宇文毓 (r. 557–560) Wudi 武帝 (r.560–578)

LIU SONG 劉宋 (420-479)

Wudi 武帝 (r. 420–422), Liu Yu 劉裕

SOUTHERN QI 南齊 (479-502)

Gaodi 高帝 (r. 479–482)

Wudi 武帝 (r. 483–493) and Gracious Consort Pei (Pei huifei 裴惠妃), posthumously Empress Mu 穆后

LIANG 梁 (502-557)

Wudi 武帝 (r. 502–549)

SUI 隋 (581-618)

Wendi 隋文帝 (r. 581–604)
Yangdi 隋煬帝 (r. 604–618)

TANG 唐 (618-690 AND 705-907)

Gaozu 高祖 (r. 618-626) and Empress Dou 竇

Taizong 唐太宗 (r. 626-649) and Empress Zhangsun 長孫皇后

Gaozong 唐高宗 (r. 649-683), Li Zhi 李治

Zhongzong 中宗 (684, 705-710), Li Xiǎn 李顯 and Empress Wei 韋皇后

Ruizong 睿宗 (r. 684-690, 710-712), Li Dan 李旦 and Empresses Liu 劉 and Dou 竇

Xuanzong 玄宗 (r. 712-756), Li Longji 李隆基

Daizong 代宗 (r. 762-779)

ZHOU 周 (690-705)

Wu Zhao 武曌 (r. 690-705)

Wu Zhao's Titles at Different Stages of Her Career

This list only includes titles mentioned in this study. It is not intended to be comprehensive.

PRIOR TO BECOMING EMPRESS

Talent (Cairen 才人), a fifth-ranked concubine under Taizong, 637–649

Lady of Luminous Deportment (Zhaoyi 昭儀), a second-ranked concubine under Gaozong, 652–655

AS EMPRESS (*HOU* 后), 655–683

Tianhou 天后 Celestial Empress, 674–683

AS GRAND DOWAGER (*TAIHOU* 太后), 684–690

Sage (Saintly) Mother, Divine Sovereign (Shengmu shenhuang 聖母神皇), 688–690

AS EMPEROR (*HUANGDI* 皇帝), 690-705

Sagely and Divine Emperor (Shengshen huangdi 聖神皇帝), 690–693

Sagely and Divine Emperor, Cakravartin of the Golden Wheel (Jinlun shensheng huangdi 金輪神聖皇帝), 693–694

Maitreya, Sagely and Divine Emperor, Cakravartin of the Golden Wheel Transcending Antiquity (Cishi yuegu jinlun shengshen huangdi 慈氏越古金輪聖皇帝), 694–695

Reign Eras from 655 to 705

REIGN ERA	TRANSLATION	DATE OF INAUGURATION
Xianqing 顯慶	Manifest Felicitation	7 February 656
Longshuo 龍朔	Draconic Conjunction	4 April 661
Linde 麟德	Unicorn Virtue	2 February 664
Qianfeng 乾封	Supernal *Feng* rite	14 February 666
Zongzhang 總章	(Name of a chamber in Bright Hall)	22 April 668
Xianheng 咸亨	Total Efficacy	27 March 670
Shangyuan 上元	Highest Origin	20 September 674
Yifeng 儀鳳	Phoenix Regulator	18 December 676
Diaolu 調露	Harmonious Dew	15 July 679
Yonglong 永隆	Forever Eminent	21 September 680
Kaiyao 開耀	Dawning Brilliance	15 November 681
Yongchun 永淳	Eternal Purity	2 April 682
Hongdao 弘道	Amplifying the Dao	27 December 683
Sisheng 嗣聖	Heir to the Sage	23 January 684
Wenming 文明	Cultured Luminosity	27 February 684
Guangzhai 光宅	Illuminated and Filled	19 October 684
Chuigong 垂拱	With Hanging Robes and Folded Hands	9 February 685
Yongchang 永昌	Eternal Prosperity	27 January 689
Zaichu 載初	Origin of Records	18 December 689
Tianshou 天授	Heaven Bestowed	16 October 690
Ruyi 如意	At Will	22 April 692

REIGN ERA	TRANSLATION	DATE OF INAUGURATION
Changshou 長壽	Protracted Longevity	23 October 692
Yanzai 延載	Extension of an Era	9 June 694
Zhengsheng 證聖	Verification of Sagehood	23 November 694
Tiance wansui 天冊萬歲	Appointed by Heaven for 10,000 Years	22 October 695
Wansui dengfeng 萬歲登封	Forever Ascending to Perform the *Feng* Sacrifice	20 January 696
Wansui tongtian 萬歲通天	Communing with Heaven for 10,000 Years	22 April 696
Shengong 神功	Divine Merit	29 September 697
Shengli 聖曆	Sage Calendar	20 December 697
Jiushi 久視	Distant Vision	27 May 700
Dazu 大足	Great Footprint	15 February 701
Chang'an 長安	Enduring Security	26 November 701

Note: Also see Hiraoka Takeo, *Todai no koyomi* [The Tang Calendar] (Shanghai: Shanghai guji, 1990), 46–105; Paul Kroll, "The True Dates of the Reigns and Reign Periods of T'ang," *Tang Studies* 2 (1984), 25–30; N. Harry Rothschild, "An Inquiry Into Reign Era Changes Under Wu Zhao, China's Only Female Emperor," *Early Medieval China* 12 (2006); A. C. Moule, *The Rulers of China, 221 BC to AD 1949* (New York: Praeger, 1957), 54–59. Some translations of reign eras are lifted from Kroll.

Acknowledgments

THIS LABOR OF LOVE HAS CONSUMED the better part of a decade. I first mentioned it, in its barest outline, to the late Antonino Forte (1940–2006), my academic idol, when he was a visiting scholar at Harvard in early 2005. I remain ever grateful for his generosity of spirit and encouragement that helped give direction to this monograph. This work also owes a profound debt to the wisdom and the ongoing guidance of Wang Shuanghuai, chair of the Wu Zetian Research Association and professor of Tang history at Shaanxi Normal University, and to his teacher and mentor, Zhao Wenrun, an emeritus professor at Shaanxi Normal. Both have been extremely generous with their time and resources.

Without access to archives and resources, this project might never have been brought to fruition. Thanks to Jiang Sheng at Sichuan University for all his kindness and help during my sabbatical year; to Liang Yongtao from Huangze Temple in Guangyuan; to the staff of the Harvard-Yenching Library; to Smathers Library at the University of Florida; to Qingyang Temple in Chengdu; and to the Research Institute for Middle Antiquity at Beijing University.

Gracious thanks to the University of North Florida for the summer research grant in 2012. I would also like to offer my gratitude to colleagues from the Department of History at the University of North Florida: Charles Closmann for his help in securing my sabbatical and David Courtwright, Theo Prousis, and Alison Bruey for suggestions that helped shape and improve the book proposal. Thanks are also due the university president, John Delaney, for his ongoing support and generosity of spirit. I am indebted to the associates of the Center for Instructional Research

Technology at the University of North Florida, particularly to the capable tandem of David Wilson and Michael Boyles, whose digital genius proved exceedingly valuable with formatting images.

My peers and friends from the Southeast Early China Roundtable (SEECR) have patiently and consistently offered thoughts, criticisms, and guidance that has helped further this undertaking—so a duly warm offering of gratitude goes out to Keith Knapp, Jeff Richey, Eric Henry, Andrew Chittick, Cynthia Chennault, Paul Fischer, and all of the other members of SEECR who cheerfully put up with five consecutive conference papers from my seemingly endless "Wu Zhao and ___" series. No more, I promise!

Thanks to my colleague, friend, and brother, Wang Hongjie, as well, who has an uncanny knack for unearthing difficult-to-find sources and seemingly always has an answer to even the most difficult questions. I am grateful, too, for the generous help offered by Dorothy Wong and Anne Kinney. And reverent thanks to Victor Mair for his sage guidance and sound advice.

Thanks, also, to Cambria Press for granting permission to print the chapter on the mother of Laozi, an earlier iteration of which appeared in *China and Beyond in the Medieval Period: Cultural Crossings and Interregional Connections.* I wish to thank Livia Kohn for allowing me to publish chapter 10, an evolved version of an essay that appeared in the *Journal of Daoist Studies.* Acknowledgments are also due to Henry Livingston for designing the original artwork that appears in the conclusion and Kelly Carlton, for allowing me to use her photograph of the statue of Wu Zhao in Huangze Temple.

Finally, I would like to express my sincere appreciation and gratitude for Suzanne Cahill's unrelenting friendship, mentorship, and support. Profound thanks are also due Kyle Fortenberry for his unswerving loyalty and insistent belief. And a profound debt is owed to a wonderful teacher and a great man who had a massive impact upon me: the late K.C. Chang, whose fierce love of myth and lore, of bronze and bone, opened the gates to me a quarter of a century ago.

EMPEROR WU ZHAO
AND HER
PANTHEON
OF
DEVIS,
DIVINITIES,
AND
DYNASTIC MOTHERS

Wu Zhao and Her Pantheon of Female Political Ancestors

> And who are my ancestors? Are they only my biological ones . . . or do I have political ancestors as well? I am proud and grateful to be an American. I cherish the values of democracy and the freedoms I enjoy in this land, and I appreciate these more every time I remember how my biological ancestors in Europe and elsewhere were oppressed. . . . In a certain sense, I have been adopted by the "fathers" of this country. Thomas Jefferson and Abraham Lincoln are my political ancestors. I imbibed their values from childhood and passed them on to my children.
>
> —SOLOMON SCHIMMEL, *WOUNDS NOT HEALED BY TIME*

IN THE TORTUOUS HALF CENTURY of her remarkable political career, China's first and only female emperor, Wu Zhao 武曌 (624–705; r. 690–705),[1] better known as Wu Zetian 武則天 or Empress Wu (Wu hou 武后), faced daunting cultural obstacles and fierce opposition.[2] Although "China did not have a written Salic Law," remarked Zhao Fengjie nearly a century ago, "nevertheless there was a prohibition, silently observed through dynasties, that a woman was not to become emperor."[3] Given these deeply entrenched cultural attitudes, Wu Zhao clearly could not and did not construct her political authority in a conventional fashion. Wu Zhao's power was constantly challenged, forcing this historical anomaly to deploy language, symbolism, and ideology in a unique and creative manner. "Liminality, marginality and structural inferiority," anthropologist Victor Turner observed, "are conditions in which are frequently generated myths, symbols, ritual, philosophical systems and works of art." Less fettered by conventional conceptions, such borderlands "are open to the play of thought, feeling and will; in them are generated new models . . . some of which may have sufficient power and plausibility to replace eventually the force-backed political and jural models that control the centers of a society's ongoing life."[4] With the keen intuition of an outsider, Wu Zhao displayed an uncanny knack for sensing the plasticity of tradition, for discerning and capitalizing on subtle gaps in structures and institutions. While male emperors like Tang Taizong (r. 626–649) paid scrupulous homage to widely acknowledged culture heroes like flood-queller Yu the Great, dynasty-founding rulers like Kings Wen and Wu of Zhou, and sage advisors like the Duke of Zhou and Confucius, Wu Zhao necessarily sought alternative sources of legitimacy both within and beyond the confines of the Confucian tradition.[5] Even as she continued to honor this canonical lineage of ideal rulers, sages, and worthies, she constructed a parallel pantheon of female divinities and paragons drawn from every ideological persuasion—including Buddhist devis, Confucian exemplars (like the mother of Mencius), and Daoist goddesses, such as the Queen Mother of the West.

In 676, when Empress Wu's ailing husband Tang Gaozong (r. 649–683) offered to abdicate in her favor, official censure was swift. "It is said in the classics that the Son of Heaven administers the path of the male *yang* essence and the empress oversees the virtues of female *yin*," a minister bluntly remonstrated. "The relationship of the empress to emperor is like that of the moon to the sun—each has its place and role."[6] Simply put, she belonged to the inner, private, familial sphere and not the outer, public, and political world of men. At different stages of her ascent to power, Wu Zhao repeatedly heard variations of this message.

Some in Wu Zhao's court and realm objected to her rule on the grounds that female authority was unnatural, aberrant, and intrinsically at odds with both human and cosmic order. When as grand dowager she seized control of the court in 684, rebels took an oath to "expunge the she-demon scourge" (*qing yao nie* 清妖孽).[7] Disgruntled scholar-poet Luo Binwang (640–684) wrote a scathing polemic that anticipated centuries of disparaging Confucian judgment,[8] vigorously attacking her subversion of traditional gender norms and the perceived frailties and flaws associated with her sex:

Miss Wu, who has falsely usurped authority to run the court, is by nature cold and unyielding, by birth lowly and obscure. . . . Innately jealous, her mothlike eyebrows allow other women no quarter. All embroidered sleeves and artful slander, her vulpine glamour beguiled the ruler. Beneath her pheasant's plumage, the former Empress Wang was trampled. This musky doe once plunged my true Sovereign into rutting frenzy, vying with his own father. Her heart is half viper and half chameleon. Her disposition is that of a ravenous jackal or wolf. . . . She is hated by men and spirits alike! Neither heaven nor earth can stand her![9]

Luo Binwang employed graphic animal imagery to show that she was monstrous, unfettered by human conventions, and utterly unfit to govern.

Likewise, those critical of her rule interpreted upheaval in the natural world as a reflection of her unnatural position of power. Several years later, when a sudden terrestrial upthrust resulted in the birth of a mountain, the grand dowager–regent, then dominating the court and making decisions of state, received an ominous warning: "Presently your majesty is a female ruler situated in the *yang* role. This opposes the principle of hard and soft in the *Book of Changes*. For this reason the terrestrial ethers were obstructed and the earth sundered."[10] Hens were rumored to grotesquely transform into roosters.[11] The reported appearance of these "chicken abominations" (*ji huo* 雞禍) can be understood as a powerful negative Confucian commentary on the grand dowager's ascendancy: the ubiquitous sightings of gender-confused fowl were manifestations of Wu Zhao's contravention of the proper social and political hierarchy. In a "predominantly patriarchal and patrilineal society,"[12] in which the Confucian prescription sequestered women almost exclusively to the inner, domestic sphere, Wu Zhao's burgeoning political involvement was judged harshly; she was routinely cast as a lewd and extravagant counterpoint to virtuous, austere male rulers, including her first husband Taizong.

Yet despite being repeatedly maligned and stigmatized, Wu Zhao would not be deterred. The ninth day of the ninth lunar month in 690 marked the culmination of her long, meticulously orchestrated political and ideological campaign. Echoing the name of a past golden age, Wu Zhao inaugurated a new Zhou dynasty (690–705), ascending to the throne as emperor.[13] An iconoclast with unprecedented ambitions, she had immediately recognized that she could not afford to ignore or casually flout tradition. Indeed, three decades of immersion in the political process had given her a keen appreciation of the power and compass of tradition.

Acutely aware of the breadth of resistance to her public political engagement, Wu Zhao capably deflected much of the virulent criticism. Overcoming these ponderous obstacles to become the sole female emperor in China's long historical pageant took tremendous originality, cold-blooded

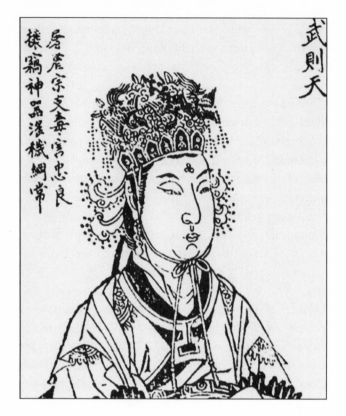

Figure I.1 Though late-fifteenth-century Ming portrait artist Zheng Zhenduo included *Wu Zetian* among eighty-eight images in a collection of ancient rulers, cultural heroes, philosophers, poets, and statesmen, he did not hold her in high regard. Consistent with the Confucian historiography, his accompanying commentary remarks upon the illicit nature of her power, her salaciousness, her lascivious character, and her toxic effect upon the loyal and worthy. (From *Portraits and Eulogies of the Ancients*)

audacity, and staggering political genius. She not only warded off this barrage of negativity but also deftly fostered an empowered female identity. To realign her culture's mythic, symbolic, and linguistic concepts in ways that sanctioned her authority was a complex undertaking that included an adroit campaign to position herself as the scion of a powerful and virtuous female pantheon. Meticulously, she developed and embraced a lineage of culturally revered female ancestors, goddesses, and paragons from different traditions, all of whom were closely associated with her person and her political power. At different junctures and to varying degrees, she drew upon each of the "three faiths" (*san jiao* 三教)—Buddhism, Confucianism, and Daoism. Elegantly rendered with her deft aesthetic touch, these affiliations significantly bolstered Wu Zhao's political authority, providing both a divine aura and tremendous normative charisma.

Wu Zhao's endorsement of these various cults waxed and waned with shifting ideological climes and political circumstances. This work will trace the timing, nature, and purpose of her connections to this eclectic assemblage of past influential women and female divinities, exploring the purposeful ties promulgated in carefully scripted political rhetoric, reinforced through poetry, celebrated theatrically in her court, and graven upon monumental steles for all to behold.

BEYOND BLOOD AND KINSHIP: FROM FAMILY TO EMPIRE

Though a wider pantheon of nature deities and gods were worshipped in ancient China,[14] K. C. Chang identifies a ruler's "individual status within a kinship system of agnatic clans and segmentary lineages"[15] as the foundation of political power in the Xia (2205–1766 B.C.), Shang (1766–1045 B.C.), and Zhou (1045–221 B.C.) dynasties. From this early juncture, ancestor worship was, in the words of sociologist C. K. Yang, "by far the most vital religious element in family life . . . a cult that contributed substantially to the integration and perpetuation of the family as a basic unit of Chinese society."[16] Oracle bone records attest to the reverent spirit with which Shang people offered sacrifices to royal ancestors.[17] Western Zhou (1045–771 B.C.) bronze inscriptions, writes Wang Aihe, "provide abundant evidence of the central position of ancestor worship," though tellingly the Zhou founders sacrificed to Shang ancestors as well as their own.[18]

Even then, the primacy of ancestral authority was already beginning to atrophy. As Richard Bendix has noted, by the end of the Western Zhou "ancestor worship had done nothing to ensure peace and prosperity," occasioning "a rise in skepticism among the Chinese aristocracy."[19] No longer did exclusive access to knowledge, ritual, and religious paraphernalia of a narrow, familial cult confer sufficient right to govern.

While ancestor worship remained significant, by the Warring States era (481–221 B.C.), as the Zhou weakened and fragmented, Constance Cook observes that the practice "lost its political saliency, and ancestral spirits were subsumed back into a larger pantheon of natural forces that could interfere with an individual's life mandate."[20] From the Han dynasty (206 B.C. to A.D. 220) onward, the centrality of these narrower consanguine ancestral cults diminished, having been supplanted by a broader vision of sovereignty. Culture heroes from a wider political tradition progressively came into clearer resolution and were often exalted as cultic divinities.

One of the means the First Emperor of the Qin dynasty (Qinshihuang 秦始皇; r. 221–210 B.C.) used to stake claim to his empire was the strategic erection of steles to stand testimony to his unmatched power and demark his vast territory. Hoping to establish a shared political tradition with conquered states, and seeking thereby to validate his authority beyond raw martial conquest, the First Emperor paired the erection of his steles with sacrifices to past leaders who were emblematic of beneficent governance: Shun, paragon of laissez-faire rule from a simpler era, and Yu the Great, altruistic establisher of the Xia dynasty, whose brilliant hydroengineering had saved China from the ravages of interminable flooding.[21]

Wang Aihe has illustrated that as early as the Han dynasty, the emperor was "the axis of the cosmos and the pivot of the empire," a figure who "claimed his legitimacy not as the descendant of the royal ancestors, but as the single moral exemplary figure representing the cosmic order in the human world."[22] This adoption of an expansive public mandate pushed ideas of rulership further from the secretive, familial notion of political authority in ancient China.

Increasingly, rulers sought to embody the grand tradition of illustrious political ancestors through reconstituting rites, resuscitating institutions, and echoing dynastic names of past eras. "Even a hundred generations hence," Confucius reputedly remarked, "the name of the heir and successor to the Zhou will be known."[23] Many aspiring dynasts chose the Zhou name. In the mid-sixth century, seeking an aura of legitimacy for his fragile regional kingdom, Western Wei ruler Yuwen Tai promulgated the *Rites of Zhou*, ordering ministers to revive Zhou institutions. In 558, his son Yuwen Yu announced the inauguration of the Zhou dynasty, calculated to evoke the pageant of virtuous kings and sage advisors of the original Zhou.[24]

Howard Wechsler has persuasively argued that by the cosmopolitan early Tang (618–907) this new, inclusive ruling philosophy—a conception succinctly expressed in the phrase "the empire is open to all" (*tianxia wei gong* 天下為公)—had fully matured. Through public rites, sacrifices, and inspection tours, renowned Tang emperor Taizong reshaped conceptions of rulership and legitimation. A new vision of political validation had gradually evolved: authority depended more on association with a great tradition of virtuous political ancestors than blood succession. Rather than simply honoring their own ancestors within family temples, emperors like Taizong solemnly recognized popular paragons like Yu the Great, King Wen, the Duke of Zhou, and Confucius. Affiliation with this lineage of kings and sages conferred the gravity of their precursors' authority upon Tang emperors. By ceremoniously revering these exemplars, the emperor became heir to their mantle of virtue. Through a public political theater that glorified culture heroes and built political ancestors into cultic icons, Tang rulers essentially fashioned a broad-based vision of sovereignty—one congruent with the diverse and pluralistic empire they governed.[25]

In his writings, Taizong emphatically extols this lineage of political ancestors. To gloss over the ugliness of the Xuanwu Gate Incident of 626 (in which he seized the throne from his father and eliminated several brotherly rivals), Taizong recast himself several years later as a staunch champion of tradition rather than an upstart fratricide in the *Golden Mirror* (*Jinjing* 金鏡).[26] With a flourish of humility, he looked to the exemplars of the past: "Whenever We contemplate the government by non-action of the Yellow Emperor or Shaohao, or the perfection of good government by Tang and Yu, We always pause to sigh with admiration, unable to stop Ourself."[27] Sinologist Denis Twitchett remarks that "Golden Mirror" "refers to the past, to the rich body of historical experience that is at the disposal of a monarch wishing to see his own policies in the actions of past rulers and the ideal models of antiquity." In short, in the process of imperial self-fashioning, of altering his ugly early image, Taizong strove to situate himself as the worthy heir, replete with studied obeisance, to this glorious lineage of political ancestors.[28]

As Jack Chen observed of putative imperial authorship of poetry in medieval China, "Emperors who sought to emulate sage-kings of legendary antiquity represented themselves in accordance with received tropes and commonplaces."[29] In Taizong's poetry, Chen sees an effort to "reiterate the familiar themes of dynasty founding, orthodox lineage and sagely rulership."[30] In one of many such poetic efforts, "On Visiting Qingshan Palace at Wugong," the ever image-conscious Taizong versifies,

> At Longlife Hill, I think upon former traces,
> The city of Feng was indeed the ancestor's base.
> Oh, I have inherited the legacies of the sages![31]

Wugong was the site where Emperor Shun bequeathed territory to the first Zhou ancestor, Hou Ji, Lord Millet.[32] Longlife Hill was the Yellow Emperor's birthplace. King Wen established Feng, not far to the west of Chang'an, as the Western Zhou capital. By reconsecrating this sacred geography, Taizong connected his person to a grand lineage of sage-kings, framing himself as their duly reverent heir. For Wu Zhao, poetry—both her own and that produced by her talented coterie of propagandists—served as a similarly important vehicle to define or redefine sovereignty, a medium that could "help mold a lasting favorable image" of her person and her rule.[33]

Written in 648, the Preface to Taizong's *Plan for an Emperor* (Difan 帝範), a valedictory manual of advice for his son and heir Li Zhi (the future Gaozong), similarly claimed their Li clan as descendants to a worthy political bloodline of virtue and good governance. Taizong declared himself the inevitable culmination of a lineage of impressive male political ancestors who had received both terrestrial and heavenly endorsement:

> The power of Yao was offered him at the spring of Cuigui.
> The black gem was presented to Yu of Xia to announce the accomplishment of his tasks.
> The vermilion sparrow presented its auspicious omen and the Zhou began its 700 years of auspicious rule.
> The spirit of the White Emperor manifested its joyful potent and Han began the foundation of its double dynastic tenure.

Then, in the wake of these two great eras, the Zhou and the Han, he establishes his own ascendancy:

> I hacked away the great leviathans, and made clear the four seas.
> Having already received the felicities conferred by boundless heaven,
>   I recklessly ascended the Great Dipper.

> Having inherited the everlasting enterprise of the glorious virtue dis-
> played by successive sovereigns,
> I continue to erect the abundant grand foundation of the precious
> register.[34]

With a characteristic blend of hubris and humility, Taizong mythologizes his political rise and dominion. Unbeknownst to him as he bequeathed these principles of rulership to his son, another benefactor of this eleventh-hour political tutelage—albeit an inadvertent one—was Wu Zhao herself. Far better than his intended student Li Zhi, she gleaned these lessons.

Contemporary scholar Jiang Yonglin termed these highly regarded ancestors (whose reputations endured throughout imperial China) "political and spiritual models," part of an official pantheon worthy of emulation.[35] Further remarking on the "public, universal nature" of the Tang dynasty, Mark Lewis has observed that "instead of being the realm of the ruling house, the empire was viewed as a public good that transcended and negated the parochialism of family ties."[36] In the ideologically pluralistic, multiethnic, and cosmopolitan early Tang, coexisting and competing Daoist and Buddhist deities surfaced alongside the familiar, deep-rooted political ancestors from folklore, myth, and Confucianism.

Consequently, tremendous normative power became vested in a ruler's political and religious connection with ancestors from each of the three faiths. By Wu Zhao's time, sovereignty had become intertwined with a far more expansive conception of the state—one based on a cult of political ancestry rather than actual consanguinity. This understanding afforded Wu Zhao the opportunity to mold a supple consensus, one capable of changing to meet her shifting ideological needs.

WITHIN THE CONFUCIAN AMBIT: WU ZHAO AND THE GOLDEN AGE

"What happened *ab origine*," suggests historian of religion Mircea Eliade, "can be repeated by the power of rites." Those possessing access to the esoteric knowledge necessary to perform these rites, Eliade asserts, hold a "magico-religious power" enabling them to recollect and reenact the powerful mythic acts of the gods, the heroes, or the ancestors.[37] Certainly, a massive political authority can accrue to such a calculated, eminently political act of recollection. From antiquity to the present day, from emperors and pharaohs to presidents and prime ministers, leaders have sought to connect their present government to an ideal golden age. Affiliation with ancient gods, heroes, and ancestors played a vital role in establishing political legitimation. Implicit in such association is the claim that the present ruler—staging the rite and evoking the ancestral political name—is its legitimate heir and will usher in the restoration of that lost golden age.

In summoning the power of the golden age, the rite provides the sense that a new prosperous era is imminent. Indeed, through such ceremonies the temporal disjuncture between the halcyon epoch of the past and the dawning era of new prosperity is suspended and blurred, creating a mythic time situated in the now. Despite paying tribute to past mythic glory, the public focus, the political limelight of such ceremonies, is squarely fixed in all its refulgence not upon the past incarnation but on the present avatar. What Eliade omits to mention (perhaps because he finds it self-evident) is that the act of staging the rite, reenacting the "mythico-ritual scenario of periodic renewal of the world," serves to consolidate the social and political ends of the host-ruler. In the very performance of the myth, what is presented as a humble genuflection to tradition is actually a calculated and purposeful retrofitting of tradition to the present moment, and as such, most often a conscious act of staggering self-aggrandizement.

Seen in this light, for a female emperor in seventh-century China, tradition—in particular, this grand tradition of time-honored political ancestors—held great potential opportunity. Though this tradition contained principles that repudiated Wu Zhao simply on the basis of her sex, it also held tremendous latent power that, if wielded in timely fashion with delicacy, skill, and rhetorical virtuosity, could be tactically marshaled to her advantage.

The ruling myth-maker orchestrating the rite, according to Eliade, seeks to collapse past and present, joining the assemblage of past gods and heroes in "a sacred Time at once primordial and infinitely recoverable."[38] Wu Zhao accomplished this difficult feat in late 689. Less than a year before she inaugurated her Zhou dynasty, she introduced a new era, tellingly called Origin of Records, simultaneously reorienting the state calendar to follow the Zhou chronometry of antiquity.[39] As emperor, she later resuscitated the imperial practice of announcing the new month (*gao shuo* 告朔) to continue, as a minister put it, "the practice of the hundred kings, and to solidify the profound regulations of past aeons."[40] "A new power which wants to assert itself must enforce a new chronology," claims Elias Canetti, for "it must make it seem as though time had begun with it."[41] Wu Zhao went further: she reset "primordial" time, situating herself at a new beginning while aligning the origin of her empire with the timeless and time-honored horological cadence of King Wen, King Wu, and the Duke of Zhou.

She worked to establish herself as the reverent heir and conscientious keeper of the enduring, glorious Confucian lineage of sage rulers. In an age in which kinship remained important, a ruler needed a worthy genealogy. She created a fictive lineage, taking King Wen of Zhou as her clan's first ancestor,[42] concocting blood ties to one of the brightest cultural luminaries in Chinese tradition. In so doing, she honored the seminal Confucian worthies while grafting herself onto their lineage.

While previous Tang rulers wistfully lauded the golden age, Wu Zhao used bureaucratic nomenclature from the *Rites of Zhou*[43] and created new characters drawn from the ornate Zhou script.[44] She realigned time to follow the original Zhou calendar[45] and greeted the new lunar year in 689 by donning ceremonial caps and vestments drawn from ancient Zhou ritual codes.[46] Ultimately, like the Yuwen, the Xianbei clan that seized control of north China and proclaimed their dynasty the Zhou (557–581), Wu Zhao's chosen dynastic epithet "Zhou" intentionally hearkened back to the halcyon days of celebrated sage rulers long honored for their morality, virtue, and perfect administration.[47] Just after Wu Zhao established her Zhou dynasty, the Duke of Zhou was posthumously invested as Prince of Meritorious Virtue and Confucius as Duke of the Reverent Way.[48] All of these measures were designed to publicly display that Wu Zhao was a worthy successor to and renovator of the golden age in both blood and spirit.

From the outset, Wu Zhao's authority was thereby intertwined with this time-honored lineage of Confucian political ancestors. Time and again, she deftly manipulated the flexibility of tradition, strategically situating herself as a champion of, rather than an opponent to, Confucian values. She was keenly aware that there was still no greater source of legitimacy and authority. Nonetheless, she knew that Chinese tradition had no provision for a female ruler and that she could never rely exclusively on this patriarchal, largely Confucian lineage of virtuous kings and sagacious ministers to valorize her person and support her sovereignty. Necessarily, she sought alternative sources of legitimacy both within and beyond the confines of the Confucian tradition.

POLITICAL ANCESTORS IN A PLURALISTIC SOCIETY:
BEYOND THE SAGE

Much as Wang Aihe describes the emperor in the Han, the ruler in the far-flung, pluralistic Tang was at the center of a "net of entangled power relations."[49] With the arrival, integration, and domestication of Buddhism, and the influx of Central Asian peoples, customs, and ideas, the number of political and ideological variables proliferated. The Tang emperor necessarily possessed a keen awareness of, and sensitivity toward, the diverse constituencies of her empire: men and women; Han and non-Han; Buddhist, Daoist, and Confucian; and newly risen families and long-established clans.

Howard Wechsler's excellent study, *Offerings of Jade and Silk*, is almost exclusively focused on Han Chinese and Confucian categories and modes of legitimation—including ancestor cults, suburban sacrifices, imperial tours of inspection, and the *feng* and *shan* rites. Wechsler illustrates that during the early Tang these traditions underwent marked transformations, becoming ever more public, open, and universal. Rulers of that era like Taizong "drew upon the newer legitimating values of Buddhism and Taoism in order to expand the conventional body of philosophico-religious legitimation that had previously been centered on Confucianism."[50] In his study on the Tang ritual code, David McMullen endorses this understanding of this increasingly multidenominational and complex era, remarking that the "the transcendental faiths of Buddhism and Daoism also exerted claims on the emperor's commitment, time and resources."[51] Naturally, as cults developed around eminent Buddhist and Daoist figures (both under and outside of state control in this pluralistic, multiethnic empire), a new collection of gods and goddesses came to be worshipped in court and country.

These developments began to evolve well before the Tang. New ideologies and the influx of non-Chinese constituencies engendered innovative models of kingship. John Lagerway has remarked that beginning in the Han, Huang-Lao Daoism (centered around the Yellow Emperor and Laozi) began "to interest the state as the key to successful government and, hence, to dynastic legitimacy."[52] A central figure in the developing Daoist pantheon, the apotheosized Laozi, Lord Lao (Laojun 老君), became one of the foremost Daoist cultic divinities.[53] Anna Seidel traces the emergence of the divine Laozi as "the supreme deity of the Daoist pantheon," a "politico-religious savior" or "messiah," to the millennial movements of the waning Eastern Han (A.D. 24–220).[54] This development marked the beginnings of a novel conception of Daoist emperorship.

During the Northern and Southern dynasties (220–581), Lord Lao emerged as a full-fledged cosmic divinity. After being blessed by the divine manifestation of Laozi on a retreat to Mount Song, Daoist master Kou Qianzhi invested Tabgach Emperor Taiwu (r. 424–452) of the Northern Wei as a Daoist priest and conferred upon him a talisman confirming his mandate, and effectively creating a "Taoist theocracy."[55] At the same time, in the south, founder Liu Yu (420–422), Emperor Wu of the Liu Song dynasty (420–478), drew sanction from the divine Laozi.[56] In the late sixth century, a Daoist master formally initiated Northern Zhou Emperor Wu (560–578) as a Daoist, gifted him a special talisman, and conferred divine blessing upon his rule.[57]

The Li family who established and ruled during the Tang dynasty claimed descent from Laozi, Li Er, whose surname they shared.[58] Franciscus Verellen remarks that "owing to the genealogical affiliation of the T'ang ruling house with Laozi, the imperial ancestor cult had become largely assimilated with the official cult of Lord Lao,"[59] or, as Timothy Barrett concludes, "Deeming themselves descendants of the sage, the T'ang emperors supported Taoism on family grounds."[60] Stories circulated at the dawn of the Tang that divine Lord Lao had revealed himself, claiming that the imperial family would last for a millennium.[61] Tang founder Gaozu (r. 618–626) honored Laozi as "Sage Ancestor."[62] Accordingly, Laozi was both a blood forebear and a political ancestor of the Tang imperial clan.

As Buddhism's popularity burgeoned in China, finding imperial patrons and sponsors, the faith came to play an important part in political legitimation. The long-existing tradition of *cakravartin* kingship emerged in China. In the cakravartin ideal, with deep roots in India and Central Asia, the ruler styled himself a champion of the Buddhist faith and even an incarnation or avatar of Buddhist divinities.[63] In his study on Buddhist (or Hindu-Buddhist) "galactic polity" in Southeast Asia, Stanley Tambiah remarks that in this tradition of sovereignty, the ruler, a "wielder of *dharma* (the moral law), *chakravartin* (universal emperor) and *bodhisattva* (Buddha-to-be), was seen as the pivot of the polity and as the mediating link between the upper regions of the cosmos, composed of the gods and their heavens, and the lower planes of humans and lesser beings."[64] Scott Pearce has also shown that by the reign of Taiwu's grandson Wenchengdi (r. 452–465) in the Northern Wei, Buddhism had become a decisive element of political legitimation. In Buddhist temples, and later in the famous statuary at Yungang, the young boy-emperor was depicted as Tathagata—so that "Buddhas became emperors and emperors Buddhas."[65] Erik Zürcher has shown that at the same time in south China, rulers of the Liu Song also styled themselves cakravartin kings.[66]

In order to purge the blood-soaked path of treachery by which he rose to power, Liang Wudi (r. 502–549) emulated political ancestor Aśoka, the legendary Buddhist cakravartin of third-century B.C. Mauryan India. He established (or renovated) Buddhist monasteries bearing Aśoka's name as sites to stage relic veneration ceremonies. Repeatedly, he held *pañcavārṣika* assemblies (*wuzhe dahui* 無遮大會), massive festal events "open to the public, regardless of gender, ethnicity, age, social status, or religious affiliation" that combined dharma lectures and vegetarian feasts.[67] On these occasions, he proffered himself and an immense hoard of gold to the Buddhist clergy, undergoing both a spiritual and a material redemption (he was redeemed, bought back from the *sangha* by the court).[68] Kathy Cheng-mei Ku persuasively argues that Liang Wudi cast himself in the image of a Buddharāja (*fowang* 佛王), "a Buddha who is also a cakravartin," as sovereign of the human realm and Maitreya incarnate.[69] This conception of Buddhist kingship, with earlier roots in the Southern dynasties, the Liu Song and the Qi (479–502), had a profound impact on Wu Zhao's own vision of sovereignty.

Reversing the Northern Zhou policy of persecution, Sui Wendi (r. 581–605) was an ardent patron and champion of the Buddhist faith, which played an integral role in his efforts to unify long-divided north and south China.[70] Like Liang Wudi, Sui Wendi styled himself a cakravartin and "claimed his legitimation by directly referring to Aśoka: repenting the bad deeds of the past," venerating Buddhist relics, and staging *pañcavārṣika* feasts.[71] When, in an imperial edict in 601, Sui Wendi initiated an empire-wide relic veneration campaign, he framed the move in the following terms: "We contemplate with awe the perfect wisdom, the great mercy, the great compassion of the Buddha that would save and protect all living creatures, that would carry across to blessed deliverance all living things."[72] He enshrined Buddhist relics in 107 different prefectures, an effort designed to emulate Aśoka's legendary erection of 84,000 reliquary *stūpas* all around his vast empire.[73] Clearly, Sui Wendi was not merely broadcasting to his newly unified realm the virtues of the Buddha, but also proclaiming his own political authority. In a patent case of his effort to style himself a Buddhist sovereign, he ordered the Indian monk Narendrayaśas to modify a Buddhist sutra to include a passage that prophesied that the Moonlight Child, Candraprabha, a Buddhist divinity, would be reborn in China, serve as king of the Great Sui, and ultimately preside as a cakravartin.[74] Sui Wendi's kingship in this fashion thus became linked to the Buddha through the dispersal of sacred relics connected with the Buddha's body.

These Buddhist and Daoist deities did not belong to the hoary lineage of political ancestors of past Confucian great-grandfathers. By the seventh century, not only did Wu Zhao have a range of male Daoist divinities like Lord Lao (the deified form of Laozi) and the Yellow Emperor to draw upon, but there were also Buddhist political ancestors like King Aśoka; furthermore, a growing cluster of Buddhist deities had developed—among whom Amitābha, Avalokiteśvara, Śākyamuni, and Maitreya were most popular.[75] Augmenting the grand lineage of Confucian political ancestors, these Daoist and Buddhist patriarchs created an impressive pantheon of male culture heroes from the "three faiths," all linked in various capacities to Chinese emperorship.

WU ZHAO'S PANTHEON OF FEMALE POLITICAL ANCESTORS

According to Sarah Milledge Nelson, in the field of archaeology the misguided assumption of the permanent and inherent androcentric nature of social and political authority has obscured the more complex reality of "negotiated power and conditional prestige."[76] To investigate the peculiar nature of Wu Zhao's political authority solely through the established lineage of male political ancestors at the heart of the Confucian matrix would fail to take into account the dynamics of ideological negotiations and shifting gender conditions in early Tang China. Although Confucian tradition carried tremendous weight in the seventh century, it was neither immanent nor all-encompassing.

With great skill, Wu Zhao fashioned a skein of relations to past women of eminence as well as a range of female divinities, complementing the traditional cult of male ancestors with a pantheon of female divinities and culture heroes. With the assistance of a talented array of propagandists and rhetoricians, she discovered in these women both deep cultural significance and great latent political power. As Stephen Bokenkamp has observed, "To be convincing her construction of legitimacy had to draw upon accepted paradigms of the medieval religious orthodoxies of the day—Confucian, Buddhist, and Daoist alike—but in a way diametrically opposed to traditional interpretations, which held that a woman, by virtue of her gender, could not properly rule."[77] Naturally, her pantheon incorporated women from each of the "three faiths."

The exploration that follows is not a broad comparative study of rulership and gender; rather, it is an investigation of the cults of female political ancestors that a single, inimitable personage, Wu Zhao, developed initially as empress, then as regent, and ultimately as emperor. In her half century of political involvement (from her emergence as empress in 655 to her deposal and the restoration of the Tang in 705), she devised and elaborated upon different roles of these forebears that enabled and enhanced the various stages of her political ascendancy. One of the aims of this study is to delineate the modifications within the cults of these female political ancestors during the turbulent arc of Wu Zhao's political career.

This work separates into four categories Wu Zhao's assemblage of divinities and eminent women:

Part I. Goddesses of Antiquity
Part II. Dynastic Mothers, Exemplary Mothers
Part III. Drawing on the Numinous Energies of Female Daoist Divinities
Part IV. Buddhist Devis and Goddesses

In each case, the study examines the different stages of Wu Zhao's lengthy political career: as empress and coruler with husband Gaozong (r. 650–683), grand dowager (684–690), and finally emperor of her own Zhou dynasty (r. 690–705). In each of these stations, the roles of these female ancestors underwent purposeful and calculated evolutions in keeping with changing political circumstances and necessities.

In part I, "The Goddesses of Antiquity," the opening chapter describes Wu Zhao's efforts to resuscitate primordial goddess Nüwa. In *The Divine Woman*, an exploration of China's wide and varied collection of female divinities, Edward Schafer muses, "Nü Kua had once ruled over all men it was thought, just as did the Empress Wu later. Mythology had become history."[78] Mythology, of course, does not simply become history. The agency of Wu Zhao reanimated the dormant cult of this goddess, shaping her mythic image much like Nüwa reputedly molded mankind from rough clay. With the help of Wu Zhao's propagandists, the shadowy creator and mender of the heavens reemerged as a significant cultic figure who played an important role in helping legitimate and magnify the late seventh-century female sovereign.

Schafer further observes that in early and medieval China "women represented metaphysical water in human form . . . the fertile, moist, receptive principle in nature. They appeared in mythology and literature as visible forms of moist soil and the watercourses that make it wet."[79] Wu Zhao's pantheon could not be without a river goddess embodying the water element and the female *yin* principle. The second chapter, "Sanctifying Luoyang: The Luo River Goddess and Wu Zhao," examines the substantial roles this riverine divinity played in the ascent of Wu Zhao and the related elevation of Luoyang. As the Luo River flows through Luoyang, so in currents of poetry and calibrated streams of rhetoric, its lovely tutelary goddess moved with fluid grace through Wu Zhao's constructions of power. Most significantly, several years before her accession to emperor in 690, an inscribed augural stone was reportedly discovered in the Luo River. The inscription told of the advent of a "Sage Mother." The grand dowager ceremoniously thanked the goddess of the Luo River for revealing and disgorging this auspicious token; she bestowed a title upon the riparian deity and took a new, grander title for herself.

Chapter 3 investigates the role that the silk goddess, Leizu, played in the female sovereign's rhetoric, particularly during the earlier years of Wu Zhao's rise. Simultaneously honoring and symbolically assuming the guise of Leizu, Empress Wu Zhao repeatedly performed vernal sericulture rites to encourage a bumper crop of silkworms and thus abundant production of silk cloth. In early and medieval China, weaving and sericulture were closely connected with female virtue. Thus, Wu Zhao's affiliation with Leizu helped project the image of a model wife and an ideal of womanly comportment to the wider empire.

The first three chapters in part II, "Dynastic Mothers, Exemplary Mothers," examine the connections between Wu Zhao's political rise and a trio of eminent women from distant antiquity who were connected with the founding of the Three Dynasties—the Xia, the Shang, and the Zhou—at the very origins of Chinese civilization. Chapter 4, "The Mother of Qi and Wu Zhao: Connecting to Antiquity, Elevating Mount Song," investigates the role of the Tushan Girl, wife of flood-queller Yu the Great, legendary founder of the Xia dynasty. Associated with Mount Song, the Central Marchmount near to Luoyang, this little-known ancestor emerged as a significant designation among Wu Zhao's wider pantheon of female deities. Chapter 5, "Ur-Mothers Birthing the Zhou Line: Jiang Yuan and Wu Zhao," explores the role in Wu Zhao's pantheon of Jiang Yuan, who divinely bore Lord Millet, the founding ancestor of the Zhou dynasty of antiquity.

The consonance between Wu Zhao and sagacious Mother Wen, the spouse of Zhou dynasty founder King Wen, occupies chapter 6. Mother Wen helped anchor Wu Zhao's Zhou dynasty to its glorious past's namesake. To justify her own political involvement, especially as empress and grand dowager, Wu Zhao and her propagandists reminded court and country that Mother Wen had assisted King Wen in administering the newly established dynasty. Most significantly, Wu Zhao, as ascending female sovereign, recrafted her genealogy so that this earlier Zhou mother became not just a political ancestor, but her blood ancestress.

As grand dowager and emperor of a vast empire, Wu Zhao worked to broadcast a vision of motherhood that reached beyond her flesh-and-blood sons, to embrace her ministers and all of her subjects. To this end, she drew on the authority that accrues to Confucian motherhood and widowhood. Chapter 7, the final chapter in part II, analyzes Wu Zhao's penchant for upholding idealized Confucian mothers from Liu Xiang's Han dynasty manual of womanly behavior, *Biographies of Exemplary Women*, to valorize her own role as mother of empire. She associated herself with Lady Ji of Lu and the mother of Confucian sage Mencius, two paragons whose timely moral guidance not only steered wayward sons toward paths of rectitude, but also provided them with keen insights into the art of governance. Finally, the chapter charts the female emperor's efforts to utilize the strong-willed martial mothers of Generals Zifa of Chu and Kuo of Zhao. Through moral suasion, one of these prescient widows of the late Warring States era (third century B.C.) instilled in her injudicious son principles of good generalship; the other saved her entire clan by remonstrating with the Zhao king, urging him not to appoint her incapable offspring. As a female ruler of a nascent dynasty surrounded by powerful non-Chinese states like the Turks, the Tibetans, and the Khitan, Wu Zhao could ill afford to appear weak in foreign relations. These strong martial matriarchs helped her project an aura of moral force and rectitude.

Part III looks at Wu Zhao's effort to incorporate a range of female Daoist divinities into her pantheon of forebears. Foremost among these deities was the Queen Mother of the West. Chapter 8 investigates the repertoire of symbols and ceremonies the female ruler developed in connection with this divinity. The Queen Mother of the West was prominently featured in poetry and rhetoric written for and about the earthly ruler. In her later years, Wu Zhao even theatrically styled herself a living incarnation of the Daoist goddess.

Chapter 9 analyzes the connection Wu Zhao contrived between herself and Mother Li, the mother of Laozi. As Gaozong's coruler and grand dowager-regent, Wu Zhao utilized Mother Li's identity as progenitor (of the Li clan, the ruling family of the Tang dynasty) to situate herself symbolically as queen mother of the imperial house. During these stages, Wu Zhao's association with this Daoist divinity helped mute criticisms of her burgeoning public presence and political role.

The final section of the third part, chapter 10, explores the conflicted relationship between Wu Zhao and Wei Huacun, the Lady of the Southern Marchmount. Apotheosized as a Daoist deity, Wei Huacun was a transmitter and revealer of sacred texts. While Wu Zhao was certainly not averse to exalting this female divinity, she was keenly attuned to shifting ideological climes. At the very height of her campaign to define herself as a universal Buddhist monarch, Wu Zhao rejected an opportunity to link herself to this Daoist goddess, choosing to suppress rather than promote Lady Wei's cult.

Buddhism played a vital role in the complex machinations of Wu Zhao's legitimation. Part IV, "Buddhist Devis and Goddesses," examines the nature and political utility of her carefully scripted connections with several Buddhist divinities. Chapter 11 traces the development, under Wu Zhao, of the cult of Māyā, the mother of the historical Buddha. As empress, Wu Zhao utilized idealized images of motherhood associated with Māyā to cast herself as a latter-day "Buddha mother" (fomu 佛母). In the Buddhist art of Wu Zhao's era, familiar images of Māyā, scenes of the Buddha's conception, birth, and paranirvāṇa, appeared with increasing frequency. And symbols from Māyā's life—like the white elephant connected with her miraculous conception—became emblematic of Wu Zhao's court.

Chapter 12 investigates the efforts of propagandists to illustrate how the female ruler was the avatar of Buddhist devi Jingguang (Sanskrit: Vimalaprabhā). In a sutra that reached China in the sixth century, the Buddha prophesies that this goddess will "obtain great sovereignty" and "be a bodhisattva who will show and receive a female body in order to convert beings."[80] Buddhist propagandists produced a commentary based on this sutra that they circulated on the eve of the inauguration of Wu Zhao's Zhou dynasty. This text meticulously cataloged proofs that Wu Zhao was the avatar of the devi, which helped exalt the female ruler and legitimize her rule as a Buddhist sovereign.

Collectively, these female divinities, dynastic mothers, and eminent women of different ideological backgrounds—complementing rather than replacing a time-honored congregation of male political ancestors—played an important role in the construction of Wu Zhao's political authority. With the help of her talented rhetoricians, Wu Zhao situated herself at the confluence of these ideological streams, a human vessel into which the collective energies and charisma of these eminent women and divinities might flow.

From the outset, it is important to be cognizant of the parameters of this study. This is not a comprehensive investigation of Wu Zhao's unprecedented and unrepeated rise to emperorship. Her creation of an assemblage of female political ancestors is but one major approach among a much wider political, religious, and ideological repertoire of stratagems. This pantheon of women was not the sole armature upon which Wu Zhao constructed her authority or maintained her power.[81]

To truly comprehend Wu Zhao's unique ascent to emperorship would require a meticulous study of gender politics in the seventh century,[82] a careful examination of the influence of Central Asian and Indian culture on Chinese gender relations and sexuality,[83] and a thorough investigation of the impact that free-flowing Silk Road traffic into cosmopolitan centers like Chang'an and Luoyang had on social norms and cultural behaviors.[84] Furthermore, Wu Zhao's political authority was a construction of dazzling complexity. A short list of some of the integral political, ideological, cultural, and religious components of the intricate edifice of her sovereignty might include: fundamental economic and agrarian practices;[85] the role of Confucian, Daoist, and Buddhist ceremony;[86] the related iconography, art, and monumental architecture that justified and enlarged her authority;[87] the manipulation of the calendar;[88] the propagation of the Buddhist faith through the new technology of printing;[89] the creation of new characters as distinctive signets of authority;[90] the political machinations underlying frequent reign era changes;[91] the strategic patronage of literature and arts;[92] the motivation behind frequent reforms of names, titles, and offices;[93] the ongoing effort to elevate and preserve her natal Wu family;[94] the instrumental use of auspicious omens;[95] the handling of military affairs and relations with martial leaders;[96] the formulation of foreign policy, including handling of embassies, raising funds from foreign sources, appointment of non-Han generals, and resettlement of non-Chinese populations within the borders of her realm;[97] the management of relations with the Confucian court, including her personal involvement in the selection and assessment process to recruit officials;[98] the orchestration of rivalries and factions at court;[99] and the instrumental use of intelligence services, torture, and violence to thwart political threats.[100]

Moreover, a parallel exploration of the extent to which Wu Zhao was able to harness the powerful regulating force of traditional male political ancestors would be necessary, a study that investigated not only her links to patriarchs of the great tradition like Yao, Shun, Yu, and King Wen, but her connections to male Daoist divinities like Laozi and the Yellow Emperor, and Buddhist deities like Maitreya, Mañjuśrī, and Vairocana.

Taken in their mind-boggling collective scope, the vast and diverse parts of this program of rulership fail to do justice to the staggering political genius of its author, Wu Zhao. No single part of this whole can come close to serving as an exhaustive explanation of her unique achievement. Many of these measures were closely intertwined. While this study mentions a large number of these strategies in their connection to Wu Zhao's pantheon of female ancestors, it does not attempt a comprehensive investigation of these interrelated elements.

In isolation, no number of prophecies auguring the advent of a Buddhist divinity in female guise, no volume of eloquent verse presenting her as a latter-day incarnation of the Queen Mother of the West, and no rhapsodic celebration of her as a throwback to the revered Confucian dynastic mothers of old can explain her dazzling, unparalleled ascent. Wu Zhao's unique status as China's first and only female emperor rested on her keen political acumen and administrative virtuosity. She exhibited a profound understanding of the different constituencies within the far-flung empire she governed. Deftly, she manipulated ceremony and symbol. Skillfully and steadily, she managed civil and military affairs. Indeed, her ideologically diverse pantheon of women is perhaps best appreciated only when situated as an original, even revolutionary, variable in a far more vast and complex political, religious, and administrative calculus.

PART I

Goddesses of Antiquity

SEEKING TO DISCERN LARGER POLITICAL PRINCIPLES in another place and time, historian William McNeill observes that "a successful revolution must invent or revive its own myths. Stability, predictability, control are otherwise impossible."[1] While McNeill's observations are drawn from Western societies in the modern era, the principles he delineates might be profitably applied to Wu Zhao's rule in the late seventh century: She could not simply invent an entirely new paradigm of political authority divorced from precedent; she could and did, however, creatively draw on a vast cultural repertoire of existing mythologies. She amassed prophecies and obscure myths connected to female deities, initially to buttress her position as empress and grand dowager and later to legitimize her new dynasty and validate her unique rule as a female emperor.

Wu Zhao was fortunate to have a large storehouse of goddess myths to draw upon. Susan Mann asserts that for a traditional culture that was ostensibly patriarchal, China possessed a wide-ranging, variegated repository of myths and folklore concerning womanhood.[2] In her study of Chinese mythology, Anne Birrell remarks that ancestral goddesses like Nüwa and the divinity of the Luo River were "more mythologically significant in terms of their function and role" than their male counterparts. She notes that these female divinities play a variety of different culture-shaping parts: creator, nature spirit, local tutelary spirit, mother or consort of a god, harbinger of disaster, donor of immortality, bringer of punishment, and dynastic founder.[3]

Mann argues that with the rise of a "Confucian moral agenda that dominate[d] the written record," these powerful ancient goddesses underwent a "civilizing process in which archaic myth was overwritten by history, literature, and the arts of popular culture," becoming "logically constituted elements" in China's patriarchal society.[4] To liberate and reclaim the original potency of these ancient goddesses, Wu Zhao attempted to reverse this process of many centuries, to un-write the texts that tamed once-powerful divinities and un-make the "civilizing process" that had harnessed them. Noting Wu Zhao's revival of cults of ancient goddesses long fallen into disuse, McNeill's remarks on successful revolutions come to mind.

In his classic *The Golden Bough*, Sir James George Frazer explains the primitive belief in an "extended self":

> The primitive believes that the self, or identity . . . is not limited to his physical being, but embraces also everything that is associated with it and everything that can evoke his presence in another person's mind. Thus, the shadow, name, footprint, gait, dress, excreta, portrait, etc. . . . are just as much an essential and integral part of him and his body, the more so because it can be evidence when he is corporeally absent.[5]

This idea of an "extended self" might profitably encompass the related realms of ceremonies, symbols, and monuments. In Frazer's sense, then, the ancient goddesses became part of Wu Zhao's "extended self," a part echoed in her rhetoric, texts, and iconography.

The three chapters in part I examine the respective roles of a trio of ancient divinities—mother-creator Nüwa; the goddess of the Luo River; and the silk goddess, Leizu—in Wu Zhao's assemblage of female political ancestors.

ONE

Wu Zhao as the Late Seventh-Century Avatar of Primordial Goddess Nüwa

VARIOUSLY KNOWN AS A DIVINE CREATOR, a savior of mankind, and a mother goddess worthy of an enduring fertility cult, Nüwa 女媧 had gained a mythic repute long before Wu Zhao's time. Suggesting a close connection to the essential female element of water, the cognate forms of *wa* or *gua* indicate a probable linkage to the snail or frog, bespeaking the primordial origins of this deity.[1] One contemporary scholar described this ur-mother, often depicted as half snake and half human (a fertile, marshy, and generative matrix that begat mankind), as a "were-snake Daoist goddess."[2] Another commentary tells of a "prestigious lamia" who "outlived the suppression and secularization of the archaic serpent women."[3] Not surprisingly, Wu Zhao discovered a valuable political immediacy in this female sovereign of hoary antiquity; by connecting herself to this mythic avatar, she gained leverage and legitimacy.

Dynamic and mutable, Nüwa played various parts in early texts. One scholar sees her as an evolution of a directional goddess who appeared on oracle bones in the Shang, a deified shamaness, rainmaker, and fertility spirit.[4] Though textual evidence intimates much earlier origins, Nüwa first appears by name in *Elegies of Chu* (Chuci 楚 辞), a Warring States–era text attributed to poet-official, Qu Yuan (343–278 B.C.), wherein the author poses the question: "How was Nü Wa's body made? How did she ascend when she rose on High and became empress?"[5] Andrew Plaks provides a provocative alternative translation—"Who created Nü-kua if she created mankind?"[6]— stating explicitly the challenge posed by a female creator divinity to patriarchal currents in later eras. Acknowledging the goddess's archaic reputation as a prolific mother-creator, annotator Wang Yi (A.D. 89–158) remarks,

"It was said that Nüwa had the head of a human being and the body of a snake and she gave birth to seventy offspring each day."[7]

In the Daoist *Liezi* 列子, a text whose dating is problematic but whose origins stem from early in the Warring States era, Nüwa is said to have "harbored the virtues of the great sages," though she lacked human form. She was cast as a savior of mankind, known for "smelting the five-colored stones to fill the holes in heaven, and breaking the legs of a turtle to support the four corners of the earth."[8] Not only was she recognized for restoring the equilibrium of a world out of kilter, but she was also known for taming the flood, stanching the inundating waters with ash and burned reeds.[9]

Compiled by Liu An (179–122 B.C.), the *Huainanzi* 淮南子 contains the passage, "Huangdi gave birth to *yin* and *yang*; Shang Pian to ears and eyes, and Sang Lin to arms and hands—events which were among the seventy transformations of Nü Wa."[10] Contemporary scholar Cai Junsheng reasonably points out that this transformation indicates that Nüwa not only predated but helped fashion the Yellow Emperor.[11] Dating from roughly a century later, the *Classic of Mountains and Seas* describes ten gods born from the guts of Nüwa.[12] In Ying Shao's (140–206) Eastern Han text, *Comprehensive Commentary on Popular Customs* (Fengsu tongyi 風俗通議), Nüwa was a creatrix, fashioning human beings from yellow earth.[13] These myths make clear that by the end of the Han dynasty, Nüwa was revered as a creator goddess. Schafer compares her to Nabatean Atargatis, "a cosmic mother goddess, with power over the fertility of living things."[14]

In Han mortuary iconography, this primeval goddess is often paired with a male divinity, her brother-husband Fuxi, their serpentine tails intertwined. As in the relief mural in the famous Wu Liang shrine in Shandong, Fuxi frequently holds a carpenter's square and Nüwa a compass, tools to fashion a world for infant humanity.[15] Painted on funerary banners and graven in relief on sarcophagi from the Han through the Tang, Nüwa and Fuxi were worshipped as primordial creators, guardian spirits and "tutelary genii of the dead."[16] Lee Irwin observes that Nüwa's signature compass serves as a symbol of social organization, marking her not only as a creator goddess, but also as "a goddess of proportion and measurement," vital to both architecture and hydro-engineering.[17]

Still, Anne Birrell, Edward Schafer, and others have noted that the autonomy and power she had possessed as a primeval goddess was diminished by the rise of the Confucian state.[18] Cai Junsheng echoes a similar

Figure 1.1 Tang-era image of Fuxi and Nüwa from Turfan, Xinjiang Uighur Autonomous Region Museum.

argument, opining, "At the time of the patriarchal clan in China, Nü Wa's activities seem to cease, and she 'died.'"[19] Once yoked to male figures, powerful female divinities like Nüwa and the Queen Mother of the West were forced to fit into a *yin-yang* schema during the Han and thereby were domesticated, diminished by emergent patriarchal mores.

Between the third and sixth centuries, the cult of Nüwa became virtually obsolete. In *Ancient China*, Edward Schafer contends that after the fall of the Han, Nüwa "faded to become a mere fairy tale being, neglected by the upper classes and ignored in state religion."[20] Yet rumors of her demise may have been exaggerated. When Cai Junsheng claims that Nüwa had "died," or Schafer asserts that "by Tang times she [Nüwa] was little remembered except by the poets, sometimes as a phantom in folktales and as a minor figure in local cults,"[21] they understate the goddess's enduring cultural resonance.

In Tang China, a powerful aura surrounding this archaic figure lingered. In an underground tomb from Wu Zhao's era, 1,600 miles west of her capital Luoyang, a painted silken funerary banner depicts Nüwa and Fuxi intertwined, with the goddess holding a compass, an instrument of celestial observation and symbol of the heavens.[22] A barrow mound next to the Yellow River bearing the name Tumulus of Nüwa that temporarily disappeared in 752 during the decadent late reign of Wu Zhao's grandson Xuanzong (r. 712–756), reemerged during the An Lushan Rebellion, prompting a diviner to observe ominously, "When graves and tombs move of themselves, the terrestrial realm will be shattered."[23] In contrast, transcendent poet Li Bo still recalled Nüwa as a creatress:

Nüwa played with the yellow earth,
Patting it into ignorant, inferior man.[24]

During the Tang dynasty, myth and history, legend and fact were frequently conflated. Whether to lavish praise upon an imperial patron or to cast seraphic radiance on a courtesan-lover, effusive Tang poets liberally sprinkled the names of Nüwa or other female divinities in their verse.[25]

Naturally, Wu Zhao availed herself of the numinous remnants of this powerful mother divinity. Literary masters vied to draw elegant associations between the goddess of antiquity and the female ruler, reviving the moribund cult of Nüwa in the process.

"REPAIRING THE SKY" WITH THE HELP
OF A PAIR OF LITERARY MASTERS

In the *Huainanzi*, amid an apocalyptic age when the barriers separating men and spirits had broken, Nüwa smelted five-colored stones to suture the sky (*bu tian* 補天). She severed the feet of a giant sea turtle to serve as pillars separating the earthly and heavenly realms, overwhelming a roiling, man-devouring dragon, and mounded ash to dam a churning freshet, delivering countless millions.[26] Her single-handed efforts to "mend the sky" helped shape Nüwa's image as a culture hero and savior of mankind.

To exalt their patron and sovereign, Wu Zhao's rhetoricians alluded to the primordial divinity's endeavors. Sundered by a string of catastrophes that struck the heart of the empire in the late 670s and early 680s, the metaphorical sky was in drastic need of mending. Gaozong, Wu Zhao's husband and coruler, was dying. In 679, an empire-wide cattle pestilence contributed to widespread famine.[27] On the fringes of the empire, Tibetans, Khitan, and Tujue Turks instigated a series of disturbances. In 681, there were widespread reports of earthquakes, floods, and droughts. During succeeding springs, in several prefectures on the northern fringe of the realm, millions of rabbits devoured seedlings before disappearing into thin air.[28] In the heart of the realm, a plague of locusts descended upon the crops, causing grain prices to skyrocket. As famine swept across the Yellow River, "the dead pillowed on each other in the streets of the two capitals [Chang'an and Luoyang]," and people resorted to cannibalism.[29]

In early 684, shortly after Gaozong's death, master rhetorician Cui Rong (653–706) delivered an encomium on behalf of the officials in Chang'an. Framing Grand Dowager Wu Zhao's regency as an auspicious new era foreshadowed by a long parade of sage monarchs, he wrote:

> Your official has heard that when the ruler acts with absolute virtue, auspicious tokens appear announcing the presence of a sage. When the ruler accords with the great *dao*, all of the numina respond. Therefore, with the actions of Yao and Shun, the Five Elders roamed the shoals of the Yellow River. With the ascendancy of King Wu of Zhou, the Four Divinities wandered the settlements of the Luo. Humbly considering your great achievement in mending the sky, Your Majesty, august Grand Dowager, has matched the earth in respectful eminence. In administering the empire, Your Majesty has devised and established a new foundation. As a result of obeying the will of heaven and acting in harmony with the people, Your Majesty has obtained extraordinary accomplishments.[30]

Cui Rong's effusive terms depict Wu Zhao as a sage possessing virtue akin to the female element earth, and merit matching savior-goddess Nüwa, the divinity evoked indirectly by his mention of "sky-mending." Tellingly,

Cui also surrounds Nüwa with a complement of worthies from the familiar set of male political ancestors—Yao, Shun, and King Wu of Zhou. In 684, Wu Zhao had just become grand dowager, and a sudden, radical departure from the familiar procession of culture heroes would have compromised rather than enhanced her authority.

Cui Rong became one of Wu Zhao's most important propagandists, rarely missing an opportunity to elegantly evoke the connection between his patron and members of her pantheon of female political ancestors. One of the aesthetic masters in a group that became known as the "literary quartet of friends" (wenzhang si you 文章四友), Cui Rong was discovered by Wu Zhao (then empress) when but a young prodigy excelling in the examinations.[31] Late in her reign, Wu Zhao asked Cui Rong to compile and edit a national history (guoshi 國史),[32] clearly demonstrating her trust in and esteem for him. After her death, Cui Rong wrote Wu Zhao's eulogy along with the "veritable records" (shi lu 實錄) for her reign.[33]

When Wu Zhao's authority as grand dowager had solidified several years later, Li Qiao (644–713)—another member of the literary quartet who emerged as an important rhetorician—compared her to Nüwa in a congratulatory memorial. His lavish panegyric reads: "her imperium is more exalted than the mending of the sky; her motherly virtue matches that of the earth."[34] By grandiose analogy, Wu Zhao's rule as grand dowager had brought about peace and stability, a remedy to the turmoil and calamities that beset the realm during Gaozong's final years. As with Cui Rong, Wu Zhao held Li Qiao in the highest esteem, specially ordering him to draft the most important compositions in court.[35] Eventually, he rose to chief minister in the later stages of her Zhou dynasty.[36]

When Wu Zhao was emperor, Li Qiao wrote the inscription for the stele of the Buddhist Great Cloud Monastery in Xuanzhou (in modern-day Anhui), which included the following lines: "She entered riding a mare, but now pilots flying dragons. From the scattered sands of dynastic decline she has forged the stones of Nüwa to repair Heaven."[37] Here, Li Qiao deftly employs the metaphor of repairing heaven to depict Wu Zhao as a latter-day Nüwa, a redeemer/heroine who remedied the ills of a chaotic, decadent time.

In conjunction with Wu Zhao's political ascendancy, Cui Rong and Li Qiao's references to "mending the sky" helped rhetorically merge divinity and earthly ruler. Like Nüwa before her, Wu Zhao delivered mankind from primeval chaos. Nüwa's name and achievements are no longer safely ensconced among the deeds of storied male political ancestors. By the later stages of her tenure as grand dowager, Wu Zhao's gender as a ruler was no longer concealed: instead, Nüwa was rhetorically employed to celebrate and amplify Wu Zhao's status as a female ruler.

NÜWA AS EMPRESS AND DOWAGER: AN INTERMEDIATE DANCE STEP

After Gaozong was interred at Qianling in late 684, libations were presented to the recently deceased emperor, set to a musical score entitled "Harmonizing with Heaven" (Juntian 鈞天).[38] Nüwa appears in the lyrics for the ritual dance that accompanied the music. This score was written at an extremely sensitive political juncture. In the second month of 684, with the support of a group of chief ministers, acting regent Grand Dowager Wu Zhao had removed her son, Li Xiǎn 李顯 (Zhongzong 中宗, r. 684 and 705–710), from the throne after just seven weeks as emperor. His nominal replacement, her youngest son Ruizong 睿宗 (r. 684–690 and 710–712), was sent to the Eastern Palace, usually the apartments of the crown prince. Wu Zhao presided over the court. She made decisions of state. In the fourth month, she exiled the deposed Zhongzong, Li Xiǎn, to Fangzhou (modern-day Hubei). In the ninth month, she launched a series of reforms to assay the temper of the court and the wider empire beyond. She changed the colors of court robes and banners to golden to match the Zhou dynasty of antiquity, altered names of offices to echo archaic designations, and declared Luoyang her Divine Capital (Shendu 神都).[39] Richard Guisso terms such measures "closely akin to those usually preceding a new dynasty,"[40] intimating Wu Zhao's future intent to assume the throne. These steps set many in court and country on edge; a spate of rebellions broke out, though they were quickly quashed.[41]

These tensions made it all the more vital to broadcast an aura of ritual tranquility and stability. Recalling Gaozong's rule with purposeful, fond nostalgia, the lyrics to the "Dance to Harmonize with Heaven" are recorded in the "Treatise of Music" in the *Old Tang History*:

The Exalted Sovereign marches in synchronicity with the *dao*;
in ceremonial garb, hands folded, he governs with effortless action.
He transformed and embraced the wild steppe tribes;[42]
his armies conquered the Korean peninsula.[43]

In ceremony, he reverently performed the *feng* and *shan* rites;[44]
in music, his splendid performances were regulated congregations of
   harmony.
Jointly enthroned with Empress Wa 娲后,
he might well be called Fuxi.

Gaozong is categorically identified with Fuxi. Grand dowager Wu Zhao was cast as his consort and coruler, Nüwa. The ceremonial dance expressly remarks that they were "jointly enthroned" (*he wei* 合位), sharing the position of ruler. And yet, not wanting to alienate Li-Tang loyalists in the court or undermine her position as dowager-regent by a rash and sudden claim to emperorship, Wu Zhao/Nüwa is still presented as an empress (*hou* 后) rather than as a sovereign (*huang* 皇). Perhaps to assuage fears, Wu Zhao/Nüwa is not yet independent, but remains partnered with a Gaozong/Fuxi. Political and military highlights of Gaozong's career are recalled, though these events also redounded to the merit of living de facto ruler Wu Zhao. She, too, had played a starring role in the *feng* and *shan* rites at Mount Tai.

The lyric "regulated congregations of harmony" (*laiyi* 來儀) is connected with the phoenix (*fenghuang* 鳳凰), a symbol of female imperial power that Wu Zhao utilized extensively.[45]

SAGELY AND DIVINE

Emphasizing the deity's role as a fertility goddess and creatress, the *Shuowen jiezi*, an etymological dictionary from the Western Han, defines Nüwa as the "Divine and Sagely (*shen sheng* 神聖) woman who gave birth to all living things on earth"[46]—an additional facet of the divinity Wu Zhao sought to emulate. In the years leading up to her establishment of the Zhou, she cast herself in the image of a sagacious mother-creator.

According to Sima Guang's *Comprehensive Mirror for the Advancement of Governance* (*Zizhi tongjian*), in 572 an official of Qi attempted to persuade the court to install Lu Lingxuan as grand dowager–regent with the argument, "Though Lu is a woman, she is nonetheless both puissant and outstanding. Since Nüwa, there has been no such woman." In Hu Sanxing's (1230–1302) Yuan-era commentary on the text, he cites a remark of Sima Zhen (679–732), a contemporary of Wu Zhao who served primarily under her grandson Xuanzong: "Nüwa was her customary name. In virtue, she was divine and sagely. She replaced Fuxi on the throne. She was also called Nüxi."[47]

For Sima Zhen, "sagely" and "divine"—Nüwa's traits in the *Shuowen jiezi*—remained attributes of the goddess. It is no surprise they had a familiar ring: The female emperor of his own time had borne the same terms in several of her titles.

In Wu Zhao's progressively grander titles, both *shen* 神 (divine) and *sheng* 聖 (sagely, saintly) played central conceptual roles. On the summer solstice in 688, presiding over the court as grand dowager Wu Zhao adopted the title Sage Mother, Divine Sovereign (Shengmu shenhuang 聖母神皇), a vital intermediate step on her path to emperorship.[48] On behalf of the court ministers, Cui Rong presented a commemoration urging her to assume this honorific designation. In this memorial, he accentuated the "mother" in her new title, framing Wu Zhao's maternity in broad, inclusive strokes. He both styled her a mother of empire and couched her authority as Sage Mother in a longer lineage of female worthies who had administered or shared in the governance of the state. At the start, Cui cites the initial passage of Laozi's *Daodejing*—"the named was the mother of the myriad creatures."[49] The petition continues:

> Without the mother (*mu* 母), compassionate love cannot fill the
> boundaries,
> Without the Sovereign (*huang* 皇), there is no one to lead and trans-
> form the empire.[50]

With this new title, Wu Zhao played two complementary roles: all-embracing, compassionate mother and capable, potent sovereign-father. In traditional China, the terse phrase "stern father and compassionate mother" (*yanfu cimu* 嚴父慈母) is often used to delineate respective parental roles.

In a subsequent passage in this same peroration, Cui Rong once again makes manifest these twinned aspects—the sagely and the divine—remarking:

> Examining into antiquity, the Sage Mother, Divine Sovereign:
> Where *yin* and *yang* harmonize, where perspicacious virtue is born;
> Where sun and moon are conjoined, where the wandering spirits
> descend:
> This is her home.
> The Turquoise Terrace of the Woman of Yusong:
> This is her rightful place.[51]

Based on the phrase "examining into antiquity" (*ji gu* 稽古), the first part of this passage appears to refer not to Wu Zhao herself but to her namesake Sage Mother, Nüwa. Strikingly, there is no Fuxi. This primordial ur-mother occupied a space that contained—and implicitly contained within herself—both sun and moon and both male and female essences. Naturally, this role of androgynous creator, of hermaphroditic god, extended to Wu Zhao. The manifest purpose of Cui Rong's rhetoric was to exalt her person. The Woman of Yusong is Jiandi, who, after eating the egg of a dark bird, gave birth to Shang founder Xie.[52] The first ancestor of every dynasty had to be born of divine means: if produced by union of man and woman, he would not be first ancestor. Male political ancestors—Fuxi, Di Ku (Jiandi's husband), and Xie—are conspicuously absent. Light irradiates only the female progenitor.

Subsequently, Nüwa appears again in Cui Rong's memorial:

Nüwa was a manifestation of divinity,
And still she administered as emperor in distant antiquity.
Taisi had a spotless reputation,
And still she alone took it upon herself to mother the exalted Zhou.[53]

Once again, Nüwa was the first link in a chain of "mothers of antiquity," a divine woman who generously deigned to descend and preside over mankind. This time, rather than the first Shang ancestress Jiandi, Nüwa followed Taisi, consort of legendary King Wen.[54] Eminently sensitive to the fluctuating political tides, lyric by lyric, verse by verse, Cui Rong helped assemble—one might even argue, create—Wu Zhao's lineage of female political ancestors.

EMPEROR WA AND THE INAUGURATION OF THE ZHOU

Yang Lien-sheng once remarked that there were only two instances in which women became emperors in Chinese history: the first being Nüwa, who "lived in such remote antiquity that her story does not seem to be reliable," and the latter Wu Zhao, "the Empress Zetian of the Tang dynasty."[55]

Nüwa's elevation to emperor seems to be fairly late. Many early texts enumerate the legendary Three Sovereigns (Sanhuang 三皇) of antiquity, culture heroes who founded Chinese civilization and ruled men. There is some contention over their identity. Most often, these three were Fuxi, Suiren (the creator of fire), and Shennong, the Divine Farmer.[56] Beginning in the late Eastern Han, however, Nüwa often replaced Suiren or Shennong. In the opening chapter of Ying Shao's *Comprehensive Commentary on Popular Customs*, "On Emperors and Rulers," he relates that "Fuxi, Nüwa, and Shennong were the Three Emperors."[57]

Nüwa's paramount position as sovereign was still recognized in the early Tang. A temple stele inscription composed by Zhu Zizhu (d. 640), an official in the late Sui and early Tang, contains the passage "mending stones in the time of Emperor Wa 媧皇."[58] The first reference in the standard histories to Nüwa as Emperor Wa appears in editorial (579–648) comments at the end of a biography in the *History of Jin* (*Jin shu*), completed in 648, during the reign of Taizong.[59] In an imperial edict that same year proposing to perform the *feng* and *shan* rites on Mount Tai, the celebrated Taizong, the Tang paragon of masculinity and political authority, addressed Nüwa as Emperor Wa, apparently with neither compunction nor qualms. The emperor declared:

> We have heard that heaven is high and earth is vast. The first to disseminate the myriad peoples were Emperor Wa and Suiren. They commenced to reverently deliberate on the Mysterious Register.[60]

Unabashedly, Taizong acknowledged Nüwa's emperorship in a public declaration to the court, not hesitating to evoke her position as a woman sovereign and her mystic role as a benevolent, generative force. For Taizong and his court, there was nothing anti-Confucian or emasculating about Nüwa's preeminent role. As a Talent (Cairen 才人), a fifth-ranked concubine, in Taizong's vast seraglio at the time, Wu Zhao perhaps gleaned an important lesson about the rhetorical force of language. If the inclusion of Nüwa could make the ceremonial plea of a male ruler more compelling, then surely the mother goddess might amplify her authority and sovereignty.

Three decades later, Taizong's son Gaozong rose from his deathbed and, unable to ride his horse to Zetian Gate to make a public announcement, took the unorthodox measure of gathering a group of commoners before the imperial basilica to promulgate an edict on 27 December 683 that changed the reign name to Amplifying the Dao.[61] The edict situates Nüwa as the originating link in the familiar lineage of male culture heroes:

> Revering the Dao, the ruler dwells in the Purple Tenuity, letting his robes hang loose.[62] Cultivating virtue, the minister exhaustively uses his loyal heart as a grindstone. When the higher maintains proper conduct, the lower respects ritual protocol—this is called edification. Only when one deviates from the path of purity, loyalty, and trustworthiness do things gradually deteriorate. In remote antiquity, though Nüwa, Suiren, and Fuxi ruled without active governance the realm was transformed. Later, the Yellow Emperor, Zhuanxu, Yao, Shun, Yu, Tang the Successful, King Wen, and King Wu all acted with absolute public-mindedness and great benevolence.[63]

Nüwa was not just one of the Three Sovereigns of distant antiquity: she was the first, foremost among a lineage of political ancestors including both sexes. In the inaugural address for this new era, Nüwa was not only independent from Fuxi—she preceded him as an independent ruler, the first of the Three Sovereigns of antiquity. She therefore becomes the first link in the proud concatenation of subsequent male rulers. Given that Gaozong died the night the new reign era was announced, it seems likely that Wu Zhao, acting as regent during her husband's convalescence, was behind this document. While this edict anticipated Wu Zhao's ascent to the imperial throne by more than six years, it served as a pointed and timely reminder that a woman had occupied the dragon throne once, and a woman could occupy it again.

It has previously been noted that in a memorial congratulating Grand Dowager Wu Zhao on her elevation to Sage Mother in 688, literary master Cui Rong pointedly remarked, Nüwa had "administered as emperor in distant antiquity."[64] Not surprisingly, once she formally ascended the throne as emperor in 690, her talented coterie of propagandists echoed with greater frequency, in edict and verse, the mythic name of Nüwa, the female ruler from the remote past. In "Panegyric for the Great Zhou Receiving the Mandate," Chen Zi'ang (661–702) praised her inauguration of the Zhou dynasty in 690, comparing Wu Zhao to Nüwa, writing: "Great indeed was the divine merit of Nüxi [Nüwa], but nothing is grander than this day!"

One of the foremost literary and poetic practitioners of Wu Zhao's era, Chen Zi'ang (like Cui Rong and Li Qiao) played an important role in fashioning a distinctive political vocabulary for his sovereign. In a series of memorials and panegyrics, he floridly celebrated prominent markers of her political ascendancy like the establishment of her Divine Capital Luoyang[65] and her construction of the Bright Hall (Mingtang 明堂),[66] in the process singing the praises of her new Zhou dynasty.

In the same panegyric extolling the inauguration of the Zhou, Chen Zi'ang later invoked Nüwa:

Heaven has ordered the Divine Phoenix
to descend and bless my Zhou.
Its color and appearance inspire reverence;
Surpassingly auspicious, its graceful deportment.
Only we have the Zhou
That so truly preserves the virtue of heaven.
When the former emperor [Gaozong] was on the verge of death,
He bequeathed [to her] the Imperium.
And the people said, "Heaven has blessed us
that we have this Emperor Nüxi [Nüwa]!
She has created the firmament and fixed the distant boundaries
    [of empire];
To distantly resound her glorious reputation.
Majestic our August Emperor,
The foremost, so admirable!
If not for heaven's mandate,
Then toward whom would the phoenix gravitate?"[67]

The association between Wu Zhao and Nüwa, according to Chen Zi'ang in this ornate tribute, is announced in the joyful collective exclamation of the populace. In Chen's vision, Wu Zhao, like Nüwa before her, was not merely founding a new dynasty, but forging a new world.

EVOKING THE NAME OF NÜWA

An essay of Li Shangyin (813–858) from the late Tang contains a conversation in which the fictitious Wife of Yidu admonishes Wu Zhao to recall the proper respective positions of female *yin* and male *yang*. Li Shangyin's fictional woman poses the rhetorical question, "My ruler knows that in the past the female was inferior to the male?" The female ruler rejoins, "Yes, I know." "In antiquity Nüwa did not formally become Son of Heaven, she only assisted Fuxi in administering the Nine Provinces," the Wife of Yidu continues. At this juncture, her line of reasoning unexpectedly swerves. Rather than conforming to Confucian boilerplate by indicating that Wu Zhao, like Nüwa in the past, should accommodate the principles of *yin* and *yang* and occupy a proper, lesser position, she asserts that unlike Nüwa, Wu Zhao is a "true Son of Heaven"—an emperor. She advises her to get rid of her male concubines, who will drain her of her *yin* energies. If Wu Zhao heeds her, Li Shangyin's Wife of Yidu contends, "Male [power] will be progressively pared down and women will increasingly monopolize authority. This is my wish."[68] Just as a stalwart Confucian minister concerned with the well-being of the state might stridently attempt to dissuade a male ruler from being drawn into the sensual inner quarters of women, where he would compromise his sociopolitical vigor, so this female advisor urged Wu Zhao not to enfeeble herself—politically or sexually—by excessive contact with her male harem.[69]

DRAGONSPAWN: A TANTALIZING TALE FROM GUANGYUAN

Wu Zetian was reputedly born in Lizhou, a prefecture based in modern-day Guangyuan, a city tucked in the rugged mountains of northeastern Sichuan. She is still honored there today with an annual 1 September Empress Day (Nü'er jie 女兒節, lit. Daughters' Day) celebration featuring colorful phoenix boat competitions with all-women crews on the Jialing River. In Guangyuan's Buddhist Huangze Temple stands an image of the apotheosized Wu Zhao crafted in the Later Shu 後蜀 (934–965).[70]

Local legend claims that one day Wu Zhao's father Wu Shiyue (577–635) was boating with his wife, née Yang (579–670), on the Jialing River, when a black dragon surged out of the waters and implanted itself in the shocked woman's womb. Falling into a semiconscious swoon, Yang dreamed that she was entangled in intercourse with the river dragon. Soon, she discovered that she was pregnant. The resulting child was Wu Zhao, a demi-dragon descended to earth. Just as Nüwa, the female emperor from ancient lore, was often depicted as half snake (or half dragon), so this legend framed Wu Zhao as a supernal being, a "true dragon, Son of Heaven" (*zhenlong tianzi* 真龍天子).[71]

Figure 1.2 Initially crafted in the Later Shu (934–965), a statue of the apotheosized Wu Zhao is seated in the Buddhist Huangze Temple in Guangyuan, Sichuan. The female emperor is still honored in this city in northeastern Sichuan province.

Not only does this legend illustrate a connection between Wu Zhao, Nüwa, and the totemic dragon, but it also situates the medieval female sovereign within a symbolic line of Chinese dragon-rulers. The Yellow Emperor of antiquity had a draconian aspect[72] and Han founder Gaozu was the reputed issue of a similar union.[73] Routinely, Chinese rulers donned dragon robes to drive home their connection to this culturally resonant totemic beast.

DENIGRATING NÜWA

When a direct confrontation with Wu Zhao was dangerous or inadvisable, ideological opponents could denigrate her proxy, Nüwa. Accordingly, a rhetorical dismissal of the creator goddess often served as a pointed, thinly veiled criticism of Wu Zhao herself. In 685, Li Shenji, a member of a lesser branch of the imperial family serving as assistant magistrate of Jiyuan County (in modern-day Henan province), composed a stele inscription that exalted recently deceased Gaozong while omitting all praise for the grand dowager. The work represents a clear effort to connect the Li family donors both to the Daoist geography of the region and Gaozong. The sacrosanct Daoist landscape of Henei is presented as follows: "Mountains are connected to Mount Wangwu, via the Clear Barrens (Grotto) Heaven; settlements are belted to the Blissful Garden, much like the grounds of Laixiang."[74] Later, amplifying Gaozong, Li Shenji remarks: "The Grand Emperor's divine merit is without flaw." [75] Laozi and Gaozong are the dual recipients of the inscription, while Wu Zhao and female political ancestors are conspicuously absent.

The aforementioned inscription was written in the immediate aftermath of the revolt of Li princes in late 684. More than 250 members of the Tang imperial family contributed to the project. The Li family members specifically mentioned in the inscription—Li Deyi, Li Ruyi, and Li Gongxie—appear nowhere else in historical records. Perhaps this is because Wu Zhao, as grand dowager and in her first years as emperor, targeted them in her extensive purge of the Li family. Disgruntled members of the Tang imperial family, especially those so close to the capital during this precarious period of incubation, posed a threat.

The tone of this stele inscription from Fengxian Observatory in Jiyuan exalted the Li family, rallying its scattered members in the aftermath of the failed uprising and recalling their glorious descent from Laozi. In addition, the inscription lauds Zhongzong, deposed in 684, while disparaging Wu Zhao:

> The Emperor's heir has protected the grand foundation of state,
> Illumining the perspicacious path of Wu Ding;[76]
> In mending rent heavens and smelting colored stones,
> He overwhelms and quells Emperor Wa.
> Passing the remote corners of the earth, he contributes precious jasper;
> He overtakes and captures Empress Ji 姬后.[77]

The emperor celebrated in the inscription is Gaozong. His rightful heir, in the eyes of Li family and Tang loyalists, was the recently deposed Li Xiǎn, Zhongzong. These lines sing the demoted emperor's praises, pointedly framing him as one who outstrips these eminent women, past and present, in virtue and capability. Rather than an incompetent and pathetic exile languishing in Fangzhou, the powerful champion of Li Shenji's imagination rivals Wu Ding, the ruler who restored the Shang dynasty; he is a potent hero capable of galvanizing the fragmented Li clan, one who might best Nüwa at her own game of "mending the heavens," stabilizing a realm rent by chaos. For good measure, this fantasy of a strong male emperor then excels Empress Ji, the consort of King Wen, founder of the Zhou dynasty of antiquity. The triumph over Nüwa and capture of King Wen's consort in the inscription reflect Li Shenji's powerful wish to overwhelm and crush the grand dowager and regent Wu Zhao, restoring his Li kinsmen to what he construed as their rightful position. The collective wishes of the Li clansmen, though graven in stone, did not come true; feckless Li Xiǎn remained in exile while Wu Zhao rose to power.

Once again, nearly two decades later, Wu Zhao's political antagonists deployed the ancient ur-mother Nüwa to undermine her modern-day avatar. And, as twenty years before, the underlying intent was the same: to restore Zhongzong and bring about the end of Wu Zhao's political prominence. Su Anheng aggressively remonstrated on several occasions to pressure Wu Zhao to abdicate.[78] In 701, in his mild "First Petition to Reinstall the Crown Prince as Emperor," Su Anheng writes: "Humbly observing the time of Nüwa, it was an era when customs were simple and straightforward. People were honest and easily administered. The ruler might simply sit with robes hanging and hands folded, and nothing needed to be said."[79] By framing Nüwa's sovereignty as rule over a simple, pastoral state in a primitive time, Su Anheng tacitly downplayed the efficacy of both Nüwa and Wu Zhao. The implication was that the complex, cosmopolitan empire of the early eighth century required the steady, strong hand of a male ruler.

Su Anheng argued by historical analogy that whereas Wu Zhao had served as regent and emperor for two decades, even Empress Lü (241–180 B.C.) of the Western Han had acted as dowager-regent for but eight years when Emperor Hui (r. 195–188 B.C.) was young and infirm, before ceding power back to him. Gently yet firmly, the petition claimed that the time had come for Wu Zhao to retire, to voluntarily abdicate the throne to her mature and worthy son.[80] A series of increasingly strident memorials ensued in an effort to oust the septuagenarian ruler from her throne.[81] Emboldened, the cheeky minister had the temerity to suggest that Wu Zhao "occupied the position of Yao and Shun, but did not follow the moral path of Yao and Shun," that "coveting her son's precious throne," she had "forgotten the deep kindness of a mother."[82]

CONCLUSION

Nüwa's presence in Wu Zhao's political rhetoric can be understood as a part of a wider strategy to include female paragons from antiquity, the illustrious repertoire of women who collectively helped legitimate and magnify her imperial authority. After all, versatile Nüwa numbered among the company of what Mark Lewis terms the "potent, wonder-working rulers at the heart of imposing order and definition on a world that otherwise collapsed into chaos."[83] Indeed, Nüwa—with the arguable exception of the Queen Mother of the West—was the only female ruler-divinity in Chinese tradition of whom such a claim might be made. In the capable hands of Wu Zhao and her propagandists, Nüwa, no longer paired with Fuxi, was largely liberated from restrictive brackets of dualistic Han Confucianism. So freed, this woman emperor and creator from shadowy antiquity now became a political ancestress of her latter-day heir and avatar, Wu Zhao. Framed with flamboyant elegance by Wu Zhao's most capable propagandists—aesthetic masters like Cui Rong, Li Qiao, and Chen Zi'ang—the affiliation of goddess and ruler was broadcast widely: carved on monumental stelae, announced to the court via memorials, and reiterated time and again in Wu Zhao's majestic imperial titles.

Alternatively, for men like Su Anheng, belittling Nüwa was part of an aggressive rhetorical campaign to undermine Wu Zhao's potency as a sovereign, to persuade the embattled woman emperor to relinquish the throne.

Sanctifying Luoyang
The Luo River Goddess and Wu Zhao

AT THE VERY BEGINNING OF HER REGENCY as grand dowager in 684, Wu Zhao designated Luoyang her Divine Capital. Naturally, she sought to utilize the cultural and political currency vested in her new seat of power. This chapter examines the role of Consort Fu (Fufei 宓妃), the goddess of the Luo River (Luoshen nü 洛神女), in magnifying Wu Zhao's political authority.

THE GODDESS OF THE LUO

"The waters of the Lo River," Edward Schafer observed of the watercourse that meanders through Luoyang, "enjoyed a reputation as venerable as those of the great Ho itself, into which it ultimately empties. They appear prominently in the earliest Chinese literature and never lost their nostalgic fascination, which depended finally on the central position of the river in the ancient plains civilization of Shang."[1] Though sacrifices were made to the river from remote antiquity, the earliest textual appearance of an anthropomorphized Luo River goddess is in "Li Sao" 離騷, the famous lyric-poem of Qu Yuan. On his celestial ramblings, the protagonist in this verse encountered various goddesses and noblewomen before meeting the lovely Consort Fu:

> I order Fenglong to ride a cloud,
> and find the location of Fufei.
> Loosening the girdle-band as my word of betrothal,
> I order Jianxiu to be the go-between.
> Numerous and confused are the separations and unions.

Obstinate and rebellious she is difficult to move.

In the evenings she returns to sojourn at Qiongshi.

In the mornings she washes her hair in Weipan stream.

She guards her beauty with arrogance.

She amuses herself every day with licentious wanderings.

Though indeed beautiful, she has no propriety.

Let us leave her and find someone else.[2]

Finding this poetic vision of the Luo River goddess too headstrong and flighty, the protagonist abandons his pursuit.[3]

Third-century commentator Ru Chun remarked that Consort Fu—in his mythic rendition the daughter of world creator Fuxi—drowned in the Luo River (Luoshui 洛水) and was resurrected as a goddess.[4] Perhaps the most evocative depiction of the Luo goddess comes from Cao Zhi's (192–232) famous "Rhapsody of the Luo Goddess" (Luoshen fu 洛神賦), written to honor his elder brother Cao Pi (r. 220–226), the first emperor of the Wei (220–265), and to exalt the sacred environs of Luoyang, where Cao Pi had fixed his capital. According to some traditions, Cao Zhi composed the poem to express his unrequited love for his elder brother's wife, Empress Zhen.[5] He describes the Luo River goddess as an arrestingly beautiful woman regally accoutered in a headdress of gold, pearls, and kingfisher feathers. "Fluttering like a swan, twisting and turning like a dragon," she shimmered, "sparkling like the sun rising from morning mists . . . flaming like a lotus flower topping the green waves." Clearly a goddess, she trails "airy trains of mistlike gauze" as she moves wreathed in a fragrant "haze of unseen orchids."[6] The ambience of Cao Zhi's evocative verse left an enduring resonance, informing Tang-era depictions of women as elegant divinities; in Wu Zhao's era, this image of the Luo River goddess as a transcendent beauty was still fresh in collective literary and poetic consciousness. Written late in Gaozong's reign (or during Wu Zhao's regency), Li Shan's (d. 689) *Selections of Refined Literature* (*Wenxuan* 文選) contained Cao Zhi's celebrated rhapsody with an accompanying commentary.[7]

Inspired by Cao Zhi's poem, Emperor Ming of Jin (r. 323–325) is reputed to have painted a picture of this bewitching river deity.[8] Originally painted by the "matchless painter" (*hua jue* 畫絕) Gu Kaizhi (345–409), a picture scroll of the Luo River goddess has been preserved in several extant Song-era reproductions. Patricia Karetzky describes the river goddess in one of

Figure 2.1 Southern Song reproduction of Gu Kaizhi's *Goddess of the Luo River.*

these reproductions as "a court beauty in her aquatic domain—slender and petite, with discreetly dressed hair studded with adornments . . . swathed in a long silk robe with fluttering scarves."[9] This pictorial image further animated Cao Zhi's literary rendering of the goddess. "From Gu Kaizhi on," Susan Nelson has observed, "dream girls and river nymphs—filmy, sylph-like beings—have been pictured in wafting clothing and lightsome attitudes."[10] Though only Song-era reproductions remain, Zhang Mingxue, among other contemporary scholars, has remarked on the consummate skill and artistry with which Gu Kaizhi recreated Cao Zhi's peerless riparian goddess.[11] More pertinent to the present exploration, Wu Hong has noted that Gu Kaizhi's invented iconographic tradition of the surpassing woman-goddess reached its zenith in the Tang.[12]

But the Luo River goddess was reckoned far more than an elegant beauty. With Luoyang as their capital, rulers of the Eastern Han and Jin (265–420) dynasties worshipped the Luo River, praying for rain, protection, and blessings. To relieve a protracted drought, an Eastern Han emperor sent an emissary to the Luo River to pray for rain.[13] During the Jin, "in spring and autumn ministers and nobles on down to common folk went to the banks of the Luo River to perform the rite of apotropaic purification."[14] Under Jin Wudi (r. 265–290), an imperial concubine suffering from an illness went to the Luo seeking ritual purification.[15] Long before Wu Zhao's time, the waters of the Luo were believed to possess great healing and evil-warding powers.

In *The Divine Woman*, Edward Schafer observes that the goddess of the Luo River appears in Tang poetry as "a pert, contemporary belle, almost a courtesan . . . a metaphor for a secular charmer," though on occasions she was also represented as "a gossamer, moonlit sylph."[16] He registers disappointment that in the usually capable hands of vaunted Tang poets the Luo River goddess is painted in a conventional manner with "tedious" strokes: slender-waisted, mothlike eyebrows, fragrant, and fragile, "tremulously white, like bleached silk, like a white lotus, like soft moonlight, like drifting snow."[17] Tang prose literature, not surprisingly, features trysts between gifted young scholars and the lovely river divinity. Du Mu's (803–852) one-chapter *Chronicle of Dragon Ladies* (*Longnüzhuan* 龍女傳) recounts a liaison between the zither-strumming literatus Xiao Kuang and the Luo River goddess.[18] In the late Tang, in poet-official Xu Ning's "Peony," the river divinity appears as one capable of generating natural beauty:

> Who doesn't adore the lovely peony?
> Divinely blessed, of all the flowers in the city it most commands
> > the gaze.
> Seemingly, it was crafted by the goddess of the Luo River:
> Who with boundless elegance and floral grace excels the roseate dawn.[19]

Luoyang is still known as the "City of Peonies" (Mudan cheng 牡丹城): the flower, like the river and the goddess, constitutes an iconic part of the image of the polis. Nonetheless, for the goddess to be a useful member of her pantheon, Wu Zhao needed something more vigorous and substantive than this evanescent poetic image.

In Daoist chronicler Du Guangting's (850–933) description of the Luo River goddess in *Register of the Assembled Transcendents of the Walled City* (composed in the final years of the Tang), it is written that the goddess "achieved the *dao* becoming a water immortal, and thereupon became ruler of the Luo River." She held floating banquets, hosting other female immortals.[20] This later representation of the Luo River divinity as a potent goddess tallies more closely, perhaps, with Wu Zhao's desired image.

ELEVATING LUOYANG, THE DIVINE CAPITAL

Luoyang, situated in the middle of the Yellow River valley in the northern part of modern-day Henan, was more proximate to the center of the Tang empire than Chang'an. With monumental architecture and elaborate symbols, Wu Zhao impressed her own distinctive ideological brand upon this city, making it her own capital.

The ancients called greater Luoyang, an area known for its rich natural bounty, the "Center of Heaven" (Tianzhong 天中). The legendary sage-kings of the Xia reputedly hailed from this region. Vestiges of Shang palaces have been excavated in the vicinity of Luoyang. In the Western Zhou, the vaunted Duke of Zhou, determined that Luoyang was a highly auspicious site upon which to build a new settlement.[21] Subsequently, in the Eastern Zhou, Eastern Han, Wei, and Jin dynasties, Luoyang served as the capital. In 605, Sui Yangdi (r. 604–618) moved the capital from Chang'an back to Luoyang. In addition, by completing the Grand Canal, linking north to south, he elevated Luoyang's role as a hub of commerce.[22]

Shortly after Wu Zhao rose to become empress in 655, the prominence of Luoyang was enhanced. In 658, Gaozong made an imperial progress eastward from Chang'an and proclaimed Luoyang the eastern capital (Dongdu 東都).[23] Chang'an, the epicenter of Tang power, was in the Guanzhong region to the west. The imperial Li family shared long-standing ties with a bloc of powerful, entrenched Guanzhong families. There were other such powerful blocs in Shandong to the east and in southern China. The daughter of a Taiyuan lumber merchant, Wu Zhao could depend upon neither support nor sympathy from these powerful blocs. Luoyang offered a central locale, a neutral venue perfectly situated between the Guanzhong and Shandong.[24]

Immediately after Gaozong was buried outside Chang'an in 684, grand dowager Wu Zhao launched a campaign to build Luoyang into a city rivaling that great Tang cosmopolis. To superimpose her present administration upon the past golden age, she implemented a series of reforms. In assigning new names to bureaucratic offices, she drew upon archaic titles from the *Rites of Zhou* and the *Book of History*. And in late autumn of 684, Luoyang was elevated from eastern capital to Divine Capital.[25]

Rhetoricians worked to exalt Wu Zhao and her Divine Capital. The famous apocryphal *Commentary on the Great Cloud Sutra*, composed in 690 by the monk Xue Huaiyi, Wu Zhao's reputed lover, and other Buddhist propagandists on the eve of her establishment of the Zhou dynasty, contains a series of prophecies geared to show her inevitable ascent as female ruler, bodhisattva, and cakravartin.[26] The *Commentary* cites a passage from the Guangwu inscription, a river-borne stone purportedly found in the Si River in 688[27] that contained the mystical words, "The King is at Luoyang." The propagandists handily interpret the king to be "the Divine Sovereign [Shenhuang 神皇, part of the title Wu Zhao assumed in 688] who reigns at the Divine Capital."[28] Elsewhere in the Guangwu inscription, it is recorded, "[She] will not run away, [she] will not fly high: [she] will be composedly seated in the center with no need to move." The propagandists analyze that "the center" refers to "the Divine Capital, which is at the 'center of the territory'; once more the meaning of the Divine Sovereign reigning majestically over Luoyang is made clear."[29]

In 690, atop Zetian Gate in Luoyang, Wu Zhao terminated the Tang and inaugurated the Zhou dynasty.[30] The state altars of grain and soil were established in her Divine Capital, and she set up seven imperial temples for the Wu clan, a number befitting an imperial clan.[31] In 691, thousands of families were moved from Guanzhong to fill Luoyang.[32] In 693, city walls were erected.[33]

Wu Zhao filled her Divine Capital with a formidable panoply of her might.[34] Completed in 694, the spectacular centerpiece of her dynastic capital was the Axis of the Sky (Tianshu 天樞), a hundred-foot pillar of bronze set on an iron mountain, surmounted by a scintillating fire pearl on a cloud canopy held aloft by a quartet of dragons. Surrounded by mysterious guardian beasts, it was deployed where all entering Luoyang could witness its splendor—outside the southern gate of the Imperial City next to Heaven's Ford Bridge at the trifurcation of the Luo River.[35] Her awe-inspiring Bright Hall complexes, joint ceremonial and administrative centers, towered over the city—elaborate ideological amalgams combining Buddhist, Daoist, and Confucian elements.[36] Arrayed before this new political and religious emblem of her authority, she set, on a monumental scale, her interpretation of the Nine Tripods (Jiu ding 九鼎), sacred vessels symbolizing moral authority and political legitimacy lifted from canonical lore.[37] The aura of her Divine Capital spread beyond the city walls.

She established nine prefectures in the Luoyang vicinity, including Zheng-zhou and Bianzhou as imperial domains.[38] Garrisons were set up in the surrounding area to fortify the new capital.[39]

SANCTIFYING THE LUO RIVER

Deifying the Luo River and worshipping its personification, the Luo River goddess, played important roles both in the sanctification of Luoyang as Divine Capital and the political ascent of Wu Zhao. The Luo River, a major tributary of the Yellow River, was at the very heart of early Chi-nese civilization—a major center of Peiligang (7000–5000 B.C.), Yangshao (5000–3000 B.C.), Longshan (3000–2000 B.C.), Erlitou (2000–1500 B.C.), and Shang culture.[40] Naturally, as Luoyang grew into a national politi-cal capital and a commercial center, the river itself gained prominence. By the Tang, after Sui Yangdi's completion of the Grand Canal, the Luo had developed into a vital artery that enabled Luoyang's growth into a flourishing center of transport. Annals record the milling commerce of the willow-lined waterways of her prosperous capital: "Sculls and boats of the empire gathered, often more than ten thousand vessels filling the canals of Luoyang."[41]

The Luo River flowed west to east, bisecting Luoyang, passing just south of the Meridian Gate to the Imperial City. Three separate bridges were constructed to span the trifurcating branches at the heart of the capital: Heaven's Ford Bridge in the center; to the north, the Yellow Path Bridge; and to the south, the Star Ford Bridge.[42]

In the fourth lunar month of 688, Wu Zhao's nephew Wu Chengsi, whose own lofty ambitions were tied to his aunt's ascendancy, had an apocry-phal inscription carved in a white stone. A man of obscure background named Tang Tongtai "discovered" the augural stone and presented it at court, claiming he had found it in the Luo River. Its inscription, rendered in royal purple, read: "When the Sage Mother appears among the people, the imperial cause will eternally prosper."[43] The delighted grand dowa-ger designated the riverine stone her "Precious Diagram" (bao tu 寶圖). The following month, she issued an imperial proclamation announcing that she would personally worship the Luo River and formally receive the Precious Diagram. She would offer ritual thanks to the Supreme Thearch of Boundless Heaven (Haotian shangdi 昊天上帝)[44] at the state altars in the southern suburb and hold an audience at her unfinished Bright Hall. Seven days later, on the summer solstice, she assumed the title "Sage Mother, Divine Sovereign,"[45] which, while short of laying titular claim to emperorship, still marked unprecedented territory for a Chinese woman: Wu Zhao had proclaimed herself a sovereign (*huang* 皇) ruler. This marked a vital step in her ongoing endeavor to secure the support of the court and populace, while at the same time gathering a sufficient critical mass of credenda (things to be believed) and miranda (things that inspire awe and admiration),[46] to take the unprecedented step of becoming a woman emperor.

Such a stone issuing from the Luo River evoked the Luo River Writing (Luoshu 洛書), a sacred and mysterious tablet of ancient lore. Like the Yellow River Chart (Hetu 河圖), the appearance of the Luo River Writing in many early texts (such as the *Analects*, the *Mozi* 墨子, the *Huainanzi*, and the Eastern Han *Lunheng* 論衡) indicated, as Mark Lewis points out, "a transfer of dynastic power and the imminent rise of a sage."[47] "The name and nature of the Luo River," as Rebecca Doran asserts, "are culturally resonant. Auspicious mystical river designs are associated with the kingships of culture heroes."[48] In the midst of Wu Zhao's lengthy and carefully engineered dynastic transition, the Luo River Writing was more apposite to the times—it depicted change while its complement, the Yellow River Chart, projected permanence.[49]

In the *Book of Changes* is the passage, "When the Yellow River disgorges the Chart and the Luo River issues the Writing, the Sage follows them."[50] In the *Mozi*, the Yellow River Chart surfaced "just prior to King Wu's establishment of the Zhou as a royal line."[51] This sacred writing was connected with mythic sovereigns like Fuxi, who created the world with the help of Nüwa, and flood-queller Yu the Great.[52] These foundational political myths were passed from one dynasty to the next. In the *History of the Han Dynasty*, it is recorded that, "When the empire is ruled in harmony with the Way, the Yellow River issues the Chart and the Luo gives forth the Writing."[53] Encoded on the Luo River Writing and the Yellow River Chart were the timeless blueprints to sage governance. The Luo River Writing was "a sacred document of remote antiquity supposedly guaranteeing the holder's possession of the Mandate."[54] Only the charismatic presence, virtue, and majesty of a sage-ruler could recover these ancient writings from the watery depths. Once revealed, these cryptic charts could impart to the ascendant sage-king a preternatural, esoteric knowledge of the workings of the natural and human worlds, of the cosmos and of governance.[55]

Thus it had been established in the classical canon that the appearance of an inscribed stone betokened the arrival of a sage-king. In popular consciousness, coruling with husband Gaozong since the emperor suffered a stroke in 660, Wu Zhao had been one of the "Two Sages" (Ersheng 二聖).[56] It remained for Wu Zhao to ceremonially reenact this powerful political myth, to draw on the lore of antiquity by discovering her own river-borne talisman that revealed her sage nature and foretold her imperial destiny. "In the Confucian ideology of the time," Antonino Forte suggests, "it [her Precious Diagram] probably represented the mythical Luoshu because it was allegedly found in the River Luo."[57] With the "discovery" of this latter-day Luo River Writing in 688, the prophesied sage rose to become a Sage Mother and a Divine Sovereign.

On the first day of the seventh lunar month of 688, to announce her advent as a sage for a new era, Wu Zhao offered a general amnesty and changed the name of the Precious Diagram to "Heaven-bestowed Diagram of the Sage" (Tianshou shengtu 天授聖圖). The Luo River was designated the Eternally Prospering Luo (Yongchang Luoshui 永昌洛水), and the Luo River goddess was given a special promotion, invested as the Marquise Who Reveals the Sage (Xiansheng hou 顯聖侯). Fishing in the sacred waters was forbidden. Wu Zhao declared that, henceforth, sacrifices to the Luo would match those offered the Four Great Rivers—the Yellow, the Yangzi, the Huai, and the Ji. The discovery site of the augural stone was honored as "Spring of the Sage Diagram," and the surrounding administrative region was denominated the Eternally Prospering Prefecture. On nearby Mount Song was bestowed the appellation Divine Marchmount (Shenyue 神嶽); the mountain's tutelary god was invested as King of the Center of Heaven (Tianzhong wang 天中王). Temples were built to honor both the river spirit and the mountain deity.[58] Not only was the river running through Wu Zhao's Divine Capital Luoyang deified, but the surrounding landscape, affixed with her labels, became part of a sacred topography.[59]

In grandiloquent verse, propagandists sought to drive home the point: the inscribed augural stone mystically arising from the Luo River presaged the coming of a new sage-ruler, Wu Zhao. In a congratulatory memorial, encomiast Chen Zi'ang gushed, "Humbly observing that Your Majesty's absolute virtue matches that of heaven, transforming even the grass and wood, heaven dared not withhold its bounty. Therefore, the Luo gave forth the auspicious diagram. The earth did not conceal its treasures, and from the river issued the mysterious tablet."[60] Stephan Kory situates Chen Zi'ang's memorial as part of a longer lineage of "panegyric memorials" written to congratulate rulers on the discovery of augural stones and other auspicious portents.[61] Such memorials were not, of course, spontaneous poetic expressions of joy. Rather, as Kory puts it, they were "institutionalized, and the qualifications of the authors who composed them were recognized by the court and the throne."[62] While none of these commemorative verses explicitly linked Wu Zhao and the Luo River goddess, collectively they reinforced a deep, personal connection between the revealed Sage Mother and the Luo River, the *yin* waters that had delivered up the augural stone.

Another talented official in Wu Zhao's court, Su Weidao (648–705)—a third member of the "literary quartet of friends" who eventually rose to become a chief minister under Wu Zhao—also wrote a verse to commemorate the "discovery" of the Precious Diagram:

> Borne on green silk, the tablet of the river;
> Atop the black altar, looking down on the banks of the Luo.
> Heaven's machinations have made manifest the imperial halting-place;
> Where, with filial reverence, she presents the sacrifice.
> Ascended to accompany the three illustrious ancestors;[63]
> With compliant heart she presents herself to the Hundred Spirits.
> As the mists lift, the sun follows the central path;
> Snow accumulates over the dust of the carriages.
> As she prepares the offering, all is eminent and exalted,
> With a song of longevity for myriad springs to come.[64]

In Su Weidao's memorial, he evokes both a numinous space shared by ruler, spirits, and ancestors, and conveys Wu Zhao's unfailing sense of ceremonial decorum.

Li Qiao, too, offered a verse to commemorate the diagram and pay homage to the Luo River, including the lines: "with an inscription like that carried on the tortoise's back, with a diagram like that carried in the phoenix's beak."[65] Reputedly, the Luo River Writing emerged on the back of a turtle and revealed its mystical design to Yu the Great.[66] The auspicious phoenix was also associated with other sage-rulers. When a phoenix arrived during the halcyon reign of the mythic Yellow Emperor in the third millennium B.C., the ruler performed a sacrifice on the banks of the Luo.[67]

Li Qiao also wrote another verse about the Luo River goddess and the augural stone disgorged by the river:

> The nine branches of the Luo flow resplendent, scintillating in their
>   beauty;
> the creatures of this trifurcated river await renewal.
> Flowers illuminate the riverside roost of the vermilion phoenix,
> as the sun reflects on Jade Rooster Ford.
> The original rites sought meetings with immortal guests,
> just so, the Prince of Chen gazed on the lovely one.
> The divine tortoise has just bestowed the auspicious [chart],
> and the green writing has again been attained.[68]

Such poems functioned to buttress Wu Zhao's concurrent purposeful political reenactment of one of the most powerful Chinese myths: the delivery of an inscribed token that symbolizes heaven's recognition and approval of a newly arrived sage-ruler. To this end, Li Qiao conjures the familiar mythic bestiary and aviary associated with the Luo Writing and the River Chart—the vermilion phoenix and the divine tortoise are present. Joining them are Cao Zhi, the prince of Chen, and, of course, the transcendently lovely goddess of the Luo River herself.

In a celebratory memorial written on behalf of the court, Li Qiao connected the Precious Diagram to the chelonian-borne Luo River Writing, calling it the "turtle writing" (*gui shu* 龜書), thereby linking Wu Zhao to Yu the Great.[69] Kory, who has translated the entire memorial, remarks that it "begins by establishing a resonant relationship between Heaven and the mandated ruler," a recurring theme that Li Qiao weaves "in and out of the piece, continually emphasizing that it is Empress Wu who possesses the mandate of Heaven."[70] Fellow member of the "literary quartet" Cui Rong chimed in as well, praising Wu Zhao's "sagely illustriousness and abundant virtue" that had brought forth the Precious Diagram.[71]

Another courtier, Niu Fengji, also presented a poem to commemorate Wu Zhao receiving the Diagram:

> The imperial diagram from the opened casket of the Luo;
> This inscribed stone is the equal of heaven.
> On an auspicious day it rose on the waves;
> Immortals and birds looked down from the mists and beheld.
> This insignificant official wishes that he might have wings,
> as the perfect ritual drum-cadence receives the phoenix.[72]

Evoking an otherworldly ambience, Niu describes the extraordinary circumstances under which this latter-day Luo River Writing was revealed. His verse catalogues all of the signs auguring the appearance of a sage-ruler: the miraculous river-borne inscribed stone, a host of approving immortals, and the phoenix.

Following Wu Zhao's imperial proclamation, a massive ten-day celebration was staged in the final month of the fourth year of Chuigong (28 December 688 to 26 January 689) for her to worship the Luo and receive the Precious Diagram, coinciding with the completion of the Bright Hall complex.[73] In its original architectural conception, the Bright Hall, a traditional emblem of the Chinese ruler as a "cosmic man" (linking heaven and earth, securing harmony between man and the celestial and terrestrial realms), was patterned on the mystic principles of the Luo River Writing.[74] In January 689, in an magnificent ceremony the likes of which the Tang dynasty had never seen, Wu Zhao presided over a host of imperial kinsmen, civil and military officials, and foreign chieftains. Arrayed before a newly constructed altar next to the Luo River, these dignitaries beheld a magnificent pageant of strange birds, miraculous beasts, and curious treasures.[75]

To a score composed for the occasion, "Music to Honor the Luo River with a Grand Sacrifice," the assembly paraded before the altar. The score included the following fourteen verses, choreographed to match stages of the elaborate rite: three preparatory hymns; one verse for the embarkment of Wu Zhao's carriage; another called "Harmony of Revelation" to honor Wu Zhao receiving the Precious Diagram; one for her ascent of the altar; a pair of verses to commemorate meat sacrifices and wine libations; another to mark the removal of the sacrificial meat stand; a verse to accompany the martial dance that ushered the audience to the altar and another for the civil dance to send them off; and, finally, three verses to see off the Luo River goddess (*song shen* 送神).[76]

To cite a single example, "Reverent Harmony," the ceremonial verse for setting out the ritual meat offerings, featured a quatrain with the following lyrics:

> Her divine merit beyond measure sets in motion *yin* and *yang*,
> Containing the myriad realms, enwombing (*yun* 孕) the eight distant
>   reaches.
> Heaven-sent tokens have shown her imperium is eternal:
> Omens and portents descend from on high, illumining this grand
>   sacrifice.[77]

The lyricists employ a language that celebrates rather than conceals the biological sex of the Sage Mother. Wu Zhao's motherhood is amplified to the point that within herself she contains, she enwombs, the entire realm. She is the sagely ur-mother and the subjects are her children.

These events were staged at a pivotal moment of grand dowager Wu Zhao's patient preparation to establish her own dynasty. Rebecca Doran observes that the veneration of the Luo River and the diagram were staged to broadcast to the widest possible audience "cosmic approval of Empress Wu's rule"; these grand ceremonies were a "part of the founding myth of the Zhou state."[78] The Luo River divinity's revelation of the augural stone was a vital element in Wu Zhao's effort to show that heaven had transferred its mandate to her. For the revered Luo River— the object of worship—was a current that ran through time, connecting present and past, linking Wu Zhao to Fuxi, Yu the Great, and the Luo River goddess.

The altar that served to stage these grand rites was constructed in the heart of Luoyang, on the north bank of the Luo River next to Heaven's Ford Bridge. There, the elders of Luoyang erected a stele called the "Record of the Heaven-bestowed Diagram of the Sage." Xuanzong razed both altar and stele in 717,[79] part of his campaign to destroy monuments like the Axis of the Sky that marked Luoyang as his grandmother's Divine Capital and the hub of her Zhou empire.[80]

FURTHER AFFIRMATIONS OF THE CONNECTION
IN TEXT AND RHETORIC

The earliest example connecting Wu Zhao to the goddess of the Luo River can be found when she was still Celestial Empress (Tianhou 天后).[81] Between 680 and 683, Cui Rong wrote a memorial on behalf of Crown Prince Li Xiǎn congratulating Wu Zhao on the discovery of an auspicious omen, a purple-stalked mushroom (zhi 芝) growing beneath the reliquary stupa of Taiyuan temple in Luoyang.[82] In this effusive memorial, he writes:

> The flowery purple-stalked zhi entwines the basilicas,
> So that it seems as if the place has become the terrace of the Queen
>   Mother [of the West].
> Fronds of purple-stalked zhi grow in the fields,
> Matching those in the dwellings of Consort Fu.[83]

The dwelling of the Luo River goddess was a site where the numinous zhi appeared. Han Confucian scholar Dong Zhongshu called auspicious omens like the zhi plant "tablets bearing the Heavenly Mandate," evidence of heaven's endorsement of a worthy sage-ruler. "When a king is about to rise to power," he remarks, "beautiful signs of good omen will first appear."[84]

Consort Fu, the Luo River Goddess, appears in the preface to the "Stele Inscription for Little Auntie Temple of the Lesser Room,"[85] written by literary genius Yang Jiong (650–693), one of the "four outstanding talents" (si jie 四杰) of the early Tang.[86] Yang nimbly connected Wu Zhao to a series of female divinities. Textually intertwining the world of men with the realm of immortals, he wonders:

> How is it that the cowry gates of the Yellow River court
> Gaze down on the capital of Feng Yi?[87]
> And the jasper altar on the river Luo
> Is set next to the dwelling of Consort Fu?[88]

Though the directive to compose the inscription for the stele came late in Gaozong's reign, the timing of the actual composition and the erection of the stele is ambiguous. Seemingly, this verse was written after the construction of the altar on the banks of the Luo. In any event, it consciously associates Wu Zhao with the river divinity.

Further evidence of the connection appears in the Buddhist *Commentary*. To justify Wu Zhao's ultimate ascent to Emperor in 690, the clever rhetoricians compiling the *Commentary* cite the prophetic *Record of Master Yitong*:

> In the Capital City (Chang'an), the Way is lofty,
> In the City of Luoyang the light is bright;
> Brilliancy pervades the Luo River,
> The dragon's flight responds to Shangtian.
> The Revealed Saint[89] holds the regency and addresses the ten thousand countries,
> Composedly seated [she] will rise to kingship and receive a thousand years.[90]

This prognostication helps clarify the title Wu Zhao bestowed upon the Luo River goddess in 688, "Marquise who Reveals the Saint." *Sheng* (聖), meaning "saint" or "sage," was not an attribute unique to any of the three faiths. In Confucian and Daoist terms, it meant sage; in a Buddhist context, it generally indicated a "saint."[91] In essence, Consort Fu bore the tablet, the sacred tally, to the surface of the Luo River, effectively passing the baton to her political heir, Wu Zhao. The saint/sage revealed by the Luo River goddess was none other than Wu Zhao herself!

Just as the precious treasure hidden beneath the cold *yin* surface of the waters of the Luo was made manifest to the world, so now the sagely sovereign presence of Wu Zhao, long concealed from public view, was revealed with sublime pomp and fanfare. When Li Qiao says in his memorial, "the hidden has been revealed in an auspicious sign,"[92] he refers not only to the omen, but to the sage-king that its presence augurs, Wu Zhao.

CONCLUSION

There is a long history in imperial China of emperors bestowing honors and titles upon gods and nature spirits (*feng shen* 封神) in conjunction with rites such as suburban sacrifices (*jiao si* 郊祀) or the sacrosanct *feng* and *shan* ceremonies. While superficially construed as a gesture of humility and homage, this act of self-exaltation effectively served to affiliate the ruler with the divinity that he or she venerated. The celebration of the Precious Diagram and the elevation of the Luo River spirit all were calculated political events staged to persuade the court and wider populace that Wu Zhao's political ascent conformed to the will of heaven and the spirits.

The ceremonial occasion upon which Wu Zhao invested the spirit of the Luo River with the title Marquise Who Reveals the Sage also served to magnify her own person. The unprecedented act of bestowing a title on the river goddess in 688 coalesced the earthly sovereign and riparian divinity into a single entity. This fusion must be understood in the context of Wu Zhao's period of incubation, her preparation to assume the throne and establish her Zhou dynasty. In performing these rites to sanctify the Luo, Wu Zhao effectively styled herself a latter-day incarnation of the Luo River goddess.

The lore surrounding the Luo River goddess sanctified Wu Zhao's Divine Capital and helped the female ruler distinctively imprint her political authority upon Luoyang. Both the goddess and the river played a central role in Wu Zhao's reenactment of a sacrosanct Chinese political myth—the emergence of an inscribed stone that presaged the advent of a sage-king. This myth was most closely connected to time-honored male political ancestors like the Fuxi, the Yellow Emperor, and King Wu of Zhou. In Wu Zhao's transmogrified performance of this canonical lore, however, the goddess of the Luo River came to the forefront. The invented act of the goddess transferring the augural tablet to Wu Zhao helped identify the grand dowager as a "Sage Mother," a ruling mother of the empire. This clever amalgamation of tradition played an instrumental role in her protracted campaign—a lengthy, carefully calculated campaign of omens and rites, of titles and apocrypha—to establish herself as emperor.

Wu Zhao never repeated the grand ceremonies staged in 688 and 689 to celebrate the revelation of the Sage Diagram and to honor the Luo River goddess. Fulfilling the augury of the inscribed stone, she took the throne as emperor in 690. In 694, ritual officials petitioned Wu Zhao to stop making offerings and cease performing sacrifices to the Luo:

> The Emperor is the father of heaven and the mother of the earth, elder brother of the sun and elder sister of the moon. Ritual matters must be reverently undertaken and decorum must be observed. According to

ceremonial protocol, the Five Marchmounts are equal in status to the Three Dukes.[93] The Four Waterways are equal to the various lords. There are no rites in which an emperor makes offerings to dukes and lords.

By this juncture, Luoyang, the heart of her sacred geography, had been built into a pan-Asian metropolis. Wu Zhao's status as emperor was secure. The Luo River goddess and the augural stone had served their respective purposes. Magnanimously, Wu Zhao assented to the request.[94]

THREE

First Ladies of Sericulture

Wu Zhao and Leizu

LEIZU 嫘祖, A DAUGHTER OF the Xiling clan, was the primary consort of the Yellow Emperor, warrior god and civilizing force of the early third millennium B.C. Regarded as an exemplary complement to the Yellow Emperor, she bore him two sons.[1] During his interregnum, Wang Mang (r. A.D. 8–23), ever keenly attuned to the complements and balance of the Five Phases, set up paired shrines for this power couple from hoary antiquity—the Yellow Emperor matched with heaven and the Yellow Empress, Leizu, with earth.[2] Shortly after the fall of the Han, in his efforts to persuade the already willing Cao Pi (Wei Wendi, r. 220–226) to elevate concubine Guo to empress, court official Zhan Qian compared her with Leizu, the Lady of Xiling, and other talented helpers/spouses like the two consorts of Emperor Shun of antiquity, Nüying and Ehuang, daughters of Emperor Yao.[3]

Curiously, none of these sources directly mentioned Leizu's greatest legacy: her role as the culture hero who discovered sericulture, invented the loom, and brought silk weaving into wider practice.[4] The advent of sericulture and silken garments were important markers. "Historians of early China," Bret Hinsch observes in his study on textile production and gender, "saw the ability to make cloth from hemp and silk as a primary distinction between civilized people and [wool- and felt-clad] savages."[5] Leizu's very name is composed of radicals for woman (女), field (田), and silk (糸). Though texts from the Song recognize Leizu as a deity renowned for teaching people to rear silkworms and reel silk, the timing of her emergence as a silk goddess is unclear, likely because her identification with silk developed relatively late.[6] In earlier texts, the Yellow Emperor himself was

credited with the creation of sericulture, prompting Dieter Kuhn to specu-
late that Leizu's emergence as First Sericulturist was closely connected to
the gendered division of labor.[7]

Leizu's emergence as a silk goddess went beyond the imperial ram-
parts. She was a widely revered cultic divinity in medieval and late imperial China. Contemporary historian Bi Xiuling has illustrated that cults of
Leizu existed in Zhejiang, Shanxi, Sichuan, and other places. For instance,
in modern-day Yanting County in Sichuan alone, the landscape is dotted
with place names closely connected to the silk goddess: Cocoon Thread
Mountain, Leizu Village Mountain, Leizu Plain, Leizu Cave, Xiling Gap, and
Silkweaver's Flats, to name a few.[8] Leizu is still written into the mountains
and valleys of the landscape.

During her first two decades as empress, Wu Zhao drew on the aura
surrounding silk goddess Leizu. While the Luo River goddess was a lovely,
anthropomorphized vision of the female element of water, Leizu represented the quintessential womanly vocation of silk weaving.

"Womanhood in early imperial China," states Francesca Bray, "was
defined by the making of cloth: with a few rare exceptions, a weaver was
by definition a woman, and a woman was by definition a weaver."[9] The
gendered division of labor in traditional China was expressed with the
terse proverb "men plow and women weave" (*nan geng, nü zhi* 男耕女織),
reflecting "a relationship of complementarity rather than subordination."
Weaving was fundamental to the well-being of family and the strength of
the state.[10] Sericulture (and other textile production) gave women in early
China a constructive economic role, empowering them within the family.

Hinsch has pointed out that in early Chinese historical writings, silk
weaving became part of the fabric of Confucian family values, not only an
essential part of women's work but a "moral activity" and a fundamental
good.[11] As Hinsch explains,

> To early Chinese, womanhood was not just an abstract passive female
> identity. A person became a true, complete, and successful woman by
> actualizing the major female roles that society expected of her. A woman
> weaving at the loom was doing far more than just producing valuable
> cloth. She was also acting out a gendered role that contributed to her
> overall social identity. Spinning, sewing, weaving, and dyeing were all
> ways of *being* a woman.[12]

Weaving was the essential enterprise of a successful, moral, and good woman, enabling her to become a "full-fledged woman by performing the ritualized behavior associated with her social identity."[13] In her *Admonitions for Women* (Nü jie 女誡; a Confucian guide to help a woman to survive and even prosper among her in-laws), Eastern Han historian and social theorist Ban Zhao (A.D. 45–116) placed "wholehearted devotion to sew and weave" at the forefront of the paragraph on "women's work" (*nü gong* 女功).[14]

RITES OF THE FIRST SERICULTURIST

The *Zhou Book of Rites* records the empress leading ministers' wives to the northern ritual precinct to perform the "opening of sericulture" (*shi can* 始蠶) ceremony—a ritualistic re-creation of Leizu's role as the primordial weaver.[15]

This rite, a gathering on the vernal equinox to jointly weave a ritual garment, served as the counterpart to the emperor's sacred field ritual (*jitian* 藉田), in which the sovereign ceremonially broke ground to inaugurate the spring planting.[16] Commencing with the reign of Han Wendi (r. 180–157 B.C.), the empress's ritual work of "weaving with her own hands" (*qin sang* 親桑) complemented the emperor's ceremonial plowing of the earth (*qin geng* 親耕).[17] This marked the beginning of the codification of plowing and weaving into imperial rites, thereby augmenting the social and political significance of these long-practiced vocations.[18] Dieter Kuhn argues that a silkworm goddess (*can shen* 蠶神) only became personified during the reign of Eastern Han sovereign Mingdi (r. A.D. 58–75).[19]

By the Jin dynasty, a wider cross-section of women were incorporated into the evolving rites: in addition to the empress, wives of lords were designated "silkworm mothers" (*can mu* 蠶母) and a widening circle of princesses, consorts, and noblewomen participated, arrayed around an elevated altar devoted to the First Sericulturist (*xian can* 先蠶), a goddess of silk.[20] The *History of Jin*, compiled by Fang Xuanling late in the Taizong's reign, records the central and supervisory role of the empress in the rites performed in the Jin in 285 and 320.[21]

Modern scholar Chen Jo-shui offers a lucid description of this vernal rite held to pay homage to the First Sericulturist and its significance:

In this ceremony the empress and the ladies involved also performed the rite of picking mulberry leaves, which were then fed to silkworms. The purpose of the rite was clear: by worshipping the divine sericulturist and doing sericultural work herself as the "first lady" of the Chinese world, the empress encouraged all women to fulfill their primary social and economic duty as cloth-producers.[22]

Only in the Northern Zhou (557–581) was Leizu, the Lady of Xiling—in what Dieter Kuhn terms "the final rationalization of the legend"[23]— explicitly designated the First Sericulturist. The Northern Zhou empress and a group of attendant women presented libationary offerings and sacrifices.[24] The *Sui History* provides a brief description of the rite:

> In the Northern Zhou ceremonial system, the empress rode in her king-fisher carriage leading the Three Consorts, the imperial concubines and a full coterie of palace women followed by the noble wives of the Three Dukes and the wives of the Three Solitaries[25] to the site of the sericulture ceremony. After offering the grand sacrifice of an ox, the empress presented a sacrifice to the First Sericulturalist, the goddess Xiling.[26]

Thus, by the Tang, Leizu's late-developing apotheosis was completed. She had finally emerged from her cocoon to become the First Sericulturist.[27]

Set in the third lunar month, the sacrifices to the First Sericulturist were an elaborate five-day event involving not only the empress but also an expanded cadre of women in a series of choreographed ceremonial activities. In the "Treatise on Rites and Music" in the *New Tang History*, the protocol for the rites is detailed. The Six Matrons (*liu shang* 六尚), directors of various branches of palace services within the inner quarters, led by the directress of ceremonies (*shangyi* 尚儀), assumed responsibility for different aspects of the rites. Female ritual specialists helped coordinate the ceremony, including a ritual receptionist (*si zan* 司贊), a communications officer (*si yan* 司言), a scribe (*nü shi* 女史), a sewing manager (*dian zhi* 典製), and a supplicant (*nü zhu* 女祝). Consorts and imperial princesses, the inner noblewomen (*nei mingfu* 內命婦), wives of court nobles, the outer noblewomen (*wai mingfu* 外命婦), and other female imperial relatives played appointed roles.[28]

Figure 3.1 With perfect symmetry and ceremonious deportment, a host of noblewomen gather to pay homage to Leizu in the First Sericulturist rites.

For three days approaching the sacrifice, the empress and other women involved in the rites fasted and underwent ritual cleansing. On the day of the sacrifice, the empress traveled in a grand chariot, leading her retinue to the ceremonial venue. In the Tang, as in the Sui, the elevated altar for the rite was not concealed in the inner realm of the Palatine City but was part of a ritual precinct three *li* north of the palaces.[29] After this public procession, all of the grand ladies were arrayed according to rank and role around the altar, where a ritual seat (*shenzuo* 神座) had been set for

Leizu. After the rite, they first adjourned to a mulberry grove, for the ritual cutting of mulberry branches. With a golden saw, the empress cut three branches; then the inner noblewomen cut five or nine, depending on rank. Next, the retinue of women headed to a silk-reeling room, where an official gave mulberry branches to designated "silkworm mothers." Leaves were stripped from the harvested mulberry boughs and passed on to select imperial concubines. This last group fed the silkworms and wove a ceremonial thread. The following day, the empress hosted a banquet for all of the participants in the main palace.[30] These rites publicly showcased the performers of the rite as exemplars of womanly virtue—none more radiant, of course, than the empress herself.

As the Chinese festival calendar became fixed by the early Tang, rites connected with sericulture and weaving became part of a seasonal biorhythm. On the date of the Buddhist Lantern Festival, women prayed for silkworms. On the seventh day of the seventh month, they prayed for technical skill in weaving. In the tenth month, offerings were made to Leizu.[31] In 635, shortly before Wu Zhao entered the palace as a concubine, Taizong's Empress Zhangsun, accompanied by a retinue of palace women, performed the rite to honor the First Sericulturist.[32] As a fifthranked Talent, languishing in Taizong's seraglio, Wu Zhao was no doubt conversant with the ceremony.[33]

WU ZHAO AND THE SILK GODDESS

From the very outset of her tenure as empress, Wu Zhao played an extremely active public role. Shortly after she supplanted deposed Empress Wang, newly appointed Empress Wu Zhao was publicly presented from atop the Gate of Solemn Righteousness to civil ministers, military officials, and foreign chieftains.[34] In the ensuing spring of 656, she performed a sacrifice to silk goddess Leizu, leading eminent ladies of the state to pick mulberry leaves and feed them to silkworms.[35] As silk weaving was the primary economic activity for women, her central role in the public performance of this spring ceremony marked her as foremost among women, the human link to the divine silk goddess.[36]

To underscore the ritual import of the event, the newly minted empress ordered the composition of a musical score, "Music for Making Offerings to the First Sericulturist." The first stanza, "Ever Harmonious," also known as "In Accord with Virtue," welcomed Leizu:

> Fragrant spring opens its festive season,
> As harmonious zephyrs pervade the splendid vernal gardens.
> Only her numinosity could explain these vast blessings,
> That benefit all creatures and make manifest her divine merit.
> Her cumulative embroidered silks fill the heavens;
> Her elegant sacrificial robes adorn the world.
> Her talents uphold this felicitous season, as, completing the libations,
>   we descend to the temporary canopy-palace.[37]

In these lyrics to receive the silk goddess, it is as if all heaven and earth are clothed in silken raiment of the deity's nimble-fingered fashioning; Leizu is cast in a celestial light, wreathed in spring zephyrs, conferring benedictions. Wu Zhao's sacrifice to the silk goddess in the spring of 656 was performed at an altar in the northern suburb (*beijiao* 北郊) of Chang'an.[38] As this ritual precinct was eleven *li* north of the Palatine City, a lengthy ceremonial procession was required.[39] Naturally, such an occasion drew a wider audience, providing the new empress greater visibility and public exposure.

When Wu Zhao ascended the altar in the northern suburban ritual precinct, "Reverent Harmony" was chanted:

> Her brilliant spirit illumines with its absolute virtue;
> Her profound merit eclipses that of the hundred deities.
> Propitious source of the season's advent,
> Her lucky threads renewed year after year.
> The realm receives the aegis of her gracious favor;
> The seven imperial ancestral temples offer their sincere veneration.
> At this moment all show utmost fervent supplication
> As the great celebration reaches its climax!

This verse credits Leizu with achievements that neatly parallel those of the central terrestrial personage involved in these rites. The earthly conduit of the goddess—the empress—ceremoniously welcomed the spring planting season, acting as "the propitious source of the season's advent." And, like

Figure 3.2 The brightest luminary in the constellation, Leizu sits surrounded by a cluster of lesser silk divinities.

Silk worm goddess

the goddess to whom she so humbly and effusively paid tribute, she spread "the aegis of her gracious favor" over the empire.

The next verse, "Expressing Respect," was sung to the accompaniment of sacrificial coins being offered to the silk goddess.

Along the celestial path, her honor guard arrayed,
as clouds gather, moving to the harmonious sounds.
Golden sacrificial vessels are placed on damask mats,
while jade currency is set aside in the fragrant pavilion.
Thus, with a heart empty of material needs and wealth,
She devotes her entire being to the common people.
All that she hopes is to extend to them enlightenment and blessings;
As at this time the offering is made with perfect sincerity.

The directress of ceremonies knelt and removed the jade coins from a round basket, rose, and passed them on to the empress, who, kneeling herself, offered them before the ritual seat that represented the goddess.[40] This genuflection emphasized both the sincerity of Wu Zhao's reverent spirit as she performed the rite and her commitment to the well-being of the common people. As "first lady" of the empire, the solemnity and dignity with which she undertook the ceremony might well initiate a bountiful year in sericulture.

> When meat dishes were presented to Leizu, "Pure Sincerity" was
>   intoned:
> The jade meat stands are positioned on the cassia mats,
> As from orchid gardens rise fragrance of hortensia.
> The eight musical notes harmonize with the song of the phoenix;
> The three libations are offered in simurgh wine vessels.
> Pure millet liquor is presented at the grand sacrifice,
> For the court and wider empire wish to confer auspicious sanction.
> Her spirit—long has it been celebrated—
> Ever bestows blessings without limit.

A larger audience, "court and wider empire," bore witness to the procession if not to the rite itself. Conveying the tremendous power and beneficence of the silk goddess, this verse depicts the venue of ritual performance as a site where the heavenly and the earthly, the divine and the mundane, converged on the principal ritual performer—Wu Zhao herself. No doubt to the throngs bearing witness to the cadenced movements of the otherworldly damask-clad beauty at the nexus of the ceremony, wrapped in a trance-like euphonic cocoon of ritual music as they beheld the empress amid the bedizening airs of flowers and incense, the boundaries between immortal goddess and mortal ruler grew ever more hazy.

Finally, after the sacrifices that concluded the rite, a parting toast of "Manifest Felicity" was offered Leizu:

> Now that the rite at the immortal altar is finished,
> Her divine chariot is about to ascend in all its majesty.
> Hopefully anticipating the dawning auspiciousness we wait assembled,
> Witnessing her myriad achievements reaching fruition.

With sincere devotion, she succors the realm;

Attending to the fundamental, she inspirits the masses.

With heart and soul I have prepared this sacrifice,

So that lands within the empire may give forth favorable signs.

Through the fond farewell bid Leizu in this concluding verse, the lyrics convey the great esteem in which the silk goddess, who succored and nourished the masses, was held. "Attending to the fundamental" (wu ben 務本) is a nod to agriculture, the "fundamental occupation" (ben ye 本業) of 90 percent of the population, of which sericulture is a signal part.

Naturally, there was a certain ritual conflation between presenter and receiver, visible supplicant and invisible object of worship. The fine qualities imputed to Leizu in the song—she is represented as divine nurturer, felicitous civilizing force, and transcendent auspicious presence—clung likewise to the newly risen empress at the center of the rite.

Wu Zhao performed these vernal ceremonies dedicated to Leizu on four occasions. Following tradition, she included wives of high-ranking ministers.[41] The First Sericulturist rites were only performed eight times in the Tang; Wu Zhao accounted for half of these.[42] The second performance occurred in 669[43]; the third in 674[44]; and the last in 675, this time on the southern face of Mount Mang, not far from Luoyang to the north, with the entire court in attendance.[45] Speculating that the final performance of these rites might be connected to Wu Zhao's assumption of the lofty title Celestial Empress in late 674, Chen Jo-shui observed that it "was the most unusual" of Wu Zhao's four offerings to the First Sericulturist, not only because of the distinctive venue, but because "accompanying her were not palace ladies, but courtiers and territorial representatives from all over the empire."[46]

AFTERMATH: TWIGS OF MULBERRY AND SILKEN GEWGAWS

As grand dowager and emperor, Wu Zhao never performed the rites to honor Leizu. In 708, during the turbulent reign of Wu Zhao's son Zhongzong, Empress Wei (d. 710), theatrically trying to fashion herself after her mother-in-law, also sought to play the ceremonial role of "first lady" and perform the First Sericulturist rites.[47] Mulberries were associated with Empress Wei, and a "Mulberry Branch Song" (sangtiao ge 桑條哥) was created in her honor. In conjunction with these rites, courtier Jiaye Zhizhong suggested that his patron, Empress Wei, had "the spirit of a woman emperor" (*di nü zhi jing* 帝女之精). The courtier framed the song within a longer line of prophetic, dynasty-legitimating verses:

> Formerly, when [Tang] Gaozu had yet to receive the mandate of Heaven, the empire resounded with "Sons of Peach and Plum." Just before Taizong received the mandate, people of the empire chanted "The King of Qin Breaks Through the Ranks." Before Gaozong won the mandate, people intoned "The Inclined Hall." Before the Celestial Empress gained the mandate, everyone sang "Enchanting Miss Wu." When Zhongzong was about to receive the mandate, the empire chanted "Prince Ying of Shizhou." Now that Empress According with Heaven [Wei] is about to receive the mandate, people all sing "Mulberry Branch Wei."[48]

Jiaye Zhizhong even referred to Empress Wei as "mother of the state" (*guo mu* 國母), confirming her ceremonial role as first lady.[49] Clearly, Wei and the courtier-rhetoricians in her faction had learned much from Wu Zhao and sought to capitalize on the ideological and political currency vested in female divinity Leizu.

Even the texture, elegance, and colorful luxuriance of silk helped associate women clad in (or proximate to) the sheer fabric with immortals and divinities. Li Qiao and other rhetoricians who had helped to celebrate and exalt Wu Zhao continued to ply their literary talents in Zhongzong's court to represent Empress Wei, the Taiping Princess 太平公主 (d. 713), and the Anle Princess 安樂公主 (d. 710)—the latter two, Wu Zhao's daughter and granddaughter, respectively—as celestial beings in the company of divinities and immortals.[50] Once again, silk played an integral part in their poetry. On poetry outings, cut silken flowers were affixed to branches to create the colorful and wondrous illusion of an everlasting spring and an immortal world, a vision mirrored in the verse of these poet-courtiers.[51] During one of these festive outings in 708 at luxurious Kunming Pool in the western suburbs of Chang'an, the gifted woman-poet Shangguan Wan'er 上官婉兒 (d. 710) sat boldly ensconced atop a tower of silk created expressly for the occasion. From that eminence, she haughtily cast down losing poems of poet-courtiers, until finally, from on high, she announced the winning verse.[52]

CONCLUSION

The First Sericulturist rites were designed for an empress—for the First Lady of the inner, domestic realm. Scholar Bi Xiuling observes that the ceremony served to confirm discrete separation of the sexes and reinforce Confucian gender roles.[53] As Wu Zhao started to play a more significant role in the outer, male political realm (first as de facto then as de jure ruler), it was no longer politically expedient to remind court and country of her complementary, feminine role. As grand dowager, she changed the name of the emperor's sacred field altar (*jitian tan* 藉田壇) to the First Agriculturist altar (*xiannong tan* 先農壇).[54] This emphasis on divine farmer Shennong (the First Agriculturist) rather than silk goddess Leizu attests to Wu Zhao's changing role. Similarly, in "Benefiting the People" (li ren 利人), the final fascicle of *Regulations for Ministers*, a political guide compiled when Wu Zhao was grand dowager, silk embroidery was relegated to the category of lesser work (*mo zuo* 末作), in contrast to the primary occupation of agriculture.[55] As grand dowager and emperor, she publicly played the traditionally male role of political decision making, determining matters of court and state and, not surprisingly, sought to distance herself from the female-identified silk goddess.

In 702, late in Wu Zhao's reign as emperor, her nephew Wu Sansi 武三思, making a bid to regain political favor amid the cacophony of his aunt's contentious court, composed a commemorative inscription for Wu Zhao's mother Madame Yang.[56] The timing of this epitaph is curious, given that Madame Yang had been dead for three decades. Wu Sansi couched Madame Yang within a chronological line of eminent women of antiquity. Like Cao Pi's courtier Zhan Qian 500 years earlier, Wu Sansi chased his praise of the virtues of Nüying and Ehuang, daughters of Yao who married Emperor Shun, with the remark: "Then there is the example of Xiling [Leizu] exalting the reputation of her clan, [two characters omitted] the palaces of the Yellow Emperor." The epitaph continues, lauding the women who helped establish the Xia and Shang dynasties.[57] Of course, Wu Sansi's flowery eulogy was intended not for deceased Madame Yang but for his aunt, the living woman emperor. For Wu Zhao—Madame Yang's living daughter—was the natural culmination, the terminus of the glorious sequence of women listed in the epitaph.

In *Myth and Reality*, Mircea Eliade remarks that "a certain tribe live by fishing—because in mythical times a Supernatural Being taught their ancestors to catch and cook fish. The myth tells the story of the first fishery, and, in so doing, at once reveals a superhuman act, teaches men to perform it, and, finally, explains why this particular tribe must procure their food this way."[58] Accordingly, a ruler who stages or reenacts this primordial fishing rite both connects with that supernatural being and is defined as the possessor of esoteric knowledge and the keeper of tradition for these fisherfolk. Thus, when Wu Zhao paid ceremonial homage to Leizu, reenacting the discovery and invention of silk weaving, she connected herself to the apotheosized cultural heroine and established herself as keeper of the original knowledge of a sacrosanct craft that defined both Chinese civilization and womanhood.

A powerful Confucian aura surrounded Leizu: as the original silk weaver and reeler, she epitomized female virtue. She also was a symbol of the economic benefit a woman could contribute to the larger household through her diligent creation of fabrics. Significantly, the First Sericulturist rite allowed Wu Zhao to play a central ceremonial role. If, as Hinsch maintains, when "women spun and wove, they performed a social role that earned them respect and status,"[59] then certainly the First Sericulturist ceremonies provided the grandest stage to publicly celebrate womanly virtue. Because female virtue had become closely intertwined with silk weaving, there was great normative political currency for the empress who personally presided over successful production of silk textiles. Hinsch remarked that Eastern Han empress Ma (A.D. 40–79) effectively "manipulated this symbolic activity . . . to construct an image of public virtue by personally demonstrating her concern with moral female occupations."[60] Wu Zhao similarly tapped into the symbolic power of this rite, broadcasting her role as the ideal Confucian wife and first lady of the empire.

In the arc of Wu Zhao's efforts to develop a cult of female political ancestors during her half century in power as empress, dowager-regent, and finally emperor, Leizu might be called a starter divinity. The goddess appeared primarily during Wu Zhao's tenure as Gaozong's empress, the first of three phases of ascending power. Leizu, in her role as the First Sericulturist, was intimately linked to an inner world of women's work and the womanly virtue of silk weaving. Once Wu Zhao left the inner quarters, more directly wielding traditionally male political authority, the silk goddess, once so prominent in her pantheon, faded into obsolescence.

APPENDIX: DAUGHTERS OF LESSER GODDESSES

In Wu Zhao's wake, a quartet of powerful women—her daughter, the Tai-ping Princess; her granddaughter, the Anle Princess; her daughter-in-law, Empress Wei; and her secretary, Shangguan Wan'er—dominated the court for seven years. Though their lofty political ambitions were ultimately thwarted, these women attempted to employ similar strategies, patron-izing literary masters to conjoin them poetically to female divinities while projecting a shimmer of paradisiacal fairylands onto their grand estates. Some of the same aesthetic masters—men like Li Qiao and Song Zhiwen (c. 660–710)—who helped connect Wu Zhao to her pantheon of female political ancestors worked closely with these women.

Evoking the avian chain spanning the Milky Way to connect Weaving Maid (Vega) to her earthly lover Oxherd Boy (Altair), poet-courtiers Li Qiao, Su Ting, and Wei Sili all waxed rhapsodic about the "magpie bridge" linking the Taiping Princess's lofty mountainside estate—a veritable otherworldly paradise—to the mundane realm below.[61] Shao Sheng identified the Taiping Princess with another immortal, Nongyu, the elegant daughter of Duke Mu of Qin (a regional hegemon in the Eastern Zhou), who rose to become an immortal, joining an ethereal flautist wandering the mountain peaks, call-ing to cranes and phoenixes.[62] In Song Zhiwen's verse praising the luxuri-ous "mountain pool" of the Taiping Princess, he gushed that his patroness:

> embodies the refined beauty of an immortal maiden
> and radiates the essence of the Wu Girl star.[63]

Edward Schafer observes that in the capable hands of Tang poets, this Wu Girl became a "star goddess par excellence, a sidereal beauty who might be recognized among the jeweled belles of an earthly court."[64] This was precisely Song Zhiwen's intent, to illuminate the Taiping Princess and cast her in celestial guise.

Lu Cangyong's series of effusive poems shed a supernal light on the grand estate of the Anle Princess, tacitly comparing its owner to moon goddess Chang E and the Weaving Maid.[65] In a collection of poems writ-ten to mark a grand banquet held at the residence of Shangguan Wan'er, courtier Zheng Yin populated the estate of the hostess, a veritable heaven on earth, with a host of minor Daoist goddesses like the Onyx Consort (Qiong fei 瓊妃) and the Jade Girl (Yunü 玉女).[66]

While these women were poetically elevated to the lofty company of immortals, they rarely sought affiliation with the same exalted tier of female divinities and immortals as Wu Zhao. As flatteringly lavish and high-sounding as these poetic allusions were, Nongyu, the Weaving Maid, and Chang E did not inhabit to the same celestial strata as Nüwa and the Queen Mother of the West. There was a calculated poetic and aesthetic logic underlying these staggered echelons of eminence: the development of these lesser pantheons of divinities to whom respective members of this quartet of eminent women were poetically yoked was commensurate with the political power the members of the quartet wielded.

PART II

Dynastic Mothers, Exemplary Mothers

IN TRADITIONAL CHINA, ONE NEGATIVE characteristic routinely associated with the archetypal woman in a position of political power was "lack of natural motherly feeling." By the Tang, there was a well-established narrative of the unnatural anti-mother.[1] Historians of subsequent eras fitted Wu Zhao into this narrative tradition of the monstrous woman devoid of human feeling, cataloging a grim litany of her abominations against her own children—smothering her infant daughter in 654, murdering her eldest son Li Hong in 675, and sending second son Li Xián 李賢 (653–684) into exile where he was pressured into suicide in 684. Though such allegations of filicide are problematic,[2] rumors of Wu Zhao's unmotherly conduct swirled even in her own time. Keenly aware of the political stakes that imbued the issue of motherhood, Wu Zhao, especially as empress and grand dowager, took proactive measures to recast her image. She engaged in an ongoing campaign to frame herself as an ideal Confucian mother, not only of her own flesh-and-blood sons but of her "political sons" throughout the vast realm.

Women were not simply victims of an oppressive patriarchal society in traditional China. They were an integral part of an evolving structure, agents who operated both within and sometimes outside the patrilineal kin parameters of Confucian society. In her work Admonitions for Women Eastern Han poet-historian Ban Zhao emphasized the importance of a woman's adherence to her Confucian role of obedience, duty, and reverence toward her in-laws; in writing a manual by a woman for women, she powerfully embodied the idea that Confucian learning was a moral force that could edify women, as well as men. She stressed competent domestic management and a mother's duty to educate her sons.[3] Women of elder generations and widows who adhered to these prescribed roles stood to gain significant influence within the larger corporate family.

Women successfully navigating the Confucian system not only exercised influence within their families but also exerted moral suasion on husbands and sons that shaped men's handling of matters within the outer political realm. Anne Kinney has shown that in early China a mother's influence upon the moral development and proper Confucian education of her sons began in utero.[4] In her study of the role of women in the literati society of the late Ming (1368–1644) and early Qing (1644–1911) Jiangnan, Dorothy Ko acknowledges that Confucian tradition offered opportunities as well as constraints for women, even in the rigid family hierarchies of late imperial China.[5]

Judith Butler theorizes that playing normative social and cultural roles according to script served women as an important "survival strategy."[6] Ban Zhao (and virtually every dowager-regent down to Wu Zhao almost six centuries later) recognized this principle and understood the importance of couching her authority in terms palatable to the Confucian patriarchs. Decades of political experience as empress and grand dowager led Wu Zhao to gain a comprehensive, nuanced mastery of the Confucian script, apprehend its plasticity, exploit its loopholes, and avail herself of every opportunity afforded by the ideology. Presiding over a Confucian bureaucracy and living in a society in which Confucian values remained deeply imbedded, Wu Zhao naturally sought to frame herself as a custodian and champion of Confucian traditions rather than an iconoclast. To this end, she actively identified and channeled virtuous female paragons of the past. Her public celebration and propagation of Confucian values conferred upon her a certain ideological authority. While the Confucian exemplars honored in texts like Liu Xiang's (79–8 B.C.) Western Han dynasty *Biographies of Exemplary Women* were not divinities akin to the Queen Mother of the West or Nüwa, affiliation with these culturally honored women helped fortify Wu Zhao's position as empress and grand dowager.

The opening chapter of *Biographies of Exemplary Women* contains seventeen "Models of Maternal Rectitude" (*mu yi* 母儀), six of whom were incorporated into Wu Zhao's pantheon of female political ancestors. The first three chapters in part II, "Dynastic Mothers, Exemplary Mothers," will examine the connections that Wu Zhao fashioned with dynastic ancestors and spouses of founding dynastic rulers featured among these exemplars of "maternal rectitude." Chapter 4 examines the connection between the medieval female sovereign and the Woman of Tushan 塗山 氏 (1.4),[7] who helped legendary Yu the Great found the Xia. Chapter 5 looks at the curious part Jiang Yuan 姜嫄 (1.2), who divinely birthed Hou Ji, the first ancestor of the Ji clan that ruled the Zhou, played in shaping Wu Zhao's image. Chapter 6 explores the significant role that Taisi 太姒 (1.6), who helped King Wen establish the Zhou of antiquity, had in magnifying Wu Zhao's political profile. The constructive roles of this trio of celebrated women in founding past dynasties made them a vital part of Wu Zhao's developing pantheon.

Chapter 7, the fourth and final chapter in part II, examines how Wu Zhao and her talented rhetoricians skillfully marshaled four widowed mothers lifted from *Biographies for Exemplary Women*—Lady Ji of Lu (1.9), the mother of Mencius (1.11), the mother of General Zifa of the state of Chu (1.11), and the mother of General Zhao Kuo (3.15),[8] to Wu Zhao's considerable advantage. Though perhaps less eminent than the dynastic mothers, this quartet of strong-willed and wise widows had been renowned for a millennium for the sage counsel they offered their sons on a range of principles including public-mindedness, loyal service to the state, diligent commitment to one's occupation, and even the art of governance.

All of these women, without transgressing Confucian boundaries or offending the protocol of the patriline, managed to wield not only significant domestic authority within the family but a measure of political influence in the state. Recognizing the tremendous normative currency vested in these idealized Confucian widows and mothers from early China, Wu Zhao strove diligently to connect her person to these paragons.

Over the centuries, many new and extended editions of *Biographies of Exemplary Women* have been compiled, loosely modeled on Liu Xiang's prototype.[9] Beginning with the *Later Han History*, assembled by Fan Ye in the fifth century, it became standard protocol in compiling dynastic histories to include a collective one-chapter biography of model women.[10] Promulgated in 645, when Wu Zhao was but one of nine fifth-ranked Talents among Taizong's bevy of concubines, the preface to the "Biographies of Exemplary Women" chapter in Fang Xuanling's *History of Jin* shows that in the early Tang, a Confucian lineage of female political ancestors was well entrenched:

> Yu rose from the bend in the Guishui River with the aid of the sisters (1.1).[11] Xia flourished with the help of the Woman of Tushan (1.4). Youxin (1.5) of Yousong amplified and solidified the foundation of Yin.[12] Tairen and Taisi (1.6) helped in the prosperous transformation of the Ji clan. Empresses Ma (8.19) and Deng[13] were respectful and frugal, so the Han court could extend its virtue. Empresses Xuan and Zhao were good and virtuous, so the Wei dynasty broadcast its fragrance. They all elevated ritual propriety in the inner quarters and graced the moon chambers with their distinguished righteousness. The Mother of Mencius (1.11) sought benevolence. . . . Wenbo (1.9) was reprimanded for making his friend hold the sword. Zifa's mother (1.14) made him share beans with his soldiers. . . . These women not only illuminated the regulations of wives, but skillfully practiced the rectitude of mothers.[14]

By design, this preface offers thumbnail introductions to many of the luminaries contained in Liu Xiang's opening chapter, "Models of Maternal Rectitude." Nine exemplary mothers from seven different entries are featured, including the majority of the Confucian female political ancestors in Wu Zhao's pantheon.[15] These paragons of motherhood were highlighted to manifest the very zenith of womanly deportment.

It is clear from the preface that even in the mind of a Confucian scholar-official in service of the Tang state, this vaunted lineage of eminent women was profoundly respected. Wu Zhao and her propagandists did not need to invent this Confucian lineage of women; more than a millennium of tradition had accomplished this already. Her task was far more delicate and thorny: it involved not only intricate rhetorical appropriation of the normative power of these past paragons, but a subtle tactical recalibration of their historical roles and meaning to justify her own burgeoning political presence.

FOUR

The Mother of Qi and Wu Zhao
Connecting to Antiquity, Elevating Mount Song

IN THE SECOND CHAPTER OF Sima Qian's *Records of the Grand Historian*, it is recorded that Qi was the son of Yu the Great, legendary founder of the Xia dynasty and flood-queller who delivered China from eight years of rain, and a woman of the Tushan 塗山 clan.[1] After their marriage, Yu remained with the Woman of Tushan for a mere four days before embarking on his tireless mission: to divert and redirect the deluge.[2]

A commentary on the *History of the Han Dynasty*, written by Yan Shigu (581–645) in the early Tang, contains a passage, purportedly from the Western Han text *Huainanzi*, about the unique birth of Qi. As Yu the Great was digging through Huanyuan Pass, part of Mount Song, he changed into a shambling bear. While bringing her hardworking husband food, the pregnant Woman of Tushan beheld this fearsome creature and fled in terror. Pursued by Yu, she turned into a stone on one of the slopes of Mount Song. When Yu demanded his son, the stone into which the Woman of Tushan had metamorphosed split asunder and delivered Qi.[3]

While touring the Five Marchmounts in 110 B.C., the celebrated emperor Han Wudi (r. 141–86 B.C.) made a special point of visiting this stone of Qi's mother. There, on the slopes of Central Marchmount (Zhongyue 中嶽), Mount Song, he established a shrine in her honor.[4] During the Eastern Han, the shrine was refurbished in 123 A.D.[5] Five centuries later, Lu Zhaolin (c. 634–689), one of the four outstanding literary talents in the early Tang, recalled Han Wudi's "homage to a stone" on Mount Song.[6] Three sets of stone *que* gates set up during the Eastern Han reconstruction—one dedicated to the mother of Qi—still survive. More than thirty feet tall and one hundred fifty feet in perimeter, the stone of Qi's mother sits at the foot

Figure 4.1 The Woman of Tushan, holding her infant son, sharing a rare moment of domestic tranquility with Yu the Great, mythic flood-queller and first ruler of the Xia.

of Mount Song's Ten Thousand Years Peak (Wansui feng 萬歲峰), one of the thirty-six peaks of the Great Room (Taishi 太室), the larger of the two major sections of the Central Marchmount.

Because Yu was so preoccupied with saving the empire from ceaseless deluge, the Woman of Tushan, according to *Biographies of Exemplary Women*, was effectively a single parent, capably raising her son and "bringing about his transformation," so Qi was "fashioned by her virtue and followed her teachings." Succinctly, the eulogy to her biography summarizes: "Tushan was wedded to Lord Yu, but after four days he went to manage the floods. Qi wailed and cried. His mother alone taught him the right order and precedence in human relationships. She instructed him to be good and in the end he succeeded his father."[7] In this manner during the Han, the Woman of Tushan was transformed into the ideal Confucian mother, selflessly raising her son and molding his character. In *The Flood Myths of Early China*, Mark Lewis observes that sage-rulers of early antiquity were often "bad fathers" who neglected or even sought to injure their offspring.[8] Consequently, the mother played a greater role in shaping the child's character. In styling herself as a caring, benevolent matriarch, Wu Zhao took women like the mother of Qi, this consummate mother of antiquity, as part of her assemblage of maternal ancestors.

PERFECT SPOUSE: THE MOTHER OF QI AS PARAGON

In the third chapter of *Biographies of Exemplary Women*, "Biographies of the Benign and Wise," it is recorded: "From ancient times, the virtuous kings invariably had an upright wife as a mate. If their consorts were upright, then they flourished; if they were not upright, then there was chaos. The success of Xia stemmed from Tushan and its ruin from Moxi."[9] From the Han forward, the Woman of Tushan was accounted part of a lineage of outstanding wives who assisted or supported their husbands in governing.

The Woman of Tushan was often associated with powerful dowagers-regent and grand dowagers. In the early late third century, following the death of Jin Wudi's empress Yang, another royal consort wrote the following encomium:

> In every aspect of women's work she excelled: she led all the concu-
> bines and maids in songs of sericulture, she successfully cultivated silk-
> worms, she skillfully unraveled the cocoons and spooled the thread. Her
> ritual deportment too was flawless: respectfully presenting offerings in
> the ancestral temple, always filial and measured in speech, and always
> gracefully adhering to the six forms of proper conduct,[10] she never
> committed a transgression. Nüying and Ehuang assisted Shun, and the
> Woman of Tushan uplifted Yu the Great. . . . Clearly my empress, though
> from a different era, held fast to the same high standard.[11]

This posthumous memorial lauded the Empress Yang with the highest Confucian praise. In managing domestic economy, engaging in women's work of weaving, and conducting herself with reverent propriety, she understood her supporting role within her in-laws' imperial clan and played that role without deviation from Confucian script.

In a song composed for the deceased spouse of Southern Qi emperor Wu
(r. 483–94), his posthumously elevated empress Mu was cast as a latter-day
incarnation of the Tushan Woman and one of the founding mothers of the
Zhou dynasty of antiquity:

> Taisi became a wife of Zhou;
> Tushan was paired with Yu.
> My empress has inherited their queenly raiment,
> renewing, repeating their plumb adherence to rules.[12]

Terms like "inherit" (*cheng* 嗣), "renew" (*chong* 重), and "repeat" (*die* 疊)
exhibit a conspicuous effort to present the empress as heir to the manifest
Confucian virtue of these female paragons, much as male rulers fashioned
themselves as political descendants of the glorious line of sage-rulers.
Indeed, the exemplars in this lineage of women are generally the spouses
or consorts of the sage-kings.

At the opening of "Biographies of Exemplary Women" in the mid-
sixth-century *History of the Wei Dynasty*, the familiar lineage appears yet
again:

> Just as the Yellow Emperor's ugly concubine Mo 嫫 brought edification
>   to his palaces,
> and Ehuang brought to fruition the great enterprise of Shun,
> so the Woman of Tushan and the Three Mothers of Zhou helped their
>   dynastic houses rise and flourish.
> It must then be said that these women matched their husbands![13]

And when a late sixth-century Northern Zhou empress took a loftier
title, the imperial writ of appointment proclaimed that she possessed
the "virtue of the Woman of Tushan."[14] Again and again, the vital female
role in securing and maintaining the prosperity of the dynastic house is
sounded.

"Biographies of Exemplary Women" in Fang Xuanling's *History of Jin*,
published at the end of Taizong's reign, contains the assertion that "Xia
flourished with the help of the Woman of Tushan,"[15] illustrating that in
Wu Zhao's time this dynastic mother from antiquity remained a fixed part

of a revered lineage of eminent women. At the end of the biography of imperial affines (*wai qi* 外戚) in this same work, it is written:

> Without the Woman of Tushan in Xia, Xie 禼 [of Shang][16] and Ji 稷 [of Zhou][17] never could have followed.
> Without Taisi residing in Zhou, the states of Yan and Qi never could have risen.[18]

And early in his reign, Gaozong wrote the inscription for a stele at a Buddhist temple to commemorate his deceased mother empress Zhangsun that described her character as possessing: "The virtue that illumines Tushan, the morality that shines brilliantly on the bight of the River Guishui."[19] Tushan and Guishui not only denote place names, but they also connote virtuous female political ancestors—the Woman of Tushan and the wives of Emperor Shun, Ehuang and Nüying. By the mid-seventh century, this lineage of eminent women, first ancestress of clans and supporting spouses of dynastic founders, had taken clear shape. This provided Wu Zhao a solid foundation upon which to further build and enhance the cult of the mother of Qi.

WU ZHAO IN THE MOTHER OF QI'S CONFUCIAN GUISE

In order to utilize the cultural weight vested in paragons like the mother of Qi to amplify her political authority, Wu Zhao's task was a delicate and complicated one. She drew on the traditional role of the Woman of Tushan (and other eminent mothers) to facilitate her unprecedented political involvement. Yet, without leaving the fold of tradition, she needed to stretch its parameters, subtly expanding the role and the power of the mother of Qi to match her own rising influence.

Initially, she was comfortable employing the familiar, time-honored Confucian image of the mother of Qi lifted from *Biographies of Exemplary Women*. During Gaozong's last years and early in Wu Zhao's tenure as grand dowager, the mother of Qi often appeared as a perfect spouse and ideal mother who upheld the Xia dynasty. This implied, of course, that Wu Zhao was a perfect spouse and ideal mother helping to support the house of Tang. In an inscription drafted prior to Gaozong's death, Yang Jiong, one of Wu Zhao's stable of literary masters, wrote, "In marrying Tushan, the virtue of his [Yu's] clan was thereupon made complete."[20] Consistent with the traditional depiction of the mother of Qi as a dutiful spouse, Yang Jiong emphasized her central role in continuing the ancestral line and enhancing the virtue of the Xia.

The mother of Qi also appears in a memorial that Cui Rong drafted: "When the virtue of earth supports heaven, the myriad sorts [of flora and fauna] are completed; when the moon complements the sun, the Four Quarters are illumined. Formerly, [the women of] Guishui assisted Shun and Tushan helped elevate the Xia."[21] Once more, Wu Zhao's support for the house of Tang was tacitly compared to the Woman of Tushan's great contribution to the establishment and continuity of the Xia.

Also during Wu Zhao's regency in 685, the wet nurse of the Taiping Princess (Wu Zhao's daughter) offered felicitations to Wu Zhao on the birth of her grandson Li Longji, the future emperor Xuanzong. In its praise of the Woman of Tushan, the memorial obliquely honored Wu Zhao: "The good fortunes of Tushan were due to the bountiful offerings made at Xia Tower."[22] In all of these instances, Wu Zhao was cast as a model of motherly deportment in the mold of the Tushan Woman rather than an independent female sovereign. The time was not yet right for her to step forth as an unadorned female power rather than a vital bulwark for male power. Once Wu Zhao moved to found her own Zhou dynasty, however, the mother of Qi was no longer utilized to present Wu Zhao as a good wife and dutiful mother to her in-laws.

The Woman of Tushan also appeared on the lengthy Coiling Dragon Terrace inscription (Panlongtaibei 攀龍台碑), written by Li Qiao in 699 on behalf of Wu Zhao to honor her deceased parents.[23] In this composition, it was not Wu Zhao herself but her mother Yang who was associated with the Woman of Tushan.[24] The inscription reads, "In the beginning, she equaled the [women of the] River Guishui; to the end she matched the achievements of Tushan."[25] By framing mother, like daughter, as heir to a glorious lineage of eminent women, Li Qiao's rhetoric cleverly merged heredity and politics and situated Wu Zhao at their apical convergence.

Wu Zhao reestablished Qi's mother as one of the significant mothers of antiquity. After the female emperor's deposal and death, the mother of Qi continued to appear in celebrations of prominent women, albeit resituated in her lesser role as an ideal Confucian mother and wife. Sometimes she served as a litmus test of sorts: Had an empress supported her in-laws in the manner of the mother of Qi? When Wu Zhao's youngest son Ruizong died in 716, officials debated whether or not the spirit tablets of his empresses Liu (d. 693) and Dou (d. 693) should be set alongside his tablet. Arguing that precedent would only allow one spirit tablet in the ancestral temple, minister Chen Zhenjie memorialized, "In my humble consideration, the Luminous and Successful Empress [Dou] possesses the virtue of Taisi, and already receives ancestral offerings along with Ruizong. However the Solemn and Brilliant Empress [Liu] is not the equal of Qi's mother and therefore should be honored in another temple."[26] Later in Xuanzong's reign, the family of Empress Dou confirmed the exalted historical reputation of their kinswoman in an epitaph composed by Pei Yaoqing (681–743) marking the spirit path of Empress Dou's younger brother. A section of the inscription reads: "My elder sister equaled the virtue of Tushan; she was the 'King Wen's mother' of her time."[27]

THE MUSIC OF HEAVEN

Qi, the son of Yu the Great, was a powerful ruler in his own right, a rider of dragons who freely traveled between the terrestrial and celestial realms.[28] Sarah Allen has observed that Qi, whose name means "beginning," was the last of the miraculously born Xia ancestors and the "first hereditary ruler in the historiography of ancient China."[29] In the *Mozi*, it was Qi, rather than his father Yu the Great, who commissioned the casting of the Nine Tripods, the mythical vessels that symbolized the ruler's virtue and the dynasty's legitimacy.[30] Like the Xia ruler, Wu Zhao commissioned the casting of the Nine Tripods, a project initiated in 694 and completed in the spring of 697.[31]

Qi, whom Anne Birrell refers to as a "god of music,"[32] either stole the music of heaven[33] or received it as a gift.[34] When Wu Zhao was still Celestial Empress, Cui Rong's aforementioned memorial to congratulate her on the discovery of an auspicious *zhi* fungus linked her with the mother of Qi and the Luo River goddess:

> The Celestial Empress transforms and contains the myriad things,
> She instructs and rectifies all within the six imperial palaces.
> The empire is suffused with the strains of Tushan
> All within the oceans look upward to receive her teachings.[35]

The "strains of Tushan" (Tushan zhi yin 塗山之音) is a reference to Qi's heavenly music. Clearly, the sound of Qi's music in Cui Rong's encomium announced the greater glory of the mother (whether the Woman of Tushan or Wu Zhao), rather than the son. As Wu Zhao at this juncture bore the title Celestial Empress and as the portentous fungus for which Cui Rong offered congratulations grew in a temple that Wu Zhao had constructed for her mother in 675,[36] he claimed it betokened her majesty.

THE APOTHEOSIS OF THE MOTHER OF QI:
TWO SISTERS AND WU ZHAO'S SACRED TOPOGRAPHY

According to the *Classic of Mountains and Seas*, "The Great Room of Mount Songgao is to the west of Chengyang. This is where the mother of Qi transformed into a stone."[37] In antiquity, wives were also known as "rooms" (*shi* 室): in a sense, a room, then, was a womb. According to the *Annals of Dengfeng*, the two main ridges of Mount Song, the Greater Room and the Lesser Room (Xiaoshi 小室) were named for the two consorts of Yu the Great, the mother of Qi and her younger sister.[38] Huanyuan Pass, the great furrow cutting through Mount Song, divides the Greater and Lesser Room ridges.[39]

From the Eastern Han to the Tang, there appears to have been scant interest in the mother of Qi and her younger sister. However, inscriptions from Wu Zhao's era testify that during the late seventh century, the female emperor and her rhetoricians resuscitated the cults of these two sisters. Wu Zhao's effort to apotheosize this pair of women began in earnest during the final years of her husband Gaozong's life. In the second lunar month of 680, Celestial Empress Wu Zhao and Gaozong retreated to the mountains south of Luoyang, visiting the Ruzhou hot springs and a series of Daoist monasteries on Mount Song. After meeting Daoist master Pan Shizheng (585–682) on the vernal equinox, they visited Songyang Monastery and the temple of Qi's mother. On both sites they ordered the erection of steles.[40] This outing marked the beginning of the elevation of the Tushan sisters.

Yang Jiong and the Shrine of Shaoyi

Shaoyi, Little Auntie, was the younger sister of the mother of Qi. In early 683, shortly before Wu Zhao and Gaozong visited Mount Song once again, Yang Jiong composed a "Preface to the Stele Inscription for Little Auntie

Temple of the Lesser Room." The young literary master described the connection between Yu the Great and the Spirit of Lesser Room:

> Lesser Auntie Temple, according to the "Treatise on Geography" in the
> History of the Han Dynasty, is Lesser Room Temple of Mount Song. The
> temple idol is the image of a woman. Following the lore of antiquity, she
> is the younger sister of the mother of Qi, the Woman of Tushan, she who
> in antiquity gave birth through a stone fissure, water and earth combin-
> ing to bring forth her achievement.[41]

Yang Jiong's inscription not only linked Wu Zhao to the Tushan sisters, but
it also helped incorporate greater Mount Song into her sacred geography,
extending beyond her Divine Capital Luoyang. As Chang'an was closely
tied to the house of Tang, Wu Zhao sought to create a separate sphere of
power. In the Lesser Room inscription, Yang Jiong cited the first emperor
of Qin's act of engraving his name on Mount Tai, indicating that a ruler's
connection with sacred marchmounts was an important part of fixing
boundaries and establishing empire. The literary master then exalted the
ridge of Mount Song: "Among mountains and peaks, the Lesser Room is the
embodiment of divine elegance. According to the Yellow River Chart and
the Treatise of the Vast Earth,[42] armor and bucklers were used to open up the
mountains. The peak gives expression to the universe, spurting forth and
gathering the yin and yang essences. . . . Carved and angular, it stands bolt
upright, eight thousand feet."[43] In the words of Jonathan Pettit, Yang Jiong
artfully evoked "an alpine landscape fit for a goddess," a mist-shrouded
otherworldly realm where ailing Gaozong might await the visitation of a
divine goddess.[44]

Cui Rong and the Stele Marking
the Shrine of the Mother of Qi

A stele inscription written by Cui Rong for Gaozong and Wu Zhao's equi-
noctial sojourn to Mount Song in 680 marked the shrine of the mother of
Qi.[45] Cui Rong, in his capacity as a tutor in the Institute for the Veneration of Literature during Gaozong's waning years, worked closely with
heirs apparent Li Xián and Li Xiǎn (later Zhongzong). Wu Zhao's relationship with the former, Li Xián, who as crown prince was exiled for

conspiring to rebel in 680 and forced to commit suicide in 684, was particularly frosty.[46] During her ascendancy, proximity to these heirs apparent and their cliques was dangerous political territory. Keenly sensitive to the shifting winds, Cui Rong—as we have seen in his memorial on the behalf of crown prince Li Xiǎn to congratulate Wu Zhao for the numinous fungus—rarely missed an opportunity to amplify the merits of the Celestial Empress.

For Cui Rong the memorial again afforded him an opportunity to ply his gifts to declare allegiance to Wu Zhao. While Yang Jiong's memorial featured Shaoyi, ethereal and lovely, descending to visit Gaozong, in a case of aesthetic one-upsmanship, Cui Rong depicted the divine mother of Qi "as an erotic prototype" of Wu Zhao herself, not merely as a supernal dream-lover descended to rendezvous with a fortunate mortal but bodily "reborn again as the sage mother of a new dynasty."[47]

Modern scholars have long recognized the ornate magnificence and rhetorical force of Cui's inscription. Timothy Barrett considers this inscription a tour de force of female power vested in Daoist lore, "a virtuoso demonstration of the amount of female imagery available in the less Confucian reaches of the Chinese tradition."[48] Though Wu Zhao still shared political authority with Gaozong in 680, Stephen Bokenkamp describes Cui Rong's composition as a manifest effort to frame Wu Zhao as a mother goddess: "couched in elegant parallel prose and studded with classical allusions," the inscription, "while nominally dedicated to the ancient goddesses," presents "Wu Zhao as mother and creator of a new heaven and earth."[49]

The following passage from the inscription displays something of the compelling rhetoric Cui Rong mustered on behalf of Wu Zhao:

> Your humble servant has carefully looked into the temple of Qi's mother, meaning the mother of the lord of Xia, Qi. In the Han dynasty, to avoid the taboo name of Jingdi, "Qi" was changed to "Kai" 開. Resultantly the name circulated, and some records call her "Kai's mother." And yet neither Gu Yewang's Yudizhi 輿地志[50] or Lu Yuanming's Records of Mount Songgao 嵩高記 followed the taboo order. Both referred to her as the Lady of Yangdi. . . .[51]

> Formerly Huaxu trod in a footprint and became pregnant with a male child. Nüdeng responded to numinous spirits and the Red Emperor

was made. The comet passed by Huazhu and the White Emperor was birthed. The moon penetrated Youfang 幽房 and the Black Spirit descended.[52]

> So scintillating the Xia! So marvelous the Woman of Tushan! She married Yu on the very morning he began to survey the earth. She was joined in matrimony at Mulberry Terrace. . . .
>
> The stone split open on the northern side, a sign of his birth. This is what Guo Pu[53] referred to as the "stone of Qi's mother to the west of Yangcheng." This is what Li Tong[54] called the "shrine of Qi's mother on the southern slope of Mount Song."[55]

This passage implicitly connects Wu Zhao to a pedigree of extraordinary women—the mother of world-creator Fuxi, the mother of the Divine Farmer, and the mothers of early mythic rulers Shaohao and Zhuanxu—culminating with the mother of Qi.

As Cui's preface reaches its climax, Celestial Empress Wu Zhao restores the shrine to a veritable abode of immortals and reveals herself to be the living avatar of the mother of Qi:

> [Her] frosty silk drags and pulls,
> [Her] cloudy brocade trips and tugs.
> [She rests on a] mandarin duck pillow with a kingfisher drape.
> [She holds a] white feather fan [and wears] azure silk shoes.
> A belt of dangling jade simurghs sways hither and thither,
> With a hairclip of pinned golden peacocks neither too long nor
>   too short.
> Her living quarters are soft and subtle;
> the yin invisible while the yang is easily seen.
> Her clothes are splendid and resilient;
> [in its design] auroras blend and clouds billow.[56]

Immortalizing Wu Zhao, Cui Rong depicts the Celestial Empress, his patron, as a divine being. Elegantly, he fuses the object of worship and reverence, the goddess, with her earthly sponsor and counterpart, the empress. In short, Wu Zhao was revealed to be the living incarnation of the Woman of Tushan, the mother of an ancient dynasty.[57]

In the first lunar month of 683, on an outing to their retreat, Fengtian Palace on Mount Song, Wu Zhao and Gaozong sent emissaries to perform sacrifices at shrines for the various divinities of the marchmount, including the shrine of Qi's mother.[58]

Given that the shrines had long lain in disrepair and the cults of the Woman of Tushan and her sister Shaoyi had fallen into obsolescence, the inscriptions reveal that both Yang Jiong and Cui Rong made a concerted effort to resuscitate these cults and invest these neglected sites with ceremonial significance. Thus, even before Wu Zhao became grand dowager, propagandists associated her with female exemplars of distant antiquity like the Tushan sisters, and sought to elevate greater Luoyang, particularly Mount Song. During her reign, Mount Song, so proximate to her Divine Capital Luoyang, emerged as the preeminent marchmount, a national center of ritual.

DAOIST ELEVATION OF THE TUSHAN WOMEN

There were no further activities on Mount Song related to the Tushan sisters for more than a decade. When Wu Zhao was emperor in 695, however, she once again paid homage to the mother of Qi and her sister. The nature and timing of her announcement venerating the mother of Qi and the various tutelary deities of Mount Song are further detailed in the "Treatise on Rites and Ceremonies" in the *Old Tang History*:[59]

In the Zhengsheng era, Zetian planned to stage an event on Mount Song.[60] Previously, she had sent emissaries to perform sacrifices [to mountain deities] in order to pray for blessings and assistance. She issued an edict designating Mount Song as the Divine Marchmount honoring its tutelary god as King of the Central Heaven.[61] His spouse was honored as Numinous Consort. In the past, Mount Song had temples dedicated to Qi of Xia and Qi's mother, and to Aunt of the Lesser Room Peak.[62] She ordered prayers and sacrifices performed at each of these sites. . . . Because during the *feng* and *shan* rites she had secured the protective blessings of the spirits of Mount Song, Zetian thereupon elevated the Divine Marchmount's King of Central Heaven to Emperor of Central Heaven and his Numinous Consort was made Empress of Central Heaven. Qi of Xia was named Perspicacious and Sagacious Emperor. The spirit of Qi's mother was invested as Grand Dowager of the Jade Capital. The spirit of the Aunt of the Lesser Room Peak was designated Lady Goldtower. Prince Jin was made Ascendant Immortal Crown Prince.[63] A temple was established for each.

Other sources clarify the timing of this titular elevation of the Tushan sisters: this occurred in the second lunar month of 696, several months after Wu Zhao performed the *feng* and *shan* rites on Mount Song,[64] the first time in Chinese history these rites were performed at a venue other than Mount Tai. Mount Song became a Daoist paradise, the Central Heaven.[65] In Daoist lore, the Jade Capital—associated in Wu Zhao's ceremony with the spirit of Qi's mother—was situated at the very center of the highest heaven where the supreme deity dwelled, presiding over a host of divinities.[66] Like "Jade Capital" in the title of Qi's mother, so Lady Goldtower, the title bestowed upon her younger sister's spirit, contained great Daoist resonance. In Shangqing Daoism, Lord Goldtower was an intermediary between heaven and humanity, a latter-day sage, a messianic incarnation of Laozi also known as Li Hong.[67] A passage in a Song-era miscellany records various titles of Laozi, including "Imperial Ruler of Goldtower."[68] Noteworthy is the emergence of a third female deity connected with Mount Song under Wu Zhao, the anthropomorphized queen of the marchmount—titularly honored as the Empress of Central Heaven (Tianzhong huanghou 天中皇后).

Jade Capital and Goldtower, terms connoting both the sisters of Tushan and Daoist paradise, often appeared in Wu Zhao's propaganda. Shangyang Palace, built in the imperial park of Luoyang during the Shangyuan era (674–676), contained both a Jade Capital Gate and a Goldtower Gate.[69] Liu Yizhi (631–687), one of Wu Zhao's famous scholars of the Northern Gate, wrote a poem styling the Palace of Nine Perfections, a summer retreat in the mountains west of Chang'an to which Wu Zhao and Gaozong occasionally adjourned in the latter's final years, as a Daoist paradise:

The imperial orchard spreads before the Golden Tower;
The Immortal Terrace stations the Jade Bells of the imperial chariot.[70]

In the second month of 684, Wu Zhao, as grand dowager, established a Daoist convent at Goldtower Pavilion, ordaining former concubines and palace girls from Gaozong's harem as Daoist nuns.[71]

In the middle of Wu Zhao's Zhou dynasty, Chen Zi'ang wrote an inscription for Laozi's tomb, a composition designed more to exalt Wu Zhao than honor the Daoist founder:

In this first year of Divine Achievement [A.D. 697] . . .
The precious Tripods have been completed.
The court is tranquil,
And the empire is at peace.
The emperor has received the way of the purple yang ether
And been invited to the Jade Capital.[72]

Also, the inscription for the "Stele for the Ascended Immortal Crown Prince," purportedly Wu Zhao's own composition, contains the passage, "The Jade Capital is a realm of deathlessness . . . the Gold Tower marks the ground of longevity."[73]

The *Complete Anthology of Tang Poetry* includes a twelve-verse poem attributed to Wu Zhao. The final stanza makes further reference to "the Golden Tower":

Use the supernal path, open the door to the heavens,
Revolve around the solar chariot, moving vestments of cloud;
Ascend the Golden Tower, enter purple tenuity,
Look toward the immortal carriage, gaze up at the regal mercy seat.[74]

These Daoist emblems for the two sisters of Tushan, Jade Capital and Golden Tower, were vested with great cultural and religious potency. As Daoism was closely linked to the founding ancestor of the Tang, Laozi, Wu Zhao's attitude toward Daoism was decidedly tepid in the years immediately preceding and following the inauguration of her Zhou dynasty. Her Daoist-ization of these two sisters in the mid-690s registers an effort to begin reconciliation with the Daoist establishment.

On a progress to Mount Song a year or two after she performed the *feng* and *shan* rites, Wu Zhao beheld once more the stele for the mother of Qi's shrine featuring Cui Rong's brilliant inscription. Later, she ordered Cui to compose another inscription for the site of the Altar of Audiences (Chaojin 朝覲), where the closing ceremony to the grand rites held at Mount Song had been performed in early 696.[75]

CONCLUSION

The emergence of the cult of the little-known mother of Qi during Wu Zhao's reign was motivated by a series of complex and interrelated political and religious concerns. A verse by late Tang poet Lu Tong attests to the rise of the Woman of Tushan from an ideal Confucian spouse to a potent cultic divinity:

> The mother of Qi is the ur-mother;
> The thirty-six peaks of Mount Song are the all-father.[76]

While the Woman of Tushan never lost her lofty reputation as an exemplary Confucian helper, she developed into a powerful local goddess, closely connected to the geography of greater Luoyang.

Wu Zhao scripted relationships with eminent mothers celebrated in the opening chapter of *Biographies of Exemplary Women*, appropriating a Confucian manual of womanly deportment to her own political advantage. The Woman of Tushan was connected with the founding of the Xia, the first quasi-historical dynasty. Exalting Qi's mother served to accentuate the role of the mother, of women, in continuing the ancestral line and enhancing a clan's virtue—particularly when Gaozong was still alive. Naturally, once Wu Zhao became emperor, this aspect of Qi's mother was deemphasized.

Anticipating the later efforts (like those of Du Guangting shortly after the fall of the Tang) to marshal various eminent women and divinities from folklore, myth, and history into a Daoist pantheon, Wu Zhao gave the Tushan sisters an initiation of sorts, investing them as Goldtower and Jade Capital, names rich in Daoist tradition.

Also, the Woman of Tushan and Shaoyi were associated with the Greater Room, the Lesser Room, and Yangdi, sites on or proximate to Mount Song. Along with Divine Capital Luoyang, Mount Song was an important part of the sacrosanct ground of Wu Zhao's Zhou revolution. In addition to the summer palaces, the ceremonies, and the Buddhist and Daoist temples that dotted greater Mount Song, her connection to these cultic goddesses helped Wu Zhao anchor her ties to this sacred topography.

Finally, Wu Zhao's manufactured connection to the mother of Qi can be understood as part of her effort to repurpose an ancient tradition and recast it in her own image. Thus, Cui Rong apotheosized Wu Zhao, depicting her as a sensual, this-worldly incarnation of the Woman of Tushan. And while traditionally Qi was credited for possessing the music of heaven, the strains of music resonated throughout Wu Zhao's propaganda for mother rather than son.

FIVE

Ur-Mothers Birthing the Zhou Line
Jiang Yuan and Wu Zhao

THE HISTORY OF THE HAN DYNASTY contains a "Table of Persons Ancient and Modern" (Gujin ren biao 古今人表). Paralleling the male "Sages" (Sheng ren 聖人) is a collection of female "Benevolent Persons" (Ren ren 仁人), including world creator Nüwa, silk goddess Leizu, and dynastic mother Jiang Yuan 姜嫄. While virtually all of the fourteen women included are consorts, mothers, or sisters of the sages, Lisa Raphals points out that this affiliation does not diminish the cultural achievements of these eminent women. Raphals musters compelling evidence from Zhou and Han sources to illustrate that "women were represented as possessing the same virtues valued in men: moral integrity, intellectual judgment, the ability to admonish a superior, courage, and chastity, in the sense of single-minded loyalty." In short, before the dominion of Confucianism, gendered virtue ethics were "not inherent to Chinese culture."[1]

Dynastic mother Jiang Yuan is also featured prominently in other Han sources. As the second entry in the opening chapter of Liu Xiang's *Biographies of Exemplary Women*, she numbers among the revered "virtuous mothers" who "were the original teachers of the legendary founders of civilization."[2] In the collective biographies of the wives of emperors contained in Sima Qian's *Records of the Historian*, Jiang Yuan, like the Woman of Tushan who helped give rise to the Xia, is portrayed as a redoubtable ancestress who played an essential role in the rise to power of the Zhou of antiquity.[3]

Raphals acknowledges that by the beginning of the Tang "the specifically Confucian intellectual hegemony" that developed after the Eastern Han brought about the "entrenchment of a gendered virtue ethic."[4] It is certainly no coincidence that Wu Zhao relied heavily upon pre-Confucian women—like Nüwa, the goddess of the Luo River, and the Queen Mother of the West—to validate and legitimize her political status. By seeking female political ancestors from a golden age, she endeavored to recall the era when legend was rampant with powerful female divinities and culture heroes. Yet, as with the Woman of Tushan, Wu Zhao also sought to draw normative power from Jiang Yuan's status as a Confucian exemplar. This chapter examines the role in magnifying Wu Zhao's political profile played by Jiang Yuan, the dynastic mother who after treading in a divine being's giant footprint, bore Hou Ji, Lord of Millet, the first ancestor of the Zhou.

JIANG YUAN AND THE MIRACULOUS BIRTH
OF HOU JI, LORD OF MILLET

Jiang Yuan was one of the wives of Ku, one of the legendary Five Emperors of remote antiquity. Ku has the curious (and dubious) distinction of having not one but two wives who conceived miraculously. Besides Jiang Yuan is Jiandi, who ate the egg of a dark swallow and birthed Xie, the first ancestor of the Shang dynasty. Sarah Allen argues that Jiang Yuan's natal clan intermarried with the Ji clan that would found the Zhou dynasty and that the two clans entered into a military alliance against the Shang, a coalition that ultimately led to the founding of the Zhou.[5]

The earliest textual appearance of Jiang Yuan is found in a poem called "The Birth of a People" from the *Book of Songs*:

She who first gave birth to our people
Was Jiang Yuan.
And how did she give birth to our people?
She performed the Yin and Si sacrifices well
So that she might not be without child.
She trod in the big toe of the Lord on High's footprint
And was filled with joy and was enriched;
She felt a movement and it soon came to pass
That she gave birth and suckled
The one who was Hou Ji.
She fulfilled her due months
And her firstborn came forth,
With no rending or tearing,

Without injury or harm.
And this revealed the miraculous,
For did not God give her an easy birth,
Was he not pleased with her sacrifice?
And so she bore her child in comfort.
She laid it in a narrow alley
But ox and sheep suckled it.
She laid it in a wood on the plain
But it was found by woodcutters.
She laid it on chill ice
But birds covered it with their wings.
Then the birds went away
And Hou Ji wailed,
Really loud and strong;
The sound was truly great.
Then he crawled in truth;
He straddled and strode upright
To look for food with his mouth.
He planted large beans,
And the large beans grew thick on the vine;
His ears of grain were heavy, heavy,
His hemp and wheat grew thick;
His gourd stems were laden with fruit.[6]

Each of these early dynasties needed a first ancestress to bear the first
male dynastic ancestor through some sort of miraculous conception. If the
founding ancestor were born by normal means, not only would he lack a
mythic aura, but he would also not be the first ancestor—instead he would
be the second. Previously, as Anne Kinney points out, only the Shang had
divine access to the supreme deity, the Lord on High (Shangdi 上帝); but
the legend of Hou Ji's divine birth "suggests the Zhou's greatness taps
from the same ancient roots as the Shang."[7] Robert Campany has observed
that through sacrifice, Jiang Yuan gained "procreative access to [Hou Ji's]
divine father" and painless childbirth. In this founding myth, however, it
is ultimately the son Hou Ji (rather than mother Jiang Yuan) who receives
credit for the creation of sacrifices, the rites that called forth agriculture—
the very foundation of Chinese civilization.[8]

Kinney observes that Hou Ji's remarkable birth and infancy are typical of the precocious gifted child destined for greatness.[9] Needless to say, in her efforts to affiliate herself with dynastic mother Jiang Yuan, Wu Zhao ignored the abandonment of poor Hou Ji, left squalling lustily in various drafty alleys, ox pens, grim forests, and icy gullies.[10]

THE RISE OF JIANG YUAN AND HER CONFUCIAN MAKEOVER

The "Annals of Zhou" in *Records of the Grand Historian* contains a biography of Jiang Yuan:

> Hou Ji of the Zhou was named Qi, the Abandoned. His mother of the Yutai clan was called Jiang Yuan. Jiang Yuan was Emperor Ku's first consort. Jiang Yuan went out on the wild fields and she saw the footprints of a giant. Her heart was full of joy and pleasure, and she felt the desire to tread in the footprints. As she trod on them there was a movement in her body as if she were with child. She went on until her due time and gave birth to a baby boy. Because she thought he was unlucky, she abandoned him in a narrow alley. All the horses and cattle that passed by avoided treading on him. She moved him into woods, but she happened to meet too many people in the mountain woods. She moved him away and abandoned him on the ice of a ditch, but flying birds protected him with their wings and cushioned him. Jiang Yuan thought that he might be a god, so she took him up at once and brought him up until he was fully grown. Because she had wanted to abandon him at first, his name was Qi 棄.[11]

Jiang Yuan's postnatal conduct in this account, while still thoroughly dreadful (she is no candidate for mother of the year), is nevertheless much improved. While she still thrice abandons infant Hou Ji, Jiang Yuan, apprehending larger providential forces at work to shelter her child, ultimately decides to rear and nurture the Zhou founding ancestor.[12]

In "Models of Maternal Rectitude," the opening chapter of *Biographies of Exemplary Women*, Jiang Yuan's historical image continued to evolve and markedly improve:

> Jiang Yuan, the mother of Qi, was the daughter of the Marquis of Tai (Taihou 邰侯). In the time of Lord Yao, she went out to see the footsteps

of a giant, took a fancy to them, trod in them, and when she returned she became pregnant, gradually becoming larger. Since she thought it strange and disliked it, she divined and offered a pure sacrifice that she be childless. At last she gave birth to a child, but considering it unlucky, abandoned it in a narrow lane. Cattle and sheep avoided it and did not step on it. Then she took it to the middle of a forest on the plains. Later woodcutters who were cutting down the forest covered it with mats. Then she took it and placed it on the cold ice but birds covered it round with their wings. Jiang Yuan, thinking this extraordinary, took the child up to return home. Because of his fate, she gave him the name Abandoned (Qi). The disposition of Jiang Yuan was mild, tranquil, and of a single purpose. She liked to sow, cultivate, and harvest. When her son grew up, she taught him to plant trees, mulberry and hemp. His temperament was intelligent and benevolent, and he could cultivate his mother's teachings. In the end he attained his fame.

Yao ordered Qi to fill the office of minister of agriculture. He raised Tai to a kingdom and enfeoffed Qi at Tai. He was given the honorary title Lord of Millet. When Yao died and Shun ascended the throne, he ordered Qi: "The common people, Qi, suffer from hunger. You, the minister of agriculture, must sow all of the grains in their proper seasons." Afterwards, his posterity from generation to generation filled the office of minister of agriculture until Wen and Wu of Zhou rose to be Sons of Heaven. The *Man of Noble Sentiments* says: "Jiang Yuan was mild and transformed others." The *Book of Songs* said:

Glorious was Jiang Yuan
Her power was without flaw
God on high succored her.
It also says:
Mighty are you Hou Ji
Full partner in Heaven's power
That we, the thronging peoples, were raised up
In all your doing.
This it says of them.

In summary: Jiang Yuan, the mother of Qi, was pure, mild, and single-minded. She stepped in the footprint and conceived. Overcome by fear,

Figure 5.1 Confucianized, a kinder, gentler Jiang Yuan instructs the young Lord of Millet in the horticultural arts.

she abandoned the child in the wilderness, but the birds and animals protected and brooded over it. Then she returned to take it up compassionately. In the end he became an assistant to the ruler and she filled her motherly duty.[13]

In this Han work, Jiang Yuan has become a paragon of Confucian motherhood. She abandoned Hou Ji due only to her fear of offending the gods with an inauspicious birth. She rescued her abandoned child, returning to edify him and transform him into a minister par excellence: she taught the Lord of Millet farming and the horticultural arts. Jiang Yuan rather than Hou Ji was the culture hero who elevated ancient China from a primitive to an agrarian society.

Like the Woman of Tushan, Jiang Yuan was retrofit into a Confucian lineage of eminent mothers and wives who had either birthed dynastic founders or assisted in the establishment of dynasties. Empress Zhen, who in her later years had fallen out of favor, was posthumously rehabilitated by son Cao Rui (r. 226–239 as Emperor Ming of Wei) and reinterred with honors. A trio of high-ranking ministers repeatedly memorialized the throne, urging that ever greater honors be heaped upon the deceased empress. These ministers contended that Empress Zhen was a latter-day Jiang Yuan and should receive her own ancestral temple:

From ancient times, the people of Zhou first made Lord of Millet their ancestor and set up a temple to worship Jiang Yuan. . . . Looking it up in the old regulations, it is fitting, according to the *Rites of Zhou*, to establish a temple for a deceased mother.[14]

Later, the same officials argued that sacrificial offerings performed and music played at Empress Zhen's temple should be "just as at the ancestral temple." To justify this homage, the ministers once again evoked Jiang Yuan:

> The people of Zhou reached back to the Lord of Millet and thereby worshipped him together with august Heaven. Tracing and recounting his kingly beginnings, they found his origins in Jiang Yuan and specially established a temple for her where, generation after generation, they offered sacrifices. This is what the *Rites of Zhou* refers to by "Play the *yize* 夷則, sing the *zhonglü* 中呂,[15] and dance the "Grand *huo*" 大濩[16] in order to make an offering to the ancestral mother." The poets eulogized her, saying, "She who in the beginning gave birth to our people [of Zhou], this was Jiang Yuan." This means she was the root of the king's civilizing influence, the source which gave birth to his people. Further, they say, "Silent was the Closed Hall,/Solid and closely timbered;/Majestic was Jiang Yuan,/Flawless her virtue." The magnificence of the Ji ancestors praised by the *Book of Songs* and the *Rites of Zhou* was as beautiful as this.[17]

The Wei ministers interpreted the lyrics of the *Book of Songs* in such fashion as to elevate the deeds of Jiang Yuan. In their hands, she became a lofty ancestress, "the root of the king's civilizing influence," the spring from whom the praiseworthy "magnificence of the Ji ancestors" issued forth.

The immediate purpose of extolling the virtuous character of Jiang Yuan was to re-present Empress Zhen as a latter-day Jiang Yuan. To make manifest the connection, the ministers lauded the recently deceased empress in effusive terms:

> As for Empress Zhen the Illustrious and Refined, she received Heaven's numinous sign and gave birth to and raised the enlightened sage. Her achievement saved the people, and her virtue filled the universe. She began all the later generations and so is the starting point for moral civilization. Such special sacrifices at a temple would be taken as another closed hall of Jiang Yuan.[18]

Ultimately the emperor agreed with the ministers' appeal and deemed his mother worthy of receiving the same sacrifices as those offered at the ancestral temple.

Later in the third century, in a eulogy written to attest to the unimpeachable good character of Western Jin empress Yang (238–274), a courtier-official cast her as a legatee of the female political ancestors in *Biographies of Exemplary Women*:

> Jiang Yuan assisted Ku.
> The consorts helped in the rise of Guishui.[19]

Another similar verse for Empress Yang read:

> In edification, she excelled Tairen and Taisi;
> As a paragon, she matched stride with Jiang Yuan.[20]

A century later, Liu Song emperor Wu (r. 420–422) honored his mother, who had died in childbirth, with a title, remarking that she was:

> Just as admirable as Jiang Yuan,
> Of a class equal to Tairen and Taisi.[21]

No longer was Jiang Yuan a suspect mother who had abandoned her prodigious offspring. Rather, incorporated into the cookie-cutter Confucian matrix of exemplary women, she emerged as an ideal wife and helper of husband Ku, one of the Five Emperors of antiquity. By the Tang, Jiang Yuan was a respected dynastic mother.

JIANG YUAN AS BLOOD ANCESTOR

Wu Zhao's affiliation with Jiang Yuan was only one part of a broader campaign to draw on the cultural potency of the idealized Zhou of yore—echoing bureaucratic titles, reinstituting ritual practice, and, ultimately, borrowing its dynastic name in 690. But in styling her own Zhou a renaissance, a neoclassical dawn, she not only sought to evoke the traditional charisma of these ancient sage-kings, but to establish herself as their blood descendant.

In the "Genealogies of Prime Ministers" section of the *New Tang History*, it is recorded that her Wu family originally descended from the ruling Ji clan of the Zhou dynasty of antiquity—of which Jiang Yuan was first ancestress and progenitor. The youngest princeling of King Ping (r. 770–719 B.C.), first ruler of the Eastern Zhou dynasty (who moved the capital from Chang'an eastward to Luoyang), was born with a "Wu" 武 character on his hand, and thus was granted a new surname to match his miraculous birthmark.[22] Fashioning a worthy genealogy, Wu Zhao claimed descent from this reinvented "Wu" prince. This served to connect her by blood to the Ji clan of the original Zhou dynasty, to the proud collection of illustrious dynastic founders and culture heroes: King Wen, Mother Wen, King Wu, the Duke of Zhou, Hou Ji, and, of course, Jiang Yuan.

Neither King Ping nor his son was particularly distinguished, and affiliation with the youngest offspring of this Eastern Zhou ruler did not offer great political advantage to Wu Zhao; she sought a more intimate link to the paramount line of ancient Zhou founders. To this end, she composed an inscription to make manifest the connection between her established predecessor, King Ping, and the earlier cultural luminaries from the Ji clan that founded the Zhou. The section of the inscription containing this crucial manufactured genealogical link read:

> The Ascended Immortal Crown Prince, styled Ziqiao, was the crown prince of King Ling of Zhou.[23] The Original Forefather's[24] heaven-mending, earth-suturing foundation accomplished two-thirds of the lofty achievement. Divine ancestor Qi [Hou Ji] first inherited the auspicious aura from [Jiang Yuan's] treading in the Supreme God's footprint and bequeathed it to posterity. His sagacious father's was of remarkable origin: in his childhood appeared the sign of the numinous mustache.[25] The white fish appeared as an auspicious token; the red sparrow descended as a lucky sign.[26]

At Wu Zhao's behest, a stele bearing the inscription was erected in 698 on Mount Goushi, a short, flat-topped hill thirty kilometers west of imposing Mount Song.[27] The original forefather refers to King Wen, and the inscription recognizes his central role in the founding of the Zhou dynasty of old. The "Annals of Zhou" in *Records of the Grand Historian* relates that during his campaign against the notorious last ruler of the Shang, a white fish leapt into the future King Wu's boat as he crossed the Yellow River and a firebird descended toward his tent as he bivouacked on the river's margin.[28] In her inscription, Wu Zhao includes both portents—the white fish and the red sparrow—signifying the Zhou ruler's rightful status as Son of Heaven. While Jiang Yuan is not directly mentioned, the Supreme God's footprint (lü di 履帝) is; her role in passing on the divine energy to her son Hou Ji and to all of Zhou posterity is the crux of this section of the inscription. Jiang Yuan's original, intimate link to the Supreme God becomes a blood component inherited by subsequent generations. It is passed on to Hou Ji, to King Wen, to King Ling with his precociously prodigious mustache, to the mercurial Daoist wanderer Prince Jin, and, ultimately, to Zhou descendant and present-day sovereign Wu Zhao.

Not only was she their political ancestor, heir to the mantle of virtue of the male paragons from the dawn of the Western Zhou, but she was their blood descendant, and the ichor of Jiang Yuan coursed through her veins.

As newly inaugurated emperor in 690, she reinvented her Wu family and set up seven ancestral temples, the designated number for the ruling clan: she named King Wen and Mother Wen First Ancestor and First Ancestress; the second temple was devoted to the youngest son of King Ping and his spouse, the members of the ruling Ji clan who first bore the Wu surname; the remaining temples were established for the past five generations of Wus beginning with great-great-great-grandfather Wu Keji, followed by great-great-grandfather Wu Juchang, great-grandfather Wu Jian, and grandfather Wu Hua, and culminating with her father Wu Shiyue. Spouses shared the temples and were invested with titles commensurate to those given husbands.[29] The dedication of these temples followed the accepted ceremonial protocol for ancestor worship, with the five most recent generations of deceased Wus filling five of the seven temple slots, leaving only two for remote ancestors. One tablet necessarily went to the youngest son of King Ping with his miraculous "Wu" birthmark, the founding Wu ancestor who linked Wu Zhao's Zhou to the Ji clan, the royal lineage of the Zhou dynasty of antiquity. Wu Zhao then chose King Wen and Mother Wen to fill the final slot—as the first ancestral couple. As blood ancestress and founding mother, Mother Wen already tied Wu Zhao to the Ji clan and her glorious namesake Zhou of yore. Mother Wen was one of the "three mothers of Zhou" celebrated in *Biographies of Exemplary Women* who had helped found the dynasty and had even assisted as a minister herself. Therefore, Wu Zhao did not grant Jiang Yuan her own ancestral temple. She had an opportunity to ensconce Jiang Yuan as a major dynastic ancestor, but declined.

And yet Wu Zhao recognized that Jiang Yuan was the wife of a god, the wellspring of the Ji line that established the Zhou, and a celebrated mother who had raised Hou Ji to be the Lord of Millet, a foundational culture hero. A strange occurrence in 701 allowed the female emperor to affiliate herself with the dynastic mother of the remote past.

THE SUPREME GOD WALKS AMONG US: DIVINE FOOTPRINT

According to the *Comprehensive Mirror*, upon hearing that a giant Buddha had left a footprint in Chengzhou (modern-day Guangdong) in 701, Wu Zhao inaugurated the Great Footprint era.[30]

In an anecdote intended to show Wu Zhao's excessive preoccupation with auspicious omens, the *Collected Records of Court and Country* from the mid-eighth century records an interesting variation of the story. The Court of Judicial Review had imprisoned in excess of three hundred prisoners in distant Chengzhou. On the night of the autumn equinox, these men fashioned an immense footprint, five *chi* (just short of five feet) in length, meant to be that of a divine being. In the middle of the night, they cried out in chorus. When the wardens investigated, the prisoners responded that they had seen a thirty-foot-tall, golden-faced god who informed them that, as they had been wrongly accused, the emperor, in her boundless mercy, would offer them amnesty. When the authorities illuminated the ground and saw the giant footprint, they reported it. Wu Zhao issued a general amnesty and changed the reign era to Great Footprint.[31] In addition to the Buddhist layer of interpretation, Wu Zhao's celebration of the giant footprint seems to hearken back to the poem "Birth of a People" in the *Book of Songs*, evoking the instance Jiang Yuan steps in the big toeprint of a god and gives birth to Hou Ji, the first ancestor of the Zhou—the female sovereign's namesake dynasty of antiquity.[32]

According to Mircea Eliade, in *Myth and Reality*, a certain inchoate awe surrounds the origin, when all is perfect and intact. Origin is divine and mythical, not something wrought by man.[33] Great authority accrues to the author of new beginnings. As the ur-mother who birthed the first ancestor of Zhou, Jiang Yuan invested the latter-day female sovereign with tremendous political power. The ideogram for her name, Yuan 嫄, consists of two parts, *nü* 女 (woman) and *yuan* 原 (origin), which yoked might be comprehended as "primordial mother."[34] Michael Puett considers Jiang Yuan's ecstatic dance in the Supreme God's footprint (in which Jiang Yuan "transgressively appropriates divine powers") a bold usurpation that led to the birth of Hou Ji, an aggressive mythic act comparable to Prometheus's theft of fire.[35] To a limited extent, with the inauguration of her Great Footprint era, Wu Zhao sought to seize upon this primordial flame to rekindle her guttering Zhou in its later years.

GHOSTBUSTER WANG TOUTS WU ZHAO AS A LATTER-DAY JIANG YUAN

Jiang Yuan also appears in a peculiar episode that appears in the Song dynasty collection, *Miscellaneous Records of the Taiping Era*. When a ghostbuster (*yiguizhe* 役鬼者) performed an exorcism and addressed the spirit of Gaozong, the medium cast Wu Zhao as a latter-day Jiang Yuan:

> In the later years of Grand Dowager Wu, within a single month several hundred palace attendants died. The grand dowager summoned ghostbuster Wang Wanche to inspect the palace. Che reported: "Because Your Majesty has long presided over the empire, the spirit of the Heavenly Sovereign [Gaozong] is displeased. Therefore, this has occurred." Wu Zhao replied, "But why?"
>
> Che answered, "I can propitiate his spirit." Thereupon, he laid a banquet before the palace hall, held a knife, and spurted water from his mouth. Then, he faced the four directions and recited incantations.
>
> After a short while, he said, "The emperor has arrived." Che then questioned the emperor: "The way of heaven has its ebb and flow. Eras of prosperity and decline alternate. Formerly, the emperor [Wu Zhao] assisted Your Majesty, presiding as a mother over the Four Seas, where she greatly amplified the transformations of Jiang Yuan and Mother Wen. Consequently, she was esteemed and honored and the ten thousand nations voluntarily submitted. This is heaven's will, not the machinations of man. Now Your Majesty's sagely spirit is on high, capable of wisely discerning between truth and falsehood. Why, then, not recognizing the real circumstance, have you so cruelly harmed living people?"
>
> From his aerial vantage, the emperor's spirit replied: "This was not my intent. This is Empress Wang's grievance being redressed. How could it stop in the inner palace? In the future it will bring ill fortune to your ruler."

Dumbfounded, the grand dowager and her attendants listened. Gloomily, she ordered the banquet removed. The following year the five princes assisted in establishing Zhongzong as ruler, moving the grand dowager to Shangyang Palace, where she died in seclusion.[36]

A year after the ominous prognostication, Wu Zhao was deposed when the coup of the Five Princes ended her Zhou dynasty.[37] Initially Wang Wanche had thought that Wu Zhao's long regency and rule had offended Gaozong's ghost. After the medium's investigation, however, it turned out that aggrieved apparition of his first consort, Empress Wang—annals relate her gruesome death a half-century earlier, having her hands and feet severed, and being cast, on Wu Zhao's order, into a wine vat, where she bled out and died horribly[38]—had wrought a terrible vengeance, killing scores of palace attendants. Well aware that Wu Zhao was listening, perhaps in an effort to soften the grim, unsettling tidings he delivered, Wang Wanche evoked both Jiang Yuan, the founding ancestress of the Zhou imperial clan, and Mother Wen, a guiding force in the establishment of the Zhou dynasty of old. In conversing with the deceased emperor's spirit, he represented Wu Zhao—then emperor of the Zhou—as one who excelled these two female political ancestors, one who had "greatly amplified the transformations of Jiang Yuan and Mother Wen."

CONCLUSION

Both before and after Wu Zhao, there is evidence that Jiang Yuan was widely recognized as the first or foremost ancestress (*xian bi* 先妣). At the beginning of Sui Yangdi's reign in 604 when officials were debating the proper number of ancestral temples, one minister mentioned that in the celebrated Zhou dynasty of antiquity separate temples were established for King Wen, King Wu, and Jiang Yuan.[39] Jiang Yuan was a woman with her own temple, where her descendants worshipped and presented her offerings. A little more than a decade after Wu Zhao's death, official Chen Zhenjie sought posthumous recognition for Ruizong's empress Dou, arguing that as Jiang Yuan had been honored at a separate temple, Empress Dou, too, might have her own temple.[40] Gao Ying (740–811) composed a late Tang inscription for a temple devoted to Jiang Yuan and Gongliu, Hou Ji's great-great-grandson, that read, in part: "Formerly, the illustriousness of Wen and Wu of Zhou had its origins in Hou Ji. And Hou Ji was born of Jiang Yuan."[41] Jiang Yuan was revered as the source from which the Zhou dynasty issued. Her name and aura had long been employed to exalt empresses.

Wu Zhao also appreciated the numinous power of Jiang Yuan. After her hierogamous union with the Supreme God, this dynastic mother of yore had carried in her a divine seed. And Hou Ji, with his legendary green thumb, had become one of the founders of agriculture, so fundamental to Chinese civilization. The Lord of Millet served as minister of agriculture under Shun, one of the Five Emperors.[42] Wu Zhao celebrated her connection with this early ancestress by inaugurating the Great Footprint era in 701 and by noting her kinship ties to Jiang Yuan and the Ji clan.

Wenmu and Wu Zhao
Two Mothers of Zhou

IN THE ANALECTS OF CONFUCIUS, when paragon King Wu of Zhou reputedly claimed, "I have ten capable ministers," he included in their number his mother Taisi, the spouse of King Wen, a woman known also as Wenmu 文母, Mother Wen.[1] As attested to by Tang and Song sources, Mother Wen was a "living name" (*sheng hao* 生號) and not a posthumous designation.[2] Not only did Mother Wen capably assist both husband and son, but she also birthed, raised, and conscientiously educated ten sons and one daughter, earning a lofty historical reputation as one of the "three mothers of the house of Zhou" (*Zhou shi sanmu* 周室三母).[3]

Taijiang and Tairen, the other two "mothers of Zhou," married eminent predynastic leaders of the Ji clan that founded the dynasty. Taijiang, a woman of the Lü clan, helped Tanfu fix the foundations of early settlements for the clan on the plains of Zhou while rearing her sons. Tairen of the Zhiren clan aided husband Wang Ji, son of Taijiang and Tanfu. During Tairen's pregnancy with King Wen, to assure her child proper moral influence in utero, this paragon of rectitude "beheld nothing evil with her eyes, heard no lascivious sounds with her ears, and did not let a single haughty word pass from her lips." While both Taijiang and Tairen were set high on pedestals, Taisi, according to *Biographies of Exemplary Women*, was the "most capable and virtuous" (*zui xian* 最賢) of the three mothers of Zhou.[4]

This chapter traces the cultic development of Taisi, the spouse of dynastic founder King Wen of Zhou and the mother of King Wu, and examines how her growing presence generated an exalted stature and political legitimacy for Wu Zhao.

Zhou dynasty romanticism

MOTHER WEN: A CONFUCIAN PARAGON OF
WOMANHOOD WITH A POLITICAL VOICE

Mother Wen appears several times in the *Book of Songs*, one of the earliest canonical classics, a work that, according to Michael Nylan, sought to "recapture the anterior halcyon days in song" by offering "unstinting praise for unimpeachable exemplars of long ago."[5] The *Book of Songs* waxes rhapsodic about the illustrious foundation of the Western Zhou dynasty under the capable rule of King Wen, King Wu, and the Duke of Zhou. These sovereigns and their spouses are artfully depicted as paragons, setting a benchmark of perfect governance to which subsequent rulers aspired. In the ode "Thoughtful and Reverent" (*siqi* 思齊), Taisi was cast as one of the virtuous founding mothers of the Zhou dynasty:

> Great dignity had Tairen,
> Mother of King Wen.
> Well loved by Lady Jiang of Zhou,
> Bride of the noble house.
> Taisi carried on the fine name.
> Hence, the multitude of sons.[6]

It is noteworthy that Taisi, Mother Wen, is revered not for the wise advice she dispensed to her husband and son, but for her fecundity, her "multitude of sons."

In the "Family Genealogies" (*shijia* 世家) of Sima Qian's *Records of the Grand Historian*, it is recorded that Taisi, "primary consort" (*zheng fei* 正妃) of King Wen, birthed King Wu second among her ten sons.[7] The "Three Mothers of Zhou" entry in the opening chapter of Liu Xiang's *Biographies of Exemplary Women* includes an account of Mother Wen:

> Taisi was the mother of King Wu and a daughter of the Si clan, a descendant of the great Yu and a native of the kingdom of Shen. She was compassionate and understood what was right. King Wen was pleased with her and went in person to welcome her at the River Wei, where he built a bridge of boats [to lead her across]. . . . From early dawn until late at night she toiled diligently and thus fulfilled her role as wife. Taisi was given the honorary title of Mother Wen. King Wen governed external

Figure 6.1 Mother Wen, with husband King Wen of Zhou, son King Wu, and mother-in-law Tairen, one of her fellow "mothers of Zhou."

affairs while Mother Wen ruled inside the palace. Taisi gave birth to ten sons. . . . Taisi diligently instructed her sons so that from the time they were small until they grew up, they never looked on harmful or mean things. . . . *The Superior Man* says: Taisi was benevolent, intelligent, and possessed virtues. . . . In final appraisal: the three mothers of Zhou were Taijiang, Tairen, and Taisi. The rise of Wen and Wu began with them. Being the most capable and virtuous, Taisi was given the title "Mother Wen."[8]

Taisi's inclusion in the opening chapter of *Biographies* fortified her stature as a Confucian paragon of maternal virtue. She was depicted as an ideal mother, a conscientious moral instructress who protected, cultivated, and educated her huge brood of sons. As a wife, she was a peerless inner helper, scrupulously overseeing her prescribed domestic sphere. Noble by birth, she was a descendant of culture hero Yu the Great, founder of the Xia dynasty. Furthermore, she was a woman of immaculate character, guided by a moral rectitude tempered by compassion and blessed with a discerning intellect. Hence, endowed by nature, noble blood, and individual disposition, Mother Wen emerged as a nonpareil in the Han, a worthy female complement to the great King Wen.

One of the earliest self-conscious articulations of a lineage of female Confucian ancestors by a woman appears in the Western Han. In Lady of Handsome Fairness Ban's (48–6 B.C.) "Rhapsody of Self-Commiseration" (Zidao fu 自悼賦), the onetime favorite of Emperor Cheng (r. 37–7 B.C.) writes:

> I spread out paintings of women to serve as my guiding mirrors;
> consulting the lady scribe, I asked about the *Odes*.
> Saddened by the augury of the hen that crows,
> I lamented the transgressions of Bao and Yan.
> I praised [E]Huang and [Nü]Ying, wives of the Lord of Yu,
> extolled [Tai]Ren and [Tai]Si, mothers of Zhou.
> Although stupid and uncouth and unable to emulate them,
> dare I still my thoughts and forget them?[9]

Cognizant of her responsibility as a consort of the emperor to act as a role model, Ban sought to pattern her demeanor upon the conduct of the women in this celebrated lineage. The mothers of Zhou continued to serve as models of maternal excellence.

Mother Wen's legacy endured. In 235, Cao Rui, Wei emperor Wendi, recalling his late mother Empress Zhen, related,

> The two daughters were consorts of Yu 虞,[10]
> and his imperial way was thereby established;
> The three mothers married Zhou rulers,
> and their sage goodness attained full brightness.
> Since these rulers received so much good fortune,
> they enjoyed the prolongation of their kingdoms.[11]

One of the "three mothers," Mother Wen helped inaugurate the ideal Zhou polity, matching King Wen as the pale light of the moon complemented the brilliant radiance of the sun. By situating his deceased mother in the company of illustrious women who had helped found ancient dynasties, Cao Rui implicitly lauded her pivotal role in establishing the Wei.

At the beginning of "Biographies of Empresses and Consorts" in *Chronicles of the Three Kingdoms*, annalist Chen Shou set the stage for examining the royal wives of the Wei era by determining their importance within the longer lineage of Confucian female political ancestors:

> In the *Book of Changes* it is written, "The proper place for the male is the outside; the proper place for the female is inside. When man and woman adhere to propriety, there is harmonious equanimity between heaven and earth." Of the wise former kings in antiquity, none failed to realize the important place of empresses and consorts, apprehending that their respective roles accorded with the virtues of heaven and earth. Formerly when he wed the two consorts of Gui, the path of Yu 虞 triumphed and prospered. When [Tai]Ren and [Tai]Si married into the Ji clan, the house of Zhou flourished. On this point, the fall or rise, the demise or survival, of dynastic houses has always hinged.[12]

[handwritten annotation: → Second guessing Confucius]

Chen Shou underscored the importance of the female role by emphasizing the codependent and complementary nature of male and female, of inner and outer; success or failure of dynastic houses hinged as much upon the character of an imperial consort as upon the emperor himself. As part of a celebrated line of ideal Confucian wives, Mother Wen (Si in the above passage) was honored for the perfect comportment and unerring propriety that could enable a husband to found an enduring dynasty.

Mother Wen was thus created in the same rigid Confucian mold as her predecessors and fellow "models of maternal rectitude," the Woman of Tushan and Jiang Yuan. As we have seen, they often appeared in conjunction. Indeed, in a late third-century eulogy, as noted earlier, the recently deceased Empress Yang traced her descent through the same exalted lineage:

> In edification, she excelled Tairen and Taisi
> As a paragon, she matched stride with Jiang Yuan.[13]

Taisi's role within this Confucian pedigree of paragons endured as a benchmark to adjudge subsequent excellence. In the lines cited above, Empress Yang is lauded for exceeding Mother Wen's capacity to instruct her sons.

More pertinent to Wu Zhao's ambitions, a tradition developed associating these illustrious female paragons with living empresses. To mark the regency of dowager empress Chu Suanzi (324–384) over young Jin emperor Mudi, courtier-official Cai Mo addressed her:

> Your Majesty, in following the proper principles of feminine deportment, has learned from the prosperous course of Mother Wen. In antiquity, the Woman of Tushan lent her radiance to the Xia dynasty and Jiandi[14] helped the house of Yin flourish. Truly, due to their manifest wisdom they helped bring about prosperity and good fortune.[15]

The former empress became a grand dowager–regent, and went on to dominate the Jin court for two decades.

Early in the fifth century, Liu Song Emperor Wu (r. 420–422) paid homage to his deceased mother by claiming that she was

> Just as admirable as Jiang Yuan,
> of a class equal to Tairen and Taisi.[16]

In an analogous capacity, Mother Wen appeared in a poem written during the reign of Emperor Wu of the Southern Qi (483–494) to honor his deceased Gracious Consort Pei (Pei huifei 裴惠妃):

> Taisi became a wife of Zhou;
> Tushan was paired with Yu.
> My empress has inherited their queenly raiment,
> Reaffirming rules and reasserting propriety.[17]

Being placed in the worthy company of Mother Wen suggested that Empress Mu had also helped establish the Southern Qi through her unswerving rectitude and punctilious observation of Confucian propriety; an empress possessing the character of a latter-day Mother Wen might directly influence both the founding and the preservation of the state. In essence, the good reputation of Mother Wen was linked to the very pinnacle of Confucian womanhood, to perfected wifely virtues and motherhood of the highest order.

That Mother Wen, the dynastic mother heralding from the Zhou of antiquity, was a personification of fully realized Confucian womanhood was not sufficient for Wu Zhao. Fortunately for Wu Zhao, a serendipitous precedent from the dawn of the Tang dynasty recast Mother Wen not as an ideal mother but as a woman who had played a constructive role in affairs of state. When Tang founder Gaozu's favorite daughter, the Pingyang Princess (Pingyang gongzhu 平陽公主, 598–623), a stalwart young woman who had helped her sire seize and occupy the Sui capital Daxing and found the Tang, passed away, her imperial father fondly remarked, "Wenmu is counted among the ten great ministers of Zhou. The princess's contribution in assisting to gain the mandate likewise marks her as an extraordinary woman."[18] Clearly, given her martial role in helping Gaozu establish the Tang, the Pingyang Princess was unlike the empresses and dowagers of the Northern and Southern Dynasties. By the early Tang, being associated with Mother Wen was no longer simply tantamount to being labeled an ideal Confucian wife and mother. The Pingyang Princess was declared an "extraordinary woman" (feichang furen 非常婦人) due to her active engagement as a field commander in the male sphere of military affairs. Drawing inspiration from this precedent, Wu Zhao seized upon the idea that Mother Wen's culturally recognized greatness resided not only in her Confucian helper role as a spouse managing the inner domestic sphere, but in her capacity as a female minister capable of extraordinary contributions in the public, political sphere.

SITUATING WU ZHAO AS THE AVATAR OF MOTHER WEN

In 666, Gaozong and Wu Zhao performed the sacrosanct feng and shan sacrifices on Mount Tai—rites performed only seven times in Chinese history. In these grand rites, the ruler (or, in this unique instance, rulers), assumed a posture of obeisance before heaven and earth, offering sacrifices to acknowledge the celestial blessings and terrestrial bounty. The stylized modesty belied the grand scope of the ceremonies, which served to confirm, before court, country, and foreign dignitaries, that the rulers possessed heaven's mandate. This was the only time emperor and empress concelebrated these rites.[19] Veteran general and senior statesman Li Ji 李勣 (594–669) sent the Two Sages—as corulers Gaozong and Wu Zhao were known at the time—a memorial urging the emperor to make his deceased forebears Gaozu and Taizong coadjutor spirits (*pei* 配) when performing the *feng* sacrifice to heaven. Li Ji not only praised the great achievements of the first two Tang emperors, but he also lauded their respective consorts, Empresses Dou and Zhangsun. The former, Li Ji claimed, "followed in the footsteps of Mother Wen" and "propagated the beautiful accomplishments of [Jiang] Yuan of Zhou"; he styled the latter, Empress Zhangsun, "equal to the ten ministers in her merit," a latter-day Mother Wen who had helped fix the dynastic foundations of the Tang. Thereafter, Li Ji logically concluded that "since the two emperors [Gaozu and Taizong] will be coadjutor spirits for the *feng* rites to heaven, it is appropriate that the two empresses [Dou and Zhangsun] serve as coadjutor spirits in the *shan* rites to earth."[20]

Though not known as a propagandist, Li Ji was a long-standing political ally of Wu Zhao. In 655, when Gaozong and Wu Zhao desperately solicited support from the "old guard" of court ministers in their effort to depose Empress Wang and elevate Wu Zhao in her stead, they were initially stone-walled. The emperor and his lover only dared to take this critical, brazen step once Li Ji tacitly condoned the move with his remark, "This is a family matter for Your Majesty to deal with. Why ask outsiders?"[21] At a pivotal juncture, the renowned statesman-general, who had capably and loyally served Taizong, helped validate Wu Zhao's rise to empress.[22] In 664, Gaozong named him grand commissioner of the Feng and Shan sacrifices.[23] Li Ji continued to serve both as a chief minister and a general until his death in 669.

Initially, when Gaozong's court deliberated, they agreed to follow Li Ji's recommendation to honor the deceased empresses, but planned to have ministers make offerings to these ancestresses.[24] However, Wu Zhao intervened, petitioning her husband en route to Mount Tai:

> Heaven and earth have fixed positions. The virtues of obdurance and pliancy are distinct. Both classics and commentaries contain examples of how, in performing rites and ceremonies, these differences are well heeded. To present secondary offerings at the jade altar tallies with the square orientation of the earth; to offer fragrant foods in jade pedestal bowls is in truth a duty for the inner apartments. Moreover, in extending honors to former empresses, how can we use ministers and officials of the outer court to perform the rites?[25]

Figure 6.2 Image of a dancing girl from a painting on the walls of Li Ji's tomb, excavated in Shaanxi in 1974.

Persuasively, she argued—in the name of Confucian propriety—that noble-women rather than ministers should perform the secondary and tertiary *shan* rites at Sheshou to honor the earth goddess and the deceased early Tang empresses.[26]

Ostensibly, Li Ji evoked Mother Wen in his commemoration in order to exalt the two deceased empresses of the early Tang. Rites to honor the dead, however, are often staged for the benefit of the living, and the *feng* and *shan* sacrifices of 666 were no exception. Li Ji's meticulously crafted peroration echoed the names of Mother Wen and Jiang Yuan and embraced the two recent empresses. Yet it was oriented toward glorifying Wu Zhao in the present, paving the way for her subsequent petition to involve herself (and a wider circle of women) in the *feng* and *shan* rites. Honoring these recently deceased women was an important gesture of stylized humility on Wu Zhao's part, one that veiled a rite of tremendous self-promotion and self-aggrandizement. Empresses Dou and Zhangsun were but placeholders, pale incarnations of Mother Wen, set up to project the accumulated charisma and political luster of the Zhou dynastic mother onto her contemporary avatar, Wu Zhao.

MOTHER WEN AND MOTHER WU

When Wu Zhao became Gaozong's empress in 655, Mother Wen had an established Confucian cult. Widely accepted as a remarkable woman whose strong moral presence was linked closely to the founding of the glorious Zhou of antiquity, Mother Wen was the perfect inner helper: a conscientious wife, a wise mother, and a diligent household manager. She was a "minister" of the inner, domestic sphere. But as the example of the Pingyang Princess shows, in the open and cosmopolitan early Tang, when women were not strictly circumscribed by Confucian gender roles, the moral authority of Mother Wen began to extend into the "outer" administrative, political, and military realms formerly accorded to men. For Wu Zhao, this extension made Mother Wen a much more compelling, efficacious, and timely political forebear.

From the very beginning, when King Wu included his mother among his "ten ministers," ambiguity had shrouded Mother Wen's role. There was always an intimation that Mother Wen was more than an inner helper confined to the familial, domestic realm; after all, she had played an active, open role in the establishment of the original Zhou dynasty. Though Mother Wen's political involvement was hitherto obscure, Wu Zhao, always eminently capable of modifying rhetoric to her ends, naturally sought to exploit this ambiguity.

In 684, when Wu Zhao became grand dowager, propagandist Chen Zi'ang referred to her as a latter-day Mother Wen, endeavoring to persuade her to remain in Luoyang and govern. Shortly after Wu Zhao deposed her son Zhongzong and replaced him with tractable Ruizong, the imperial funerary cortege planned to bear Gaozong's corpse westward, to a tomb site in the mountains northwest of Chang'an, where the first two Tang sovereigns, Gaozu and Taizong, were buried. Initially, Wu Zhao planned to accompany the procession; on the eve of the journey, however, Chen Zi'ang petitioned her to remain in Luoyang and bury Gaozong in the vicinity. To secure this objective, he lavishly praised her for the stability she had lent the imperial house:

> When the redoubtable emperor departed this world and left behind us officials, the ten thousand nations were shaken and alarmed, the common folk rent asunder with grief. Because Your Majesty is a quick-apprehending sage, you have undertaken the burden of the ancestral temples, conforming to the wishes of the empire. None but hope to receive your sagely transformations. . . . Moreover, Your Majesty, the august grand dowager, with the virtue of Mother Wen, has assisted in glorifying the dynasty, in both military affairs and great matters of state making decisions and promulgating edicts so that the country now flourishes as it did in the time of Yao and Shun.[27]

Chen Zi'ang's "Mother Wen" was not simply an inner helper who, through subtle behind-the-scenes remonstrance, served as a moral compass to guide her husband in the outer realm of politics and statecraft. To tally with Wu Zhao's preeminent role in court, his rendition of Mother Wen capably superintended "great matters of state," wisely charting the country's political and military course. Ultimately, Wu Zhao remained in Luoyang to preside over the court while puppet Ruizong accompanied his father's funerary procession.[28]

Another source also indicates that during Wu Zhao's first years as grand dowager, Mother Wen was on her mind. In the *Analects*, Confucius qualified his remark, "King Wu said, 'I have ten capable ministers,'" with the disparaging opinion that "with a woman amongst them there were, in fact, only nine."[29] In contrast, Wu Zhao publicly recognized Mother Wen's constructive political contribution. First promulgated in 685, her political treatise *Regulations for Ministers* advocated total and unswerving loyalty of minister to ruler.[30] In the preface, she explained the structure of the text: "To commemorate the ten great ministers of the Zhou dynasty, I have written ten fascicles."[31] In Confucian scholar Zheng Xuan's Eastern Han commentary on the *Analects*, Mother Wen's name was placed first among the ten ministers.[32] For Wu Zhao, too, there was no doubt about Mother Wen's importance: Taisi was one of her son's ten ministers, a full-fledged member of their learned company.

Later in Wu Zhao's tenure as grand dowager, Cui Rong presented a petition on behalf of a general to persuade her to hold a ceremonial banquet, in which she was once more compared with Mother Wen:

> Helping in the rise of the Yin, Youshen[33] irradiated the dynastic
>   enterprise,
> Supporting the ascendancy of the Ji clan, Taisi aided their meritorious
>   success.[34]

In 688, Cui Rong again used the name and aura of Mother Wen in a memorial to persuade Wu Zhao to take the title Sage Mother, Divine Sovereign:

> Taisi had a spotless reputation,
> And alone took it upon herself to mother the exalted Zhou.[35]

Portending Wu Zhao's own rise as emperor, he mentions dynastic mother Taisi immediately following Nüwa. In each of these appearances of Mother Wen from Wu Zhao's time as dowager-regent, the original mother of Zhou is presented as playing an important part in the founding of the ancient dynasty. In 690, with a bit of further assistance from Mother Wen, Wu Zhao would inaugurate a new Zhou dynasty.

MOTHER WEN AS BLOOD ANCESTOR

Previous chapters have remarked upon Wu Zhao's effort—first as grand dowager and then as emperor—to invoke through names, titles, ceremonies, and monuments, the return of a golden age. To conjure a neoclassical air of majesty, she selected "Zhou" for her dynastic epithet. Like many newly risen dynasts of humble origins before and after her, she concocted a genealogy moored in antiquity.[36] As noted in the previous chapter, Wu Zhao selected the youngest son of King Ping (eighth century B.C.) for one of her early ancestors. The princeling was given the new surname, Wu, to match the extraordinary "Wu" 武 birthmark on his hand.[37] This served two purposes: First, it enwrapped the first Wu with a miraculous aura. Second, it grafted Wu Zhao's clan to a branch of the grand Ji clan, founders of the glorious Zhou of yore. Her kinship line became even more venerable than that of the house of Tang, which only traced its descent back to the Daoist sage Laozi in the sixth century B.C. Through the Wu princeling, Wu Zhao traced her ancestry back to dynastic founder King Wen of the Ji clan and his eminently capable spouse, Mother Wen. Not only did Wu Zhao claim political affinity to this paragon from the remote past, but she also declared her consanguinity to Mother Wen.

When Wu Zhao established her new Zhou dynasty, to broadcast these ties with her Zhou kinsmen, she not only elevated recently deceased family members but also bestowed grand titles upon Mother Wen and her distant ancestors from the Zhou of antiquity. In the ninth month of 690, just four days after Wu Zhao inaugurated her Zhou dynasty, she established seven temples for her natal Wu clan—the number appropriate to a ruling dynastic family. At the first ancestral temple, the female emperor honored King Wen of Zhou, designating him Emperor Wen and First Ancestor (Shizu 始祖); his spouse, Mother Wen, was named Empress of Decorated Resolve (Wending huanghou 文定皇后). Thus, in the foremost ancestral temple of Wu Zhao's Zhou dynasty, Mother Wen and King Wen, founders of the original Zhou, were jointly presented sacrifices.

In the next ancestral temple, offerings were made to King Wu—not the celebrated martial conqueror who had defeated the Shang, but the Wu princeling with his curious birthmark, reportedly Wu Zhao's fortieth-generation ancestor, who had branched off the Ji clan to found a new family.[38] He was named Emperor Kang (Kang huangdi 康皇帝), the Perspicacious Ancestor (Ruizu 睿祖), while his spouse was designated Empress of Salubrious Kindness (Kanghui huanghou 康惠皇后).[39] Early in 691, to correspond with their new elevated titles as First Ancestors of the new Zhou, the tomb (mu 墓) of King Wen and Mother Wen was redesignated an imperial mausoleum (ling 陵).[40]

Wu Zhao's reinvented origin was confirmed in the Coiling Dragon Terrace stele inscription, composed in 699 by Li Qiao at Wu Zhao's behest to honor her parents. In this elegant exercise in mythmaking, the aesthetic master relates the marvelous birth of Wu Zhao's father: Wu Shiyue emerged from the womb surrounded by five-colored mists; on the skin of his back were moles arrayed in the pattern of the Big Dipper.[41] This curious constellation of moles recalls the 72 moles on the thigh of Han founder Gaozu (r. 206–195 B.C.), mystic nevi that signaled his future ascendancy.[42] The inscription then relates the story of the "Wu" marking the hand of the prodigal youngest son of King Ping.[43]

Once again, this connection was not only political, but familial. Wu Zhao situated herself as Taisi's heir, at once a blood descendant and a wise mother of state in Mother Wen's image. This connection to the golden age of the original Zhou helped cloak her inventive political authority in the guise of tradition. When Wu Zhao established her Zhou dynasty and honored Mother Wen as First Ancestress, she herself became, in effect, the "mother of Zhou" for the new era she inaugurated in 690.

FOR MOTHER AND DAUGHTER: MOTHER WEN IN THE STELE INSCRIPTION OF WU SANSI

Wu Zhao's nephew Wu Sansi composed a commemorative inscription in 702 for Madame Yang, the female emperor's mother. The inscription situated Mother Wen within the familiar political lineage of women who had helped found and govern dynasties:

> Your humble subject has heard that the two principles [*yin* and *yang*] have complementary virtues. . . . The two glorious orbs are equally brilliant, the Jade Hare [moon] matching the Golden Crow [sun]. In the celestial orbit, the Widow Star is in ascendancy. . . . Guishui harmonized with the virtue of Ehuang. Then there is the example of Xiling exalting the reputation of her [affinal] clan, [two characters omitted] the palace of the Yellow Emperor. The splendid match with Southland elevated the tents of Xia. Thereafter, the uprightness and consistency of Tairen helped fix the foundation of King Wen. The diligence and assiduousness of Taisi secured the smooth transition of authority to King Wu.[44]

Wu Sansi placed his great aunt, Madame Yang, and by extension ruling emperor Wu Zhao herself, within this wider assemblage of female political ancestors. Women were often identified by their place of origin. Ehuang, a consort of Emperor Shun, was associated with Guishui. Xiling is a reference to silk goddess Leizu, spouse of the Yellow Emperor. Southland (Nantu 南土) is likely the homeland of the Tushan Girl, consort of Yu the Great, founder of the Xia. Mother Wen, Taisi, was the final and pivotal link between Wu Zhao and this glorious classical lineage of female paragons. Wu Sansi's rhetoric not only affirms the great contributions of these women in establishing past dynasties, but values them as "equally brilliant" compared with their celebrated male counterparts—Shun, Yu, and King Wen.

CONCLUSION

Mother Wen developed into a significant figure. In calculated synchronicity with her own rise, Wu Zhao and her propagandists reinvented Mother Wen in a process tailored to link and exalt these two mothers: the sagacious dynastic mother of a halcyon golden age to the wise parent of the newly inaugurated Zhou dynasty. Their affiliation meant different things at different stations of Wu Zhao's political career. At times, the relationship suggested that Wu Zhao, like Mother Wen, possessed attributes of an ideal Confucian wife and mother—virtue, intelligence, and diligence. Mother Wen's role as one of King Wen's "ten ministers" helped justify Wu Zhao's burgeoning participation in government as empress and grand dowager.

When Li Ji linked the empresses of Gaozu and Taizong to Mother Wen on the eve of the *feng* and *shan* sacrifices, it enabled Wu Zhao's participation in these ceremonies. When Wu Zhao was grand dowager, Chen Zi'ang styled her a second coming of Mother Wen, intimating that she was not merely a "minister" but a dynastic mother capable of managing affairs of state. Most importantly, when Wu Zhao established herself as a female sovereign, Mother Wen—as her blood ancestor and political forebear—played a central role in her wider political strategy to fashion a neoclassical legitimacy by connecting both her person and the state she ruled to the Zhou dynasty of old.

SEVEN

Four Exemplary Women in Wu Zhao's Regulations for Ministers

WU ZHAO PRODUCED AN IMPRESSIVE array of normative Confucian texts that prescribed proper behavior for women. Before she was empress, as Lady of Luminous Deportment, a second-ranked concubine, Wu Zhao composed *Instructions for the Inner Realm* (Neixun 內訓) in 654.[1] Subsequent works for women attributed to the prolific Wu Zhao include a hundred-chapter *Ancient and Recent Rules for the Inner Quarters* (Gujin neifan 古今內範) and an abridged ten-chapter version of this text titled *Condensed Essential Rules for the Inner Chambers* (Neifan yaolue 內範要略), a hundred-chapter edition of *Biographies of Exemplary Women*, a separate twenty-chapter *Biographies of Filial Daughters* (Xiaonü zhuan 孝女傳), and a one-chapter *Biographies of Tutors and Wet Nurses* (Baofu rumu zhuan 保傅乳母傳).[2] Wu Zhao was not the only seventh-century author of instructional manuals for women. During Taizong's reign, Empress Zhangsun is credited with compiling a ten-chapter *Essential Regulations for Women*, while Taizong's renowned chief minister Wei Zheng authored an *Abridged Biographies of Exemplary Women* (Lienü zhuan lue 列女傳略) of seven chapters.[3] In the century following Wu Zhao, two new classics for women were composed, both modeled on canonical texts for men: Madame Cheng wrote the *Classic of Filial Piety for Women* (Nü Xiaojing 女孝經) and the Song sisters composed *Analects for Women* (Nü Lunyu 女論語).[4] Unfortunately, none of the manuals credited to Wu Zhao is extant.

Wu Zhao did not style herself as the latter-day incarnation of these exemplary women, as she did with certain goddesses. Rather, as Gaozong's empress and first lady of the realm, she lent her authorial voice of moral instruction to the illumination of these past models of perfect deportment, projecting them as cynosures for women of her era to emulate. Implicitly, this suggested that she possessed, internalized, and served as arbiter of those prized Confucian virtues: she was chaste, filial, benign, wise, austere, modest, obedient, and righteous. During her tenure as empress, when most of these works were produced, textual reinforcement of these sanctioned behaviors served to represent her as an ardent champion of Confucian values.

Though Wu Zhao's hundred-chapter edition of the text is lost, a quartet of women from *Biographies of Exemplary Women* (presumably, women included in Wu Zhao's version, as well as in Liu Xiang's) have fortunately surfaced in one of the female ruler's extant writings from a later stage of her political career, a political treatise titled *Regulations for Ministers*. The curious appearance of these four women—the mother of Mencius 孟母, Lady Ji of Lu 魯季, the mother of Zifa 子發母, and the mother of General Kuo of Zhao 趙將括母—and the fashion in which they are deployed provide hints as to the manner in which Wu Zhao drew upon the normative ideological sanction of celebrated Confucian women in past eras. Looking at the roles of these women in *Regulations for Ministers*, several interrelated factors become apparent. First, the two texts had very different target audiences: her *Biographies* was written to instruct women of the inner palace and wives of ministers in proper womanly behavior, while *Regulations* demanded total loyalty from officials in her court. Second, the timing was different: Wu Zhao's hundred-chapter rendition of *Biographies* was promulgated when she was empress; *Regulations* was compiled when she was grand dowager and continued to be disseminated once she became emperor in 690. Though these widowed mothers neither helped establish new dynasties nor bore divine sons who founded revered lineages, Wu Zhao discovered a fresh political potency in these wise, principled women.

CONTEXT AND PURPOSE OF THE FOUR FEMALE EXEMPLARS IN *REGULATIONS FOR MINISTERS*

Wu Zhao's *Regulations for Ministers* eclectically blended Confucian, Legalist, and Daoist writings, along with texts from martial traditions, into an elaborate justification of authoritarian power. Her text, two chapters of five fascicles each, features imperatives from ruler to ministers, guiding instructions gleaned from an array of three dozen texts. Denis Twitchett contends that this work reinforces the ruler-minister relationship "on a very personal level by stressing the amalgamation of the concept of 'loyalty' toward ruler with that of filial piety within family."[5] Emphasis upon these two paramount virtues, loyalty and filial piety, buttressed the Confucian ideology of order and hierarchy. Modern scholar Li Hexian remarks that the text provided an ideal blueprint for the ethical code of ministers, creating the image of a perfect machine in which each cog knew and capably performed its role. Such mutual interdependence, coordinated effort, and unswerving loyalty is necessary to administer a vast empire with multitudinous tasks.[6] To this end, the opening fascicle, "The Same Organism" (Tongti 同體), articulates a vision of the body politic, the state, in which the ruler is the "heart-mind" (xin 心) and the ministers function as the body (ti 體), the arms and legs.[7]

Ministerial loyalty reached its full expression in single-minded and wholehearted civic duty. In the fourth fascicle, "Public-mindedness and Rectitude" (Gongzheng 公正), to properly fulfill their duty to Wu Zhao, loyal ministers are instructed to "exhaust their will for the ruler and the dynasty, paying no mind to private familial affairs." Wu Zhao's authorial voice continues, "There are ten thousand principles to administer the people. But effective governance stems from a single source. What is that source? Simply, it is public-mindedness."[8]

Curiously, though their target audiences may be different, *Regulations* and *Biographies*—one, a political treatise designed to foster a culture of total loyalty among court ministers, and the other, a guide to dutiful and chaste behavior for women—appear to have been closely linked. In the mid-670s while still empress, Wu Zhao formed the scholars of the Northern Gate, an extra-bureaucratic group that compiled Confucian texts and other political treatises geared toward amplifying her political authority. The biography of Liu Yizhi (631–687), a leading member of this cadre of unofficial advisors who later became one of Wu Zhao's chief ministers, records that the group was involved in the joint compilation of these two normative manuals—*Regulations* and *Biographies*—among others.[9] In a passage that underscores her political ascendancy during Gaozong's waning years, Wu Zhao's biography in the *New Tang History* also pairs the texts:

In the emperor's [Gaozong's] later years, his illness grew increasingly severe and his humors were out of kilter, so that all of the affairs of the empire were determined by the empress. The empress thereupon, in order to foster greater peace and civility in governance, gathered a large group of Confucian scholars into the Inner Palace. They compiled and edited *Biographies of Exemplary Women, Regulations for Ministers, New Instructions for the Hundred Offices*, the *Book of Music*, etc., overall more than a thousand chapters.[10]

In these accounts, and several others in the official Tang histories, *Regulations* immediately follows *Biographies*.[11] Compiled by Wu Zhao and the scholars of the Northern Gate, these two texts were linked by shared authorship and purpose.

The decade that Wu Zhao worked together with the scholars of the Northern Gate on these normative texts was decisive in her political career. Gaozong's protracted illness worsened, prompting growing tensions about succession. She faced powerful antagonists in court. Domestically, the country endured a series of grim catastrophes—droughts, pestilence, scourges of locusts, and invasions.[12] For Wu Zhao and the Tang dynastic house, these were precarious times. Amid this volatility, she sought to stabilize her own position through circulation of this series of normative texts.

In the late 670s, to guide her wayward second son, heir apparent Li Xián, Wu Zhao—exemplifying the concerned Confucian mother—presented him with two works: *Orthodox Patterns for Princes* (Shaoyang zheng fan 少陽正範) and *Biographies of Filial Sons* (Xiaozi zhuan 孝子傳).[13] She also established the *Classic of Filial Piety* (Xiaojing 孝經) as a compulsory examination text in 678.[14] The ambitious crown prince surrounded himself with a coterie of tutors and portrayed himself not as an obedient princeling and filial son but as one ready to assume the mantle of a Confucian monarch. In 679, he allegedly plotted to murder a soothsayer who had suggested he was not cut in the mold of an emperor. Shortly thereafter, hundreds of suits of black armor were found in his palace, indicating a plot to usurp the throne.[15] Li Xián was banished and forced to take his own life in 684, shortly after Gaozong's death.[16]

By the time *Regulations for Ministers* was composed in 685,[17] dowager-regent Wu Zhao had recently deposed her feckless third son Zhongzong and relegated the nominal emperor, her timid youngest son Ruizong, to the palace of the crown prince while she "presided over court and issued edicts" (*linchao chengzhi* 臨朝稱治).[18] Her paramount concern in this text was not with defining proper filial conduct for her flesh-and-blood sons, but rather, as the name of the text suggests, with designating behavioral expectations for men in court, demanding of these political "sons" absolute civic duty and undeviating loyalty.

As emperor in 693, Wu Zhao elevated *Regulations* to canonical status, placing it alongside the *Book of Rites*, the *Book of History*, and the works of Confucius as a compulsory text for all officials taking the civil service examinations.[19]

WU ZHAO, WIDOWED DOWAGER: DRAWING ON THE CONFUCIAN AUTHORITY OF WIDOWHOOD

In her work on the station of women in early Tang China, Duan Tali observes that widows and mothers enjoyed a particularly high status. Despite the injunction contained in the Confucian three obediences (*san cong* 三從) that a mother submit to her eldest son after the death of her husband, in reality a Tang widow "exercised tremendous authority within the family, not only as the true head of household, but also as heir to her husband's prestige and social status." A widow was responsible for managing the family estate and keeping it intact.[20] As widow (after Gaozong's death in 683), mother, and regent, Wu Zhao was perfectly poised to command the filial devotion and loyalty of blood sons and "political sons"—that is, court ministers and countrymen—alike.

Given the enduring influence and vitality of the Confucian system, texts like *Biographies* continued, in the words of Josephine Chiu-Duke, "to shape the Tang perception of maternal responsibility." Such works presented women—especially mothers—as "a crucial positive force of society in general and of the state in particular."[21] Jennifer Holmgren has classified an entire category of women found in *Biographies* as "learned instructresses who advise men on social and political matters."[22] Tang mothers (at least those mothers honored in epitaphs or celebrated in their sons' official biographies) patterned themselves upon these exemplars and, like these wise instructresses of the past, were well-versed in the art of governance. They guided their sons to successful careers in bureaucratic service, often urging their offspring to relinquish frivolous pursuits like hunting and falconry in order to wholeheartedly devote themselves to the state. In this sense, mothers wielded influence beyond the inner, domestic sphere. Inheriting the tradition of wise and upright motherhood touted in *Biographies*, these Tang mothers set public service and duty as a greater good than private, familial interest.[23] This persona of the public-minded mother who placed loyalty to state above family, thus reflecting strong Confucian values, held a powerful political resonance for Wu Zhao as ruler.

Rather than offering filial devotion to men, these sagacious mothers had, by virtue of the edification and guidance they had provided their offspring, earned and duly received filial piety from their sons. By affiliating herself with this lineage of wise instructresses possessing profound knowledge of the political sphere, Wu Zhao identified herself as a motherly sage, the fitting object of filial devotion.

At the opening of the preface to *Regulations*, Wu Zhao portrays herself as a dutiful widow, declaring, "Humbly, I take the Celestial Sovereign's brilliant edicts and follow their wisdom, seeking wise and capable men on every side." Gaozong had taken the title Celestial Sovereign (Tianhuang 天皇) in 674, when Wu Zhao was made Celestial Empress.[24] Far from claiming an autonomous authority, Wu Zhao represented both her promulgation of *Regulations* and her growing public political presence as the requisite actions of a dutiful Confucian widow of the imperial Li family.

Later in the preface to *Regulations*, Wu Zhao depicts herself as a model Confucian mother, announcing her "determination to rear and nurture, without partiality, children and ministers alike."[25] Thus, from the very beginning of this political manifesto, Wu Zhao sought to extend her maternal aegis beyond her own children. The preface continues, "The compassion and love of a mother for her sons runs especially deep. Though the son may already have accumulated loyalty and goodness, still the mother wishes to offer exhortation and encouragement."[26] As articulated in *Regulations*, Wu Zhao's overarching motherly love, her avowed concern for the character, improvement, and well-being of her children, was not reserved for flesh-and-blood sons but embraced all her ministers and subjects, her political sons, in court and in country.

LESSONS OF THE LOOM: TWO MODELS OF MATERNAL
RECTITUDE IN *REGULATIONS FOR MINISTERS*

Immediately after emphasizing the profound "compassion and love of a mother for her sons" in the preface to *Regulations*, Wu Zhao pointedly alludes to two episodes from the opening chapter of *Biographies*. In all likelihood, these famous episodes, no doubt familiar to every official in her court, also held a prominent place in her own hundred-chapter version of *Biographies*. Wu Zhao's terse reference reads: "In the past though Wenbo was already a man of distinction, his mother still offered the metaphor of the axle; though Mencius was already a worthy man, his mother added the lesson of her cut weaving to instruct him."[27]

The model of maternal rectitude featured in the exemplum of the axle is Lady Ji of Lu, also known as Jing Jiang 敬姜, a widow of the late Spring and Autumn era (sixth century B.C.). Not only was she represented prominently in the opening chapter of *Biographies*, but she also appears in other Warring States and Han sources, such as the *Book of Rites*, the *Narrative of States* (Guoyu 國語), and *Accounts of the Warring States* (Zhanguo ce 戰國冊). Jing Jiang is consistently depicted "as a woman of considerable expertise, who operates within (and appears to approve of) the gender codes of her society, but with no loss of acumen in expressing her views on both state and domestic affairs to her male relatives."[28]

In her biography, the longest of the 125 in Liu Xiang's work, "the metaphor of the axle" is but one in a series of instructive episodes through which she imparted wisdom to her son.[29] Contemporary scholar Zhou Yiqun has observed that Jing Jiang "was acting on behalf of family interest and ultimately speaking in patriarchal authority."[30] Certainly, her powerful influence within her affinal family derived from her perfect adherence to Confucian principles. To wield such "patriarchal authority" with efficacy and confidence required far more than a widowed woman ventriloquizing time-honored Confucian principles: it took profound understanding of the classics, mastery of language, an adept grasp of rhetoric, a nimble tongue, and an opportunity provided by familial circumstances.

To shape young Wenbo's character, Jing Jiang expounded on the humility and sagacity—the willingness to receive remonstrance and the meticulous self-cultivation—of Zhou paragons like King Wu and the Duke of Zhou.[31] When Wenbo became minister of the state of Lu, she

Figure 7.1 Lady Ji of Lu used the "weaving-government analogy" to explain statecraft to her son, even when he was a minister of state.

instructed him not only on the finer points of ritual propriety but on the art of statecraft.

Wu Zhao's "metaphor of the axle" in *Regulations* was a reference to what Lisa Raphals terms the "weaving-government analogy," an extended conceit that Jing Jiang used to explicate to Wenbo the nature of good governance in which different parts of the loom corresponded to different interdependent administrative offices.[32] Raphals has scrupulously demonstrated that in Liu Xiang's original text, Jing Jiang draws a correspondence between eight parts of the loom and the same number of central and local bureaucrats—from the director of messengers (*da xing* 大行), moving fluidly from hand to hand like the shuttle (*kun* 捆); to the general (*jiang* 將), playing the role of the selvedge (*fu* 幅), the vital straight border of woven cloth that keeps the pattern regular. Her intricate analogy culminates with the minister (*xiang* 相), the axle (*zhou* 軸), one who "can fill an important office, travel a long road, and is upright, genuine, and firm."[33] In late imperial China, a seventeenth-century thinker, Song Yingxing, observed that weaving and government share a common vocabulary: *zhi* (治) means "to govern" or "to reel silk"; *luan* (亂) means "civil disorder" or "raveling a skein"; *jing* (經), "canonical texts" or "warp threads"; and *lun* (論), "philosophical discourse" or "silk yarn."[34] Providing women a measure of political and moral purchase, this shared language reflects not only the metaphorical potency of weaving but the literal centrality of the weaving art in Chinese society.

Following this weaving-government analogy in *Biographies*, Lady Ji of Lu offered her grown but misguided son further counsel, once again evocatively through the figurative language of weaving. When Wenbo urged her to stop weaving and enjoy a relaxed and prosperous life, Jing Jiang sighed, "Lu is done for!" Vehemently, she remonstrated that in former times, the diligence of queens and noblewomen in weaving ceremonial apparel set standards for commoners' wives to properly clothe their families. Virtue and diligence trickle down from top to bottom; so, too, do self-indulgence and sloth. If Wenbo as a minister of state failed to grasp this essential thread, the state of Lu was doomed.[35]

As we have seen in the chapter on Wu Zhao and Leizu, in early China weaving was women's work performed in the inner, familial sphere. In the "Domestic Rules" (Neize 內則) chapter of the *Book of Rites*, it was famously recorded that "men do not speak of the inner, women do not speak of the outer."[36] Within the inner sphere, women wielded tremendous influence. In Confucius, Lady Ji of Lu found an unlikely champion. When the sage, who held Jing Jiang in high esteem, learned of her didactic engagement in the public and political realm, he remarked:

> Disciples, note! The woman of Ji was not licentious. The *Odes'* saying "Women have no public charge, but tend their silkworms and their looms," means that a woman has public charge by virtue of her weaving and spinning. If she leaves them, she contravenes the rites.[37]

Her sage advice to her son in the outer, public sphere was articulated through the metaphorical vehicle of weaving; without ever quitting her loom, Jing Jiang capably imparted instruction on statecraft. While male and female spheres may have become rigidly delineated in later imperial China, in Jing Jiang's time inner (*nei* 內) and outer (*wai* 外) were "relative and relational terms."[38] Honored as an exemplar of Confucian propriety, the Jing Jiang celebrated in Wu Zhao's era, much like the strong-willed matriarch in Warring States and Han texts, was, in addition, as Lisa Raphals frames her, "a decisive and powerful woman who did not hesitate to intervene in either family matters or affairs of state."[39]

Comprehending at last his own role and responsibility as minister, Wenbo humbly bowed to his mother in acknowledgment that her intricate metaphor had elucidated the mechanisms of governance. Wu Zhao no doubt hoped that, upon receiving the instructions in her didactic political manual, her ministers would respond similarly. Indeed, from the reference to Jing Jiang and the nature of *Regulations*, it seems that the text was an effort to condition just this manner of ministerial response: humble acceptance of the wise dictates of the mother.

The renowned mother of the Confucian sage Mencius is the other central figure from the opening chapter of *Biographies* who appears in the preface of *Regulations*. Wu Zhao's pithy remark—"though Mencius was already a worthy man, his mother added the lesson of her cut weaving to instruct him"[40]—is an encapsulation of the best known of instructions the mother of Mencius imparted to her callow son. A more substantial version of the story of Mother Meng is recorded in *Biographies*:

Once when Mencius was young, he had just returned home from studying. Mother Meng was weaving. She asked how far his studies had progressed. Mencius answered, "About the same as before." Mother Meng then took a knife and cut her weaving. Terrified, Mencius asked the reason. Mother Meng responded, "My son's waste of his time studying is like me cutting my weaving. The superior man studies to establish his reputation; he makes inquiries in order to amplify his knowledge. This is because if his purpose is fixed, then it will bring security and tranquility; if it wavers, it can cause long-lasting harm. If you waste your time now, you will not be able to avoid becoming a laborer, and will meet with catastrophes and worries. How is that different from a weaving woman quitting her work mid-thread? How could she then make clothes for her husband and son, or provide food so they don't starve? A woman who quits on that which she depends on to eat is like a degenerate man who gives up on his cultivation of virtue. If he does not end up a thief, he'll end up a lackey." Mencius was terrified and thereafter studied assiduously morning and night, without cease. He served his teacher Zi Si and became a famous Confucian scholar known empire-wide.[41]

Figure 7.2 In her political manual *Regulations for Ministers,* Wu Zhao utilized the mother of Mencius to cast herself as a mother of empire who instructed her myriad sons to adhere to Confucian principles.

Once again, weaving plays a central part in delineating female virtue. For the mother of Mencius, industrious textile production marked the fulfillment of her office as widow and mother—she wove not merely for livelihood, but to sustain her son's education.[42] "Mencius's mother is not simply a weaver of cloth," Robin Wang asserts, "but the weaver of Mencius' intellectual, spiritual, and moral landscape."[43] She admonished her son that his haphazard work ethic would prove calamitous and inevitably reduce him to a lowlife. Conversely, diligent application to study might allow him to cultivate virtue and become a fully realized, superior man. Officials who read *Regulations* were familiar with the episodes from *Biographies* and did not need the whole story recounted. For them, the message was simple: undertake your office with assiduous, civic-minded devotion; otherwise, as a son, a man, and a minister you are a failure.

Wu Zhao's pairing of Lady Ji of Lu and the mother of Mencius in the preface was not unusual. Robin Wang has noted that the mother held "the primary authority in the shaping of the mind, character and personhood of her offspring."[44] Lisa Raphals observes that a widow often "took on a didactic 'male' role and excelled in the education of her son."[45] Josephine Chiu-Duke has remarked on the repeated appearances of both paragons of motherhood in Tang epitaphs, representing the continuity of an established vision of motherhood.[46] She has also shown that in Wu Zhao's time mothers frequently were honored for raising sons to be public-minded, incorruptible officials, whose "filial conduct and loyal service reinforced each other without contradiction."[47] And if the mother in question was at once widow-emperor, political mother, and author, there was no possibility of contradiction: loyalty and filial piety could be yoked together and marshaled toward single-minded service to state.

Composing epitaphs to eulogize eminent women, poet-courtiers contemporaneous to Wu Zhao often compared the deceased with Jing Jiang and the mother of Mencius. In 682, Yang Jiong wrote an epitaph for the wife of the duke of Pengcheng (d. 682), eulogizing her "comportment remindful of the mother of Mencius" and her "admonitory presence of a Jing Jiang."[48] Shortly after Wu Zhao's death, Su Ting, a censor during the latter days of her rule (who rose to become a chief minister under Xuanzong), composed an epitaph inscription that praised a senior princess for her "diligent study of the mother of Mencius and ritual knowledge of Jing Jiang."[49] Zhang Yue, a powerful chief minister under Xuanzong, commemorated a woman named Qin who died in A.D. 721 as a "Mother Meng for this age."[50]

By Wu Zhao's time both Jing Jiang and the mother of Mencius enjoyed long-standing repute as "intelligent, eloquent and authoritative mothers and mothers-in-law praised for the good upbringing they gave their sons and for their impeccable administration of the house."[51] Like the revered duo of wise, virtuous mothers of yore, Wu Zhao (as grand dowager) enacted the role of a dutiful widow. It was not desire for power and prominence, but a conscientious accountability to her deceased husband and affinal family that morally compelled to play a vocal and assertive role. Though as grand dowager and emperor Wu Zhao dramatically surpassed these women in terms of her overt political engagement, these widely revered female role models helped to pave the way for and justify her open, public involvement as mother of the realm.

Immediately after the reference to these two paragons of "Maternal Rectitude," the preface of *Regulations* continues:

> Recently, instructions for self-cultivation have been compiled for the heir apparent and for the princes. But as yet no model rules for providing information on loyalty and guidance of goodness have been set forth for the assembled nobles and the ranks of those appointed to officer.[52]

In this transition from motherly concern for the well-being of her flesh-and-blood children to a symbolic matriarchal preoccupation with her "children" of the larger empire, the preface shifts to the central theme of the text: the paramount importance of ministerial loyalty. As Wu Zhao set it forth in the preface, "Now in the leisure of my mornings, my mind wanders to questions of policy and government."[53] It is here the two exempla of the axle and the cut textile serve to bridge her transformation from conscientious mother of the imperial princes to ur-mother of a wider polity.

The affiliation between Wu Zhao and two celebrated instructors, Lady Ji of Lu and Mother Meng, politically savvy sage mothers who grasped the essence of statecraft and imparted that knowledge to their sons, legitimized her role in government. She situated herself as a patron of Confucian learning and an enthusiastic champion of Confucian values, a strategy that she used effectively, time and again, to deflect criticism from the court. She insinuated herself into tradition, so that to attack her was to attack these paragons of Confucian principle and virtue. And who would dare criticize Mencius' mother?

Most significantly, in the mother of Mencius and Jing Jiang, Wu Zhao drew well-known models from *Biographies* who were pertinent to the crux of her political manual: instructing ministers on the paramount importance of loyalty to ruler and to state. Like those mothers of old, she was a widow concerned with the education of her sons—for their moral education and their performance in the public realm. But as dowager, she considered the realm to be her in-laws' estate and took her ministers and subjects as political sons. Therein lies a primary difference: the two paragons from *Biographies* instructed their consanguine sons; in *Regulations*, Wu Zhao edified her political sons. Just as the flesh-and-blood sons of Jing Jiang and Mother Meng bowed humbly upon receiving profound lessons from their iconic Confucian mothers, so Wu Zhao's political sons, receiving her instructions, were to genuflect before their mother-ruler.

MARTIAL MATRIARCHS: THE MOTHERS OF ZIFA AND GENERAL KUO

The mothers of Zifa and General Kuo of Zhao, two figures from Liu Xiang's *Biographies*, both appear in the penultimate fascicle of *Regulations for Ministers*, "Good Generals" (Liang jiang 良將).[54] Unlike the abbreviated references to Jing Jiang and the mother of Mencius in the preface to *Regulations for Ministers*, the entire biographies of these two women are lifted from Liu Xiang's work and tactically deployed in Wu Zhao's political treatise.

In his fascicle-by-fascicle summary of *Regulations*, Denis Twitchett remarks that "Good Generals" "reminds us that the empress ruled a state in which the military played a vital role, in which her great commanders were as important to the sovereign as were her civil ministers, equally essential to the smooth exercise of power."[55] While the subsequent Song dynasty may have "exalted the civil and disparaged the military" (*zhongwen, qingwu* 重文輕武), the Tang often employed the most talented men both as generals in the field and ministers in the court (*chujiang ruxiang* 出將入相).[56] The all-encompassing loyalty and self-abnegation demanded in *Regulations* applied to generals as well as ministers.

During Gaozong's final years and into Wu Zhao's tenure as dowager-regent, incessant incursions from a nomadic confederation of Turks—galvanized under strong leadership of the Ilterish Qaghan (Ashina Gumalu 阿史那骨篤祿) who founded a second Turkish khanate (683–734)—plagued the western and northwestern fringes of the realm. The Khitan and Tibetans also harassed the northern borders.[57] As a woman in a position of paramount power, Wu Zhao could ill afford to be perceived as weak. While she had no desire to broadcast a bellicose image to peoples of the periphery and foreign states, she needed to project a strong, confident presence. The demeanor of her generals served as the most visible external manifestation of her martial prowess. Many of Wu Zhao's military leaders were non-Chinese generals (*fanjiang* 蕃将).[58] In "Good Generals," these military officers are repeatedly and emphatically reminded of their duty to the state.

The first of the two women to appear in *Regulations*, the mother of Chu general Zifa, numbers among the models of "maternal rectitude" in the opening chapter of *Biographies*, situated between the two aforementioned paragons, Lady Ji of Lu and the mother of Mencius. Because Zifa failed to share rewards and spoils with his rank-and-file troops, his mother refused to open the household gate to allow him entry. Zifa's mother imparted to her self-absorbed son the importance of sharing with his men "in sweetness and bitterness alike."[59]

Regulations relates, in its virtual entirety, the account of Zifa's mother from *Biographies*:

> In the distant past, when Chu general Zifa attacked Qin, his supply lines were cut off. He sent a messenger to report to the king. The messenger

then asked after Zifa's mother. His mother asked the messenger, "Are the rank-and-file soldiers in good fettle?" The messenger replied, "The soldiers have to divide a measure of pulse into sections to share." She also asked, "And the general—is he in good condition?" The man answered, "Day and night the general sups on tender meats and fine grains." Later, when Zifa destroyed Qin and returned, his mother closed the gate to the family compound and did not allow him entry. She sent someone to reprimand Zifa with the words:

"Can it be that my son hasn't heard of King Goujian of Yue's attack on Wu? When guests presented him with a cask of fine wine, the king ordered them to dump it into the river. Though the aromatic taste was completely diluted, the king's virtuous act so inspired officers and men that partaking of the river waters they felt as though they were intoxicated. In battle each fought fiercely as five.

"On another occasion, someone presented him [Goujian] with a beautifully wrapped package of parched rice cakes. The king again divided them among his men. The men split them up and ate them. While there was scarcely enough for each man to enjoy a mouthful, men and officers had the air of being surfeited. Embracing the king's graciousness, each fought with the strength of ten of the enemy.

"Now, with my son as general, rank and file men divvy up grains of pulse, while he alone enjoys tender meats and fine grains morning and night. Why? How can a leader send others to confront scarcity and death while he alone enjoys plentitude and health? Even if victory is gained, martial principle is lost. You are no longer my son. Do not enter my gate."

Zifa acknowledged his faults, then was allowed to enter. Thereafter as a general, he partook of sweetness and bitterness alike with his soldiers, in peace and peril sharing equally in their toil and travail. Embracing his grace and virtue, his men contended to be the first to brave the arrows and stones of the enemy. Subsequently, word of his meritorious reputation spread with each passing day. Those such as the mother of Zifa can truly be said to understand the way of the general.[60]

Lisa Raphals remarks that the mother of Zifa, clearly a strong-willed and principled matriarch, assumed "the admonitory role of a Sunzi-style strategist."[61]

Figure 7.3 Though her son may have held a general's rank, the mother of Zifa of Chu, a martial matriarch par excellence, deploring the conduct of her well-fed and selfish scion, did not allow him to cross the threshold of the family home.

Immediately following the account of Zifa's mother in "Good Generals" is the detailed story of the mother of General Kuo of Zhao lifted from the third chapter of *Biographies*:

Formerly, in the time of King Xiaocheng of Zhao, Qin attacked Zhao. The Zhao ruler sent Zhao Kuo to replace Lian Po as general. Zhao Kuo's mother sent a petition, stating: "Kuo is not capable of serving as general. In the beginning I served his father.[62] When Kuo's father was appointed general and people presented him food, for every ten parts he kept for himself, he would distribute one hundred parts to friends and soldiers. When the king gifted him gold and silks, he shared it all with officers and soldiers. On the day he received his orders, he ceased inquiring about family matters.

"Now, when Kuo was appointed general, he faced east.[63] His troops and officers dared not look at him. He hoarded the gold and silk the king bestowed upon him at home. When he sees good fields and nice residences he buys them. In ability and spirit, father and son are unalike. I strongly request that Your Majesty revoke his appointment." But the king answered, "My decision is already made." Kuo's mother responded, "If it is Your Majesty's final decision to send him and he fails to meet your standards, may I avoid punishment by implication." The king replied, "Yes."

Figure 7.4 Wu Zhao's pantheon featured another wise and prescient matriarch, the mother of General Kuo of Zhao, who placed the highest premium upon civic duty and loyalty to state.

Kuo then departed to replace Lian Po as general. In forty-odd days, as his mother had anticipated, the Zhao soldiers met with defeat. Kuo was killed and his troops were routed. Because of the prescience of Kuo's mother, the King of Zhao did not sentence the family to clan extermination. Those such as Kuo's mother can be said to anticipate the mechanisms of success and failure.[64]

Consistent with the remainder of the text, these two accounts categorically valorized public-minded civic duty and disparaged self-serving behavior that benefited private, familial interests.

The mother of Zifa upbraided her adult son, imparting a powerful message of public-spirited conscientiousness, setting the errant young man on the proper course to become a successful martial leader. Zhao Kuo's mother goes even further. Repudiating her son, she directly petitions and speaks with the king of Zhao. Twitchett remarks that these back-to-back biographies in "Good Generals" very likely "reflect the personal input of the empress," and that the "two anecdotes about generals and their mothers" served to "obliquely justify . . . [female] intervention in this masculine sphere."[65] Just as Jing Jiang only instructed Wenbo on matters of public administration through weaving, so these martial matriarchs justified their intervention in military matters through dutiful familial involvement: one played the time-honored role of the wise widowed mother instructing her grown son; the other's public rebuff of her son's self-centeredness saved her entire clan from execution.

Perhaps the message conveyed by the inclusion of these martial matriarchs was not so oblique to those ministers for whom *Regulations*, a text Wu Zhao elevated to canonical status, became compulsory reading. Herself a dutiful widow with grown sons, Wu Zhao possessed knowledge of military affairs, and could offer wise instructions to generals and sagely admonitions to her political sons. And like the mothers of Zifa and Zhao Kuo, Wu Zhao stridently placed public good above self-interest, something she expected (or, rather, demanded) of all her children. But Wu Zhao issued her instructions from a position of supreme power. Unlike Kuo's mother, she did not need to petition the King of Zhao: she was the one appointing civil and military officers, receiving foreign emissaries, sending campaigns against peoples raiding the margins of her realm, and ordering public works projects. While it is true that in *Regulations*, Wu Zhao's didactic authorial voice subsumes and incorporates the normative moral weight and power of the words of these long-celebrated Confucian paragons, the message was broadcast from the female ruler's raised dais. Accordingly, her words were amplified a thousandfold, reverberating empire-wide from her Divine Capital, with a stentorian voice that carried to the harbors of Panyu in the free-wheeling south, the frontier garrisons of the northeast, and the bustling oases in the far west.

BEYOND MOTHERHOOD

Both the abbreviated references to Lady Ji of Lu and the mother of Mencius in the preface of *Regulations* and the full accounts in "Good Generals" reflect Wu Zhao's effort to create a wider paradigm of motherhood, one that reached the entire court and country. As empress and grand dowager, she had long styled herself mother of the empire. In an edict promulgated shortly after Gaozong's death, at roughly the same juncture *Regulations* was crafted, she announced, "I gaze as a mother over the realm" (zhen mu lin Chixian 朕母臨赤縣).[66]

As Gaozong's coruler, Wu Zhao had been recognized since 660 as one of the Two Sages.[67] In 688, established as a wise instructress, not so much by the rhetoric in *Regulations* as by her three decades' experience handling matters of court, the sage became a sage mother. When a cryptic augural stone was found in the Luo River bearing the inscription, "When the Sage Mother is close to the people, the imperial cause will eternally prosper," she assumed the title "Sage Mother, Divine Sovereign."[68] Wu Zhao maintained the moral authority of the mother of Mencius and Jing Jiang, but she had quit the weaving chamber and now presided over court and country. As both ruler and mother she became the recipient of convergent filial piety and loyalty. Wu Zhao's assumption of the title Sage Mother marked the political realization of a broader motherhood, one extending to all the subjects of her empire, bringing to fruition the vision of maternity articulated in *Regulations* several years earlier.

One of the brilliant aspects of *Regulations*—the core of Wu Zhao's political philosophy—was the elevation of loyalty to the pinnacle of the hierarchy of Confucian virtues, supplanting filial piety. Throughout *Regulations*, loyalty (*zhong* 忠) and filial piety (*xiao* 孝), the two paramount Confucian virtues, are conjoined. Twitchett observes that the text stresses "the amalgamation of the concept of 'loyalty' toward ruler with 'filial obedience' within the family." But these two attributes are not equal: the primacy of loyalty is made manifest and filial devotion is relegated to a "lesser loyalty."[69] Such classification of degree is spelled out explicitly in the opening fascicle:

> The minister serving his ruler is like a son serving his father. The deportment and reverence are the same. But though father and son are extremely close, they are not of one body like ruler and minister. There have been fathers without sons; there have been families without fathers. Yet there has never been a ruler without ministers, or a country without a ruler.[70]

The bond between ruler and minister is stronger and more indispensable than that between father and son. Summarizing, Lü Huayu observes that loyalty, associated in *Regulations* with public interest and the common weal, is presented in the text as a greater virtue than filial piety.[71] Father and son are separate beings. The ruler and ministers are a single entity, interdependent, inseparable parts of the body politic. In effect, the role of ruler both incorporates and supersedes the role of parent.

In the second fascicle, "Absolute Loyalty" (Zhi zhong 至忠), state and ruler are once again placed above family and parents. The traditional family was a corporate body bound by patriarchal structures—entrenched and hierarchical ties of blood kinship that severely restricted roles of women. By elevating loyalty over filial piety in *Regulations*, Wu Zhao functionally allowed her authority to operate outside, or even above, the patriarchal structures of Confucian relationships. As an object of universal loyalty that transcended kinship bonds, as the governing mind-heart of a large single organism, she effectively circumvented the strictures of traditional social relationships. Family, albeit important, was secondary. A prospective impediment to absolute loyalty, family was relegated to the lesser realm of the private and personal, hence the diminished status of filial piety. Loyalty to the state was a necessary precondition for the cultivation of filial piety. Only once the foundation of state was stable might a family be united by humane bonds of filial piety. Family, the text forcefully asserts, is born of the state:

> In antiquity loyal officials served their ruler first and then their parents; they placed the nation first and the household second. Why? The ruler is the root of the parents. Without the ruler, the parents would not exist. The nation is the foundation of the household. Without the nation, the family could not be established. Thus, it is from the ruler that the parents receive their existence. It is due to the state that the family is established. Therefore, the ruler is first and the parents second. The state is first and the household second.[72]

With no radical departure from traditional texts, Wu Zhao philosophically undercut any undue emphasis upon the female gender. At the apex, as "the ruler," Wu Zhao was not a woman at all, but the nexus of the shared body of the nation, toward which absolute loyalty must be granted.

CONCLUSION

With a clever turn of logic, Wu Zhao lifted a quartet of paragons—the mother of Mencius, Lady Ji of Lu, and the mothers of Zifa and Zhao Kuo—from their usual stations in *Biographies of Women*, the Confucian woman's guide to proper behavior, and transplanted them in *Regulations for Ministers*. Each of these women, carefully chosen by Wu Zhao and the scholars of the Northern Gate, used the moral suasion of her position within the inner, domestic sphere to intervene in the outer, political domain of men.

Their message of public-mindedness justified their intrusion: each of these women guided less capable sons to dedicate themselves to wholehearted loyal service to state while eschewing private, familial ambitions. Relocated in *Regulations*, the carefully culled references to these four women were designed to represent Wu Zhao as a matriarch wise in the ways of governance—a sage mother, as the title she assumed in 688 announced. With rhetorical virtuosity, the conduct of these four women was not upheld for women to direct them in proper motherly deportment but set forth to dictate behavioral expectations to ministers, to instruct them in absolute loyalty to ruler and state. In *Regulations*, a minister was, by definition, one who "exhausts his energy in anxiety for the country and concern for the people."[73] As imperial commands of the realm's mother-ruler, these instructions carried the weight and force of canonical edicts. Wu Zhao was not only owed the unswerving filial devotion due a parent, but also the absolute loyalty that a subject paid to a ruler.

With her deft rhetorical engineering of the "ascendancy" of loyalty over filial piety in *Regulations*, she situated herself not within the narrow consanguine confines of family, but as a sage mother, a mother of all mothers, whose brood extended beyond her immediate imperial offspring to the court and far beyond palace walls to her myriad subjects, Han and non-Han, of the larger empire.[74] These ideal Confucian mothers, in essence, became vehicles that helped move Wu Zhao beyond motherhood, beyond gender: in *Regulations*, she becomes a forceful authorial voice of power issuing instructions to her myriad officials and subjects.

PART III

Drawing on the Numinous Energies of Female Daoist Divinities

DEPENDING ON THE IDEOLOGICAL CLIMATE and political vicissitudes, Wu Zhao's patronage of Confucianism, Daoism, and Buddhism waxed and waned at different junctures of her corule with Gaozong, her regency, and her reign as emperor of the Zhou. From the outset, however, Wu Zhao had a conflicted relationship with the Daoist establishment. On the one hand, Daoism was the ideology most amenable to female power, glorifying the latent force of the female water element, illuminating the potency of the mother, and prescribing that the Daoist sovereign cleave to "the role of the female."[1] On the other hand, the ruling Li clan claimed Laozi (Li Er 李耳) as a blood ancestor, thus insinuating the figure of the Daoist sage into the apparatus of Tang legitimation. In this respect, Daoism impeded her from establishing her own dynasty.

Many passages in the *Daodejing*, the canonical Daoist text attributed to Laozi, testify to the awesome female power contained in the *dao*. One cryptic prescription for Daoist governance announces:

The spirit of the valley never dies.
This is called the mysterious female.
The gateway of the mysterious female is called the root of heaven
    and earth.
Dimly visible, it seems as if it were never there, yet use will never
    drain it.[2]

Another section speaks of a nameless, silent, amorphous, primordial entity that might be styled the *dao*, but might also be called "mother of the world" (tianxia mu 天下母).[3] And again, we are told, "the female always overcomes the male with stillness."[4] Throughout the text, the passive, the unseen, the submissive, the nebulous, the hidden, and the low-lying (like the female-identified element water) invariably overcome that which is in motion, visible, strong, and active. That female overcomes male is a cosmic and natural principle. For all of these reasons, Kristofer Schipper contends that "the body of the Tao is a woman's body."[5] Edward Schafer terms this "aqueous" and "inchoate" female entity the "Lao-tzu Goddess," remarking that she might be considered "the ancestress of all of the water goddesses of China."[6]

Wu Zhao was keenly attuned to this advantageous Daoist prescription for her exercise of power. As Gaozong's empress, she had her only daughter, the Taiping Princess, ordained as a Daoist priestess.[7] As grand dowager, one of her reign era names projected the image of the Daoist ideal of "effortless action" (wuwei 無為). Inaugurated in 685, her Chuigong (With Hanging Robes and Folded Hands) era referenced the "Successes of Wu" (Wucheng 武成) chapter in the Book of History, in which King Wu (of her namesake Zhou dynasty) simply "let his robes fall and folded his hands, and the empire was perfectly ruled" (chuigong er tianxia zhi 垂拱而天下治).[8]

In part II, it was mentioned that in "Same Organism," the opening fascicle of Wu Zhao's treatise, Regulations for Ministers (promulgated the year Chuigong was inaugurated), Wu Zhao described ruler and ministers as interdependent parts of the body politic—she, the still mind-heart (xin 心); they, the active body (ti 體). Drawing on classical authority to delineate her vision of the ruler-minister dynamic, the text continues:

> The Yellow Emperor had four officials who investigated the Four Quarters. Therefore Shizi 尸子 records: "The Yellow Emperor had four eyes."[9] Thus we know the position of the emperor is respected and exalted, like the nine levels of heaven, mysterious in the extreme. The ruler can not solely attend to the affairs of the ten thousand areas, therefore she installed the various ministers to act as her claws and teeth, her ears and eyes.[10]

Ministers served as her extended senses, instruments for gathering intelligence. Wu Zhao remained mysterious, unseen, and withdrawn, a vessel into which secrets and intelligence might be poured. As mind-heart of a shared body politic, she rhetorically adopted a traditional female posture of passivity and motionlessness. Her stillness and occupation of the interior locale—in short, her very femininity—imbued Wu Zhao with power. The mysterious *dao* resides in characteristics that are essentially female: in all that is weak, soft, yielding, motionless, and passive.

In addition to this textual acknowledgment of the power vested in the feminine realm, Daoism is rife with female deities. Timothy Barrett has noted that Tang Daoism, which assigned both importance and power to women, had incorporated an array of female divinities, including the Queen Mother of the West, the mother of Qi, the Mysterious Woman (Xuannü 玄女), and the mother of Laozi.[11] Edward Schafer has observed that through elegant similes and "veiled transformation," skilled fourth- and fifth-century poets began to summon "glimpses of the celestial world," leading their readers to a hallucinatory terrain populated by Daoist divinities.[12] Such ethereal landscapes and their godlike denizens underwent further sophistication in Tang verse. As Schafer puts it,

> In T'ang times, when the monarchs claimed descent from the revered author of the *Laozi*, already elevated to the status of a cosmic divinity, when princesses of the blood—like high-born abbesses in medieval Europe—took holy orders, when highly competent poets did not disdain to renew themselves through periodic retreats in hermitages attached to great Taoist friaries, this noble heritage was even more refined and elaborated.[13]

To win over the female sovereign, poet-officials in Wu Zhao's court evoked astral wonderlands populated by a colorful array of immortals.

Though Daoism, with both its powerful intrinsic female element and its rich tradition of female deities, offered Wu Zhao a potent ideological tool to express her authority, the Daoist establishment's close identification with the Tang dynastic house severely hampered her utilization of the faith. In order to show other powerful aristocratic families that they were not merely martial upstarts of mixed Han Chinese and central Asian blood, the Li imperial family had claimed descent from the Daoist sage and founder Laozi.[14] This claim and their patronage of the Daoist establishment bolstered Li prestige and anchored the newly risen Li family in Chinese tradition.[15] As empress and grand dowager, Wu Zhao's credibility as a ruler who protected and honored the Daoist establishment was predicated upon her connection to her Li in-laws. As she approached the inauguration of her own Zhou dynasty, however, this credibility rapidly deteriorated, particularly as she looked to the rival Buddhist faith for validation. Charles Benn notes that Wu Zhao "fully supported the T'ang Taoist ideology" as empress, but as her political power grew, her attitude toward the Daoist church grew progressively more tepid; by the time she founded the Zhou in 690, while "she was not hostile to Taoism, she did not foster or patronize it much either."[16] Naturally, Wu Zhao's shifting needs influenced the development of the cults of Daoist goddesses within her pantheon.

Part III examines the emergence among Wu Zhao's political ancestors of two powerful female Daoist divinities, the Queen Mother of the West and the mother of Laozi. Chapters 8 and 9 explore the respective roles that these female deities played in amplifying Wu Zhao's political authority. Chapter 10 looks at the rationale behind Wu Zhao's calculated decision not to enshrine a powerful Daoist transcendent, Wei Huacun.

EIGHT

The Queen Mother of the West and Wu Zhao

FROM PRIMITIVE SPIRIT TO DAOIST MONARCH

From an array of different ancient directional goddesses who appear on Shang oracle bone inscriptions, the Queen Mother of the West comes into clear resolution in the *Zhuangzi* (a Warring States–era text) as a woman who had attained the *dao*.[1] As Elfriede Knauer frames it, "after a long break she becomes a powerful shaman and teacher of privileged human beings and a mediatrix between the heavenly and earthly realms."[2] For Xunzi (312–230 B.C.), she was a divine teacher who instructed legendary flood-queller and Xia founder, Yu the Great.[3] In the *Classic of Mountains and Seas* (a text likely dating to the first century B.C.), a vision of a primitive and potent Queen Mother is evoked:

> A deity who presides over a mountain wilderness in the west and lives among wild beasts. In these accounts she is described as a human with unkempt hair, a panther's tail, and tiger's fangs, and she has a retinue of feline beasts and birds that bring her messages and food . . . Her mountain realm is designated as being in the west, and it is said to be the sacred range of Kunlun.[4]

Anne Birrell remarks that this potent goddess, ruling over an earthly domain, possessed "divine control over all living things" and the capacity to visit "awesome catastrophes on the world."[5]

From this primitive incarnation as a "ruthless goddess of prey,"[6] the Queen Mother evolved during the Han, becoming a beautiful ageless divinity, an immortal monarch celebrated in both popular and elite culture, replete with headdress, staff, and scepter. She emerged as "the first personified female deity to predominate as the focus of popular religious devotion."[7]

In Liu An's *Huainanzi*, she presented an elixir of immortality to Yi the Archer (Hou Yi 后羿), though it subsequently was stolen by moon goddess Chang E.[8] This late Western Han text also contains a passage in which the Queen Mother snapped her headdress, precipitating a string of catastrophes—an episode, Michael Loewe suggests, demonstrating that she wielded some control over the cosmic order and the movement of the constellations.[9] Liu Xiang's *Biographies of Immortals* (Liexian zhuan 列仙傳) viewed the Queen Mother as "creator of Heaven and Earth, molder of all things that are created, mistress acknowledged by all those who ascend to Heaven or descend to Earth."[10] To alleviate a drought during the waning years of the Western Han, in 3 B.C., adherents of the Queen Mother carried sheaves of millet to honor her, indicating that she had already emerged as a cultic divinity, perhaps a rain goddess or agricultural deity.[11] The cult endured: Episodes in the Jin and Sui official histories report that as far west as Kokonor (near Qinghai Lake), the faithful worshipped at shrines dedicated to the Queen Mother, who, in the guise of a rain goddess, delivered the afflicted from drought.[12]

Colorful lore grew around her. According to esoteric master Guo Xian's *Record of Penetrating Mysteries* (Dongming ji 洞冥記, c. first century A.D.), the Queen Mother made a cameo appearance two centuries earlier during Han Wudi's reign, appearing astride a simurgh (*luan* 鸞), turning darkness to daylight as she traversed the heavens singing a lilting paean to spring.[13] The Queen Mother's mountain lair in the Kunlun Mountains had evolved into a western paradise.[14] Western Han teller of supernatural tales Dongfang Shuo (c. 160–93 B.C.) rode one of her wind-striding horses.[15] The *Biography of King Mu* (Mu tianzi zhuan 穆天子傳) describes King Mu of Zhou (c. tenth century B.C.) and the Queen Mother banqueting and exchanging gifts atop Mount Yan.[16] There are also stories of the Queen Mother sharing intimacy, peaches, and the secrets of immortality with Han Wudi.[17] Eight hundred years later, these divine/mortal trysts remained alive in the Tang literary imagination. Association with a goddess conferred tremendous power upon a mortal ruler. As Near Eastern historian Henri Frankfort frames it, "only those kings were deified who had been commanded by a goddess to share her couch."[18]

A rich iconographic tradition developed around the Queen Mother of the West.[19] Marshaling evidence from a series of Han tombs beginning in the first century B.C., Wu Hung convincingly argues that the Queen Mother supplanted Nüwa as "the embodiment of *yin* force."[20] In southern China, beginning during the Northern and Southern Dynasties era, the Queen Mother, coupled with male counterpart King Father of the East, appeared on many elaborate decorative mirrors.[21]

Suzanne Cahill has observed that by the Tang there was a well-established literary tradition "commemorating visits to cultic centers of archaic goddesses." Tang poetry, she notes, abounds with scenarios containing "allusions to legends concerning the goddess [the Queen Mother of the West] and mortal Chinese rulers, an epiphany of the goddess, and some communication between the divine and human realms." Tang poets frequently riffed on the rapturous delight of hierogamous dalliances between King Mu or Han Wudi and the Queen Mother of the West. Studded with references to earlier encounters between mortals and the timeless goddess, one of Li Shangyin's poems rhapsodically describes a visit to the shrine of the Queen Mother on Mount Hua.[22] Cahill has shown that during the Tang several marchmounts had shrines or temples dedicated to the Queen Mother.[23] Tang poets like Chu Guangxi (c. 707–760), Liu Fu (c. early ninth century), Liu Yuxi (772–842), Liu Cang (fl. mid-ninth century), and Wu Rong (fl. late ninth century) all rapturously described the Queen Mother's immortal grace.[24] Though these poets herald from the mid- to the late Tang, dating from after Wu Zhao's demise and death, their verses collectively describe the cult of a deity still worshipped, reflecting her continuing cultural resonance.

In her extensive work on the goddess, Cahill has illustrated that, by the Tang, the Queen Mother of the West had developed into the highest female divinity in the Daoist pantheon,[25] a powerful patron deity of women who possessed "control over immortality and power to mediate between the divine and human realm."[26]

Through ceremony and symbol, in decorative silk and polished jade, Wu Zhao linked herself to the Queen Mother of the West. Though these connections were not always explicit, they were presented through culturally legible rites and gestures understood by court and country alike.

SHARED CEREMONIES AND SYMBOLS:
CONNECTED BY JADE, PHOENIXES, AND SILK

In the *Classic of Mountains and Seas*, it is recorded that the Queen Mother of the West lived on Jade Mountain.[27] As a medium, jade symbolizes incorruptibility and eternal life.[28] A substance of beauty and power, jade (*yu* 玉) shares a radical with "king" (*wang* 王). When King Mu of Zhou and the Queen Mother exchanged gifts atop Mount Yan, he offered her a white jade token.[29] There is another story dating from the Han of a scholar-recluse who rescued a messenger of the Queen Mother of the West, a golden sparrow. In return, assuming human guise and making known his position in the Queen Mother's service, a yellow-liveried man presented his rescuer four white jade rings and promised that his savior's offspring would rise to become eminent officials.[30] In 676, Cui Shen, the prefect of Chuzhou, presented thirteen treasures of state at the court of the Celestial Emperor and Celestial Empress—as Gaozong and Wu Zhao were known at the time. The fourth treasure consisted of two jade rings belonging to the Queen Mother of the West.[31] Thus, Wu Zhao came to possess this jade token of the Queen Mother, at once an emblem of the divinity's magical power and a tally of political authority.

Through this precious medium of white jade, one can find further connections between the earthly ruler and the celestial sovereign. The *Miscellaneous Records of the Taiping Era* relates a story in which the Queen Mother of the West presented a white jade—seemingly her preferred ceremonial medium—*guan* 琯 ritual tube to Emperor Shun. In the Han, the white jade *guan* was found under Shun's shrine. Ritual specialists learned how the ancients used the ceremonial *guan* as an instrument to harmonize men and spirits. The technique was called "regulation of the phoenix" (*fenghuang yi* 鳳凰儀).[32] *Yi* can mean "to regulate" or "regulator," a kind of ritual instrument (*yi qi* 儀器).[33] When Gaozong offered to abdicate to Wu Zhao in 676, a phoenix, a potent auspicious omen of female imperial power, was sighted in Chenzhou, prompting the inauguration of Phoenix Regulator,[34] a reign era whose name tacitly announced Wu Zhao's instrumental role in securing harmony between the celestial and terrestrial realms.

There are further indications that the phoenix was an important symbol of power for both the Queen Mother of the West and Wu Zhao. Wu Hong has remarked that in the Wu Liang shrine, the Queen Mother wore a "crown of five phoenixes" (*wu feng guan* 五鳳冠).[35] According to one source, likely from the sixth century, atop Kunlun—the mountain citadel of the Queen Mother—there was a massive bronze pillar that reached the heavens. Atop the pillar was an immense bird, facing southward. This regal avian's outstretched wingspan sheltered the Queen Mother to the west and the King Father to the east.[36] Though it is not clear whether this monumental creature was a phoenix, it seems likely that this image inspired Wu Zhao to crown both of her Bright Hall complexes with massive phoenixes, their wings outspread.[37] Wu Zhao crowned her first Bright Hall complex, completed in 688, with a ten-foot-tall gilded iron phoenix poised for flight.[38] Wu Zhao named her second Bright Hall, completed in 696, Penetrating Heaven Palace (Tongtiangong 通天宮), and topped it with a finial phoenix taking flight, twice as large as the first.[39] The name Penetrating Heaven provides another curious link between Wu Zhao and the Queen Mother of the West. In 110 B.C., when Han Wudi, the Queen Mother's mortal lover, performed the *feng* and *shan* rites on Mount Tai, he constructed a Penetrating Heaven Terrace (Tongtiantai 通天台) to commune with immortals.[40] The name of her ritual complex betokened a liminal site at the confluence of the mortal realm and the world of spirits.

A shared involvement in sericulture and weaving provides further suggestion of linkage between the earthly ruler of the late seventh century and the Daoist goddess. In his *Annals of Revelations of Diverse States* (Bieguo dongming ji 別國洞冥記), Dongfang Shuo records the Queen Mother of the West picking mulberry leaves. During the ceremonial gathering of mulberry leaves in the Eastern Han, imperial ladies wore a *sheng* 勝 (lit.: victory), the signature crown of the Queen Mother.[41] Appearing as "two spools joined by a horizontal rod," to each "attached a twirl of thread," the "victory" headdress of the Queen Mother of the West may have represented a weaving implement, the brake pedal of the loom.[42] A Tang mirror housed in the Kyoto Museum features just such an image, accompanied by the inscription "golden victory headdress" (*jin sheng* 金勝).[43]

As empress, Wu Zhao performed the First Sericulturist rites to honor the silk goddess on four occasions between 656 and 675, leading palace women and wives of high-ranking officials to pick mulberry leaves in a vernal rite.[44] In the sericulture rite, before a large assembled audience, the empress knelt humbly in front of an empty ritual seat representing the goddess. In the collective imagination, that empty place might be filled by the Queen Mother of the West, with her loom-inspired headdress, rather than Leizu. Wu Zhao's public ritual homage made manifest her connection to these female divinities. To all those present, the empress's repeated public performance of the sericulture rites were ceremonial acts that evoked the aura of these two divinities, and identified the female sovereign with them.

Wu Zhao shared a series of culturally resonant symbols and rituals with the Queen Mother of the West. The Chuzhou prefect's presentation of the rings of white jade illustrates that political supporters of Wu Zhao sought emblematic connections between their Celestial Empress and the Queen Mother of the West. The phoenix developed into an important symbol of harmonious order and regulatory authority. Wu Zhao's performance of the First Sericulturist rites honored the Queen Mother of the West and silk goddess Leizu and in turn helped link the empress to both divinities. Notably, most of these shared symbols appear during Wu Zhao's time as Gaozong's empress, a time when she, in the words of Eugene Wang, "eagerly maintained the imperial clan's interest in Daoism."[45]

CONNECTED BY CELESTIAL LIGHT: THE QUEEN MOTHER IN THE POLITICAL RHETORIC OF WU ZHAO

Ever willing to draw upon efficacious symbols of majesty, Wu Zhao incorporated both celestial orbs, male sun and female moon, into her repertoire. Like the Daoist goddess, the female sovereign appropriated celestial symbols from hoary myth: the sunbird (*yang niao* 陽鳥, the mythological three-legged solar crow, with origins dating back to the Eastern Yi culture in the third millennium B.C.)[46] and the pair of lunar denizens, the hare and the toad.

Michael Loewe has remarked that during the Han dynasty, the crescent moon with toad and hare and the solar disk encircling a sunbird or crow became recurring symbols associated with the Queen Mother of the West.[47] In Sima Xiangru's (179–127 B.C.) "Rhapsody of a Great Man," written for Han Wudi, the Queen Mother of the West is described as possessing a three-legged crow, which served her as a messenger.[48] In the Eastern Han and into the Northern and Southern Dynasties, the hare, toad, and sunbird joined the nine-tailed fox in the Queen Mother of the West's impressive train of courtiers, her flamboyant immortal bestiary.[49]

The solar crow, the Queen Mother's avian messenger, also played a prominent role in Wu Zhao's court. *Miscellaneous Records of the Taiping Era* includes the following story:

> In the era of the Celestial Empress, a three-legged bird was presented as tribute. Someone in the court said, "One of the legs is fake." The Celestial Empress laughed, and ordered the scribe to record it in the annals, remarking, "What's the use of examining whether it's real or fake?" The *Tang History* recorded, in the first year of Tianshou [690] somebody presented a three-legged bird. The Celestial Empress took it to be an auspicious omen of the House of Zhou. Ruizong remarked, "The front leg is fake." The Celestial Empress was displeased. Shortly, one leg fell off.[50]

Aware of the great political currency invested in auspicious omens, men vied to present Wu Zhao with sunbirds and other such tokens that, broadcast properly, announced heaven's endorsement of her rule. Such presentations, of course, also afforded these men a path of rapid career advancement.

There is further evidence that Wu Zhao consciously augmented her political luster with images of celestial illumination: Three of the twelve new characters created for Wu Zhao in 689 upon the inauguration of the Origin of Records reign era—"sun" ⊘, "moon" 囝, and her invented name Zhao 曌—reflect a conscious effort on Wu Zhao's part to, like the Queen Mother of the West, affiliate herself with both celestial bodies.[51]

In 697, according to Shi Anchang's investigation of funerary epitaphs and other inscriptions, the character for moon changed from 囝 to 囲.[52] In appearance, the character *chu* 出 resembles a crouching animal, such as the moon's traditional inhabitants, the hare or the toad. This creature parallels the solar crow, found in the new character for sun.[53] The toad is pressed flat, legs splayed to the sides. In this character can be discerned an effort by Wu Zhao to draw on a deeply ingrained mythological tradition, to associate herself with the Queen Mother or, perhaps, Chang E, the goddess of the moon, who oversaw the efforts of the lunar toad and jade hare to brew the elixir of immortality.

The sunbird and the new characters for "sun" and "moon" were part of Wu Zhao's deliberate composition of a repertoire of common symbols she shared with the Queen Mother of the West. These characters became unique signets of Wu Zhao's imperial sovereignty, symbols indelibly imprinting her image on language. They appeared in many guises—as part of the state calendar, as representations of celestial bodies, and as signs to remind ministers of her authority. The solar crow and the lunar denizens were familiar motifs, and those in Wu Zhao's court viewing edicts bearing the new characters at once understood the consonance between their female ruler and the Queen Mother.

IN THE IMAGE OF THE QUEEN MOTHER:
AGELESS, TIMELESS, BEAUTIFUL

In her waning years, Wu Zhao's thoughts turned to the promises of longevity and immortality offered by Daoist elixirs. She looked once more to the Queen Mother of the West. In the Tang imagination, the Queen Mother was no longer a primitive beast-woman presiding over a jagged border peak but a vital goddess who eternally projected youth and beauty. Shortly after the fall of the Tang, Daoist hagiographer Du Guangting provided a physical description of the Queen Mother of the West: "Her age might have been around twenty. Her celestial appearance eclipsed and put in the shade all others. Her numinous complexion was unique to the world."[54]

When Wu Zhao, in her mid-sixties, became emperor, she took great pains to project immutability. Like any emperor, Wu Zhao was deeply preoccupied with her mortality and strove to broadcast an image of vitality, timelessness, and agelessness. A wizened, toothless crone does not project the image of a potent, charismatic leader. In a concerted effort to conceal her mortal blemishes, her wrinkles and creases, Wu Zhao, like many Tang women, expertly applied powders, rouges, creams, ointments, mascara, and oils to disguise the ravages of time.[55] Her secular power was buttressed by the sense that the sovereign was, like the Queen Mother, otherworldly, not beholden to the same limits of space and time as other mortals. She linked her physical self to the state ritual calendar, tying the inauguration of the Protracted Longevity era in 692 to her personal rejuvenation:

Although the grand dowager had passed through many springs and autumns, she excelled at applying cosmetics and adornments to herself, so that even her own attendants did not feel her decrepit. On the bing-xu day of the ninth month she issued an imperial edict announcing that her lost teeth had regrown. On *geng-zi* [23 October 692], she went to the Zetian Gate, declared a general amnesty, and changed the reign era to Protracted Longevity. The sacrifice to the earth god was changed to the ninth month.[56]

The sacrifice to the earth god, which had corresponded with breaking the ground and planting in the early spring, was now shifted to the final month of autumn, synchronizing larger terrestrial and the celestial patterns with her dental regeneration, her springtime in her autumn years.

In 700, Wu Zhao's inauguration of the Distant Vision era celebrated the good health and longevity of the seventy-six-year-old female emperor:

> The grand dowager commissioned Hongzhou monk Hu Chao to concoct a longevity potion. After three years it was completed, wasting millions of cash in the process. When the grand dowager imbibed it, the process of aging seemed to reverse itself. On *gui-chou* [27 May 700], she declared an empire-wide amnesty and changed the reign name to Distant Vision.[57]

"Distant vision" comes from Daoist savant Laozi: "When a ruler possesses the mother of the state, he can then endure. This is the way of distant vision and longevity, of deep roots and firm stems, by which one lives to see many days."[58] "Distant vision" means never growing old, maintaining clear wit and perspicacity. Wu Zhao's rejuvenation occasioned the change of a reign era and a five-day congratulatory feast, at which her subjects raised many a cup to toast her long life and good health.[59]

CREATING A DAOIST PARADISE ON EARTH: FEATURING WU ZHAO AS THE QUEEN MOTHER OF THE WEST AND ZHANG CHANGZONG AS PRINCE JIN

In the last seven or eight years of Wu Zhao's life, she turned—as so many Chinese rulers did in senescence—toward Daoism in an aggressive quest for immortality.[60] In *Shaping the Lotus Sutra*, Eugene Wang observes that Wu Zhao's growing obsession with prolonging her life played a part in her growing interest in Daoism in the post-695 period.[61]

Under Wu Zhao, the Queen Mother of the West became closely identified with Mount Song, the Central Peak of the Five Marchmounts, located close to the female ruler's political center, Luoyang. Mount Song's emergence as a ritual center was made manifest as early as the first lunar month of 683, when, on an outing to a newly completed mountain palace on the slopes of the Central Marchmount, Wu Zhao and ailing Gaozong sent emissaries to offer sacrifices at the nearby shrine devoted to the Queen Mother of the West.[62] For the "Two Sages," such a sacrifice enhanced the sense that their summer palace in the crags of Mount Song was a tribute to and localized manifestation of the legendary supernal mountain aerie of the Queen Mother of the West. As grand dowager, Wu Zhao designated Mount Song the Divine Peak.[63]

A verse of legendary Tang poet Li Bo (701–762) further illustrates that in the imagined topography of the Tang, Mount Song was transformed into a Daoist fantasia. To commemorate the ordination of Wu Zhao's granddaughter, Princess Jade Verity (Yuzhen gongzhu 玉真公主, 692–762), as a Daoist priestess, he envisioned that:

> Whenever she enters the Lesser Room,
> The Queen Mother will certainly be there to meet her.[64]

Both in Wu Zhao's worship and Li Bo's poem, the Queen Mother dwelt not on the snow-capped peaks of Kunlun but on nearby Mount Song, making her a local and accessible deity.

A second mountain in the region was also associated with the Queen Mother of the West. Situated even closer to Luoyang, Mount Goushi was a short, flat-topped hill thirty kilometers west of the imposing Mount Song. In Du Guangting's biography of the Queen Mother, he records that "the Queen Mother was born at the Yi River [near Luoyang] in the Divine Continent (Shenzhou 神洲) [China]. Her surname was Gou 緱,"[65] the same as that of Mount Goushi.

Du Guangting's work also contains a biography of the Immortal Maiden of the Gou clan, who shared a surname with the Queen Mother and heralded from Southern Marchmount, Hengshan. In her nineties, this maiden was cultivating the *dao* in dangerous wilderness solitude at the altar of famous Daoist Wei Huacun, who sent her a long-tailed, talking green bird with a red-capped head, which resembled a mourning dove. This messenger bird informed the Immortal Maiden of Gou that "The surname of the Queen Mother of the West was Gou. . . . In Henan there is a Mount Goushi.

That was where she cultivated the *dao*."[66] In all likelihood, this connection between the Daoist goddess and Mount Gou prompted Han Wudi, so intimately connected in myth and legend with the Queen Mother, to stop at Mount Gou in 110 B.C.[67]

In the seventh month of 675, when Wu Zhao's eldest son, Crown Prince Li Hong, was buried in the vicinity of Mount Goushi, Goushi County was established.[68] By the Tang, these sources attest, the Queen Mother was identified with more readily accessible local sites like Mount Goushi and Mount Song, in addition to faraway Kunlun.

Perhaps the greatest influence the Queen Mother of the West exerted on Wu Zhao is evidenced in the emergent cult of Prince Jin (Wangzi Jin or Wangzi Qiao, c. sixth century B.C.), the son of Eastern Zhou ruler King Ling (r. 571–545 B.C.), during the later stages of Wu Zhao's tenure as emperor.[69] In Daoist lore, Prince Jin had risen from a recluse to an "ageless demigod."[70] Disgusted with his father's maladministration—to protect the royal palaces in Luoyang, King Ling planned to dam the rivers, diverting the floodwaters eastward to submerge the dwellings of the common people—Prince Jin remonstrated, and was banished. In the end, however, King Ling's plans were not implemented, and the cast-off prince became a folk hero. This high-minded noble became an ascetic, playing a flute as he roamed the Yi and Luo river valleys in exile. Lord Fuqiu, a wandering immortal, taught Prince Jin the art of crane riding, a skill usually reserved for spirits and divinities. Finally, from the bald crown of Mount Goushi, Prince Jin ascended to become an immortal, taking leave of his contrite father, the Zhou court, and adoring throngs on the seventh day of the seventh lunar month, spiraling skyward on a red-capped crane to join the company of Daoist gods above. On the site where Prince Jin departed, King Ling erected an Ascended Immortal Observatory (Shengxian guan 升仙觀). Shrines were erected to Prince Jin both on Mount Song and on Mount Goushi.[71] Two of the peaks on the Greater Room of Mount Song are called Zijin, after Prince Jin, and Fuqiu, after his Daoist immortal instructor.[72] Over time, a regional cult of Prince Jin developed; he emerged as a local tutelary divinity.[73]

Once Wu Zhao became emperor, Mount Song loomed even larger. In early 696, she performed the sacrosanct *feng* and *shan* rites on the Divine Peak.[74] Shortly thereafter, on the equinox, she honored the deity of Mount Song as Emperor of the Center of Heaven and elevated Prince Jin to become Ascended Immortal Prince (Shengxian taizi 升仙太子). On her return trip to the Divine Capital, she stopped by Mount Goushi and, seeing the shrine devoted to Prince Jin in a state of disrepair, ordered it restored and named Temple of the Ascended Immortal Prince.[75]

En route to Mount Song in the first month of 699, Wu Zhao once again sojourned at the temple on Mount Goushi.[76] Beside the temple she had established several years earlier, she ordered the erection of a commemorative stele dedicated to Prince Jin. The elegant strokes of the stele's title characters are a series of beautiful, ornate birds.[77] Wu Zhao composed a preface to the stele that celebrates the efficacy of the *dao* and the auspicious geomancy of Mount Goushi. The preface includes a history of Prince Jin and proofs that heaven endorses her Zhou dynasty.[78]

It is beyond the scope of this book to exhaustively analyze the implications of this rich and important work upon Daoism, but several sections warrant particular attention. Wu Zhao begins her benediction upon the blessed ground of Mount Goushi by imagining a host of immortals setting out from the west gate of Luoyang and paying homage to the Queen Mother of the West. There are other intimations of the Queen Mother: in the section on Wu Zhao's decision to restore the Daoist immortal's temple, she mentions that the year before she composed the inscription, she sent an emissary to Mount Goushi to offer a sacrifice to Prince Jin. On the very day the rite was performed, the strains of an immortal's flute, like the mellifluous call of a phoenix, could be heard from the distant heavens; an immortal astride a red-capped crane descended from on high, no doubt Prince Jin offering his thanks.[79]

To understand Wu Zhao's sudden interest in the cult of this lesser Daoist immortal and its connection to her worship of the Queen Mother of the West, it is important to look at the emergence of two favorites in her court, Zhang Yizhi and Zhang Changzong. According to the Sui manual of the sexual arts, the *Prescriptions from the Heart of Medicine* (Yixinfang 醫心方)—citing an earlier text, the *Secret Instructions of the Jade Chamber* (Yufang bijue 玉房秘訣)—the Queen Mother of the West secured her everlasting youth through nurturing her *yin* essence by copulating with young boys.[80] Septuagenarian Wu Zhao, influenced by the Daoist notion that young male *yang* essence could rejuvenate old female *yin* essence, summoned Zhang Changzong and Zhang Yizhi into her inner quarters in 697. These dashing brothers, skilled in music and well-versed in poetry, accoutered in colorful silks and wearing vermilion rouge, rapidly emerged as Wu Zhao's male favorites. Soon court officials served as personal valets for the Zhangs' mothers; and Wu Zhao's kinsmen addressed the Zhangs reverently as "Fifth Master" (Wulang 五郎) and "Sixth Master" (Liulang 六郎), all the while vying for the honor of stabling their horses.[81] In 698, Wu Zhao set up the Institute for Reining Cranes (Konghejian 控鶴監), with Zhang Yizhi as director.[82]

The significance of this new office, Reining Cranes, soon became apparent. In 700, Wu Zhao's nephew Wu Sansi (d. 707), the prince of Liang, proclaimed that Zhang Changzong was the incarnation of Prince Jin. Thereafter, Wu Zhao ordered that Zhang Changzong don a feathered garment, play a flute, and prance around the court astride a wooden crane.[83] The feathered raiment may well have been the extraordinary "flock of kingfishers" cloak (Jicuiqiu 集翠裘) worth "more than a thousand gold" presented at Wu Zhao's court by emissaries from Guangzhou (Nanhai commandery 南海郡), a garment she bestowed upon Zhang Changzong.[84]

In his obsequious effort to further exalt Zhang Changzong, Wu Sansi wrote the "Verse of the Immortal Cranes" (Xianhe pian 仙鶴篇), which included the lines:

Riding the immortal crane into the firmament whither soars he?
From Mount Goushi in the seventh month he flies into the distance . . .
mysteriously ascending into the boundless emptiness.[85]

Literary master Cui Rong responded to Wu Sansi with another effusion stitching together Zhang Changzong and Prince Jin:

I have heard that once a guest wandered the heavens,
And parting the clouds descended to the imperial realm.
After three years the lofty visitor departed,
But a thousand years later returned once again.
In the past he encountered Duke Fuqiu;
Today he is like Ding Lingwei.[86]
Just so the palace attendant [Changzong] in talent and appearance!
But his name is not that of the hidden archivist.
Commanding respect, summons issue from the dragon gate-tower
And with deep gratitude, people pay respects before the tiger gate.
When her vermilion seal is impressed, the golden tripods[87] are presented;
When the wine arrives, the jade goblet is raised.

Figure 8.1 This eighteenth- or nineteenth-century Korean silk screen painting of the Queen Mother of the West banqueting amid fairy maidens and phoenixes conjures a sense of a Daoist paradise not unlike the fairyland Wu Zhao and her rhetoricians wrought in poetry and verse 1,100 years earlier.

Flanked by imperial guards with banners and pennons,
in feathered raiment beside the imperial countenance.
Where have the past altars gone?
So refulgent this new dynastic era!
The Han ruler preserved the secrets of the immortals;
Huainan cherished the machinations of the dao.
Now every morning the cranes of Mount Gou
Fly toward the walls of Luoyang.[88]

Both Duke Fuqiu and Ding Lingwei are Daoist immortals. The "archivist" refers to Laozi himself. And Huainan is Daoist loremaster Liu An. Luoyang is depicted as a Daoist paradise, drawing cranes from nearby mountains. The ultimate point Cui Rong establishes in this poem is the extended conceit that the cumulative Daoist incense churned up by the polychrome crane wings of Zhang Changzong in the guise of Prince Jin perfumed not the ousted Tang dynasts associated with Laozi but Wu Zhao in her incarnation as Queen Mother of the West.

A body of literary masters including Song Zhiwen and Li Qiao—members of the Institute for Reining Cranes—produced the 1300-chapter *Pearls and Blossoms of the Three Faiths* (Sanjiao zhuying 三教珠英), an anthology that sought to systemically gather an encyclopedia of Buddhist, Daoist, and Confucian wisdom. Because of the rumors swirling around the institute, however, many argued the project was little more than an elaborate diversion to cover the riotous carousing, boisterous feasting, and other lascivious goings-on in the inner palace, a transparent effort to squelch the cacophony of criticism from the court.[89]

The emergence of Mount Goushi as a ritual center, associated with both Prince Jin and the Queen Mother of the West, can be understood in terms of Wu Zhao's ongoing effort to transform greater Luoyang into sanctified ground connected to her imperial person and indelibly imprinted with her image. The rising cult of Prince Jin signaled a shift in Wu Zhao's imperial favor from Buddhist utopias, in the first half of her Zhou dynasty, to Daoist paradises during her later years.

In 698, Wu Zhao made her son Li Xiǎn (the once and future emperor Zhongzong), heir apparent once again. This decision effectively signaled her intention to return the empire to the house of Tang.[90] Rather than deal with the constant pressures of her dissension-ridden court, in her later

years Wu Zhao retreated to her mountain villas or indulged in the flamboyant gaiety the Zhangs provided in her inner quarters.

This desire to remove herself from the infighting and factionalism of
her court is reflected in her poem "Shizong" ("Stony Torrents") written
in 700:

Drenched in cloaks of mist, stop.

Take joy in feasting

Admire the creek-lover's wisdom, the charity of hills.

And then, on jeweled saddles,

As twilight falls, above the roiling world, we'll fly away.[91]

In her tone, one readily detects Wu Zhao's escapist delight in the comfort-
ing vastness of the mountains and dales south of Luoyang. Stony Torrents
is a gorge near Mount Song. On the same outing, Wu Zhao commanded
those in her entourage to write poems to commemorate the occasion. Not
only did Wu Sansi cast Zhang Changzong as Prince Jin in his "Verse of the
Immortal Crane," but he also tacitly elevated his aunt Wu Zhao to the station of a Daoist immortal.

From this place, layered with several thousand cliffs and ravines,

My sovereign ascends mounted on a crane, riding a dragon.[92]

Elsewhere in the poem, he mentions, as one of the crane's destinations,
"Green Fields" (Qingtian 青田), one of the thirty-six lesser grotto-heavens
in Daoism, located on a mountain in Zhejiang.[93] Similarly, Li Qiao's poem
"Crane" (he 鶴) features a crane, presumably ridden by a Daoist immortal,
soaring from "Green Fields" to the "Vermilion Within" (Danjin 丹禁) of
the imperial palaces.[94] And if Zhang Changzong was Prince Jin, then who
in the Daoist pantheon could Wu Zhao be other than the Queen Mother of
the West?

Suzanne Cahill has illustrated that on this famous outing to Shizong,
poet-courtier Yao Chong (650–721)[95] drew upon images like King Mu of
Zhou's "westward procession culminating in a supernatural feast," in order
to transform Wu Zhao's entourage into a company of Daoist immortals.
Yao Chong's poem on the occasion indicates that Wu Zhao excelled two

rulers of the past with whom the Queen Mother of the West was closely intertwined, King Mu and Han Wudi:

> Long ago, a Zhou king declined the bounty of the Turquoise Pond,
> And a Han ruler felt anxious and ashamed before the Jade Tree Palace.
> Now, on the other hand, we have auspicious mists paired with beautiful breaths,
> Which can follow the light palanquin: altogether profuse.[96]

While these male rulers of the past were ill at ease in the immortal presence of the Queen Mother of the West, Yao Chong implies, his own sovereign was in her element.

The poem of favorite Zhang Yizhi commemorating the outing to Stony Torrents more explicitly linked his patroness to the Queen Mother:

> With alacrity, six dragons rear their heads in clarion announcement
> As the Seven Sages join the Yellow Emperor, gathering in the shade of the Ying River.
> Thousand *zhang* 丈 tall[97] pines thatched with wisteria form an emerald canopy.
> The entire mountainscape echoes with birdsong and strains of flute,
> As white cloud and bluebird, emissaries of the Queen Mother,
> Part the hanging vines and creepers that make men's hearts grow wild.
> As the evening sun settles in a secret crevasse deep in the mountains
> with airy nonchalance a zephyr blows falling flowers earthward.[98]

This association was not unique. Citing many instances in which Daoist priestesses and recluses were explicitly affiliated with the Queen Mother in verse, Cahill asserts that Tang poems sometimes "compare especially lofty or talented priestesses and adepts to the Queen Mother."[99]

Wu Zhao's desire to associate herself with the Queen Mother of the West was most readily apparent in her later years: in her establishment of the Institute of Reining Cranes, in the development of Mount Goushi into a cultic center for Prince Jin, in Zhang Changzong's theatrical portrayal of this crane-riding Daoist immortal, and in her recurring role as Queen Mother of the West in the poetry of her courtiers. Assuming the part only after she had ceded the empire back to her son, she played the Queen Mother of the West to Zhang Changzong's Prince Jin. Seemingly, this role as the Queen Mother of the West functionally did little to amplify her political authority and, indeed, might better be understood as a playful diversion during her waning years.

Imperial poetry outings like the picnic to Stony Torrents continued after Wu Zhao's deposal and death in the court under uxorious Zhongzong and his empress Wei in the Jinglong 景龍 era (5 October 707 to 4 July 710). Jia Jinhua has noted that, continuing a tradition from Wu Zhao's court, poet-officials "took poetry as a political tool whereby they obtained favor from the emperor, empress, and other members of the royal house in order to gain high political position in court."[100] While Zhongzong's puissant spouse Empress Wei was identified with the Queen Mother of the West less frequently than Wu Zhao, on an outing to Xingqing Pool, courtier Zhao Yanzhao wrote the following verse on her behalf:

> I hope to attend the Queen Mother of the West forever;
> As an attendant I feel ashamed without Dong[fang] Shuo's talent.[101]

Styling himself a second-tier Dongfang Shuo (the quirky Western Han esoteric master), to Empress Wei's Queen Mother, Zhao sought to curry her imperial favor.

CONCLUSION

Through sericulture rites, jade tokens of authority, phoenixes, and lunisolar radiance, Wu Zhao linked herself to the Queen Mother of the West. These culturally legible symbols identified Wu Zhao with the potent Daoist goddess, amplifying her authority with the divinity's mythic aura. In her final years of rule, attended by the flamboyant Zhang brothers, Wu Zhao styled her inner palace a Daoist paradise on earth, over which she presided as Queen Mother of the West. This colorful theater, while it may have served as a welcome distraction from her factionalized court, did little to rekindle the fading power of her Zhou dynasty.

NINE

The Mother of Laozi and Wu Zhao
From One Grand Dowager to Another

Among Wu Zhao's pantheon of female political ancestors, the mother of Daoist founder Laozi proved problematic, presenting singular opportunities and yet posing serious difficulties. This chapter examines, with attention to specific context and timing, the various strategies Wu Zhao devised to exalt the mother of Laozi in ways that might redound upon her own political authority.

THE MOTHER OF LAOZI

Perhaps the clearest sense we have of Laozi's mother as a mortal being comes from the genealogical records of the Li family in the *New Tang History*. In this Northern Song Confucian text, she is not a divine goddess but a woman of the Yishou clan named Yingfu, married to Censor-in-Chief Li Qian (c. eighth century B.C.) during the Eastern Zhou dynasty. Her son Laozi, then known as Li Er, served under King Ping as a royal scribe. The clan name Li does not derive from the plum (*li* 李) tree she grasps while birthing Laozi; rather, it originates from an earlier female ancestor from the state of Chen who, along with her son Li Zhen, ate "fruits of wood" (*mu zi* 木子) while fleeing the notorious last Shang king, Zhou (c. eleventh century B.C.). The characters for "fruits of wood" were combined to derive the new clan name Li (*mu* 木 + *zi* 子 = 李).[1]

In balance, Song Confucians present a diminished image of Laozi. Conversely, Daoist traditions elevate the mother of Laozi to divine status, in preparation for the coming of Laozi. Catherine Despeux categorizes the mother of Laozi as one of "a number of major goddesses who played a key role in religion," along with the Queen Mother of the West and Mazu, the protectress of fishermen and merchants.[2] Daoist hagiographer Du Guangting listed Laozi's mother first in his *Register of Assembled Transcendents*. The text provides a four-stage evolution of this divinity. First, this "mother of the Dao," initially known as the Jade Maiden of Mystery and Wonder (Xuanmiao yunü 玄妙玉女), arose from creation—from the merging of primordial *qi*, the "virginal culmination of the *dao* 道," with the essence of the universe.[3] Second, after taking human female form, she gave birth to Laozi from her left side, while clutching a plum tree. As a result, she was known by the earthly name of Mother Li (Li mu 李母) and gained the celestial title Sage Mother Goddess (Shengmu yuanjun 聖母元君). Third, she expounded the crux of the Daoist teachings to Laozi, gaining the title Goddess of the Great Unity (Taiyi yuanjun 太一元君). Finally, having passed on her wisdom to her prodigious offspring, with a caravan of chariots and an entourage of attendants, she ascended to the highest cerulean reaches as Grand Dowager of the Anterior Heaven (Xiantian taihou 先天太后), where "she presides as benevolent ancestor over the wider universe."[4]

In the *Book of Transformations of Laozi* (Laozi bianhua jing 老子變化經), a text dated to the Eastern Han, it is recorded, "By the transformation of Heaven and Earth he [Laozi] is incarnated in the womb of Mother Li."[5] This passage prompted Kristofer Schipper to remark, "Cosmogony, the creation of the universe, and the pregnancy of Laozi's mother do here coincide."[6] In the *Secret Jade Tally Record* (Yuzhang bi jue 玉章秘訣), another work by Du Guangting, the mother of Laozi plays what Anna Seidel terms "the primordial role of the mother demiurge":[7]

> Some believe that it is she who is the greatest and the most venerable. She controls Heaven and Earth, harmonizes *yin* and *yang*, employs Wind and Rain as her servants. She makes the five planets advance and retreat, arranges the cold and the heat, wields power over Qian 乾 and Kun 坤 and rules over all immortals of the three realms. Life and death of men, rise and decline of generations, all proceed from her. It is from the Holy Mother of Laojun that Heaven, Earth and all beings have received life.[8]

Du Guangting's tenth-century perspective illustrates that the mother of Laozi was a powerful Daoist divinity who filled multiple roles: world creator, mother-educator of Laozi, and transcendent divinity. These multiple roles—mother, demiurge, and divine goddess—would all prove important to the affiliation Wu Zhao sought with the mother of Laozi.

MOTHER LI AND HER SON IN EARLY TANG DAOISM

Shortly after establishing the Tang dynasty, to enhance their prestige among the great clans of the day, the imperial Li family claimed descent from the Eastern Zhou Daoist sage Laozi, with whom they shared a surname.[9] In the truculent wake of their military seizure of the empire, such ideological and kin connections helped legitimize the newly risen Lis (with their central Asian background), by anchoring their authority in indigenous Chinese political and cultural tradition.[10] Daoist prophecies and miracles, including the appearance of Laozi, played an important role both in the legitimation of the first Tang emperor, Gaozu, and in the founding of the dynasty, creating what Charles Benn calls "an aura of mystique for the royal house" that was "uniquely destined" for power.[11] In 620, Gaozu honored the Daoist forefather-divinity as "Sage Ancestor" (Shengzu 聖祖).[12]

Lest anyone doubt the kin connection, one Ji Shanxing told the Tang court that on Ram's Horn Peak (Yangjiaoshan 羊角山), he had encountered an old man riding a white horse who had declared himself to be Laozi. The venerable rider then instructed Ji to inform Gaozu that he (Laozi) was the emperor's ancestor and that once the emperor pacified the realm his scions would rule for a thousand years. Gaozu marveled, and built a temple in Laozi's honor.[13] Thus the Tang dynasts "accepted Laozi as a deity, claiming that his divine guardianship and grace protected the dynasty and caused it to prosper."[14] In 625, Gaozu formally elevated Daoism over Buddhism, an ideological hierarchy reconfirmed by Taizong in 637.[15] The divine Laozi manifested himself twice during the corule of Gaozong and Wu Zhao, in 662 and 679, both times on Mount Beimang, overlooking Luoyang to the north.[16] Overall, the reigns of the first three Tang emperors witnessed not only Laozi's emergence as a Tang ancestor, but the elevation of divine Laozi as "creator of the cosmos, a universal deity who promised salvation for all mankind." Daoism was placed "over Confucianism and Buddhism in the official rankings of the three doctrines."[17]

Naturally, the promotion of the cult of Laozi greatly publicized and politicized the Daoist ideology. Yet despite the ascendancy of Laozi as apotheosized sage and ancestor of the imperial Li clan, his mother remained little more than a shadowy presence until the reign of Gaozong and his powerful empress and coruler Wu Zhao. As with the elevation of the cults of Nüwa, the mother of Qi, and the Queen Mother of the West, it was no accident that the rise of the cult of the mother of Laozi coincided with the political ascendancy of Wu Zhao.

THE ELEVATION OF THE MOTHER OF LAOZI AT BOZHOU IN 666

In 637, Taizong restored the Laojun (Laozi) Temple in Bozhou, reputed birthplace of the Daoist sage, and endowed it with land revenues to pay for performing rites there.[18] This site developed into an early Tang center for the worship of both Laozi and the mother of Laozi.

As mentioned earlier, from 660, when Gaozong was stricken with a serious illness, until his death in 683, Wu Zhao often assisted him in his public duties as emperor. She sat behind a curtain in the audience hall and deliberated upon administrative decisions with her husband. Because the emperor and empress jointly made decisions and wielded political influence, people called them the "Two Sages."[19] In the second month of 666, returning from their execution of the *feng* and *shan* rites on Mount Tai—as empress, Wu Zhao had deftly maneuvered her way into an unprecedented role in these grand ceremonies—the Two Sages stopped at the Laojun Temple in Bozhou and bestowed an exalted title upon the Tang founder: Grand Superior Emperor of Mysterious Origin (Taishang xuanyuan huangdi 太上玄元皇帝). According to Hu Sanxing's (1230–1287) commentary in the *Comprehensive Mirror*, Guyang County in Bozhou prefecture, 898 *li* from Luoyang, housed a shrine to Laozi. On this occasion, the Two Sages changed the name of Guyang County to Zhenyuan (True Origin) County.[20] In addition, all citizens of this county who shared the Li surname with the Daoist founder and the Tang dynasts were specially granted a year's tax relief.[21]

Du Guangting's account presents the Two Sages' stop in Bozhou as part of a watershed Daoist movement rather than a simple homage to the renowned sage:

> In the second year of the Longshuo era (662), the emperor ordered Xu Lishi, the vice prefect of Luo prefecture and duke of the state of Qiao, to build Shangqing Abbey on Mount Mang in order to ward off demons.

When this meritorious achievement was complete, the Grand Superior One [Laozi] appeared once again, and the entire court presented a memorial to offer their congratulations. The emperor was delighted. At the beginning of the Qianfeng era (666), when the emperor's *feng* sacrifice in the east was complete, the imperial chariot returned to Bozhou, and the emperor personally visited Laozi's temple. He respectfully presented the honorific title "Emperor of Nebulous Origin" (Hunyuan huangdi 混元皇帝) and made the Sage Mother "Grand Dowager of the Anterior Heaven." Guyang County was subsequently renamed "True Origin County."[22]

In another text, Du Guangting similarly recorded that "under the Great Tang dynasty, she [Mother Li] was venerated posthumously and given the title Grand Dowager of the Anterior Heaven."[23] On the momentous nature of this title, Charles Benn remarks: "In the *Daodejing*, *xiantian* 先天 refers to the Dao which precedes creation in time and is taken to be the mother of the world. The Emperor thus recognized Laozi's mother as the personification of the Dao and cosmic progenitor."[24] The timing of this elevation of Laozi's mother can best be understood in conjunction with Wu Zhao's rising political presence, unprecedented in the *feng* and *shan* rites.

Gaozong's "Imperial proclamation to exalt Laojun [Laozi] with the honorific title Emperor of Primal Origin" corroborates Du Guangting's account:

It is proper that the origin of mysteries be expounded to make manifest the merit of the Original Sage (Yuan sheng 元聖). Thus, we shall posthumously designate him [Laozi] Grand and Superior Emperor of Primal Origin (Taishang yuanyuan huangdi 太上元元皇帝), and denominate the Sage Mother as Grand Dowager of the Anterior Heaven. Temples, shrines, and halls [dedicated to Laozi] shall be repaired or built, with a director and an aide installed at each to make sacrifices. In addition, Guyang County shall be changed to True Origin County.[25]

Though the dating of this proclamation is unclear and the title is slightly altered from that one mentioned in Du Guangting's account, on no other occasion during Gaozong's reign did he bestow titular honors upon Laozi. This proclamation was issued in the second month of 666, on the return of the imperial cortege from Mount Tai. Benn has observed that the director and aide "customarily managed the affairs of imperial ancestral temples" and other temples related to state cultic sacrifices. These sacrifices, involving not only imperial kinsmen but a wider circle of high-ranking court ministers, were usually held at the imperial ancestral temple in the capital. On this singular occasion, however, they were held in Bozhou to honor Laozi and Laozi's mother.[26] Mother and son were not only elevated as universal, cosmic divinities, but they were honored as ancestors of the ruling clan. Naturally, the prestige and authority of Gaozong and Wu Zhao, the earthly sovereigns who honored them, was augmented as well.

MOTHER LI IN WU ZHAO'S GROWING PANTHEON OF FEMALE DIVINITIES

Late in Gaozong's reign, while the Two Sages remained corulers, Wu Zhao's control over her ailing husband was increasingly apparent. During the emperor's final years, the pair retreated to the hot springs and craggy peaks of Mount Song, an area dotted with Daoist temples and Buddhist monasteries.[27]

On the vernal equinox in 680, when Gaozong and Wu Zhao visited Mount Song, encomiast Cui Rong composed an inscription for a stele erected at the temple of the mother of Qi. Though Wu Zhao still ostensibly shared political authority with the dying Gaozong at this juncture, Stephen Bokenkamp describes Cui Rong's composition, studded with references to female divinities, as a clear-cut endeavor to project the empress as the "mother of gods."[28] In the inscription, Cui Rong deftly frames the proper celestial orientation of the mother of Laozi and the Queen Mother of the West as consonant to and parallel with the harmonious earthly rule of Wu Zhao:

> Examining the Northern Dipper (Beidou 玉斗) with the armillary sphere, the residence of Mother Li is near the Northern Culmen (Beiji 北極);[29] and in the Stone Chamber of the Golden Terrace,[30] the dwelling of the Queen Mother is on the Western Mount.[31] When the pneumas act as mother, the myriad things all sprout forth. When the moon acts as mother, its glowing countenance shines down on all. When the earth element acts as mother, above and below merge and produce greatness. When the empress acts as mother, state and family are successfully formed.[32]

Though Gaozong was still alive, Cui Rong's inscription clearly focused upon the exaltation of Wu Zhao, affiliating her with an array of female divinities from antiquity, among them Mother Li. With a flourish—"When the empress acts as mother, state and family are successfully formed"—Cui Rong situated Wu Zhao as heir to these cosmic mothers. In this collection of worthy celestial mothers, Mother Li was the polestar. In Cui Rong's elegant metaphor, just as Mother Li presided over the supernal realm above, so mother-empress Wu Zhao oversaw the harmonious earthly empire below.

TWINNED MOTHERS OF LI AND GRAND DOWAGERS: A TIMELY REAFFIRMATION

In 683, during Gaozong's final months, when the Two Sages visited a Daoist monastery converted into a summer palace on Mount Song, they inaugurated the Amplifying the Dao era, decreeing the construction of Daoist monasteries in every prefecture.[33] After Gaozong's death, however, the relationship between his widowed empress and the Daoist establishment became much more conflicted.

In 684, mere months after Gaozong's demise, grand dowager Wu Zhao deposed her son Li Xiǎn (Zhongzong) and replaced him with weak-willed Ruizong, her youngest son Li Dan. Presiding over the court in the ninth month of 684, Wu Zhao launched a series of reforms that imitated the archaic titles, nomenclature, and court colors of the Zhou dynasty of antiquity.[34] The reform most troubling to Daoists was the titular elevation of Wu Zhao's natal kinsmen to princely rank. Any advancement that threatened the paramount position of the Li family—given their fictive blood ties to Laozi—implicitly jeopardized the entire Daoist establishment.

Indeed, the collective anxiety of the Daoist establishment is reflected in Du Guangting's *Historical Records Exalting Daoism* (Lidai chongdao ji 歷代崇道記):

> In the inaugural year of Wenming (684), when the Celestial Empress desired to make all of the Wus princes, Taishang 太上 [Laozi] appeared on the August Heaven Plateau in the Fangxing hamlet of Longtai town, Wenxiang County, in Guozhou prefecture.[35] He sent Wu Yuanchong[36] to transmit the following report to the Celestial Empress: "The empire has been long blessed and enjoyed great peace. It is inappropriate for

you to seize the throne." The Celestial Empress let the matter rest and ordered the temporary palace in Wenxiang converted into the Temple of Worship of the Immortals (Fengxian guan 奉仙觀).[37]

The appearance of the divine Laozi and the transmission of his message might best be understood as part of a wider political and ideological discourse (or negotiation) between the dowager-regent, court, and empire. Sensing the time was not yet appropriate, Wu Zhao pulled back, content to style herself an exemplary Confucian widow, assiduously working to manage and preserve the family estate for posterity.[38] There is further evidence that Daoists, worried that Wu Zhao's rise might jeopardize their faith, rallied behind the Li family. In 685, ostensibly to commemorate recently deceased Gaozong—but perhaps reflecting the apprehension of the imperial Li clan and Daoist establishment alike—250 Li family members commissioned a statue of Laozi at the Daoist monastery near the grand dowager's newly proclaimed Divine Capital.[39]

Ever astute at reading the shifting ideological landscape, Wu Zhao initially took steps to mollify the disquietude of the Daoists. Immediately after Gaozong's death, she bestowed upon her deceased husband the title Heavenly Great Emperor (Tianhuang dadi 天皇大帝), a former title for Laozi in his divine aspect.[40] And in her inaugural address to promulgate the Guangzhai era in the autumn of 684, Wu Zhao bestowed upon the mother of Laozi the honorific title Grand Dowager of the Anterior Heaven,[41] reaffirming the title granted the Daoist goddess in 666:

> Now, the Mysterious Original One (Yuanyuan zhe 元元者) is the wellspring from which the imperial house issued. Embracing the Way and its virtues, it is effortless; crowning all spirits and immortals, it is unfathomable. Brilliant and wondrous beyond measure, its benevolence extends to the myriad matters. So how is it that while this precious son is made manifest in the imperial apartments, the Original Mother (Xianmu 先母) still has no honored position? I hereby present the honorific title Grand Dowager of the Anterior Heaven. It is fitting that at Laojun Temples her honored image be respectfully erected in order to receive our sincere offerings.[42]

Far from a gratuitous recognition of Laozi's mother, this announcement represents Wu Zhao's efforts to define, at one remove, her own paramount position. In the ninth month of 684, she was de facto ruler, issuing edicts and making decisions of state, while the nominal emperor, Ruizong, simply remained in the crown prince's apartments, minimally involved in court politics.

Why would Wu Zhao once again ceremoniously bestow upon Laozi's mother a title that had been granted eighteen years earlier? The timely attachment of this title reaffirmed that Wu Zhao, like Laozi's mother, was a grand dowager, allowing the future female sovereign, at this critical juncture, the time to consolidate her tenuous control over the court. Thus, Wu Zhao underscored her station as a mother of empire—and avoided, for the moment, alienating the Daoist establishment.

The title was all the more poignant because Laozi had no father, only a demiurgic mother. With Gaozong gone, the empire had no father—only a powerful, all-seeing mother.

FROM SAGE MOTHER TO EMPEROR:
PHASING OUT LAOZI'S MOTHER

Later in this period of incubation as grand dowager, Wu Zhao mustered ideological support anticipating her establishment of a new dynasty, assuming the title Sage Mother, Divine Sovereign, on the summer solstice in 688.[43] Everyone in court and country heard the echo of the well-known title of Laozi's mother, Sage Mother Goddess. Even as Wu Zhao marshaled Buddhist propaganda and constructed sky-piercing Buddhist monuments, her choice of nomenclature signaled that she was not entirely unsympathetic to the Daoist establishment. Her identification with Laozi's mother still carried potent political resonance, helping confirm Wu Zhao in her roles as grand dowager presiding over the imperial family and Sage Mother ruling the empire. From 688 until she formally claimed the throne in 690, Wu Zhao's propagandists often used the epithet "Sage Mother" in their rhetoric.

"Sage Mother" was not merely a Daoist title of Laozi's mother. Contemporary scholar Gu Zhengmei has remarked upon the Buddhist overtones in Wu Zhao's usage of the character *sheng* 聖, contending that the "sage" in Wu Zhao's new title was closely linked to Buddhist sainthood and to a Khotanese tradition of Buddhist kingship.[44] Wei-dynasty dowager empress Feng (馮太后, 442–490) had styled herself a "saintly mother" (*shengmu* 聖母) after succoring Buddhist monks in the late fifth century.[45]

Simultaneously, Wu Zhao may have been claiming to be a sagacious Confucian mother of empire, like King Wen's wife, Mother Wen. In short, "sage" or "saintly" mother was a multivalent political concept that straddled the many current coexisting ideologies.

In 689, Wu Zhao demoted Laozi from Emperor of Primal Origin to Lord Lao (Laojun).[46] Though there are no records of a commensurate reduction in title for Laozi's mother, once Wu Zhao established her Zhou dynasty in 690, she immediately jettisoned the title Sage Mother and, reflecting her paramount stature, designated herself Sagely and Divine Emperor,[47] a title that effectively muted her gender. Laozi's mother was too intimately identified with the Li clan and the Tang dynasty. Once Wu Zhao attained the position of emperor, it was no longer politically advantageous to emphasize her role as widowed mother of the imperial Li clan. Thus, although she neither disparaged nor severed ties with the Daoist goddess, Wu Zhao also realized that Laozi's mother no longer offered the sort of legitimation she sought.

During her fifteen years as emperor, there are few records of Wu Zhao making any effort to amplify her connection with the mother of Laozi. Among his measures designed to reestablish the Tang dynasty and erase the reforms of his mother, Zhongzong restored Laozi's lofty title in 705.[48]

CLUES FROM EMPEROR XUANZONG'S
DAOIST RITUAL INNOVATION

In 743, Xuanzong, known for compiling and standardizing ritual protocol, introduced by imperial decree a new major state sacrifice: the practice of worshipping the divine Laozi in a rite at the Taiqing Palace, a refurbished temple complex in Chang'an. This ceremony reconfirmed Xuanzong's kinship with the venerable Daoist sage. Victor Xiong remarks that "in his decree on initiating Taiqing Palace worship, Xuanzong honored Laozi's father and mother with the posthumous titles . . . while emphasizing the blood relation between Laozi and the imperial family of Tang."[49] This elevation of status is recorded in the *Old Tang History*:

> On the *ren-zi* day of the third month of Tianbao 2 (11 April 743), Xuanzong personally offered a sacrifice and bestowed honorific names at the Temple of Mysterious Origin. By imperial edict he posthumously honored

the father of Sage Ancestor Emperor of Mysterious Origin 聖祖玄元皇帝 [Laozi], Zhou censor-in-chief Li Jing, as Emperor Emeritus of the Anterior Heaven 先天太上皇 and the mother, from the Yishou clan, as Grand Dowager of the Anterior Heaven. The temple remained fixed in his ancestral village in Qiao commandery 譙郡.[50]

On the surface, it appears peculiar that Xuanzong, an emperor seeking to reestablish patriarchal Confucian rule, would publicly honor Laozi's mother. After Wu Zhao's deposal and death, a divided court and a series of palace coups marred the restoration of the Tang. Female relatives and in-laws of the Li family—the Taiping Princess, the Anle Princess, and Empress Wei—held sway over court and politics. Xuanzong's ascent to the throne in 712 marked the termination of half a century of court domination by powerful women.[51] On closer analysis, the intent of Wu Zhao's grandson was not to exalt the celestial status of a Daoist female divinity. Rather, in keeping with Xuanzong's own ideological agenda, it was a calculated effort to retrofit this divinity into a patriarchal ancestral framework. This is perhaps a perfect example of what Richard Kagan refers to as the constant effort of "general literary and official Confucian circles" in early and medieval China "to place all female deities into a context of subservience to more powerful male divinities who were themselves rationalized reflections of the social order."[52] Under Wu Zhao, Laozi's father was never mentioned. To mention the earthly father reduced the mystical aura surrounding Laozi's mother. In affirming a position within the ancestral order for Laozi's little-known father, Xuanzong joined a long tradition of those seeking to diminish female ancestresses, goddesses, and divinities by yoking them to male counterparts.

CONCLUSION

At the beginning of the Tang, the new imperial Li family, with mixed Han Chinese and non-Han blood, drew upon Daoist sage and founder Laozi to construct an identity grounded in indigenous Chinese tradition. In the aftermath of Wu Zhao's extraordinary involvement in the *feng* and *shan* rites at Mount Tai in 666, the Two Sages honored the mother of Laozi at Bozhou with an exalted title—a measure that helped normalize Wu Zhao's open political involvement. While a dying Gaozong sought peace of mind and immortality on Mount Song, Wu Zhao rose in political eminence, honoring a growing pantheon of female divinities that included Mother Li, the mother of Qi, and the Queen Mother of the West. During her time as grand dowager—a critical incubation period for the establishment of her own dynasty—Wu Zhao designated Laozi's mother as a kindred spirit, a fellow grand dowager, and an affiliate who helped confirm her status as mother of empire. Mother Li helped connect Wu Zhao to her imperial Li in-laws, to the Daoist establishment in particular, and to a wider Chinese cultural tradition.

But her affiliation with Laozi's mother was more than a means of affiliating herself with the Li imperial clan. On a primordial level, her connection to this female divinity helped define Wu Zhao as a demiurgic force. Kristopher Schipper has illustrated that in the Daoist conception of creation, "there was no father creator," only a mother. Furthermore, of unclear etymology, the *jun* 君 of Laojun "can designate woman as well as man." In mythology, *jun* often referred to female deities. Schipper concludes that "Lao-chün is Lao Tzu before his birth . . . is the body of the Tao before birth; Lao Tzu is the Old Child and the Old Master of this world. It is the Mother in whom and through whom this transformation is accomplished. The Tao has taken form in her. Through her the Tao has been revealed."[53] At once precursor, embodiment, and progenitor, Mother Li was Laozi before Laozi. Through this association, Wu Zhao, too, becomes a generative force, a mother of the Dao.

Wu Zhao's affiliation with Mother Li lasted as long as this identification was politically expedient. As Wu Zhao renegotiated her political authority, however, building a broad multiethnic, pluralistic coalition as she prepared to set up her own Zhou dynasty, she relied increasingly on Buddhism and masked her gender. Her identification with Mother Li, a figure tightly bound to Tang legitimation and indigenous Chinese culture, became a political liability. Consequently, once Wu Zhao established her Zhou dynasty in 690, Mother Li vanished from rhetoric and rites.

TEN

Rejected from the Pantheon
The Ill-Timed Rise of the Cult of Wei Huacun

THIS CHAPTER EXAMINES THE RISE and fall of the cult of Wei Huacun 魏華存 (252–334), Lady of the Southern Marchmount (Nanyue furen 南岳 夫人), during Wu Zhao's decades as empress, grand dowager, and emperor. As we have seen, Wu Zhao, possessing surpassing political acumen, was acutely responsive to shifting ideological climes; tempered by political circumstance, her measured patronage of Daoism ebbed and surged. The women who composed her pantheon were not static dramatis personae. At various junctures along the arc of her political career, the particular qualities that emanated from the different divinities and eminent women became more or less desirable, expedient, and efficacious.

As empress and to a lesser extent as grand dowager, Wu Zhao honored Lady Wei alongside a pantheon of other female Daoist divinities. Once emperor, however, even when the perfect opportunity arose, Wu Zhao chose not to publicly magnify the cult of Lady Wei.

LADY OF THE SOUTHERN MARCHMOUNT

Wei Huacun was a signal figure of medieval Daoism. Many hagiographies of this celebrated Daoist divinity have been written: James Robson, drawing on the work of Isabel Robinet, lists no fewer than twenty-five![1] Du Guangting's biography of the foremost Daoist goddess, the Queen Mother of the West, contains a curious story connecting Lady Wei to the renowned Daoist center Maoshan (Mount Mao, in Jurong County, near Nanjing in modern-day Jiangsu), the seat of Shangqing 上清 (Highest Clarity) Daoism. According to this source, 250 years before her birth, Lady Wei visited mortal Mao Ying (who would emerge as god of Mount Mao and patron deity of Shangqing Daoism), and remained behind as his "divine wife."[2] Isabel Robinet refers to Lady Wei as a master of Daoist liturgical practice, the "first patriarch" of the Shangqing movement.[3] Perhaps more aptly, Russell Kirkland and Livia Kohn dub Lady Wei Shangqing's "first matriarch."[4]

The mortal Wei Huacun heralded from Rencheng in Shandong, born to a wealthy office-holding family in the Jin dynasty. Even while married to a local office-holder, as an adept in the Celestial Masters (Tianshi 天師), she served as a libationer (jijiu 祭酒). With the chaos that ended the Western Jin, her family fled to Jianye (near Nanjing). After her two sons rose to become officials, she devoted herself single-mindedly to Daoist wanderings, cultivating the dao near Linchuan (in modern-day Jiangxi), and ultimately attaining it at the Southern Marchmount.[5]

Hagiographies record that after sloughing off her mortal form in 334, Lady Wei became a female immortal, joining other Daoist divinities like the Queen Mother of the West and revealing scripture to male devotees like mystic Yang Xi (330–386). In Daoist chronicler Tao Hongjing's (452–536) *Declarations of the Perfected* (Zhen'gao 真誥), the apotheosized Wei Huacun received the titles of Lady of the Southern Marchmount and Primordial Ruler of the Purple Vacuity (Zixu yuanjun 紫虛元君).[6] By the early Tang, she had developed into a major revelatory deity revered locally and nationally.

With the rise of Tang, given the ruling Li family's fictive kin connection to Daoist sage Laozi, a wide pantheon of Daoist divinities blossomed. As her popular and liturgical reputation broadened in the centuries following her death, Wei Huacun became widely regarded as a cultic figure.

There is strong circumstantial evidence that during the reign of Gaozong, the Two Sages promoted Shangqing Daoism and the cult of Lady Wei.[7] Gaozong and Wu Zhao ardently supported the Daoist establishment: they patronized efforts to compile a Daoist canon, oversaw widespread construction of state-sponsored monasteries, bestowed titles upon Daoist divinities, and ordained imperial family members.[8] In 662, Gaozong ordered the construction of a Highest Clarity Palace atop Mount Mang near Luoyang. When the palace was completed, a manifestation of divine Laozi appeared.[9] In 674, Gaozong took the title Celestial Emperor and Wu Zhao became Celestial Empress, drawing loosely on a tradition of Daoist kingship.[10]

In Gaozong's final years, both celestial sovereigns embraced Daoism with a greater fervor, reflected in their support of Wang Xuanhe (fl. late seventh century), a Daoist chronicler whose works focused on "production of ency-clopedias and integrative summaries of the religion."[11] At this critical time of the integration and synthesis of Daoist teachings, Wang composed two of the numerous hagiographies celebrating the emergence of Wei Hua-cun as a cultic divinity: *Realities and Categories of Highest Clarity* (Shangqing daolei shixiang 上清道類事相), an encyclopedia of Daoist practices and institutions, and *A Bag of Pearls from the Three Caverns* (Sandong zhunang 三洞珠囊), a miscellany on everything from celebrated Daoist practitioners and cosmology to asceticism and diet.[12] Not by chance did Wang Xuanhe compose this pair of biographies for Lady Wei in 683; in Chengdu that same year, he engraved prefaces that Gaozong and Wu Zhao had composed for Yin Wencao's (622–688) lost 7300-chapter Daoist canon.[13]

Meanwhile, Wu Zhao and her dying husband Gaozong sought out Shangqing patriarch Pan Shizheng, a master of self-cultivation, breath con-trol, and longevity. The ailing emperor asked the ascetic what the moun-tain possessed that he needed. The venerable Daoist famously responded, "The mountain has clear springs and pine trees—what is lacking?"[14] In his final days, Gaozong changed the reign era name to Amplifying the Dao. He issued a decree establishing Daoist monasteries in every prefecture and bestowed titles on octogenarians and nonagenarians.[15]

Despite the imperial patronage of Shangqing Daoism, there is little direct evidence of a cult of Lady Wei during Gaozong's reign. Indeed, although Cui Rong's stele inscription for the Temple of the Mother of Qi includes references to the Queen Mother of the West and the mother of Laozi (and even mentions obscure female figures from antiquity like the mothers of Fuxi and Shennong), it makes no mention of Lady Wei.[16] In the first lunar month of 683, on an outing to their mountain retreat, Fengtian Palace on Mount Song, the celestial sovereigns honored the Queen Mother of the West and the Mother of Qi—they even paid respects at the shrines of oxherd Chao Fu and hermit Xu You—but they did not pay homage to Lady Wei.[17]

THE CULT IN HUAIZHOU

Despite the absence of clear-cut imperial patronage during the early Tang, a "diffusion of cults to the memory of Lady Wei . . . came to dot the Chinese landscape": there were shrines exalting this visionary divinity at Southern Marchmount Hengshan, in Huaizhou, and in Fuzhou.[18]

Wei Huacun was linked to Huaizhou prefecture 30 miles northeast of Wu Zhao's Divine Capital, centered in present-day Qinyang County in Henan.[19] In the Western Jin, Lady Wei accompanied her husband to this area when he served as district magistrate of Xiuwu, a county in northeastern Huaizhou.[20] In 289, four divine beings, among them Wang Bao, Perfected One of the Clear Barrens (Qingxu zhenren 清虛真人)—whose name echoes the cavern heaven on Mount Wangwu (on the northwest fringe of the region in present-day Yangcheng, Shaanxi)—descended and initiated twenty-four-year-old Lady Wei, revealing to her cryptic heavenly texts. In 350, immortal Wei Huacun underwent her apotheosis on Mount Wangwu; before assuming full divine duties, she spent two additional months of purification there, culminating with festive music and song among a collection of Daoist divinities.[21]

Shortly after Gaozong's death, Lady Wei's cult in Huaizhou surfaced. The Huaizhou region was invested with rich symbolic significance. Sui Yangdi remarked in a 604 edict that he had considered constructing a "new Luoyang" in Huaizhou.[22] In 657, shortly after Wu Zhao became empress, Luoyang was elevated to Eastern Capital. To create a greater metropolitan region worthy of the new capital, Gaozong and his new empress appended to Luoyang's territory four counties in Huaizhou prefecture—Heyang, Jiyuan, Wen, and Wangwu.[23]

The Daoist ambience in the area was dense. Renowned poet Bo Juyi (772–846) once versified, "Of the splendid mountains and rivers of Jiyuan, Lord Lao has long known."[24] A sacred mountain associated with the Queen Mother of the West and other divinities, Mount Wangwu was perhaps the most notable feature of the region's Daoist topography.[25] In Shangqing tradition, the Lesser Clear Barrens Grotto (Xiaoyou qingxu 小有清虛) on Wangwu was foremost among the thirty-six Daoist cavern heavens (dongtian 洞天), earthly paradises impervious to pestilence, sickness, and death.[26] The main peak of Wangwu, Celestial Altar (Tiantan 天壇), was "a locus for assemblies of transcendent officials of all the mountains and Grotto-Heavens who examine and judge the students of the Dao."[27] In Li Yi's early ninth-century poem "Climbing the Celestial Altar to View the Sea at Night," Laozi and the Queen Mother both appear atop Wangwu in full immortal splendor.[28] Du Guangting's one-chapter Records of Traces of Saints on Celestial Altar Peak of Mount Wangwu (Tiantan Wangwushan shengji ji 天壇王屋山聖跡記) contains an account of the Queen Mother of the West presenting the Nine Tripods to the Yellow Emperor before the altar on the mountain's crown.[29] Both the larger region and Mount Wangwu itself were closely connected to Wei Huacun and to a wider lineage of Shangqing worthies.

Twelfth Shangqing patriarch Sima Chengzhen (647–735), who imparted wisdom to a series of Tang emperors including Gaozong, Wu Zhao, and Xuanzong, lived on Mount Wangwu for much of his career.[30] When, late in life, the venerable master of the Dao headed southward to Mount Tiantai in Jiangsu, Emperor Xuanzong personally went to Wangwu and saw him off with a poem.[31] Upon the Daoist patriarch's return, Xuanzong ensconced him in an abbey on Mount Wangwu, where Sima Chengzhen remained until his death.[32]

During Wu Zhao's years as grand dowager, Huaizhou was abuzz with Daoist activity connected to the cult of Lady Wei. The *Commentary on the Great Cloud Sutra*, Buddhist propaganda circulated by Wu Zhao on the eve of her establishment of her Zhou dynasty in 690, contains a passage that likely refers to Lady Wei. Among the many events in the narrative mustered as evidence foretelling the ascent of Wu Zhao is the passage: "in the Wenming year [684] at Huaizhou, a cloud of five colors suddenly arose from the Yellow River. On the cloud was a person who proclaimed herself the Mysterious Woman (Xuannü 玄女). She announced that Heaven had delegated her to present the divine cinnabar refined nine times to the grand dowager."[33] That same year Wu Zhao had conferred the title Grand Dowager of Anterior Heaven upon the mother of Laozi. The Mysterious Woman appeared "on the site of Lady Wei's future shrine."[34] Though the Mysterious Woman was also the name of a separate Daoist goddess, given Lady Wei's connection to the area, it seems probable that the Mysterious Woman was another name for the apotheosized Lady Wei. While the *Commentary* represents a subsequent effort by Wu Zhao's propagandists to resituate this avatar of Lady Wei seamlessly into a Buddhist narrative, the appearance of the Mysterious Woman in 684 was a Daoist event.

The region's position as a cultic center for the Daoist divinity is also made apparent in an epitaph carved for Lady Wei in Huaizhou at the same juncture. In 688, Lu Jingchun composed a shrine inscription for Lady Wei at Mujian village in Henei County of Huaizhou.[35] Lu's local residency is confirmed in a passage in the "Treatise on the Five Phases" in the *New Tang History* under "fish abominations" (*yu nie* 魚孽), explaining that when the rotted beam of a watermill on Lu Jingchun's Jiyuan estate was being replaced, a live sheatfish was found in the damp, decaying wood.[36] Not only does the shrine inscription contain a biography of Lady Wei, but anticipating her role as rain goddess in Song cults, it includes a prayer requesting the Daoist goddess to quench the drought that afflicted the area.[37] With local connections and an estate in Jiyuan, Lu Jingchun was both a member of the Huaizhou elite and a literary practitioner of broad learning.[38]

Though it is impossible to know whether Wu Zhao was familiar with the content of Lu Jingchun's inscription, she was aware of this talented fellow's presence in greater metropolitan Luoyang. Within two years after he composed the Mujian inscription on Lady Wei—mere months into her newly minted Zhou dynasty—Wu Zhao appointed him official scholar of the Ministry of Rites (Sili boshi 司禮博士). Furthermore, by imperial edict, she requested that he edit official state histories and compile ceremonial regulations on auspicious and inauspicious events. Always seeking to harness such literary gifts, Wu Zhao attached great importance (shenzhong 深重) to Lu Jingchun.[39]

Yoshiko Kamitsuka suggests that the amplification of the cult of Lady Wei in Huaizhou a mere two years before Wu Zhao ascended the dragon throne was part of the "preparatory work" for her rise to become emperor.[40] Yet the content of the Mujian inscription does not exalt Wu Zhao. Her efforts to bring Lu Jingchun into her Luoyang court, employing him among her growing stable of literary masters, suggest she was monitoring rather than patronizing the cult of the Daoist goddess.

Otagi Hajime has remarked on the emergence of Huaizhou as a center for female Daoists. In addition to the cult of Lady Wei revealed in Lu Jingchun's inscription, another stele in Runzhou, erected in 677 for Daoist master Wei of Renjing Abbey, lists 134 Daoist nuns and female adepts among the donors. The surname the Daoist abbot shares with Lady Wei may represent a long-standing Wei family kin connection both to the Daoist faith and to the region.[41]

WU ZHAO, FLOWER MAID, AND THE CULT OF LADY WEI IN FUZHOU

The cult of Lady Wei in Fuzhou (modern-day Jiangxi) has already received close scrutiny from a bevy of scholars. Suzanne Cahill, Yoshikawa Tadao, Edward Schafer, Russell Kirkland, and James Robson, among others, have examined both the rise of the cult of Wei Huacun in Jiangnan and the role in its development of Huang Lingwei 黃靈微 (640–721), also known as Flower Maid (Huagu 花姑), the Daoist priestess who restored Lady Wei's shrine in the late seventh century.[42]

Perhaps the best sources for understanding the connection between the changing status of the cult of Lady Wei during the political ascendancy of female ruler Wu Zhao are a pair of commemorative inscriptions composed by Yan Zhenqing (709–785) while serving as a prefect in Fuzhou. While Song Confucians viewed Yan as a moral pillar whose renowned bold calligraphic strokes reflected his unbending rectitude, later Daoists revered him as a lofty transcendent who had partaken of the nectar of immortality. After serving as a high-ranking court official and becoming embroiled in an intense partisan dispute under Daizong (r. 762–779), Yan was demoted to prefect and sent southward, where he served in a succession of offices.[43] In Fuzhou, a region rich in Daoist lore of spirits, magic swords, and mysterious grottoes, he refurbished the local altar and shrine of Lady Wei and wrote an inscription honoring her.[44] In a second inscription, the prefect commemorated Huang Lingwei, the female adept who had located and restored the same shrine of the Lady Wei seventy-five years earlier.[45] Both inscriptions are preserved in the Complete Anthology of Tang Prose.[46]

While she might be classified as a "medieval renunciant,"[47] Huang Lingwei was not an obscure local figure. Works of later Daoist scholars show that like the goddess whose shrine she restored, she also joined the company of Daoist immortals upon her death.[48]

As in Huaizhou, the cultic site in Fuzhou was connected with a stage of Lady Wei's mortal existence. At some point, either during her southward flight or her late-life peregrinations, Lady Wei settled in Fuzhou and erected an altar, "an out-of-doors precinct for the performance of sacred rites."[49] Yan Zhenqing's inscription exalting Lady Wei reveals that like the Southern Marchmount in Hunan, Fuzhou was a sacred site for the Daoist transcendent, a locale where "the Lady attained a significant stage on her spiritual ascent towards self-realization."[50]

From the overlapping accounts in Yan Zhenqing's two inscriptions and Du Guangting's bibliography, it is possible to reconstruct the efforts of the female Daoist adept Huang Lingwei to locate and restore Lady Wei's altar. Providing a framework to understand the significance of and motivation behind Huang Lingwei's endeavors, Suzanne Cahill has observed that practice of "good works" could help a Daoist subject attain transcendence. Restoring a shrine was a "good work" of the highest order, an act that might "constitute the subject's mature practice and principal contribution to the faith."[51]

In the tenth month of 693, three years into Wu Zhao's Zhou dynasty, with the guidance of a mysterious Daoist master named Hu Chao from neighboring Hongzhou prefecture, Huang Lingwei discovered a lost altar of Wei Huacun in the lush, tangled overgrowth of Dark Tortoise plateau. The altar was located near the remains of a legendary stone tortoise that gave the plateau its name—a chelonian marauder that purportedly had trampled crops until incensed locals lopped off its head. Beneath the altar, Huang Lingwei discovered relics of the Daoist divinity—a votive image, an awl, a knife, an oil vessel, and several dozen lampstands. Thereafter, she repaired the altar.[52]

Though Dark Tortoise plateau was 700 miles from Luoyang, Wu Zhao, known for her intelligence-gathering network, got wind of the exhumed relics. According to Yan Zhenqing's inscription, "When the Celestial Empress[53] heard this, she gathered the relics into her inner quarters."[54] Russell Kirkland observes that "despite the fact she shared Huang's apparent disassociation from the patriarchal tradition," Wu Zhao "neither honored Huang Ling-wei for her achievement, nor favored the shrine with official recognition or economic support." Kirkland attributes that decision to her "highly limited" interest in the matter.[55]

While the female sovereign neither officially recognized Huang Lingwei's restoration of the shrine nor celebrated the cult of Lady Wei, there is another explanation for Wu Zhao's inaction. In other circumstances, given her penchant for grandiose ceremony, for amplifying her sovereignty with symbols or omens, she might well have parlayed these Daoist relics to her political advantage. That Wu Zhao chose to confiscate and conceal the relics was a matter of timing.

As mentioned earlier, Antonino Forte has convincingly illustrated how the *Commentary*, propagated on the eve of the inauguration of Wu Zhao's Zhou dynasty in 690, forwarded evidence that the woman emperor was both a cakravartin and a living bodhisattva.[56] In the fourth month of 691, Wu Zhao formally elevated Buddhism over Daoism.[57] In the second month of 693, Laozi's *Daodejing* was discontinued as an examination text in her court.[58] In the ninth month, just a month prior to the discovery of the

Daoist relics in Fuzhou, Wu Zhao had the seven Buddhist treasures cast and added to her already grand imperial title the designation "Golden Wheel" (Jinlun 金輪)—thereby broadcasting that she was a cakravartin, a wheel-turning universal monarch.[59] Huang Lingwei discovered the relics of Lady Wei in late 693, at the very moment the campaign to project Wu Zhao as a Buddhist sovereign overseeing a far-flung cosmopolitan and international empire reached its crescendo.

While Wu Zhao likely appreciated the potential political utility of this discovery, she downplayed the unearthing of the relics. Ideological machinations, not indifference, underlay her decision to sequester them. Ever the pragmatist, Wu Zhao took the relics into custody, for if the ideological climate changed, she could one day utilize them to her advantage. In addition, her possession of these sacred relics prevented potential rivals and enemies from themselves employing the artifacts as symbols of legitimation.

Had Huang Lingwei unearthed the sacred relics of Lady Wei a decade earlier, Wu Zhao and her opportunistic propagandists might well have, with grand pomp and ceremony, given full play to the latent capacity in Daoism to exalt the female, honoring the Daoist priestess from Fuzhou and elevating Lady Wei still higher among her growing pantheon of Daoist divinities, inviting the Shangqing goddess to share sweet dew with the Queen Mother of the West and Laozi's mother.

Further evidence of Wu Zhao's close attention to the events in Fuzhou in 693 is reflected in her subsequent efforts to seek out and employ Huang Lingwei's mentor, Hu Chao, who had helped reveal Lady Wei's shrine. Several years after confiscating the relics of Lady Wei from Dark Tortoise plateau in Fuzhou, the septuagenarian ruler hired the esoteric master to brew a longevity potion.[60] In 700, he also helped Wu Zhao perform an important Daoist expiatory rite, "tossing the dragons" (tou long 投龍), on Mount Song.[61]

After discovering the altar, Huang Lingwei uncovered several more sacred sites connected with Lady Wei in the region. However, only after the Tang dynasty was restored in 705 did Fuzhou emerge as a court-sanctioned cultic center of Wei Huacun. Unfortunately for Huang Lingwei, she never received her due recognition in her mortal body. Under Ruizong and Xuanzong, Lady Wei's shrine was reconsecrated by male Daoist official Ye Fashan (616–720).[62] Nonetheless, Flower Maid continued to wander the forests and mountains of the region, locating and restoring holy sites, until she rose to join the host of Daoist transcendents in 721. A century after Yan Zhenqing, in a poem to an official in Jiangnan, Buddhist monk Guanxiu (832–912) evoked the Daoist transcendent once more: "The strains of the Flower Maid's flute cause jade to rise up and dance."[63]

CONCLUSION

As Celestial Empress (her title from 674 until Gaozong's death in 683), Wu Zhao enthusiastically patronized Daoism. Yet Lady Wei, one of medieval Daoism's most eminent personages, never seems to have found a niche in Wu Zhao's burgeoning pantheon of female deities. As she and Gaozong wandered the mountains in the vicinity of Luoyang, they did not accord to the Lady of the Southern Marchmount the reverence offered other Daoist goddesses.

As grand dowager, Wu Zhao's patronage for Lady Wei and for Daoism itself was also measured. Though the Mysterious Woman who appeared in Huaizhou in 684 desiring to present refined cinnabar to Grand Dowager Wu may have been the incarnation of Lady Wei, there is no decisive evidence of imperial sponsorship for her cult in the region.

Nor as emperor did Wu Zhao sponsor the emergent cult of Lady Wei. Her extensive campaign to define herself as a Buddhist sovereign dictated her apparent apathy toward the potential political and religious significance of the relics revealed by Huang Lingwei. Accordingly, under Wu Zhao, neither the cultic site at Fuzhou nor the sites in Huaizhou devoted to Lady Wei were imperially sanctioned.

However, the female ruler recruited men involved with each locale into her service, and was keenly aware of both sites. Lu Jingchun, the local literatus who had framed the inscription honoring Lady Wei in Henei, came to Luoyang to serve as an official. Daoist master Hu Chao, after helping Huang Lingwei reveal the hidden shrine in Fuzhou, concocted elixirs of longevity and performed rites of expiation for Wu Zhao. This instrumental utilization of mystic and literary talent reveals an important aspect of the female ruler's renowned political acumen: she was an extraordinary judge of talent.[64] Even Song Confucian Sima Guang grudgingly praised her capacity to recruit capable men, remarking: "She possessed keen oversight and was an excellent judge of character. Therefore, at that time talented and virtuous men competed to be employed by her."[65] A few years before Lu Jingchun composed his shrine inscription, when disgruntled poet-scholar Luo Binwang had written a scathing polemic attacking her character and questioning her legitimacy, reviling her "vulpine glamour," her "ravenous disposition of a jackal or wolf," and her cold-blooded heart that was "half viper and half chameleon,"[66] the grand dowager's wry response was telling: "Ministers, this is your fault! How is it that a man this talented has been cast out and isn't serving in office?"[67]

Rather than allow a literary master like Lu Jingchun to wield the calligraphy brush against her, she sought to employ his talent to armor her authority. Instead of permitting a gifted esoteric mystic like Hu Chao to wander the wilderness revealing sacred shrines and gaining a lofty reputation for his miraculous powers, Wu Zhao sought to bring him into the fold and utilize his unique talents to her own ends.

In sum, there were three major reasons that Lady Wei did not become a major figure in Wu Zhao's pantheon of female divinities. The most significant reason was poor timing: as empress, Wu Zhao "fully supported the T'ang Taoist ideology," but once she founded the Zhou, Charles Benn observes, she "abolished the Taoist ideology of the T'ang and inaugurated her own ideology based on Buddhism.[68] The emergence of the two local cults of Lady Wei coincided with Wu Zhao's aggressive campaign to redefine herself as a Buddhist monarch.

Second, the two local cultic centers of Lady Wei in Huaizhou and Fuzhou did not correspond with Wu Zhao's reorientation of sacred space. As Celestial Empress and Celestial Emperor, Wu Zhao and Gaozong frequently visited Mount Song, not far south of Luoyang. Mount Song emerged as the preeminent marchmount. As grand dowager and emperor, Wu Zhao considered Mount Song an important part of her sacred geography, dwarfing Mount Wangwu to the north. Many imperial clansmen of the Li family who opposed Wu Zhao's ascendancy were tied to Daoist circles in the Huaizhou region.

And finally, many of the other female divinities Wu Zhao honored were associated with motherhood and creation. Nüwa created the world. The Queen Mother of the West lived on the highest mountain peak and was foremost among female Daoist deities. Mother Li birthed Lord Lao, the Daoist founder and deity. Jiang Yuan begat the Ji clan that founded the Zhou. While she was a divine teacher capable of bestowing esoteric revelations,

Wei Huacun was not a creatress.[69] She was not a mother goddess. She did not give birth to an ancient line of rulers whose very name resonated with political legitimacy. She was not royalty. Geographically, she was more closely connected with Jiangnan and the Southern Marchmount than the heartland: the Yellow and Luo river valleys. Seemingly, therefore, from the vantage of Wu Zhao, the political value of this outsider was limited.

Her handling of Lady Wei's relics serves as a powerful reminder that Wu Zhao was not simply a religious and political gadfly, capriciously flitting among Confucianism, Buddhism, and Daoism. She was a pragmatist, a political animal, reading and purposefully adjusting to shifting ideological terrain.

PART IV

Buddhist Devis and Goddesses

IT IS TEMPTING TO CONSIDER Wu Zhao a Buddhist monarch. Her mother, née Yang, a descendant of the pro-Buddhist Sui imperial family, was a devout believer.[1] After the death of her first husband, Taizong, Wu Zhao spent several years in a Buddhist convent.[2] During the half century of the reign of her husband Gaozong, her tenure as grand dowager, and her Zhou dynasty, more than 1,600 state-sanctioned Buddhist monasteries were established.[3] In 690, shortly after inaugurating the Zhou, Wu Zhao issued an edict formally elevating Buddhism above Daoism.[4] In 692, she placed a Buddhist prohibition on the butchering of animals.[5] As emperor in 694, she transferred supervision of Buddhist rites from the Court of State Ceremonial, which oversaw foreign affairs, to a branch of the Ministry of Rites, which superintended ceremonial matters for Confucianism and Daoism. In doing so, she made official what had long been a reality in China: Buddhism was no longer a foreign faith.[6] Her ardent patronage prompted Chen Jinhua to remark that Wu Zhao's ideological support prompted Chinese Buddhism to undergo "immense and rapid" growth, leading to an "unprecedented climax."[7]

Wu Zhao lavishly patronized Buddhist art, commissioning the creation of many Buddhist sculptures, perhaps best represented at the Longmen caves near her Divine Capital Luoyang and the Dunhuang grottoes on the frontier of her empire.[8] Her "unstinting patronage," Patricia Karetzky remarks, "led to a period of unprecedented creativity in Buddhist art."[9] Luoyang was filled with grand monuments of Buddhist pacifism, like the Axis of the Sky and the firmament-piercing five-story pagoda containing an 880-foot Buddha in her Bright Hall complex.[10]

She supported an esoteric Buddhist cult of Avalokiteśvara (Guanyin 觀音), in which eleven-headed Avalokiteśvara and thousand-armed Avalokiteśvara deployed their far-reaching compassion and magical powers to protect the state. Another manifestation of this bodhisattva was Amoghapāśa, Guanyin of the Unfailing Lasso, who rescued sentient beings with his rope and taught believers prayers that promised health, prosperity, and protection. Amoghapāśa's cult flourished in Wu Zhao's time.[11] The iconographic tradition of the savior bodhisattva Dizang (Sanskrit: Kṣitigharba) also developed dramatically during her half century in power.[12]

Wu Zhao took imperial titles trumpeting grandiose Buddhist majesty, like "Golden Wheel," intimating that she was a cakravartin of the highest order,[13] or "Maitreya" (Cishi 慈氏), the Buddha of the future, a messianic figure.[14] As sovereign, she staged huge communal Buddhist feasts, inviting noble and humble, men and women, young and old.[15] She held relic veneration ceremonies that whipped the masses into a frenzy of devotion.[16] She also set up an inexhaustible storehouse (wujin cang 無盡藏) to invite boundless almsgiving from the faithful, to project the immeasurable power of the Buddha, and to manifest her magnanimity as sovereign.[17]

She brought in a talented multinational team of Buddhist scholars from India, central Asia, and oasis states along the Silk Road to translate Buddhist scripture from Sanskrit into Chinese. Wu Zhao worked closely with the monks of the palace chapel (neidaochang 內道場), giving Buddhist religious leaders access to the innermost corridors of power, the imperial palace.[18] Many of these monks functioned as propagandists, working to support her sovereignty and amplify the Buddhist faith.

Her patronage of Buddhism, reflecting at once fervent piety and elaborate spectacle, prompted one scholar, perhaps the result of his ingesting too much Confucian boilerplate, to harshly rebuke the cruelty, the excess, and the "megalomaniac tastes" evidenced in the lavish Buddhist ornamentation of "usurper Wu."[19]

A great deal of recent scholarship has emphasized the vital role that Buddhism played in legitimizing Wu Zhao's political authority. Chen Yinke argued that Wu Zhao necessarily relied on Buddhism for political sanction, as the Confucian tradition provided her no blueprint for her political legitimation.[20] From its origins, though it was far from egalitarian, Buddhism did not have as many structural and institutional limitations for women as Confucianism. Early Indian Buddhist sutras often contained debates in which clever women bested and rhetorically outflanked men. There is also an androgynous aspect to Buddhism: some texts see Buddhahood as "neither male nor female, beyond gender altogether."[21] Naturally, Wu Zhao availed herself of the ideological space afforded by these blurred gender lines.

In his biography of Wu Zhao, Hu Ji remarks that to validate her position as female ruler, Wu Zhao effectively "utilized the Buddhist canon to fight against the patriarchal impulse—the conception that the 'male is honored and the female denigrated' (nanzun nübei 男尊女卑)—at the core of Confucian ethics."[22] Stanley Weinstein contends that given the inbuilt androcentric nature of Confucianism and the Li family's claimed descent from Laozi, Wu Zhao naturally looked to Buddhism to sanction her political authority, because this ideology alone "had no vested interest in the maintenance of the T'ang."[23]

Richard Guisso maintains that Buddhism, which "permeated the lives of the ordinary people of the T'ang," was a key persuasive element in validating Wu Zhao's sovereignty in the eyes of "the vast majority of the people."[24] Similarly, Sen Tansen contends that between 685 and 695, Wu Zetian secured critical support from Buddhist clergy to legitimize her authority and her formal role as "emperor" of China.[25]

Nonetheless, Wu Zhao's construction of political and ideological authority was necessarily pluralistic and multivalent, reflecting the constituencies within her empire and the complex cosmopolitanism of her age.[26] Immediately after cataloging Wu Zhao's efforts to define herself as a Buddhist sovereign in their biography of the female ruler, coauthors Wang Shuanghuai and Zhao Wenrun remark: "Wu Zetian's utilization of Confucianism, Buddhism, and Daoism all stemmed from a singular motivation: to buttress her authority through propagating the legitimate position of her Zhou dynasty, instilling a social consciousness and moral standard compatible with her rulership, and stabilizing the social order."[27] While Buddhism certainly played a key role in Wu Zhao's sovereignty, her gender and the resultant fragile nature of her power forced her to utilize language and ideology in a uniquely inventive fashion.

Given Wu Zhao's vast support and sponsorship of the Buddhist faith, one would expect to find her pantheon of female political ancestors populated by an array of Buddhist goddesses. There are several good reasons for the relative scarcity of such divinities. First, Buddhism was neither egalitarian nor free of patriarchal influence. Within the Buddhist faith, limitations bound women in the *sangha* (the monastic community) and the lay community alike. Buddhist nuns were subjected to different, more stringent rules of ordination than monks, creating a "fundamental asymmetry" between the sexes, making them a "second order."[28] Second, if one were to seek out or recruit eminent Buddhist goddesses and past female exemplars to develop a tradition of illustrious ancestresses, the seeker might be hard-pressed to discover in Buddhist scripture any women or goddesses readily adaptable for religious emulation in China. Few of those women who appeared had gained any deep or lasting cultural purchase in China. In the Central Kingdom, Queen Śrīmālā would never be a household name like the Queen Mother of the West or the mother of Mencius.[29]

Undeterred, Wu Zhao creatively linked herself and her rulership with several Buddhist devis and goddesses. Just as she had associated her person and her rule with mother divinities from Confucianism and Daoism, she connected herself to the mother of the historical Buddha, Māyā. Also, in her effort to complement the dynastic ancestresses, exemplary mothers, and Daoist goddesses with a powerful Buddhist devi of commensurate magnitude, one worthy of her own elevated status as emperor, Wu Zhao worked with a talented stable of Buddhist propagandists to draw connections to Vimalaprabhā, a bodhisattva-goddess of pure light.[30]

ELEVEN

Dharma Echoes of Mother Māyā in Wu Zhao

MOTHERS AND MOTHERHOOD, as we have seen, played a crucial role in the construction of Wu Zhao's pantheon of political ancestors and in the development of her political persona. Wu Zhao discovered in Nüwa, Laozi's mother, and the mother of Mencius powerful ancestresses who exerted an enduring cultural moment, and accordingly, with rhetorical and poetic panache, she cloaked herself in their several guises. Not surprisingly Māyā (Moye 摩耶), also known as Great Māyā (Mohe Moye 摩訶摩耶) or Pure Wonder (Jingmiao 淨妙), the mother of the Buddha, joined these other mother goddesses and exemplary mortal mothers.

With a small "m," *māyā* has traditionally been translated as "illusion." Victor Mair, in his investigation of the transformative impact that Buddhism exerted on Chinese thought and literature in the early Tang, has shown that *māyā*, while containing intimations of ruse and subterfuge, is vested with a potent demiurgic energy connected to magic, power, and creation.[1] Certainly, some of this mystical creative energy clings to the mother divinity Māyā with her capital "M."

A noble of the Devadaha kingdom in modern-day Nepal, Māyā married king Śuddhodana (also known as King Baijing or King Jingfan) of the Shakya clan, ruler of a small kingdom in northern India and southern Nepal. Legend has it that after twenty childless years, Queen Māyā was transported in a dream to a Himalayan lake. There she was bathed and perfumed by devis, and a rider atop a white, six-tusked elephant circled her three times. The supernal elephant then implanted the future Buddha in her womb. From her dream, Māyā awakened pregnant, and eventually, in Lumbini (southern Nepal), she gave birth through her right flank to a

Figure 11.1 En route to implanting himself through Māyā's flank, the Buddha descends from the heavens on a supernal elephant. Early Tang image from cave 329 of the Mogao grottoes at Dunhuang.

prodigy destined for greatness. A week afterward she died and ascended to become a divinity in her own right.[2]

According to *Sutra of Great Māyā*, translated into Chinese by Tanjing in the late fifth century, when the Buddha experienced his *paranirvāṇa* (his final death and release from the cycle of suffering), the divine Māyā, utterly distraught, descended to earth to lament his passing. In one last miraculous act, before his funeral procession and cremation, the Buddha rose and uttered to her words of consolation.[3] This marked a distinctively Chinese iconographic and textual transposition: Māyā eclipsed the Buddha's senior disciple Kasyapa as the chief mourner. After attaining enlightenment, the Buddha paid a three-month visit to his deceased mother, illustrating both his filial devotion and tremendous supernatural powers.[4]

This scene became a recurring motif in Chinese Buddhist art, notably during Wu Zhao's time.

In the *Flower Garland Sutra*, Māyā also appears as one of the fifty-three Buddhist mentors who guide pupil-protagonist Sudhana on the path to Buddhist goodness and truth. In this text, as a virtuous teacher possessing great determination, wisdom, and supernatural powers, she is described as the "mother of all bodhisattvas" (*zhu pusa mu* 諸菩薩母).[5] Māyā was not just the Buddha's mother; she was also a Buddhist divinity and sage. In drawing on the ideological currency vested in this mother-teacher-goddess, Wu Zhao availed herself of each of these offices.

ARTISTIC AND SCRIPTURAL INTEGRATION OF MĀYĀ INTO THE CHINESE BUDDHIST TRADITION

Part of an iconographic tradition with roots in first-century B.C. India, visual representations of Māyā's divine conception and the birth of Buddha appear in China as early as the second century A.D.[6] In the funerary art of a late Eastern Han tomb, among the series of auspicious omens, a depiction of an immortal astride a white elephant was included with the *qilin* and phoenixes.[7]

Stone carvings from the fifth and sixth century provide further evidence. The sides of the stupa pillar in one of the Yungang caves feature scenes of the Buddha's life, including his divine birth.[8] A stele dating to 525 from Xingyang, between Luoyang and Zhengzhou, contains an image of Māyā birthing the Buddha from her left armpit.[9] Several late Northern Wei steles feature pictorial narratives of the Buddha's life, including images of the white elephant's visitation of Māyā and her abnormal lateral birthing—the "celebrated nativity scene."[10] By the Tang, the day of the Buddha's birth was celebrated as a festival.

Between visual and textual representations, the name and story of Māyā became a part of Chinese Buddhist culture. Tanjing's *Sutra of Great Māyā* related the dream visitation of the elephant and Māyā's pure birth of the Buddha. On the façade of a cave temple at Baoshan (in modern-day Henan), an inscription dating to the late sixth century cites the sutra, still well-known in Wu Zhao's time.[11] In his catalog of Buddhist sutras completed during the Two Sages' reign in 664, Buddhist chronicler Daoxuan listed several versions of the text.[12] It was also recorded in the

Great Zhou Catalog of Buddhist Scriptures, compiled at Wu Zhao's imperial behest in 695.[13]

In a sense, the white elephant became a symbol not only of Māyā and the conception of the Buddha but of the powerful grasp of Buddhism. In 509, when dowager empress Hu (d. 528) dominated the Wei court in Luoyang, the Buddhist state of Gandhāra offered the Northern Wei a white elephant as tribute. Mounted atop the regally caparisoned pachyderm was a Seven Treasures palanquin with a five-colored canopy door. Unfortunately, the elephant did not take well to the new burden and ran amok, destroying houses, uprooting trees, and smashing down walls—an unforeseen turn of events that terrified the local populace. Dowager empress Hu sequestered the harried behemoth in a section of the city that became known as White Elephant Ward.[14]

Māyā is also found in many early Daoist texts. In a fragment of a Daoist text from the fifth century or earlier, *Inner Chapters of Mystery and Wonder* (Xuanmiao neipian 玄妙內篇), sage-divinity Laozi entered the mouth of an Indian queen, Qingmiao 清妙 (Pure Wonder)—whose name closely echoed Māyā's Chinese name Jingmiao, and was born from her armpit on the fourth day of the eighth month, the Buddha's birthday.[15] In the mid-fifth-century Daoist *Book of the Inner Exegesis of the Three Heavens* (Santian neijie jing 三天內解經), Laozi commanded Daoist mystic Yin Xi to transform into a white elephant and then into a yellow sparrow that flew into Qingmiao's mouth and became the body of the Buddha.[16] "Wonder" (*miao* 妙) was a powerful attribute. The name of the mother of the historical Buddha, Māyā, is sometimes transcribed in Chinese with the same *miao* 妙 used in the name of the Indian queen. These sources reflect a Daoist effort to co-opt the birth story of its ideological rival, Buddhism, and provide a strong indication of Māyā's growing cultural resonance in the centuries leading up to the Tang.

A SILLAN PROTOTYPE? SEONDOK'S MOTHER AS AN EARLY SEVENTH-CENTURY INCARNATION OF MĀYĀ

Queen Seondok 宣德 (r. 632–647), the first female ruler of Silla (57–935), one of the Three Kingdoms of the Korean peninsula, was an ardent champion of the Buddhist faith. The posthumous title she chose for her father, long-ruling Sillan king Jinpyeong 真平王 (r. 579–632), was Clear Purity

(Baijing 白淨; Korean: Baekjeong), an epithet used in the Buddhist canon for the Śākyamuni's father, Śuddhodana. Seondok's mother was known as Lady Māyā, echoing the name of the Buddha's mother.[17] The idea that Seondok was the child of Māyā enhanced her sovereign credibility, even raising the possibility that the Sillan queen was the Buddha incarnate.

Seondok's connection to the blood lineage of the historical Buddha was reinforced by other sources. In the Buddhist history *Omitted Events of the Three Kingdoms Period* (Samguk Yusa 三國遺事), monk-scholar Iryeon (1206–1289) recorded that during Seondok's reign, Buddhist pilgrim Jajang traveled to Mount Wutai and encountered there an incarnation of the bodhisattva Mañjuśrī. The bodhisattva said, "As your nation's sovereign is a member of India's Kshatriya (Chinese: *chali* 刹利) class, she already received a prophecy (Chinese: *shouji* 授記) from the Buddha."[18] If not tantamount to the brazen claim to be Buddha incarnate, it at the least implied that Seondok "was descended from the royal Śākya clan."[19]

Wu Zhao was aware of this female Buddhist ruler from Silla. During Seondok's reign, when Wu Zhao was a young Talent in the imperial seraglio, the Sillan ruler frequently sent embassies to Taizong's court seeking a military alliance against threats from Koguryo and Paekche.[20]

WU ZHAO'S ROLE AS EMPRESS: BUDDHIST MOTHERHOOD

In the early 660s, when Wu Zhao and Gaozong coruled as the Two Sages, a Buddhist monk named Yuanze, from Tiangong Temple in Luozhou (in the precincts of then Eastern Capital Luoyang), wrote the *Preface to the Former Collection of Miraculous Records of the Forest of Zen* (Chanlin miaoji qianji xu 禪林妙記前集序). In this introduction, Yuanze related the familiar story of the Buddha's descent astride the white elephant, where he entered his mother's right side. Of this miraculous conception, a Brahman immortal prognosticated, "Your dream is clear as sunlight: you will give birth to a king. You dreamt of a white elephant, and will certainly bear a sage son." Thereafter, a changed Māyā grew more tranquil and compassionate by the day.[21]

Wu Zhao's motherhood was clearly connected to the Buddhist establishment. When her eldest son Li Hong became ill in 656, shortly after her ascent to empress, she and Gaozong prayed to the compassionate Buddha for his deliverance. When the child recovered, they built an ornate complex, the Temple of Western Light (Ximingsi 西明寺) to express their gratitude.[22] When their second son was born, famous Buddhist pilgrim Xuanzang ceremonially took him as a disciple and bestowed the title Prince of Buddha Light (Foguang wang 佛光王) upon the child.[23] In 662, when Wu Zhao gave birth to Li Dan (Ruizong), the last of her four sons, she placed a jade guardian Buddha in his nursery.[24]

MĀYĀ AND WU ZHAO AS RULER

Return of the White Elephant

Elephants were sacrosanct in early and medieval Asia, a multivalent symbol of strength, auspiciousness, wisdom, peace, and prosperity.[25] From the earliest lore in the Hindu classics, elephants, particularly white elephants, were mounts for gods and kings.[26] During the reigns of Gaozong and Wu Zhao, seven of the thirteen tributary embassies from Linyi (modern-day southern Vietnam) presented elephants.[27] At the Two Sages' court in 672, an emissary from a small state in Southeast Asia reported that when the ivories of a certain four-tusked elephant were cleansed, the salubrious wash water possessed the power to heal sickness and cure disease.[28] As emperor, Wu Zhao set up six palace corrals where huge elephants were stabled.[29]

Even after Wu Zhao inaugurated the Zhou dynasty and proclaimed herself emperor, she symbolically maintained ties with Māyā. On 5 October 693, Wu Zhao's nephew, Wu Chengsi, led five thousand people in requesting that Wu Zhao append an exalted Buddhist title, Cakravartin of the Golden Wheel (*jinlun* 金輪), to her already grand designation, Sagely and Divine Emperor.[30] Eight days later, Wu Zhao formally added the title and arrayed the seven Buddhist treasures (*qi bao* 七寶)—the golden wheel, the white elephant (*bai xiang* 白象), the woman, the horse, the pearl, the military official, and the hidden official—for her entire court to see.[31]

Of these treasures, the white elephant, a symbol of the Buddha's miraculous conception, was listed second only to the golden wheel of the cakravartin. The elephant's importance is made manifest yet again in the Preface to the *Great Zhou Catalog of Buddhist Scriptures*, completed in 695 by some of Wu Zhao's chief Buddhist propagandists. There, amid the copious praise for their ruler, is written:

She descended to be born, riding on her original vow; she greatly gives succor, pouring forth her great compassion. The Golden Wheel while ascending turns, and she governs and bends the Four Continents; the Precious Elephant (baoxiang 寶象) goes in flight, and she resounds and spreads in the Eight Extremities.[32]

Like the golden wheel, the elephant was a powerful symbol of sovereignty. The treasure served as a symbolic instrument to extend the reach of Wu Zhao's political and ideological authority. The flight of the precious elephant recalls the white elephant's original descent to earth—the Buddha's vehicle to his own conception.

The white elephant appeared yet again, not merely as a symbol of Buddhist authority on display for the court but in the tangible flesh-and-blood form of a powerful pachyderm striding down the main avenue of Luoyang. In the fourth lunar month of 697, after several years of design, craftsmanship, and casting, the monumental Nine Tripods (Jiu ding), a potent traditional symbol of a ruler's legitimacy and virtue,[33] were set before Wu Zhao's recently completed ritual and administrative center, Communing with Heaven Palace (Tongtiangong 通天宮). To array the bronze tripods in their requisite spaces, prime ministers and nobles led a procession of more than 100,000, including a martial force in full regalia. In the midst of this spectacular parade before the awestruck populace, a white elephant and great oxen dragged the giant vessels, aided by human pullers who chanted a "Tripod-Dragging Anthem" composed by Wu Zhao, as they heaved.[34]

The anthem, inscribed on the eighteen-foot-tall central tripod, traced the proud and familiar lineage of male political ancestors at the heart of Chinese tradition:

Fuxi and Shennong first emerged,
The Yellow Emperor and Hao acted in timely fashion;
Yao and Shun followed in their footsteps,
Tang and Yu availed themselves of the times.
The empire was enlightened and populated,
Within the seas there was harmony and peace;
From distant antiquity heaven has sent a mirror,
Squarely to fix an exalted foundation.[35]

In conjunction with her installation of the tripods, this paean helped to situate Wu Zhao as the present-day counterpart to this ancient genealogy. Several millennia had elapsed since the remote era of these sage-kings. Antonino Forte has shown that Communing with Heaven Palace was an ideological amalgam: a Buddhist pagoda set atop a Confucian administrative hall.[36] I have also argued elsewhere that "closer analysis of the personnel she [Wu Zhao] put in charge of the production process [of the tripods], the religio-political circumstances surrounding the erection of Communing with Heaven Palace, and the evolving nature of the tripods' use" all indicate a strong Buddhist imprint on Wu Zhao's vessels.[37] And, of course, the white elephant at the forefront of the parade evoked Māyā's dream (and the Buddha's divine conception), helping lend a Buddhist aura to the festive spectacle.

White elephants were a precious rarity. In the *Tang Administrative and Legal Compendium of the Six Ministries*, an institutional history compiled under Xuanzong thirty years after Wu Zhao's death, white elephants are placed alongside dragons and phoenixes in the category of "greatly auspicious" omens warranting the congratulations of the entire court.[38] Tang histories reveal that these prized white elephants came from faraway Persia, from the remote country of Tanling in the southern seas, and from Piao (modern-day Burma).[39] The tripod-pulling elephants likely came from Piao, where the white elephants were reputed to stand one hundred *chi* (roughly 100 feet) tall.[40]

Textual Amplification

Between 695 and 699, Khotanese Śikṣānanda (Shichanantuo 實叉難陀, 652–710), South Indian Bodhiruci (Putiliuzhi 菩提流支, d. 627), Sogdian Fazang (643–712) and other Buddhist monks translated a huge volume of Buddhist scripture, including a new eighty-chapter version of the *Flower Garland Sutra*.[41] When it was completed in late 699, Emperor Wu Zhao personally composed the preface.[42] One passage from this new rendition reads:

> Lady Māyā, her prestige and virtue singularly remarkable, sends forth light from every pore, illuminating countless worlds. There are no obstructions, so that everything is brilliantly illuminated and nothing remains unseen. She eliminates all the vexation and distress. . . . Within

her stomach are all the manifestations of three thousand worlds. Among the countless Jambudvīpas contained within are capitals and settlements, each containing gardens and forests, all with different names.[43]

It is tempting to suggest that the translators made a directed effort to link Wu Zhao's penchant for luminous imagery to the powerful image of radiant, all-encompassing Māyā conjured in the above passage.

In 703, eight years after the famous pilgrim Yijing (635–713) was warmly welcomed to Wu Zhao's court after a quarter century of wandering the Buddhist world, he presented his translation of the fifty-chapter *Mūlasarvāstivāda Vinaya*, a work originally written in India in the second century A.D. Far from being reform minded (in this work and others on the Vinaya, the rules of conduct for Buddhist monks and nuns), Yijing sought to restore old school, "unspoilt" Indian rigidity in both external (sartorial rules) and internal (moral conduct) domains to combat the slackening of Buddhist discipline in China. Particularly strict were the regulations for Buddhist nuns. Like their Indian counterparts of old, they were forbidden to bathe naked and had to wear more layers of robes (five) than monks (three).[44] Yijing perhaps seems an unlikely candidate to advocate the power of a female ruler.

However, in all of his many translated Vinaya manuals, Yijing upheld "thrice purified" (*sanjing* 三净)[45] Māyā as a scintillating paragon of womanly virtue and a perfect model for nuns to emulate. An epic annunciation of Māyā's divine conception and birth of the Buddha is contained in the preface to Yijing's *Mūlasarvāstivāda Vinaya*:

> Sleeping, Lady Māyā dreamed that a six-tusked white elephant descended into her stomach. At that time, the vast earth was riven with six types of tremors and quakes, giving forth a great brilliant illumination that filled the entire world. All of the dark and gloomy recesses in the world, those that even the awesome light of the sun and moon couldn't penetrate, became plainly visible. . . . And when the Buddha was born, the great earth quaked emitting brilliant luminosity everywhere.[46]

In Yijing's preface, both conception and birth are stupendous events casting immeasurable pure light everywhere. In the opening chapter of *Matters of Renunciation in the Mūlasarvāstivāda Vinaya*, Māyā, also called "divine mother" (*shenmu* 神母), has a version of the familiar "greatly auspicious" (*da ji* 大吉) dream in which the Buddha rides the elephant to enter her womb. As before, the blinding, demiurgic light irradiates, "exceeding that of the solar and lunar wheels, reaching up to the Trāyastiṃśa [Thirty-third] Heaven."[47] Yijing's *Miscellany from the Mūlasarvāstivāda Vinaya* also contains a comparable passage in which Māyā shines far brighter than either of the celestial bodies, male sun or female moon.[48]

To the Buddhist faithful, the earth-sundering, light-emitting paroxysms accompanying Māyā's dream conception likely recalled a happening in 686 that played a significant role in Buddhist propaganda, helping justify Wu Zhao's ascent to emperor and establish her Zhou dynasty—the violent terrestrial upheaval that gave rise to Mount Felicity (Qingshan 慶山).[49] This event, which many in the court saw as a fell sign that the Five Elements were drastically out of kilter because the grand dowager was presiding over the court, is described vividly in Ouyang Xiu's *New Tang History*: "Amidst great wind and rain, thunder and lightning, a mountain burst forth 200 *zhang* [1617 feet] tall."[50] Forte has shown that this event played an important role in two vital pieces of Buddhist propaganda—the *Commentary on the Great Cloud Sutra* in 690 and an interpolated version of the *Rain of Jewels* sutra. In both texts, the emergence of Mount Felicity is interpreted as evidence that Wu Zhao was the being designated in the Buddha's prophecy that a cakravartin and a living bodhisattva in a female body would rule China.[51]

The *Mūlasarvāstivāda Vinaya* also associates Māyā's conception and the Buddha's birth with immeasurable, far-reaching radiance. Wu Zhao invented her own image as a light bringer in similar, scintillating fashion. In an inscription Li Qiao composed in 699, the female sovereign's grandmother, while praying at a riverside shrine, discovered a small stone the size of a swallow's egg inscribed with purple characters for sun and moon; she swallowed the stone and became pregnant with Wu Shiyue, Wu Zhao's father.[52] Twinned celestial spheres also radiate prominently from Wu Zhao's chosen Zhao 曌, an invented character that featured the sun and moon presiding over the void, illuminating all.[53] The reach of this refulgent light was, of course, a metaphor for the limitless extent of her political authority.

To better apprehend the resonance of Māyā worship during Wu Zhao's reign, it is important to revisit one of the terms mentioned in Yijing's rules for Buddhist nuns: "divine mother" (*shenmu* 神母).[54] In common usage long before the Tang, "divine mother" was a fairly standard term for Māyā, appearing more than one hundred times in the Chinese Buddhist canon. It is used most frequently in the phrase "descended into the divine mother's womb" (*jiang shenmu tai* 降神母胎). Māyā's divinity is tied to her mother-hood, and to the birth of her celebrated son.

"Divine Mother" also appears in Śikṣānanda's *Flower Garland Sutra*[55] and in a biography of Buddhist pilgrim Sanzang compiled in 688, when Wu Zhao was grand dowager.[56] Noting Wu Zhao's ties in dharma and blood with the Sui imperial Yang family, Chen Jinhua has observed that the title of the nun-guardian of Sui Yangdi's son Yang Jian, Zhixian, Divine Mother, was closely echoed in Wu Zhao's 688 title "Sage Mother, Divine Sovereign."[57]

Beginning when Indian monk Jñānagupta (She'najueduo 闍那崛多) coined the term while translating the *Sutra on the Collection of the Buddha's Original Practices* for the Sui imperial family, some Buddhist texts use "sage mother" (*shengmu* 聖母) rather than "divine mother" for Māyā.[58] In the hundred chapter *Pearl Forests of the Dharma Garden*, completed by Daoshi in 668, when Wu Zhao was known as one of the Two Sages, Māyā is called "sage mother."[59] The *Lalitavistara Sutra*, translated by Indian monk Divākara when Wu Zhao was grand dowager, also used "sage mother" for Māyā.[60]

MĀYĀ, THE PARANIRVĀṆA, AND WU ZHAO

Around the time the *Sutra of Great Māyā* was translated into Chinese, scenes involving Māyā's role in her son's paranirvāṇa began to appear in Chinese Buddhist art. On a stele dated 471, now housed in the Shaanxi Provincial Museum in Xi'an, there is a series of six scenes from a nativity cycle, includ-ing what Patricia Karetzky describes as "the conception which shows Maya sleeping in a Chinese-style house with the disc ensconced elephant above her"; and another of "the birth with the child emerging from the capacious sleeve of Maya's Chinese robe."[61] Some scholars have argued that the Māyā in cave 5 of the Xiangtangshan site in Henan represents onetime empress and grand dowager Li Zu'e (c. 550s), who had lost two sons and a daughter in the cutthroat Northern Qi court of the mid-sixth century.[62] Māyā began to take the shape of a Chinese queen.

A stele in Yishi (in modern-day southwestern Shanxi not far from Taiyuan) features a four-panel depiction of the Buddha's *paranirvāṇa*. In bas-relief, Māyā is depicted in the first two, first lamenting over her son's closed coffin and then hearing the Buddha's miraculous last words of comfort. Erected in 692, this plinth bears the inscription: "Stele with Scenes of the Paranirvāṇa Reverently Erected at the Great Cloud Temple of the Great Zhou Dynasty on Behalf of the Sagely and Divine Emperor."[63] The stele marked the local fulfillment of Wu Zhao's imperial order on 5 December 690, that Great Cloud temples be founded in every prefecture.[64] The choice to showcase Māyā and feature the Buddha's paranirvāṇa on this stele honoring the newly minted female ruler was decidedly strategic.[65]

The paranirvāṇa scene in the fresco in cave 146 of the Mogao grottoes at Dunhuang, dating from the same period as the Great Cloud Temple stele, features the miraculously risen Śākyamuni and mother Māyā who, in the description of art historian Alexander Soper, is depicted as a Chinese queen.[66]

Buddhism did not exist on a textual level alone. In both popular and elite traditions, the wide circulation and visibility of Māyā images helped her cult proliferate. Pervasive in Wu Zhao's time, such images were an important vehicle to project the miraculous power of the Buddha and his mother, stoking the ardor of the faithful.

GROTTO OF THE BUDDHA'S MOTHER ON MOUNT WUTAI

One of the four sacred Buddhist mountains, Wutai, the Mount of Five Terraces in Shanxi, was a hub of religious activity during the early Tang. Given its distinctive shape, Wutai neatly fit the description of the five-peaked mount in Mahācīna (great China) where the Buddha had prophesied the appearance of Mañjuśrī (Wenshu 文殊), the bodhisattva of transcendent wisdom.[67] On Wutai, rulers encouraged construction of temples and pagodas; pilgrims flocked to sacred sites. In 660, the Two Sages ordered the refurbishing of temples on Wutai.[68] That same year, the corulers traveled northward to Wu Zhao's ancestral home in Bingzhou, not far south of the mountain, where she bestowed silks upon local officials and elders and invited their wives to her private quarters in the temporary palace.[69] The sanctification of Wu Zhao's hometown coincided with an effort to upgrade the temples and monasteries on Mount Wutai. In 676, eminent Kashmiri monk Buddhapālita (Fotuopoli 佛陀波利) traveled to the mountain seeking Mañjuśrī. He encountered a venerable old man, who bade him return to the mountain with the Dhāraṇī Sūtra of the Buddha's Crowning Victory. Seven years later, Buddhapālita presented this sutra to Wu Zhao and Gaozong.[70]

High up on the southern peak of Wutai, a mountain exalted by Wu Zhao, there is a unique limestone cave called "grotto of the Buddha's mother" (Fomu dong 佛母洞). A well-lit outer chamber constricts to a narrow, polished channel that leads into the inner chamber, the dark womb. It is believed that those who crawl in through the aperture can emerge reborn, cleansed of their sins. Isabelle Charleux describes the unique cave and the curious associated rite:

> The door leading to the cave is shaped like a *yoni*. Within the cave there is an outer chamber with a high ceiling, followed by a narrower chamber and a one-way narrow corridor (5–6 meters long, 30–40 cm. large) leading to a third small chamber allowing room for two people to stand. A monk, nicknamed "the midwife," assists the pilgrims and advises them how to crawl in. Inside, the pilgrims are informed that they are within the womb of the Mother of Buddhas; and when they come out they are told that they have been reborn. They must pay a fee to enter the narrow passage, and an additional fee for "ransom" to leave the grotto.[71]

ANOTHER MANIFESTATION OF MĀYĀ
IN THE DECADES AFTER WU ZHAO

There is evidence that other noblewomen in the Tang drew on the charisma of the devi Māyā. Recalling the propitious day of the famous emperor Xuanzong's birth, mid-Tang poet-courtier Gu Kuang (725–814) composed a "Song for the Fifth Day of the Eighth Month":

> On the fourth day of the eighth month, a brilliant star came out,
> as Māyā bore into this world the Buddha;
> On the fifth day of the eighth month, auspicious ethers rose anew,
> when the Luminous and Successful grand dowager gave birth to
> a sage son.[72]

This was likely written early in Gu Kuang's career, during the reign of Xuanzong. "Luminous and successful" was part of the posthumous title of Xuanzong's mother, Consort Dou (d. 693), the spouse of Ruizong. She gave birth to Xuanzong on the fifth day of the eighth month of 685.[73] Even Xuanzong, who had an ambivalent, and at times adversarial, relationship with the Buddhist establishment, would like to hear verse in which his mother and the mother of the Buddha were uttered in the same breath.[74]

CONCLUSION

Queen Māyā played a substantial role in the ornate construction of Wu Zhao's political authority. The female ruler honored the Buddha's mother—often, if obliquely—so that the mother-sage-goddess from Nepal 1,200 years past became a part of her pantheon. Like many other aspects of the Buddhist faith that reached Tang China via the oasis states of the Silk Road, Māyā became a shared component of a pan-Asian culture, a celebrated mother honored across all Buddhist Asia.

As empress, Wu Zhao utilized idealized images of motherhood and maternity associated with Māyā to depict herself as a latter-day "Buddha mother" (*fomu* 佛母), one deeply concerned with her children's well-being. In Buddhist art, scenes of the Buddha's conception, birth, and *paranirvāṇa* were familiar motifs, images that often served to magnify Wu Zhao's ideological profile. Symbols from Māyā's life, like the iconic white elephant, became central emblems in Wu Zhao's court. And finally, to illuminate the majesty of their sovereign, Wu Zhao's capable propagandists borrowed the rhetorical language used in Buddhist scripture to celebrate the incandescent Māyā.

TWELVE

Bodhisattva with a Female Body

Wu Zhao and Devi Jingguang

PERHAPS NO SINGLE PIECE OF propaganda was more important to Wu Zhao's attainment of emperorship than a Buddhist text, the *Commentary on the Meanings of the Prophecies About the Divine Sovereign in the Great Cloud Sutra* (Dayunjing shenhuang shouji yishu 大雲經神皇授記義疏; hereafter *Commentary*). Propagated on the eve of her accession to the dragon throne in 690, this four-fascicle text explicated a series of prophecies that helped to legitimize the inauguration of Wu Zhao's Zhou dynasty. This elaborate, well-orchestrated collective effort on the part of Wu Zhao and her Buddhist propagandists introduced a new figure to her pantheon of female political ancestors, the Devi of Pure Radiance (Jingguang tiannü 淨光天女; Sanskrit: Vimalaprabhā).

THE *GREAT CLOUD SUTRA*, THE *COMMENTARY*, AND THE DEVI

This chapter owes a profound debt to Antonino Forte, whose meticulous work, *Political Propaganda and Ideology in China at the End of the Seventh Century*, illustrated how the *Commentary* forwarded proofs that Wu Zhao was both a Buddhist monarch and a bodhisattva. Collaboratively composed by Wu Zhao's notorious monk-lover Xue Huaiyi (d. 695) and nine orthodox Buddhist monks working at the palace chapel in Luoyang, and circulated on the eve of Wu Zhao's accession to emperor, the *Commentary* was masterful propaganda abounding in prophecies that foretold the inevitability of her ascent.[1] Acknowledging the efficacy of such Buddhist auguries, Jacques

Gernet observes, "The role of prophecies in the accession of Wu Tse-t'ien is amply known. This form of propaganda, practiced by Buddhist monks, was plainly very effective."[2] The *Commentary* played just such a critical role in Wu Zhao's campaign for emperorship, then reaching its crescendo in the autumn of 690.

Translated into Chinese from an earlier Sanskrit version in the late fourth or early fifth century, the original *Great Cloud Sutra* (Dayunjing 大雲經; Sanskrit: Mahāmegha sutra) was by Wu Zhao's time an accepted part of the Buddhist canon.[3] "Great Cloud" was both the name of bodhisattva Mahāmegha (along with legendary Indian sovereign Aśoka, one of the great preachers who helped propagate the Buddhist faith) and a metaphor for the all-encompassing, far-reaching power of Buddhism.[4] The reason Wu Zhao and her Buddhist supporters were so irresistibly drawn to this sutra was simple: the fourth fascicle contains a conversation between the Buddha and devi Jingguang, Pure Radiance, a goddess the Buddha predicted would descend to the mortal world and become a powerful monarch, a bodhisattva with the body of a woman, and a great champion of the Buddhist faith.[5] According to the Buddha's pronouncement, this devi was the incarnation of a queen Hufa, protector of Buddhist law, and she would be reborn in the future as another earthbound queen, Zengzhang 增長.[6] In short, contained in the *Great Cloud Sutra* there was a lineage of female Buddhist political ancestors who moved fluidly between earthly and divine realms, a line connected not by blood but by a canonical prophecy and shared, ardent devotion.

Availing themselves of the correspondence between Wu Zhao's ascendancy and the Buddha's prediction, the Buddhist propagandists constructed a text substantiating clauses lifted from the original *Great Cloud Sutra* with fragments from other texts and miraculous events to form a catalog of prophecies foretelling their female sovereign's imminent emergence as an earthly sovereign, while also identifying her as the predicted incarnation of the Devi of Pure Radiance. Her reign, the Buddha claimed, would be a perfect era of greater peace without distress or disease during which all in the vast empire would voluntarily convert to the Buddhist faith.[7] To identify Wu Zhao as the chosen one fulfilling the prophecy, the *Commentary* deftly interweaves Buddhist and Daoist works, an array of apocryphal and canonical texts, songs, and legends.

WU ZHAO, THE DEVI, AND THE PROPHECIES

Before the *Commentary* was presented to Wu Zhao, but during the Chuigong reign era (685–688), in the midst of what Forte terms "the *Dayun jing* [Great Cloud Sutra] operation,"[8] a Convent of the Devi (Tiannü nisi 天女尼寺) was established in Luoyang.[9] Forte surmises that the Devi in question was Jingguang.[10]

Presented in 690, the *Commentary* is full of auguries that purport to show that "the *Dayun jing* preached by the Tathāgata pertains fundamentally to Shenhuang,"[11] to the Divine Sovereign, to Wu Zhao. While the Devi of Pure Radiance is a major character, the rhetoricians marshaling proof in the *Commentary* interwove many other pieces of evidence foretelling the advent of a female emperor. From the Daoist *Prophecy of Master Ma of the Central Peak* is cited: "The saintly wife helps the luminous husband and her mercy spreads in all of the earth." Just as Jingguang in the original *Great Cloud Sutra* had once been an earthly queen dutifully assisting her husband, so Wu Zhao had aided Gaozong. This "prophecy"—one of many recent lesser "prophecies" garnered in the *Commentary* to support the Buddha's claim in the *Great Cloud Sutra*—is explained as a prediction that not only anticipated Wu Zhao's support of husband-emperor Gaozong but attested to the boundless reach of her benevolent grace.[12]

In the cryptic *Tiancheng Weft of the Jade Plan of the Lady Ziwei*, composed sometime after 678, Lady Ziwei, apparently a Daoist divinity named after a constellation, similarly foretells Wu Zhao's ascent and the coming of an age of greater peace.[13] One song embedded in the *Commentary* reads, "Her body is formed by the crossing sevens"; the propagandists explicate, "That is the character for woman," suggesting the equation 七 × 七 = 女.[14] employed every available scrap of supporting evidence, including rebuses.

As proof Wu Zhao was the avatar of Vimalaprabhā, the Devi of Pure Radiance, the realization of the Buddha's prophecy, propagandists cite the line in the *Great Cloud Sutra* that maintains "[Jingguang] shall obtain a quarter of the places governed by a cakravartin king" as a clear-cut reference to Wu Zhao. After all, the commentators pointed out, Wu Zhao was currently the de facto ruler.[15]

Among their diverse sources, the exegetes utilized the apocryphal Guangwu inscription, an augural stone reportedly discovered in the Sishui River in Henan in 688, which contained further prophecies of the accession of Wu Zhao.[16] In the enigmatic lines of the stone's inscription— "a person who has the virtue of earth (*tu de* 土德) will reign with maximum prosperity"—they gleaned proofs that Wu Zhao was the female ruler the Buddha had prophesied in the *Great Cloud Sutra*.[17] The "virtue of earth" is associated with the *yin* principle, the female. The opportunistic propagandists even interpreted a reference to a popular song, "Enchanting Miss Wu" (Wu Meiniang 武媚娘). Since the song followed a ditty entitled "Flourishing Tang" (Tangtang 唐唐) that appeared in the Guangwu inscription, the commentators reason that it was "clear that the Divine Sovereign [Wu Zhao] would govern the world," succeeding the first three Tang rulers.[18]

Elsewhere in the original *Great Cloud Sutra*—accentuated in Wu Zhao's *Commentary*—the Buddha claims of the devi that "all the countries of Jambudvipa (Yanfuti 閻浮提)[19] will be obedient to her; there will be none that dare resist or oppose her." Not surprisingly, the commentators find this to tally perfectly with the present atmosphere of Wu Zhao's court:

> This makes it clear that at present the Great Ministers, the Hundred Families, all those who are loyal and sincere, obtain offspring and prosperous years, and have no weaknesses; all are happy, without the sorrows of sickness and calamity. . . . With extraordinary virtue, the Great Sage spread her transformation to all parts of the world. All among the four barbarians will come and submit.[20]

Wu Zhao, as the descended Pure Radiance, presides over a carefree realm, a Buddhist paradise on earth.

In the original *Great Cloud Sutra*, the Buddha tells the devi, "You will destroy or subdue the outer doctrines and the perverse and heretical views." Cleverly, after the fact, Huaiyi and the commentators explained the violent, forcible tonsure of Daoists in 685 as the fulfillment of this prophetic mandate.[21] So, brutal repression was glossed over as the realization of a preordained event.

The Buddha in the *Great Cloud Sutra* considered the devi Jingguang a bodhisattva, a merciful and compassionate being who had fully attained

Buddhist enlightenment, remaining in the suffering world to help liberate other sentient beings from the cycle of birth and rebirth. In the original sutra, the Buddha spells out the prophecy to Jingguang: "You will in reality be a bodhisattva who will display and receive a female body in order to convert beings." To help clarify to court and country why a woman was about to take the throne and to further confirm that Wu Zhao was the devi reincarnate, the helpful commentators remark: "Now, the form that a bodhisattva assumes to benefit beings is not fixed, and he/she answers beings according to their impulses. This is the reason why she now has a female body."[22]

Though the Buddhist faith presented Wu Zhao certain opportunities, she also needed to creatively surmount inherent obstacles. The Five Impediments (*wuzhang* 五障) restricted women from the five highest tiers of political and religious power: being a cakravartin, a god-king, a Brahmā king, a nonregressing (*avaivartika*) bodhisattva, and the Buddha.[23] Blurring and rationalizing Wu Zhao's gender, the *Commentary* helped circumvent these obstacles and justify her ascent to power, defining her (with the Buddha's blessing) as a bodhisattva.

There is another factor to consider. In the early Tang, perhaps influenced by Wu Zhao's political ascendancy and patronage, statuary of bodhisattvas underwent what art historian Patricia Karetzky terms a "process of feminization." The images of the bodhisattva grew more beautiful, their "slender but fleshy body . . . in a graceful, contrapposto pose with protuberant belly, with clinging drapery revealing anatomical forms, and delicate feminine facial features but for the deftly drawn wispy moustache and goatee."[24] Whether Wu Zhao initiated and influenced this trend or merely benefited from it, these androgynous images helped validate her claim.

Elsewhere in the *Commentary*, her rhetoricians revealed the fulfillment of another of the auguries of the Buddha that purportedly presaged Wu Zhao's incarnation as a living bodhisattva. The *Great Cloud Sutra* contains the prophecy that the reborn Vimalaprabhā would "teach and convert the cities and villages" and "observe the Five Precepts." The commentators conclude that as Wu Zhao "teaches and converts men" and "has received and observes the Five Precepts," the Buddha's prediction refers to her.[25]

At the end of the *Commentary*, the propagandists pose three rhetorical questions to confirm their identification of Wu Zhao with Jingguang. The first asks, given the powerful female grand dowagers in Chinese history over the centuries, why the prophecy from the *Great Cloud Sutra* specifically referred to Wu Zhao. Corroborating evidence is provided, much of it drawn from a series of augural stones found in the years immediately preceding the promulgation of the *Commentary*. For instance, the propagandists interpreted the inscription discovered in the Luo River in 688 that read "when the Sage Mother appears among the people, the imperial cause will eternally prosper"[26] in such a way as to validate Wu Zhao as a sovereign in her own right, yet also to portray her as one who had dutifully secured (and would continue to build upon) the foundation established by the first three Tang rulers.[27] Another cryptic augural stone mentioned in the *Commentary* purportedly reads, "Stopping unique woman, good fortune in the ten thousand directions," "a female leader for thousands and thousands," and "my daughter only person for thousands and thousands of years."[28] The commentators assembled such fragments from recently discovered augural stones to advance the proposition that Wu Zhao—not past grand dowagers like Empress Lü of the Western Han or some fortunate dowager-regent in the unforeseen future—was the prophesied one. Commentators also present a revelation inscribed on the prophetic "Diagram Regurgitated by the Dragon" (Longtu tu 龍吐圖). This augural stone foretold the coming of a Mother and Sagely Thearch (Mu sheng di 母聖帝) versed in the Way and preordained to rule. In the supple handiwork of the rhetoricians, it is maintained that this divine mother-ruler is none other than Wu Zhao.

In a text called the *Illustration of Opposing Backs* (Tuibeitu 推背圖), the propagandists located still further revelations. The text mentions a "female leader" who will resuscitate the Tang, "guide and purify the Four Seas," and "put in order and make uniform the Eight Directions." Again the framers of the *Commentary* sought to assuage fears of the Tang dynasts and their allies, claiming that Divine Sovereign Wu Zhao "establishes rightness and revitalizes the saintly action of the imperial family."[29]

Such examples are far from a comprehensive catalog of the evidence mustered by those who compiled the *Commentary*. They set forth many other proofs that identified Wu Zhao as the devi Jingguang incarnate—which was, after all, as Forte puts it, "the raison d'être" of the text.[30] On 17 August 690, a mere two months before she established the Zhou dynasty and declared herself Sagely and Divine Emperor, Wu Zhao issued an edict ordering the dissemination of the *Commentary* throughout the realm.[31] Shortly after she formally took the throne as emperor, Wu Zhao ordered the establishment of a Great Cloud monastery in every prefecture. Buddhist monks were ordered to take to the lectern and to broadcast the revelations to the wider lay community.[32] To get the news out that Wu Zhao was Pure Radiance incarnate, the avatar of Vimalaprabhā, the *Commentary* was trumpeted throughout the empire, to court and country, to *sangha* and lay communities.

ELEVENTH-HOUR PURE LIGHT

The name "Pure Radiance" appears both in the title and text of the one-fascicle *Great Spell of Unsullied Pure Radiance* (Chinese: Wugou Jingguang tuoluoni jing 無垢淨光大陀羅尼經; Sanskrit: Raśmivimalaviśuddhaprabhā-dhāranī).[33] By Wu Zhao's imperial proclamation during her final year in power, Tokharian (from the Tarim Basin in modern-day Xinjiang) monk Mitraśānta translated this sutra from Sanskrit into Chinese.[34] The *Great Spell* promised that if seventy-seven copies were placed in so many miniature pagodas, they could help the believer secure longevity, attain rebirth in paradise, and gain other rewards. Barrett speculates that this dhāranī may have been involved in funeral rites, helping assure the deceased of protection and blessings.[35] Chen Jinhua suggests that Wu Zhao may have offered patronage for translating this spell due to "personal concerns and fears . . . heart-felt repentance for some heinous crimes that she had committed in the course of seizing and solidifying supreme power, her strong desire to lengthen her life and to neutralize all her bad karma in order to escape punishment in the after-life."[36] Mass production of stupas and written spells, just like repetition of Buddha images in temples and grottoes, projected the sacred power of the Buddha and testified to the religo-political authority of the sponsoring ruler. After Wu Zhao's death, the sutra spread rapidly to the Korean peninsula and Japan.[37]

Michael Welch has remarked that "Pure Radiance" (he renders it "Pure Light") in the title of this spell suggests a connection between Wu Zhao and the Devi of Pure Radiance, with whom the sutra shared a name.[38] Curiously, the dhāranī may have come from the beginning rather than the end of Wu Zhao's Zhou dynasty: in *Lives of Eminent Monks*, Song dynasty Buddhist historiographer Zanning dates the *Great Spell of Unsullied Pure Radiance* to her inaugural reign era, Heaven Bestowed, immediately following the *Commentary*'s publicized claim that the female ruler was the prophesied incarnation of the Buddhist goddess.[39] Though there is no explicit

Figure 12.1 Shimmering with beatific radiance, devi Vimalaprabhā may have resembled the apsara in this Dunhuang wall painting. Mid-Tang image from cave 158 of the Mogao grottoes at Dunhuang.

mention of the goddess in the spell, the echo of the devi's name in the title escaped no one.

OTHER TRACES OF PURE RADIANCE

Wu Zhao frequently utilized concepts that had multiple, overlapping layers of meaning. Naturally, she sought to harness the lexical power vested in the name Pure Radiance both to bolster her new dynasty and amplify her sovereignty.

Illuminating Her Personal Name
and Inaugural Reign Era

Both of the components of the name of the devi Vimalaprabhā, purity (*jing* 淨) and radiance (*guang* 光), express positive Buddhist attributes. Du Doucheng notes that the meaning of "pure" (*jing*), approximates the meaning of "empty" (*kong* 空), such as in compounds like "cloudless sky" (*jingkong* 淨空).[40] This emptiness, void, or space corresponds with the bottom half of Wu Zhao's chosen name, Zhao 曌, the invented character that represented her evolved self. Buddhist emptiness is not nothingness—it is limitlessness. To take this a step further, the devi's "radiance" (*guang* 光) is close in meaning to "illumination" (*ming* 明), the top half of Wu Zhao's name. In this sense then, Pure Radiance was vested in her new name Zhao, which was announced on 25 December 689 (part of a larger collection of new characters), shortly before the promulgation of the *Commentary*.[41]

Hu Ji suggests that the name of Wu Zhao's inaugural reign era, Heaven Bestowed (Tianshou 天授), was chosen to succinctly express that she was the "Celestial Devi Bestowed with the Prophecy" (Tiannü shouji 天女授記).[42] A similar rationale underlay the naming of a Buddhist monastery established in Luoyang in the second year of Heaven Bestowed (6 December 690 to 25 November 691), the Monastery of the Buddha's Bestowed Prophecy (Fo shouji si 佛授記寺).[43] At the advent of Wu Zhao's Zhou dynasty, not only was every memorial and commemorative plaque marked with the reign name Heaven Bestowed but the very landscape was studded with monasteries named to remind the faithful and unbelievers alike that the woman emperor was the prophesied avatar descended to earth.

A Poetic Evocation of a Wandering Bard

During the reign of Wu Zhao's grandson Xuanzong, Cui Shu (704–739) composed a poem, "Examining the fire pearl atop the Bright Hall," about the ornamental finial that capped Wu Zhao's administrative and ceremonial center in Luoyang:

> On this central spot stood the many-storied edifice;
> Rising into the void, its crowning fire pearl:
> By night like the full moon's twin,
> By day, a solitary star.
> Making the Heavens so pure (jing 淨) and radiant (guang 光)
>   it is hard to extinguish.
> Clouds emerge gazing the yearning emptiness
> From a distance, I recall an era of greater peace
> A national treasure in this famed capital.[44]

Though Wu Zhao had passed away, Cui Shu, wandering in obscurity near Mount Song,[45] evoked "pure" and "radiant" in connection with her Buddhist-ized ritual center.

A Confucian Connection

Far from Wu Zhao's center of power in Luoyang, in distant Suizhou prefecture (near Suining in modern-day Sichuan), one of her most avid propagandists, Yang Jiong, wrote a stele inscription for the ancestral hall of the local temple of Confucius, including the passage:

> When the Pure and Radiant Child
> descended to wander the old grounds of Ji Dan,[46]
> the supernal phenomena will illumine the numens,
> looking down on the realm of Paoxi 庖犧 below.[47]

A Yuan dynasty (1279–1368) Buddhist work explains that Confucius was known as the Pure and Radiant Child bodhisattva (Jingguang tongzi pusa 淨光童子菩薩).[48] Apparently, from Yang Jiong's inscription, this appellation for the legendary sage was known in Wu Zhao's time. How curious that the title of Confucius should echo that of the Buddhist devi. If Wu Zhao was herself Pure Radiance, it is almost as if the great Eastern Zhou sage were her son, and as though his title were part of a subtle effort to subordinate Confucianism to Buddhism.

Not Enough Room for Two Devis
in this Here Divine Capital

Aware of the lofty reputation of the Buddhists in Henei (northern Henan in modern-day China), sometime prior to 694, Wu Zhao ensconced a venerable Buddhist nun from the region—who called herself the Future (Tathagata) Pure Radiance (Jingguang rulai 淨光如來) and claimed to subsist on a single grain of rice and seed of hemp per day—in Unicorn's Hoof Temple (Linzhi si 麟趾寺) in Luoyang.[49] The vaunted nun claimed to be 500 years old and to have met Wu Zhao's monk-lover Xue Huaiyi two hundred years earlier.[50] Possibly, this opportunistic woman was trying to situate herself as the next incarnation of Vimalaprabhā at a juncture when the female sovereign had begun to identify herself more closely with Maitreya, the future Buddha.

Sima Guang's *Comprehensive Mirror* recorded that by night, along with her band of more than a hundred salacious disciples, this nun would savor extravagant meat dishes to the accompaniment of sultry erotic songs.[51] When the nun failed to predict the conflagration that consumed Wu Zhao's Bright Hall in late 694, Wu Zhao sent her back to Henei in disgrace. When Wu Zhao learned of her excesses, she recalled the nun and made her a palace slave.[52]

LUNAR PURE-RADIANCE: BODHISATTVA IN A FEMALE BODY

Apparently the evidence gathered in the *Commentary* was not sufficient to persuade the Confucian establishment of Wu Zhao's claims to Buddhist legitimation or even to convince the diffuse Buddhist faithful that she was both cakravartin and bodhisattva—transcending her sex and unbound by the restrictions of the Five Impediments. In another instance that makes manifest Wu Zhao's deft circumnavigation of these strictures, her Buddhist supporters retranslated the *Sutra of the Rain of Jewels* (Baoyu jing 寶雨經; *Ratnamegha sutra*), an interpolated rendition of a text that had arrived in China in the sixth century or before.

On 7 October 693, Xue Huaiyi and a multinational coalition of Buddhist monks—including a Sillan royal, central Asian translators, and monks from various parts of India and Uḍḍyāna (Wuchang 烏萇)—presented the *Sutra of the Rain of Jewels* to Wu Zhao.[53] In this version, the Buddha conversed with a light-emanating, cloud-riding divinity named Lunar Radiance (Chinese: Yueguang 月光; Sanskrit: Candraprabha) and prophesied that, during an age in which Buddhist law had fallen, he would be reborn in a female body in Mahācīna (great China). In this calculated forgery, the Buddha tells this prophesied king, "Since in reality you will be a bodhisattva, you will manifest a female body and you will be the sovereign head. . . . Your name will be Lunar Pure-radiance (Yue Jingguang 月淨光)."[54] Forte suggests that the name "Lunar Pure-radiance" was chosen to echo Wu Zhao's established identification as Pure Radiance, "the object of the Buddha's prophecy in the *Commentary*."[55] In the dexterous hands of the propagandists, the considerate Buddha then waives two of the usual Five Impediments, allowing her to become a cakravartin and an avaivartika, a nonbacksliding bodhisattva who goes straight to nirvana despite her female body.[56]

In timely fashion, the *Sutra of the Rain of Jewels* reconfirmed and reemphasized Wu Zhao's identification as a cakravartin and a bodhisattva—this time as the reincarnation of Lunar Pure-radiance, perhaps a cousin to Jingguang. Six days after the presentation of the sutra, Wu Zhao made it official: she took the audacious step she had foregone three years earlier, announcing to the realm that she would add Golden Wheel to her title, thereby formally becoming a cakravartin, a universal monarch holding sovereignty over the four continents of the Buddhist world.[57] Whereas Chinese kingship considered the emperor a sanctioned agent of heaven, in this Buddhist tradition of cakravartin kingship, the emperor was not merely a representative and a political ancestor of divinized culture heroes but an incarnation of Buddhist divinities.[58]

This lineage from the *Sutra of the Rain of Jewels* (male devaputra Yueguang → Yue Jingguang, the bodhisattva with a female body) is not as purely female as the progression (Queen Hufa → Devi Jingguang → Queen Zengzhang/Wu Zhao) advanced in the *Commentary*. As the propagandists framing the *Commentary* remind their audience, however, merciful bodhisattvas can assume any form to succor humanity.[59] In this sense, Wu Zhao's new claim, perhaps representing a corporate decision acceptable to orthodox *sangha* and a bit less offensive to the Confucian establishment, was perhaps not so revolutionary after all. In 693, she was cast not as part of a lineage of female divine and semidivine champions of the Buddhist faith but as the avatar of a male devaputra and a bodhisattva who "manifested the body of a woman."

IDENTIFICATION WITH OTHER DEVIS

Besides connecting Wu Zhao to the Queen Mother of the West, several lines of a poem attributed to Wu Zhao's favorite Zhang Yizhi link Wu Zhao to a female Buddhist divinity. The symbolic scenic description "as the evening sun settles in a secret crevasse deep in the mountains, with airy nonchalance a zephyr blows falling flowers earthward"[60] refers to a conversation between a devi and Śāriputra (Shelifu 舍利弗), a male disciple of the Buddha, contained in the *Vimalakirti Sutra*.[61] When the goddess spills down flowers, a blow of petals like those evoked in Zhang Yizhi's verse, they are shed by authentic bodhisattvas but adhere to spiritually unrealized disciples, including Śāriputra, causing them to violate the Buddhist prohibition against ornamental display. When Śāriputra saw the power of the female divinity, he asked why she did not slough her female body. "The form and shape of my female body does not exist," the devi responded, "yet does not not exist."[62] Gender, in the words of the Buddhist devi, had "no fixed form" (*wu ding xiang* 無定相). She underscores this by turning Śāriputra into a woman, illustrating that "all phenomena are neither male nor female."[63] In Zhang Yizhi's verse, with this subtle "allusion to perspective, gender, and transcendence," Wu Zhao was connected to a powerful Buddhist devi, at once amplifying, blurring, and transcending gender.[64]

WU ZHAO AS MAITREYA AND VAIROCANA

Given Wu Zhao's fluid movement through (and transcendence of) the gendered terrain of her era, it is instructive to look at the significant iconic and textual roles that two male-identified Buddhist divinities—Maitreya (Mile 彌勒; Cishi 慈氏), a messianic figure of pure dharma and infinite compassion, and all-seeing, all-illuminating cosmic Vairocana (Lushena 盧舍那)—played in her legitimation as a Buddhist sovereign.

Wu Zhao and Maitreya

Though Wu Zhao's Buddhist kingship built upon traditions developed under Liang Wudi and Sui Wendi, her gender added a unique dimension to her sovereignty. While in Tang China Maitreya was male, he played a significant part in Wu Zhao's legitimation as a Buddhist sovereign. Buddhist sutras compiled at Wu Zhao's behest in the 690s forwarded proofs that she was the reincarnation of Maitreya in a female body.

Xue Huaiyi and the canny anthologists behind the *Commentary* maximized the ideological capital of the document, presenting Wu Zhao as a divinity incarnate, a prophesied pro-Buddhist champion who would elevate the faith. Therefore, rather than limiting themselves strictly to the prophecy in the *Great Cloud Sutra* that foretold the majestic earthly reincarnation of devi Jingguang, they tentatively identified Wu Zhao with Maitreya as well.[65]

The Buddhist establishment in medieval China was far from uniform. Competing schools apprehended Buddhist teachings in different fashions and at different levels: lay and *sangha*, popular and elite. Forte has observed two very disparate strands of Buddhism built into the *Commentary*—a mainstream teaching represented by most of the orthodox *sangha* and a heterodox, millenarian vision driven by charismatic Xue Huaiyi. Though their objectives were starkly different, both wings collaborated on the *Commentary* and both jointly touted Wu Zhao as a champion who would propagate the Buddhist faith.

One of the most frequently cited supporting texts in the *Commentary* was an apocryphal one-chapter work from the late sixth century entitled the *Sutra of Attestation* (Zhengming jing 證明經). Incorporated in this sutra was an apocalyptic text known as the *Sutra of Primal Causes* (Benyin jing 本因經), which Forte terms a work of "Maitreyan millennialism" akin to the *Book of Revelation*, an "authentic expression of popular religiousness formed in a messianic environment."[66]

In the fourth fascicle of the original *Great Cloud Sutra*, the Buddha says to Pure Radiance, while she is in the mortal guise of an earthly queen, "You shall reign over the territory of a country in the body of a woman." Naturally, Wu Zhao's propagandists seized upon this declaration as a prophetic sign that presaged Wu Zhao's sovereignty. To explain this "proof," the framers of the *Commentary* cited the *Sutra of Attestation*.

In this text, the bodhisattva Samanthabhadra begged Maitreya to build a silver tower in her (his) Guidance City (Huacheng 化城), a magnificent structure topped by a silver pillar and crowned by a golden bell graven with "an inscription for ten thousand generations." This is followed in the *Commentary* by the blunt assertion that the Maitreya (Cishi 慈氏) in this passage designates none other than the Divine Sovereign (Shenhuang 神皇), Wu Zhao.[67] Shortly thereafter, the propagandists explain that "Guidance City is the *mingtang*."[68]

The Maitreya of the *Attestation Sutra* who constructs the Guidance City is a Buddhist avenger, descending upon the mortal world "to cure and eliminate all filth and foulness," to purge those who have transgressed Buddhist law.[69] One of the goals of extremists like Xue Huaiyi was to identify Wu Zhao as the avenging head of an army of devas smiting enemies of the Buddhist faith. Naturally, this radical proposal was opposed both by the Confucian court and the mainstream Buddhist establishment. This extremist ambition compromised the comparatively modest aim of orthodox monks to identify Wu Zhao as a cakravartin and a bodhisattva.

Forte suggests that there is a "double level of truth": uninitiated "simple people" among the Buddhist faithful might accept at face value the "vulgar truth" that Wu Zhao was Maitreya; "learned exponents of official Buddhism," however, were well aware that the primary claim in the *Commentary*—that Wu Zhao was a bodhisattva—superseded that lesser, tentative assertion.[70]

In the interpolated version of the *Sutra of the Rain of Jewels*, presented in 693 immediately before Wu Zhao formally assumed the title cakravartin, the Buddhist propagandists never identified the woman emperor as Maitreya. As Wu Zhao's Buddhist ambitions reached their crescendo a little more than a year later, however, it seems that Xue Huaiyi and the radical sect of Maitreyists briefly gained sway.

Emboldened by her successful campaigns in 690 and 693 to project herself as bodhisattva and a cakravartin, Wu Zhao took a more brazen step. On 23 November 694, Wu Zhao inaugurated the new reign era Verification of Sagehood and appended Maitreya (Cishi 慈氏) to her already grand title. Taken in its entirety, her grandiloquent title was Maitreya, Sagely and Divine Emperor, Cakravartin of the Golden Wheel Transcending Antiquity.[71] Formally, she claimed to be the incarnation of the future Buddha Maitreya.

Two weeks later, Wu Zhao and Xue Huaiyi cosponsored a three-day *pañcavārṣika*, a limitless Buddhist festival that turned into an unmitigated disaster. Xue Huaiyi delineated in ox blood a 200-foot image of Maitreya, but a violent wind shredded it to ribbons. Amid the festivities, either a careless worker (the Buddhist version) or the righteous wrath of heaven (the Confucian interpretation) sparked a conflagration that burned Wu Zhao's Bright Hall complex to the ground. Though in the aftermath of the catastrophe Buddhist supporters persisted in identifying Wu Zhao as Maitreya, the resultant uproar tempered Wu Zhao's grandiose Buddhist ambitions and quashed the extremist aims of the heterodox faction. In the months that followed, Xue Huaiyi, after initially being reappointed commissioner of works for the construction of a new *mingtang* complex, was murdered under suspicious circumstances.[72] Wu Zhao discarded her new title, Maitreya.[73] Forte saw these events as a "political crisis" and "turning point." Wu Zhao's ideological support for the Buddhist establishment shifted, becoming more somber, conservative, and inclined toward mainstream Buddhism.[74] For all the millennial bombast in the *Attestation Sutra* and Wu Zhao's new title, there is no indication that once Wu Zhao identified herself as Maitreya, there were any purges to cleanse the "filth who had transgressed Buddhist law."

In both volume and scale, the reign of Wu Zhao marked the pinnacle of monumental Maitreya iconography.[75] The most extraordinary example, constructed by local elite working in conjunction with the community of *sangha*, is the 105-foot giant statue of Maitreya in cave 96 at Dunhuang. Almost 1,100 miles from Luoyang, this monumental image serves as a powerful testament to local support for Wu Zhao as emperor.

A Brief Discussion of Wu Zhao and Vairocana

Without doubt, the most stunning of the Longmen grottoes is the outdoor amphitheater of Fengxian Temple. From its lofty vantage, the temple's centerpiece, a fifty-two-foot statue of Vairocana, presides over the Yi River. An inscription records that as empress Wu Zhao contributed 20,000 strings of her own cosmetics money to support the construction of this grand image of Vairocana, a project completed in 676.[76] Given Wu Zhao's patronage, many scholars have remarked on the feminine aspect of the fifty-two-foot statue, speculating that Vairocana may have been carved in Wu Zhao's image.[77] The statue possesses a beautiful face, perfectly composed and serene, neither distinctly male nor female. Ning Qiang, among others, asserts that the inscription assumes a "feminine tone," describing Vairocana's "beautiful aspect" (*li zhi* 麗質) and "rosy complexion" (*hong yan* 紅顏).[78] Patricia Karetzky concurs, contending that the statue itself possesses a "new sensuality . . . apparent in the delineation of a distinctly feminine face, with highly arched brows, almond-shaped half-closed eyes, pursed full lips and three rings of flesh around the throat."[79]

Other scholars disagree. Wen Yucheng maintains that "rosy complexion" is a standard indicator of the androgynous beauty of a Buddhist figure rather than a sign of femininity.[80] Guo Shaolin points out that Wu Zhao's contribution of rouge and powder cash would have only covered a fraction of the elaborate project and that she was still only empress at the time.[81] Historian Zeng Qian argues that Wu Zhao's support for, and ideological investment in, the construction of Vairocana has frequently been overstated, contending that Fengxian Temple was primarily constructed at Gaozong's behest to secure posthumous blessings for his deceased parents.[82] Amy McNair, an art historian who has devoted a good part of her career to studying the Longmen grottoes and the donors who commissioned their construction, assesses, "Glamorous as the idea might be that in looking on this seventh-century face we see the very features of the only woman to rule China in her own right, a colossal portrait seems to fit better the reputation for megalomania she earned at the end of her life and not the role she sought at the time the shrine was made."[83] In any event, Wu Zhao contributed to the construction of this colossal Vairocana and was an enthusiastic patron of carvings in the Longmen grottoes.

CONCLUSION

In the *Commentary*, Wu Zhao's propagandists employed the "great cloud" as an emblem for the awesome breadth of her sacred and secular power. The anthropomorphic figuration of this great cloud, Wu Zhao is depicted as casting a "benevolent shade," anointing the realm with her salubrious "sweet rain," intimating plentitude and fecundity—which might be understood as a potent expression of female power (shade and water being associated with *yin*). All-embracing, Wu Zhao is "like a mother who rules over the ten thousand countries and educates milliards of men as her own children," like a great cloud whose "rain-of-one-taste permeates the inner and outer so that there is no [place however] distant which is not watered."[84] The prophecy's chosen, Wu Zhao, was a mother goddess and a great rain bringer. And yet, even here, there was a clever ideological flexibility: at the same moment the propaganda presents Wu Zhao as a Buddhist thearch and the divine avatar of Pure Radiance, she is also cast as a responsible Confucian ur-mother, a mother of empire, nurturing numberless political offspring.

The *Commentary* is by far the most striking document connecting Wu Zhao to a female Buddhist political ancestor: it claimed to establish that she was the avatar of Vimalaprabhā, the devi the Buddha had foreseen in the *Great Cloud Sutra*. Rebecca Doran has commented that "Wu Zhao's selection of Jingguang as her previous incarnation suggests both her perception of the need to address her gender identity and the possible fluidity or equality of the genders via the doctrine of reincarnation."[85] As the *Commentary* was being compiled, Wu Zhao was keenly aware of the attendant challenges her biological sex posed to her assumption of emperorship; there is perhaps no greater testament to that awareness than the six-year incubation period, the meticulous planning and cataloging of proofs that culminated with the *Commentary*'s revelation that Wu Zhao was Vimalaprabhā.

In ritual, statuary, and rhetoric, Wu Zhao affiliated herself with Maitreya and Vairocana, both celebrated, male-identified figures in the Buddhist world. In both cases, however, she was but a temporary vessel, a placeholder (albeit an anomalous and prophesied one), a female body in which these male deities were made manifest. Though Vimalaprabhā was not so high profile as these other Buddhist divinities, she represented Wu Zhao's most unapologetic and ambitious strategy to validate female sovereignty on its own merit, without elaborate gender-shifting. Wu Zhao's affiliation with this Buddhist ancestress was audacious, because it connected her emperorship to, and traced it through, a line of illustrious female ancestors, queens, and devis, culminating with her foretold ascent to the throne.

Conclusions

STEPPING BACK TO BEHOLD THE cumulative might of the diverse pantheon of female political ancestors Wu Zhao culled in a half century as empress, grand dowager, and emperor, we are confronted with a staggeringly eclectic and pluralistic congregation of virtuous exemplars, renowned mothers, and numinous goddesses. Constructively and positively, this tour de force of culture heroes helped shape the contours of Chinese family, society, and religion. With elegant force and bedazzling panoply, Wu Zhao and her coterie of resourceful propagandists vividly rendered the collected women of her pantheon for all to witness—in text, symbol, image, and monument.

Foremost in this worthy assemblage, from the fecund depths of folklore and myth, emerged a trio of ancient goddesses. Embodying this archaic lore, mother goddess Nüwa fashioned mankind from earth and mended the rent heavens. Sometimes considered one of the Three Sovereigns who had first governed China, Nüwa offered Wu Zhao a conveniently nebulous mythic template of female power. As grand dowager, at a pivotal stage in her campaign to become emperor, Wu Zhao ceremoniously honored the Luo River goddess, ritually and rhetorically binding the dazzling water beauty to her own person, to Luoyang, and to the Luo River Writing, an ancient tally of political authority. Finally, performing the First Sericulturist rites as empress, Wu Zhao summoned Leizu, spouse of the Yellow Emperor, to reinforce her position as first lady of the empire.

A host of exemplary women followed, revered paragons from the classical canon. Honored as a model mother and wife, the Tushan Girl was connected to the founding of the Xia dynasty in the remote past and with the central peak of the Five Marchmounts, Mount Song, located not far south of Wu Zhao's political heart, Luoyang. By drawing affiliations with Jiang Yuan, the mother who miraculously birthed the first male ancestor of the Zhou dynasty of old, Wu Zhao tacitly connected herself to that halcyon era. The female sovereign found in Mother Wen, the spouse of King Wen (first ruler of that earlier Zhou), a culturally revered mother-administrator upon whom she might pattern herself. Lifted from *Biographies of Exemplary Women*, paragons like the mother of Mencius, Lady Ji of Lu, and the mother of General Zifa of Chu, offered Wu Zhao not only their Confucian status as models of maternal rectitude, but also their reputations as mothers who placed civic commitment above private, familial concerns. Wu Zhao's affiliation with these women helped validate her claim to be a sage mother, a mother of state, demanding loyalty and obedience from her countless political sons.

Female Daoist divinities in Wu Zhao's pantheon also helped amplify her political authority. In casting herself as a latter-day incarnation of the Queen Mother of the West, Wu Zhao drew on the avian iconography and the divine ethers of the great Daoist goddess. To help confirm ties to her imperial in-laws as grand dowager–regent, Wu Zhao bestowed the honorific title Grand Dowager of Anterior Heaven upon the apotheosized mother of the sage Laozi (from whom the Tang dynasts claimed descent).

Wu Zhao also included a Buddhist mother goddess and a devi among her assemblage of political ancestors. The mother of the Buddha, Māyā, already a goddess of pan-Asian renown, offered Wu Zhao an alternative model of motherhood resonant with the myriad Buddhist faithful. Calling upon powerful and widely disseminated Buddhist propaganda, she also styled herself the avatar of devi Vimalaprabhā, Pure Radiance, whom the Buddha had prophesied would appear on earth as a female sovereign.

To what extent, and in what ways, did Wu Zhao's pantheon of female ancestors help in the establishment and maintenance of her Zhou dynasty? This concluding section identifies a series of significant ways in which this collection of ancestresses played constructive roles in facilitating Wu Zhao's ascent to emperor and her political authority.

The scope of her selection of female ancestors, canvassing each of the "three faiths" of the time—Confucianism, Buddhism, and Daoism—enabled her a certain ideological flexibility in keeping with her cosmopolitan, multiethnic, and religiously diverse empire.[1] Wu Zhao maintained political and personal ties with each of these "faiths." Her Bright Hall complexes in Luo-yang were elaborate ideological amalgams, combining Buddhist, Confucian, and Daoist symbols.[2] Just prior to the inauguration of her Zhou dynasty in 690, she held an open meeting at which a Confucian literatus lectured on the *Canon of Filial Piety* (Xiaojing 孝經) to a wide assembly of Confucians, Daoists, and Buddhists, who then held a joint discussion.[3] From 698 to 701, dozens of scholars working in Wu Zhao's Institute of Reining Cranes created *Pearls and Blossoms of the Three Faiths*, a vast 1,300-chapter work combining the aggregate wisdom of these teachings.[4] With impeccable timing and a keen awareness of audience—in keeping with the shifting religious vicis-situdes of the half century in which she rose from empress to grand dowa-ger and finally to emperor—Wu Zhao moved fluidly among and between the three faiths, tactically honoring cults in accordance with political and ideological fluctuations. Such dogged pursuit and obsessive maintenance of power, of course, reflects the consensus-building might of a political genius.

Not only did her broad, pluralistic pantheon of women provide ideo-logical flexibility, but it also offered such a remarkable variety of cults that Wu Zhao was able to select an apt paragon for every occasion, a suitable divinity for each stage of her fifty-year political career. Exemplary wives and ideal mothers helped add luster to her role as empress; strong-minded women with administrative and political experience lent validity to her regency as a grand dowager presiding over the court; and celebrated dei-ties shed a beatific radiance upon her emperorship.

Early in her political career, as empress, Wu Zhao drew on the cultur-ally legible moral suasion of women like the mother of Mencius and Lady Ji of Lu, to project the image of the perfect wife. As grand dowager, when she vigorously built Luoyang into an international polis symbolizing her ascendancy, the cults of the Luo River goddess and the Tushan Girl—deities long connected to her reoriented sacred topography—also rose into promi-nence. And as emperor, courtier-officials like Cui Rong and Chen Zi'ang poetically compared Wu Zhao with Nüwa, while Buddhist propagandists broadcast the claim that she was the prophesied avatar of a devi. In her final years, Wu Zhao transformed her court into a veritable Daoist para-dise, theatrically assuming the role of Queen Mother of the West.

Wu Zhao was able to plumb a deep, culturally embedded vein of mythic female potency. To a remarkable extent, she reactivated long-dormant female deities. Commenting on the *Classic of Mountains and Seas*, a work dating from a millennium before Wu Zhao's time, Anne Birrell notes that, unlike other canonical texts that "portray female gender in ways that fulfill male aspirations for female subordination," women in this text were "accorded privileged status" and possessed disproportionate "prestige in terms of power, authority and influence."[5] Birrell placed thirty-seven female-identified individuals and groups from the text—including Nüwa and the Queen Mother of the West—into sixteen different categories of women, including mother, queen, shaman, warrior, ancestress, and giantess. Birrell also catalogs eighteen different functions that these women performed, including founding ruler, divine consort, cultural hero, cosmological controller, medium, and nurturer.[6] Long before Wu Zhao's time, then, Chinese culture contained a tremendous lode of primordial female potency. However, between 600 B.C. and the first century B.C., as Birrell points out, women were all but "eliminated from canonical literature . . . written out of the mythological record." Male authorship and male-dominated schools of thought reflecting patriarchal, Confucian mores "socially removed women from the role of actively shaping and transmitting sacred mythic narratives."[7] As a result, "the mythic roles of ancestress, foundress, and female ruler become in the patriarchal system the male ancestor, founder, and emperor."[8] Wu Zhao successfully mined this powerful vein. She resuscitated cults of deities like Nüwa and the Queen Mother of the West that had been long dormant, sublimated under an accretion of Confucian tradition. She supplemented these chthonian female divinities with reshaped images of exemplary Confucian women and Buddhist devis.

Wu Zhao's gathering of female political ancestors helped mainstream the image of the transcendent goddess, beautiful and powerful. These familiar women served to validate her person and her unique role as female emperor; their presence provided a sense that they always had been and always would be politically eminent. These women were all traditionally revered at both elite and popular levels. Calculated positive affiliation with such culturally honored divinities and exemplars redounded to Wu Zhao's merit, amplifying her name and extending the compass of her influence. Far from iconoclastic, the repeated appearance of these beloved, long-worshipped deities and female luminaries helped anchor Wu Zhao in tradition. While a male ruler might automatically claim his role as heir to the grand pedigree of gods and men, these women offered her a normative purchase that no man could claim.

Chen Jo-shui observes that, as empress, Wu Zhao, in "symbolic efforts to display her solidarity with women and remind people around her of the importance of women in Chinese life," frequently included an enlarged circle of women on the ceremonial stage—the *feng* and *shan* sacrifices and the First Sericulturist rites.[9] In an era already known for strong, independent-minded women less beholden to Confucian mores, the prominence of the goddesses and paragons reinforced the sense that women in positions of power and influence constituted a cultural norm.

Wu Zhao's intrepid and lordly presence seems to have trickled down, reverberating widely in culture and society. Patricia Karetzky has remarked that during the early Tang, congruent with Wu Zhao's ascendancy, the female figure in pictorial representation evolved from "the dominant image . . . of an undistinguished, slight, passive young girl" into a woman rendered with increasing distinction, differentiation, individuality, and sensuality.[10] "Wife-fearing" (*wei qi* 畏妻) was widespread in the early Tang: many stories feature imperious termagants tongue-lashing their cowering husbands.[11] Attired in tight-fitting Central Asian garments, bold, self-assured women of the period rode through the streets of Chang'an and Luoyang without veils and played polo.[12] The cult of chastity, a powerful Confucian force in late imperial China, lacked social and cultural currency in the Tang, prompting Gao Shiyu to observe that "woman's initiative . . . found expression outside of marriage in pre-marital and extra-marital sexual intercourse, which seems to have been quite common. The female almost always took the initiative and displayed great bravery."[13] The vanity industry flourished, offering myriad elaborate hairstyles, beauty marks, decorative mirrors, cosmetics, and elegant clothing.[14] Less than half a century after Wu Zhao's time, one anecdote tells that lovely courtesans inspired the celebrated painter Han Gan (c. 706–783) to adorn Buddhist temple walls in Chang'an with elegant, lifelike bodhisattvas and devis.[15] In the pluck and élan of Tang women, the cultic aura of these goddesses appears to have radiated well beyond the palace walls.

The women of Wu Zhao's pantheon took on many guises and manifestations, repeatedly surfacing in poetry and memorials, in symbol and iconography. The abundant connections between the female sovereign and these women—articulated sometimes with subtlety, sometimes with pomp and garish fanfare—served as a composite apotheosis, imbuing Wu Zhao with an aura of the divine. The illustrious bevy of goddesses and cultural

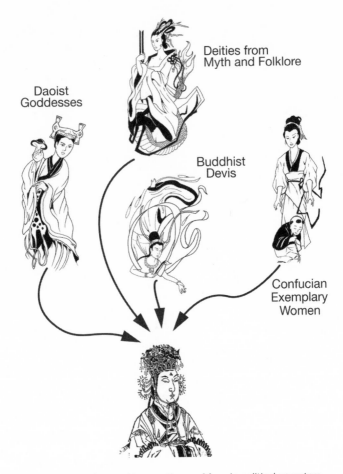

Daoist
Goddesses

Deities from
Myth and Folklore

Buddhist
Devis

Confucian
Exemplary
Women

Figure C.1 Wu Zhao and her pantheon of female political ancestors.

luminaries helped normalize Wu Zhao's own political eminence: the woman emperor simply seemed a present-day extension and culmination of this glorious lineage.

In Chinese tradition, tremendous power was vested in motherhood. Many of the women in Wu Zhao's pantheon, divine and mortal, were celebrated mothers. Nüwa was a world creator, a mother goddess par excellence. The cult of Buddha's mother, Māyā, which flourished under Wu Zhao's patronage, resonated with the Buddhist faithful, both Chinese and non-Chinese, in the multiethnic empire. And in an era when Tang emperors claimed descent from Laozi, the cult of Laozi's mother grew apace.

Wu Zhao also venerated paragons of maternal rectitude in *Biographies of Exemplary Women*—Jiang Yuan, the Tushan Girl, Mother Wen, Lady Ji of Lu, the mother of General Zifa of Chu, and the mother of Mencius—as her forebears.

In early and medieval China, given the central import of filial piety, mothers—especially grand dowagers—were accorded great respect. Particularly in Wu Zhao's capacity as empress and grand dowager, motherhood was exalted. In "Female Rulers in Imperial China," Yang Lien-sheng argues that the role of grand dowager became institutionalized by the Eastern Han, in large part as a result of the importance of mothers within the patriarchal system.[16] Richard Guisso underscores this point, observing that "if the Five Classics fostered the subordination of women to man, they fostered even more the subordination of youth to age. Thus, in every age of Chinese history where Confucianism was exalted, the woman who survived, the woman who had age and the wisdom and experience that accompanied it, was revered, obeyed, and respected . . . even if her son were an emperor."[17] Susan Mann reinforces this concept, remarking that "motherhood and widowhood force women to the foreground of the power politics in China's patriarchal system."[18] In Tang society and culture, mothers exerted a great sway, and by the final decade of Gaozong's life, Wu Zhao possessed all the attributes a woman needed to exercise power: age, experience, and social position.

Beyond these observations, Roger Ames and David Hall point out that while Western sexism tends to be dualistic, with gender construction reflecting "institutionalized male dominance," sexism in traditional China was "correlative"—with interdependent, complementary aspects like *yin* and *yang*, earth and heaven, and inner and outer providing a discursive space that allowed women a greater range of opportunities.[19] During Wu Zhao's time as grand dowager and emperor, she and her rhetoricians fully availed themselves of this space, siphoning off the collective maternal force of these exalted ancestresses and redirecting it onto her physical and political persona, casting her as a sage mother, a mother of state, a political mother to her 100 million subjects, Chinese and non-Chinese alike.

Associations with martial matriarchs—like the mothers of General Kuo of Zhao and General Zifa of Chu—illustrated not only that Wu Zhao was public-minded but that she was tough. Righteously wielding a keen sense of civic responsibility that placed the well-being of the state over family, these stalwart mothers browbeat misguided sons into following the proper course of action.

There were also other paradigms of motherhood. On the fringes of the empire, central Asian steppe cultures (that profoundly influenced the Tang) held mothers in highest esteem. The notorious Sogdian general, An Lushan (d. 757), famously remarked to Xuanzong, "Central Asian peoples esteem the mother above the father."[20]

The Book of Songs contains the verse, "Clever men build cities, clever women topple them . . . disorder does not come from Heaven; it is wrought by women."[21] As creatures restricted to the inner, domestic, familial sphere, women in the Book of Rites were "not to speak of the outside."[22] Even in the Tang, Wu Zhao needed to overcome deep-seated cultural opposition to a woman's political involvement—let alone her rule.

This intrinsic cultural opposition to powerful women brings us to an additional manner in which Wu Zhao's political ancestresses contributed to her authority: many of these goddesses and women had played political and administrative roles or were involved in governance. Goddess Nüwa was reputed to be an ancient sovereign. Mother Wen was one of the "ten ministers" of King Wen. Wise instructresses from Biographies of Exemplary Women were well-versed in statecraft. Following the Buddha's prophecy, Vimalaprabhā was said to be reborn as an earthly female sovereign. Such connections helped challenge and surmount the deeply embedded cultural notion that women and power do not—and should not—mix.

Womanhood was interwoven with textiles in ancient and medieval China. Through weaving, the virtuous woman might show her moral fiber, work ethic, economic worth, and character. With its integrated process of "disentangling, ordering, smoothing and combining," its "timeless continuity of long, strong warp threads and the regular patterning of the weft," weaving, Francesca Bray makes clear, transcended the technical, material, social, or economic realm: it was a vocation and a process with powerful moral and political implications. As Bray puts it, "from these moral threads were woven the fabric of Chinese civility."[23]

Not a few of Wu Zhao's female political ancestors, both divinities and renowned mortals, were rendered intertextually with weaving, an intricate, multifaceted art that by the Tang had developed its own rich metaphorical language that gave women discursive license to encroach upon the male domain of politics. Manifesting a sense of civic duty and a profound grasp of the principles of governance, Lady Ji of Lu and the Mother of Mencius used weaving to instruct their wayward sons. The *sheng* headdress of the Queen Mother of the West may have represented a weaving implement, the brake pedal of the loom. Leizu is credited with the invention of sericulture. In four public performances that helped establish her as "first lady" of the Tang empire, Wu Zhao honored the silk goddess in the First Sericulturist rites. Both in a narrow Confucian sense and a pervasive cultural sense, these connections with weaving helped depict Wu Zhao as an ideal public-minded woman.

Jack Chen has observed that Taizong's extensive appropriation of cultural forms—poetry, calligraphy, political theory, historiography, and myth—for the purpose of imperial "self-fashioning" contributed greatly to his rise to power, favorably reshaping his image while constructively reinventing his sovereignty. This process helped enable Taizong to poetically "rewrite the history of sovereignty, reperforming and negating the past and inscribing the significance of the Tang in cultural memory for generations to come."[24]

Wu Zhao learned a great deal from the modus operandi of her first husband. Just as Taizong and his propagandists ingeniously enlarged his political charisma with the cumulative force of several millennia of celebrated male culture heroes and sage emperors, so Wu Zhao, aided by poets and rhetoricians of every ideological persuasion, tactically enhanced her visibility and political amplitude by imbuing herself with the aggregate majesty of female paragons and goddesses. This was not, of course, the consequence of spontaneous fabrication. Rather, the product of inventive statecraft, performative flair, and calculated ideological deployment, Wu Zhao's pantheon evolved over decades, ever responsive to the ebb and flow of political and ideological exigencies.

This fabricated pantheon of women conferred upon Wu Zhao an aura of divinity. In symbol and rhetoric, she shaped herself into a living goddess. She became the human vessel into whom the cumulative charisma and vital force of these eminent women and divinities flowed. The cultural resonance, maternal potency, demiurgic energy, divine splendor, and traditional weight of these female ancestors combined to support Wu Zhao's political ascent and authority, and helped to generate her inimitable power.

Wu Zhao's Pantheon of Female Political Ancestors

DYNASTIC MOTHERS

Mother Wen (Wenmu 文母), known also as Taisi 太姒, the spouse of King Wen
Woman of Tushan 塗山氏, also known as the mother of Qi (Qimu 啟母)
Jiang Yuan 姜嫄

GODDESSES OF ANTIQUITY

Nüwa 女媧
Leizu 嫘祖
Goddess of the Luo River (Luoshen nü 洛神女), also known as Fufei (Mifei) 宓妃/妃

EXEMPLARY MOTHERS

Zifa mu 子發母, mother of General Zifa
Meng mu 孟母, mother of Mencius
Lady Ji of Lu (Lu Ji 魯季), also known as Jing Jiang 敬姜
Mother of General Kuo of Zhao (Zhao jiang Kuo mu 趙將括母)

DAOIST DIVINITIES

Mother Li (Li mu 李母), Grand Dowager of the Anterior Heaven (Xiantian taihou 先天 太后)
Queen Mother of the West (Xiwangmu 西王母)
Wei Huacun 魏華存, Lady of the Southern Marchmount (Nanyue furen 南岳夫人)

BUDDHIST DEITIES

Vimalaprabhā (Jingguang tiannü 淨光天女), also known as the Devi of Pure Radiance
Māyā (Moye 摩耶, Moye furen 摩耶夫人)

Glossary of Chinese Places, Names, and Terms

Those not included among rulers or in bibliography

PLACES

beijiao 北郊
Beimang shan 北邙山
Beiyuan 北苑
Bingzhou 并州
Bozhou 亳州
Chang'an 長安
Chengzhou 成州
Chenzhou 陳州
Chixian 赤縣, China
Chuzhou 楚州
Danjin 丹禁
Dengfeng 登峰
Dongdu 東都, Eastern Capital (Luoyang)
Dunhuang 敦煌
Emeishan 峨嵋山
Fangxingli 方興里
Fangzhou 房州
Fengtian Palace 奉天宮
Fo shouji si 佛授記寺
Fuzhou 撫州
Goushi, Mount 緱氏
Guangyuan 廣元
Guishui River 媯水
Guozhou 虢州
Guyang 谷陽
Hanyuan Basilica 含元殿
Henan 河南

Henei 河內
Hengshan 恒山, Northern Marchmount
Hengshan 衡山, Southern Marchmount
Heyang 河陽
Hongzhou 洪州
Huaihe 淮河
Huaizhou 懷州
Huanyuan Pass 轘轅關
Huashan 華山, Western Marchmount,
    Mount Hua
Huaxu 華胥
Huoshan 霍山
Jialing River 嘉陵江
Jianchang 建昌
Jiangsu 江蘇
Jianye 建業
Jintai 金臺
Jishan 箕山, ridge of Mount Song
Jiyuan 濟源
Junji Peak 峻极峰
Jurong 句容
Kunlun 崑崙
Kunming Pool 昆明池
Linchuan 臨川
Linru 臨汝
Linyi 林邑
Linzhi si 麟趾寺

GLOSSARY OF CHINESE PLACES, NAMES, AND TERMS

Lizhou 利州
Longmen 龍門
Longtai Town 龍臺鄉
Luoshui 洛水
Luoyang 洛陽
Luozhou 洛州
Luyi 鹿邑
Mangshan 邙山
Maoshan 茅山
Mujian 木澗
Nanhai commandery 南海郡
Nanjing 南京
Nanyue 南岳
Piao 骠
Putuoshan 普陀山
Qianling 乾陵
Qiao commandery 譙郡
Qimushi 啟母石
Qingshan 慶山
Qingtian 青田
Qinyang 沁陽
Qishan 岐山
Rencheng 任城
Renjing Abbey 仁靜觀
Runzhou 潤州
Ruzhou 汝州
Shaanbei 陝北
Shangqing Abbey 上清宮
Shangyang Palace 上陽宮
Shanxi 山西
Shazhou 沙州
Shendu 神都, Divine Capital
Shenyue 神嶽, Divine Marchmount
Sheshou 社首
Shizong 石淙, Stony Torrents
Si River 汜水
Songshan 嵩山, Mount Song
Songyang Monastery 嵩陽觀
Songzhou 宋州
Suining 遂寧

Suizhou 遂州
Taiqing Palace 太清宮
Taishan 泰山, Mount Tai
Taishi 太室
Taiyuan 太原
Tanling 曇陵
Tiangong Temple 天宮寺
Tiannü nisi 天女尼寺
Tiantai 天台
Tianzhong 天中
Tongtiangong 通天宮
Tongtiantai 通天台
Wangwu 王屋
Wansui feng 萬歲峰
Wanxiang shengong 萬象神宮
Wen 溫
Wenshui 文水
Wenxiang County 閺鄉縣
Wugong 武功
Wutaishan 五臺山
Wuyue 五嶽, Five Marchmounts
Xiangtangshan 響堂山
Xiaoshi 小室, Lesser Room
Ximingsi 西明寺
Xingqing Pool 興慶池
Xingyang 滎陽
Xiuwu 修武
Xuanzhou 宣州
Yanfuti 閻浮提
Yangcheng 陽城
Yangjiaoshan 羊角山, Ram's Horn Peak
Yi River 伊
Yishi 猗氏
Yungang 雲崗
Zetian gate 則天門
Zhendan 振旦, China
Zhengzhou 鄭州
Zhenyuan 真源
Zhongyue 中嶽, Mount Song

NAMES AND TERMS

An Lushan 安祿山 (d. 757)
Anle Princess 安樂公主
Ashina Gumalu 阿史那骨篤祿
bai xiang 白象

Baidi 白帝
Baijing 白淨
Ban Jieyu 班婕妤
Ban Zhao 班昭 (A.D. 45–116)

bao tu 寶圖
Beidou 玉斗
Beiji 北極
Beimen xueshi 北門學士
ben ye 本業
Bo Juyi 白居易 (772–846)
Boyi 伯夷
bu tian 補天
Cai Mo 蔡謨
Cairen 才人
can mu 蠶母
Cao Zhi 曹植
chali 刹利
Chang E 嫦娥
Chao Fu 巢父
Chen (state) 陳
Chen Zhenjie 陳貞節
Chen Zi'ang 陳子昂 (661–702)
Cheng Chubi 程處弼
Cheng Tang 成湯
chi 尺
Chu Guangxi 儲光羲 (c. 707–760)
chujiang ruxiang 出將入相
Cishi 慈氏, Maitreya
Cui Rong 崔融 (653–706)
Cui Shen 崔侁
Cui Shu 崔曙 (704–739)
Cui Xuanwei 崔玄暐
Dajiaye bodhisattva 大迦葉菩薩
Daoshi 道世
Daoxuan 道宣
Dayunjing 大雲經
Degan 德感
Di Renjie 狄仁傑 (630–700)
Difan 帝範
Ding Lingwei 丁令威
Dizang 地藏
Dongfang Shuo 東方說 (c. 160–93 B.C.)
dongtian 洞天
Dongwang gong 東王公
Du Gongzhan 杜公瞻
Du Guangting 杜光庭 (850–933)
Du Mu 杜牧 (803–852)
Du Yu 杜預 (222–285)
Ehuang 娥皇
Erlitou 二里頭

Ersheng 二聖
Fajing 法經
fanjiang 蕃将
Fazang 法藏 (643–712)
Feng Yi 馮夷
feng 封 and *shan* 襌 rites
fenghuang 鳳凰
fengshen 封神
Foguang wang 佛光王
Fomu dong 佛母洞
Fomu 佛母
Fotuobatuoluo 佛馱跋陀羅
Fotuopoli 佛陀波利
Fowang 佛王
Fuqiu 浮丘
Gao Ying 高郢 (740–811)
Gao'an changgongzhu 高安長公主
   (649–714)
gong 公
Gongliu 公劉
Gu Kaizhi 顧愷之 (345–409)
Gu Kuang 顾况 (725–814)
Gu Yanwu 顧炎武 (1613–1682)
Gu Yewang 顧野王 (519–583)
guang 光
Guanxiu 貫休
Guanyin 觀音
Guo Pu 郭璞 (276–324)
Guo Wei 郭威
Guo Xian 郭憲
guoshi 國史
Han Gan 韓幹 (c. 706–783)
Hao Chujun 郝處俊
Haotian shangdi 昊天上帝
Heichi Changzhi 黑齒常之
Hetu 河圖
Hou Ji 后稷
Hou Yi 后羿
hou 后
Hu (dowager empress) 胡太后
Hu Chao 胡超
Hu Sanxing 胡三省 (1230–1302)
Hu Yanqing 胡延慶
hu 胡
Huagu 花姑, Flower Maid
Huan Yanfan 桓彥范

Huang Lingwei 黃靈微 (640–721)
huangdi 皇帝
Huangfu Mi 皇甫謐 (215–282)
Huaxu 華胥
Huazhu 華渚
Hufa 護法
Huizhi 慧智
Ji Dan 姬旦, Duke of Zhou
Ji Shanxing 吉善行
Ji 姬
Jiandi 簡狄
jiao si 郊祀
Jiaye Zhizhong 迦葉志忠
Jihu 稽胡
Jing Hui 敬暉
jing 淨
Jingfan 淨飯
Jingguang rulai 淨光如來
Jingguang tongzi pusa 淨光童子菩薩
Jingmiao 淨妙
Jinjing 金鏡
Jinlun 金輪
Jinpyeong 真平王 (r. 579–632),
    Sillan king
Jinque dijun 金闕帝君
Jiu ding 九鼎
Kongfuzi 孔夫子, Confucius
Konghejian 控鶴監
Kun 坤
Laojun 老君
Laozi 老子
li 里
li 李
Li Bo 李白 (poet)
Li Bo 李渤
Li Chunfeng 李淳風
Li Daoyuan 酈道元
Li Deyi 李德异
Li Duozuo 李多祚
Li Er 李耳
Li Gongxie 李公協
Li Hong 李弘
Li Ji 李勣 (594–669)
Li Jingye 李敬業
Li Qian 李乾

Li Qiao 李嶠 (644–713)
Li Ruyi 李儒意
Li Shangyin 李商隱 (813–858)
Li Shan 李善
Li Shenji 李審幾
Li Tai 李泰 (618–652)
Li Tong 李彤
Li Xián 李賢 (653–684)
Li Xiǎn 李顯 (Zhongzong 中宗,
    r. 684 and 705–710)
Li Yi 李益
Li Zhaode 李昭德
Li Zhen 利貞
Li Zu'e 李祖娥
Liezi 列子
ling 陵
Lingbao 靈寶
lingtai 靈臺
Liu An 劉安
Liu Cang 劉滄 (fl. mid-ninth century)
Liu Fu 劉复 (c. early ninth century)
Liu Xi 劉歆
Liu Xiang 劉向
Liu Yizhi 劉禕之 (631–687)
Liu Yuxi 劉禹錫 (772–842)
Longshan 龍山
Longtu tu 龍吐圖
Lu Jingchun 路敬淳
Lu Ji 魯季, Lady Ji of Lu
Lu Tong 盧仝
Lu Yuanming's 盧元明
Lu Zhaolin 盧照鄰 (c. 634–689)
luan 鸞
Lunheng 論衡
Luo Binwang 駱賓王
Luoshu 洛書
Lushena 盧舍那, Vairocana
Mao Ying 茅盈
Mazu 媽祖
miao 妙
Mile 彌勒, Maitreya
ming 明
Mingtang 明堂
Mituoshan 彌陀山
Mohe 靺鞨

Moxi 末喜

mu yi 母儀

mu 墓

mu 母

muzi 木子

nan geng, nü zhi 男耕女織

nanzun nübei 男尊女卑

nei mingfu 內命婦

nei 內

neidaochang 內道場

nei mingfu 內命婦

nian hao 年號

Nihon Shoki 日本書紀

Niu Fengji 牛鳳及

Nongyu 弄玉

nü gong 女功

Nü jie 女戒

Nüdeng 女登

Nüying 女英

Pan Shizheng 潘師正 (585–682)

Panlongtaibei 攀龍台碑

pei 配

Pei Songzhi 裴松之

Pei Yaoqing 裴耀卿

Peiligang 裴李崗

Pingyang Princess 平陽公主 (598–623)

pusa 菩薩

Putiliuzhi 菩提流支, Bodhiruci

Puxian pusa 普賢菩薩, Samanthabhadra

Qi 棄, Hou Ji

qi 氣

qi bao 七寶

Qian 乾

Qibi Heli 契苾何力

Qijuzhi fomu 七俱胝佛母

qilin 麒麟

Qingmiao 清妙

Qiongfei 瓊妃

Qiwu Sui 綦毋邃

Qu Yuan 屈原 (343–278 B.C.)

Quan Xiancheng 泉獻誠

que 闕

rui shi 瑞石

san cong 三從

san jiao 三教

Seondok 宣德 (r. 632–647), Sillan queen

Shangdi 上帝

Shangguan Wan'er 上官婉兒

Shangqing 上清

Shao Sheng 邵昇

Shaoyi 少姨

Shazha Zhongyi 沙吒忠義

She'najueduo 闍那崛多, Jñāngupta

Shelifu 舍利弗

shen 神

sheng 勝

sheng 聖

shengmu 聖母

Shengmu yuanjun 聖母元君

Shengxian taizi 升仙太子

Shi Jiao 尸佼

shi lu 實錄

Shichanantuo 實叉難陀, Śikṣānanda

shouji 授記

side 四德

Sima Chengzhen 司馬承禎 (647–735)

Sima Qian 司馬遷

Sima Xiangru 司馬相如 (179–127 B.C.)

Sima Zhen 司馬貞 (679–732)

Song Yingxing 宋應星

Song Zhenzong 宋真宗 (r. 997–1022)

Song Zhiwen 宋之問 (c. 660–710)

Su Anheng 蘇安恆

Su Ting 蘇頲 (680–737)

Su Weidao 蘇味道 (648–705)

Sun Furen 孫夫人, Lady Sun

Taijiang 太姜

Taiping Princess 太平公主

Tairen 太任

Taiyi yuanjun 太一元君

Tanfu 亶父

Tang Lingze 唐令則

Tangtang 唐唐

Tanjing 曇景

Tao Hongjing 陶弘景 (452–536)

Tiangong Temple 天宮寺

tiannü 天女

Tianshi 天師

Tianshu 天樞

Tianzhong huanghou 天中皇后

Tiele 鐵勒
Tongtiangong 通天宮
tou long 投龍
Tuibeitu 推背圖
Tujue 突厥
Uḍḍyāna Wuchang 烏萇
wai mingfu 外命婦
wai qi 外戚
wai 外
Wang Ji 王季
Wang Jian 王建 (r. 907–918)
Wang Wanche 王萬徹 (fl. late seventh
    century)
Wang Xuanhe 王懸河
Wang Yi 王逸
Wangzi Jin 王子晉, Prince Jin (Ziqiao
    子喬) (c. sixth century B.C.)
Wei Daijia 韋待價
Wei Fashi 魏法師
wei qi 畏妻
Wei Shou 魏收
Wei Shuxia 韋叔夏
Wei Sili 韋嗣立
Wenshu 文殊
wenzhang si you 文章四友
Wu Chengsi 武承嗣
Wu Hua 武華
Wu Jian 武儉
Wu Juchang 武居常
Wu Keji 武克己
Wu Meiniang 武媚娘
Wu Rong 吳融 (fl. late ninth century)
Wu Sansi 武三思, Prince of Liang 梁王
Wu Shiyue 武士彠 (577–635)
Wu Yuanchong 鄔元崇
Wuchang 烏萇, Uḍḍyāna
wujin cang 無盡藏
wulun 五倫
Wutai 五臺山
wuwei 無為
wuxing 五行
wuzhang 五障
wuzhe dahui 無遮大會
Xi Weiguo si 西魏國寺
xian can 先蠶
Xiang Zong 項宗

xiantian 先天
Xiao Deyan 蕭德言 (558–645)
Xiao Kuang 蕭曠
Xiao shufei 蕭淑妃
xiao 孝
Xiaojing 孝經
Xie Shouhao 謝守灝 (1134–1212)
Xiling 西陵
Ximingsi 西明寺
Xu Lishi 許力士
Xu Shao 許紹 (d. 621)
Xu You 許由
Xuanmiao yunü 玄妙玉女
Xuannü 玄女
Xuanwu Gate 玄武門
Xue Huaiyi 薛懷義 (d. 695)
Xue Ji 薛稷
Xunzi 荀子 (312–230 B.C.)
Yan Chaoyin 閻朝隱
Yan Shigu 顏師古 (581–645)
Yan Zhenqing 顏真卿 (709–785)
Yandi 炎帝
Yang Jian 楊㦮
Yang Jiong 楊炯 (650–693)
Yang Xi 楊羲 (330–386)
Yangdi, Lady 陽翟婦人
Yangshao 仰韶
yang 陽
yang niao 陽鳥
Yao Chong 姚崇 (650–721)
Ye Fashan 葉法善 (616–720)
Yidu, wife of 宜都內人
Yijing 義淨 (635–713)
Yin Wencao 尹文操 (622–688)
yin 陰
Yingfu 嬰敷
Yishou 益壽
Youfang 幽房
Youshen 有莘
Yuan Shuji 袁恕己
Yuanze 元則
Yue Jingguang 月淨光
Yueguang 月光, Candraprabha
yuezhuo 鷟鷟
Yujing 玉京
Yunü 玉女

Yuwen Jun 俞文俊
Yuwen 宇文
Yuzhen gongzhu 玉真公主 (692–762)
Zengzhang 增長
Zetian Gate 則天門
zhang 丈
Zhang Changling 張昌齡 (d. 705)
Zhang Changning 張昌宁
Zhang Changzong 張昌宗
Zhang Jianzhi 張柬之
Zhang Yizhi 張易之
Zhang Yue 張說 (663–730)
Zhao Yanzhao 趙彥昭
Zhao 罃

Zhaomu 趙母, Mother Zhao
Zheng Xuan 鄭玄
Zheng Yin 鄭絪
Zhiren 摯任
Zhixian 智仙
zhong 忠
zhongwen, qingwu 重文輕武
Zhu Fonian 竺佛念
Zhu Zizhu 朱子奢
zhuan 篆
Zhuangzi 莊子
Zhuanlun wang 轉輪王, cakravartin
zi lai 子來

Notes

1. While in most secondary scholarship she is known as Wu Zetian 武則天 or Empress Wu 武后, throughout this work I use the self-styled designation Wu Zhao she assumed in 689. For historical records of her assumption of the name Zhao, see *Zizhi tongjian* [Comprehensive Mirror for the Advancement of Governance], comp. Sima Guang (Beijing: Zhonghua, 1995), 204.6263 (hereafter *ZZTJ*); and *Xin Tang shu* [New History of the Tang], comp. Ouyang Xiu (Beijing: Zhonghua, 1997), 76.3481 (hereafter *XTS*).

Throughout this work, depending on the juncture of her half-century political career, I refer to Wu Zhao as empress, grand dowager, or emperor. When speaking in general terms, I call her "emperor." She has earned this designation. See also "Titles at Different Stages of Wu Zhao's Career."

2. For a study on the obstacles Wu Zhao faced in her ascendancy to emperor, see Rebecca Doran's excellent dissertation "Insatiable Women and Transgressive Authority: Constructions of Gender and Power in Early Tang China" (Harvard University, 2011). Doran illustrates how female political power in traditional China was consistently—through successive constructions and reconstructions of Confucian narratives—identified with deviousness, greed, and hypersexuality; these intense, deep-seated male fears developed into a well-established tradition that systematically delegitimized Wu Zhao and other powerful Tang women, transforming them into caricatures of lawlessness and evil, "remembered primarily in terms of excess, cruelty, vapid symbolism, and dalliance with much younger male consorts" (7). Played out for more than a millennium, this "negative 'canonization'" (28) makes it difficult to look at the actual construction and nature of the female sovereign's political authority. See also Guo Shaolin, "Lun guren de Wu Zetian diwei guan" [A Discussion of Wu Zetian's Position from the Perspective of the Ancients], in *Sui-Tang Luoyang* [Sui and Tang Luoyang] (Xi'an: Sanqin, 2006), 263–75.

3. Zhao Fengjie, *Zhongguo funü zai falüshang zhi diwei* [The Position of Women in Chinese Law] (Shanghai: Shangwu, 1927), 111, translation by Yang Lien-sheng in "Female Rulers in Imperial China," *Harvard Journal of Asian Studies* 23 (1960–61): 50.

4. Victor Turner, *The Ritual Process: Structure and Anti-structure* (Ithaca: Cornell University Press, 1969), vii and 128.

5. This is not to suggest that male rulers did not look beyond the purview of Confucian tradition for legitimation. For instance, Taizong styled himself a Central Asian Heavenly Qaghan (Tian kehan 天可汗) as well as a Chinese/Confucian Son of Heaven. See Pan Yihong, *Son of Heaven and the Heavenly Qaghan: Sui-Tang China and Its Neighbors* (Bellingham: Western Washington University Press, 1997); and Marc Abramson, *Ethnic Identity in Tang China* (Philadelphia: University of Pennsylvania Press, 2008), chap. 5. The primary point is that conception of emperorship naturally evolved with the increasingly complex ideological and ethnic composition of the empire.

6. *Jiu Tang shu* [Old Tang History], comp. Liu Xu (Beijing: Zhonghua, 1997), 84.2799 (hereafter *JTS*). These are the words of official Hao Chujun, recorded in his biography.

7. *JTS* 67.2491; see also note 9 below. This oath is included in the biography of Li Jingye, the chief rebel in the uprising against grand dowager–regent Wu Zhao in 684. For more on Luo Binwang, see Volker Klöpsch, "Lo Pin-wang's Survival: Traces of a Legend," *T'ang Studies* 6 (1988): 77–97. Luo Binwang did not make it to the end of the year.

8. It is impossible in a footnote to do justice to Confucius or Confucianism. As Mario Poceski observes in *Introducing Chinese Religions* (New York: Routledge, 2009), "For over two millennia the Confucian tradition occupied a central position and exerted significant influence on various spheres of life in China, including politics, culture, society and religion" (34). Still, some explanation of what is meant by "Confucian" in this work is necessary. Based on the teachings of the Eastern Zhou sage Confucius (551–479 B.C.) from Lu (modern-day Shandong), Confucian thought (or Confucianism) was an ethical system, an ideology that reinforced, in state and family (in political and social principle), the normative authority and rectitude of hierarchy. Confucius famously offered the following counsel to a regional ruler who asked him about the art of governance: "Let the ruler be ruler, the subject a subject; the father a father, the son a son" (slightly altered from *The Analects*, Confucius, trans. D.C. Lau (New York: Penguin, 1979), 114, XII.11. In essence, know your role! This vision of harmony and order drawn from hierarchy is reflected in the five Confucian relationships (*wu lun* 五倫): the minister shall be unswervingly loyal to the ruler; the son shall be duly filial to the father; the younger brother shall embrace the elder with fraternal spirit; the wife shall submit to and obey the husband; and friends shall treat one another with reciprocal kindness. The idea that the female is subordinate to the male is concomitant with the very core of this ideology. Confucius is often attributed authorship of many of the Five Classics (*Book of Songs, Book of Changes, Book of History, Book of Rites,* and *The Spring and Autumn Annals*). He is also credited with composing the *Doctrine of the Mean* and the *Greater Learning*. Perhaps the sage is best known for his *Analects*, fragments of his wisdom collected by disciples and immortalized. Confucius honored the past. In this canonical matrix, Yao, Shun, Yu, King Wen, King Wu, and the Duke of Zhou—the illustrious company of long-honored political ancestors—are time and again exalted and upheld as cultural heroes and exemplars.

9. *Quan Tangwen* [Complete Anthology of Tang Prose], comp. Dong Gao (Beijing: Zhonghua shuju, 1996), 199.2009–10 (hereafter *QTW*). Luo Binwang's polemic also appears in *JTS* 67.2490–91 and is excerpted in *ZZTJ* 203.6421–22.

10. *ZZTJ* 203.6442. This admonishment came from court minister Yuwen Jun.

11. *XTS* 4.87–88, 34.880, 889; *Taiping guangji* [Miscellaneous Records of the Taiping Era], comp. Li Fang (Beijing: Zhonghua, 1996), 463.3785, 361.2866–67 (hereafter *TPGJ*). These fowl were the invention of Song Confucians. They do not appear in the *Old Tang History*. These chickens were a culturally legible reference to the famous quote in the "Speech at Mu" in the *Book of History*, where it is written, "When the hen crows to greet the dawn, the family is doomed."

12. To coin a phrase from Yang Lien-sheng, "Female Rulers in Imperial China," 48.

13. *JTS* 6.121; *XTS* 4.90.

14. David Keightley, "The Making of Ancestors: Late Shang Religion and Its Legacy," in *Religion and Chinese Society*, vol. 1, *Ancient and Medieval China*, ed. John Lagerway (Hong Kong: Chinese University Press, 2004), 41–42. Keightley divides the Shang gods into six groups, three that might be considered shared with other peoples (nature spirits like the river deity He, Former Lords like Wang Hai, and the high god Di) and three that were connected to the Shang royal family.

15. Kwang-chih Chang, *Art, Myth and Ritual* (Cambridge, Mass.: Harvard University Press, 1983), 107.

16. C. K. Yang, *Religion in Chinese Society* (Berkeley: University of California Press, 1967), 29.

17. Herrlee Creel, *The Birth of China* (New York: Frederick Ungar, 1961), 175–80.

18. Wang Aihe, *Cosmology and Political Culture in Early China* (Cambridge: Cambridge University Press, 2000), 60.

19. Richard Bendix, *Kings or People: Power and the Mandate to Rule* (Berkeley: University of California Press, 1978), 53.

20. Constance Cook, "Ancestor Worship During the Eastern Zhou," in *Early Chinese Religion*, part 1, *Shang Through Han (1250 BC–220 AD)*, ed. John Lagerway and Mark Kalinowski (Leiden: Brill, 2009), 238.

21. Martin Kern, "Announcements from Mountains: The Stele Inscriptions of the First Emperor," in *Conceiving the Empire: China and Rome Compared*, ed. Fritz Heimer-Muschler and Achim Mittag (New York: Oxford University Press, 2008), 233–34.

22. Wang Aihe, *Cosmology and Political Culture*, 207.

23. Modified based on Confucius, *The Analects*, 66, II.23.

24. *Beishi* [History of the Northern Dynasties], comp. Li Yanshou (Beijing: Zhonghua, 1997), 9.330–36 (hereafter *BS*).

25. Howard Wechsler, *Offerings of Jade and Silk: Ritual and Symbol in the Legitimization of the T'ang* (New Haven: Yale University Press, 1985), ix–x and 95–104. For more on the development and patronage of the cult of Confucius in the early Tang, see also John Shryock, *The Origin and Development of the State Cult of Confucius* (New York: Paragon), 131–36. Shryock notes the expansion of the cult of Confucius under Taizong. By his imperial order, every prefecture and district established a Confucian temple. In addition, worship extended to a broader range of Confucian disciples, whose tablets were set in these temples. During the early Tang, though both worthies were honored, there was an ongoing dispute among courtier officials as to whether Confucius or the Duke of Zhou was more deserving of the posthumous title Foremost Sage (*xian sheng* 先聖). See also *XTS* 15.373–74.

26. For more on this incident, see Andrew Eisenberg, "Kingship, Power and the Hsuan-wu Men Incident of the T'ang," *T'oung Pao* 80 (1994): 223–59.

27. Translation drawn from Denis Twitchett, "How to Be an Emperor: T'ang T'ai-tsung's Vision of His Role," *Asia Major*, Third Series, 9, no. 1–2 (1996): 18–19; cf. *Wenyuan yinghua* [Flowers and Blossoms of the Garden of Literature], comp. Li Fang (Beijing: Zhonghua, 1982), 360.1845–46 (hereafter *WYYH*). I have slightly modified the translation and changed Wade-Giles to pinyin.

28. Twitchett, "How to Be an Emperor," 8n5.

29. Jack Chen, "The Writing of Imperial Poetry in Medieval China," *Harvard Journal of Asiatic Studies* 65, no. 1 (2005): 57.

30. Ibid, 89.

31. *Quan Tangshi* [Complete Anthology of Tang Poetry], comp. Peng Dingqiu (Beijing: Zhonghua, 1995), 1.4 (hereafter *QTS*), translation by Chen in "The Writing of Imperial Poetry," 90.

32. *Shi ji*, comp. Sima Qian (Beijing: Zhonghua, 1995), 4.112 (hereafter *SJ*). See chap. 5 of this volume for more on Hou Ji.

33. Chen, "The Writing of Imperial Poetry," 97.

34. Translation by Twitchett in "How to Be an Emperor," 53–55. I have changed Wade-Giles to pinyin. The *Difan* was initially brought back by the Japanese embassies from Tang China. Twitchett's translation is from a Japanese version printed in Kyoto in 1668 and officially republished by the Tokugawa bakufu in 1830 (Twitchett, 48).

35. Jiang Yonglin, *The Mandate of Heaven and the Great Ming Code* (Seattle: University of Washington Press, 2011), 78.

36. Mark Lewis, *China's Cosmopolitan Empire: The Tang Dynasty* (Cambridge, Mass.: Harvard University Press, 2009), 226.

37. Mircea Eliade, *Myth and Reality* (New York: Harper and Row, 1963), 13–15.

38. Ibid., 18–19.

39. *ZZTJ* 204.6462.

40. *JTS* 22.873.

41. Elias Canetti, *Crowds and Power*, trans. Carol Stewart (New York: Seabury, 1978), 397.

42. *ZZTJ* 204.6467. The nature and purpose of Wu Zhao's fictive kin ties with the dynastic founders of the original Zhou dynasty are addressed in chaps. 5 and 6 in this volume.

43. *ZZTJ* 203.6421.

44. *XTS* 6.120, 76.3481; *ZZTJ* 204.6263–64; *QTW* 96.996.

45. *ZZTJ* 204.6462. See also *XTS* 4.89, 36.559; *JTS* 6.120.

46. *ZZTJ* 204.6456–57.

47. For the establishment of the Northern Zhou, see *BS* 9.330–36. After the fall of the Tang, during the tumultuous Five Dynasties, Guo Wei established another ephemeral Zhou dynasty (951–960).

48. *XTS* 4.91, 15.374. For annual sacrifices, descendants of these cultural worthies were enfeoffed with 100 households each.

49. Wang Aihe, *Cosmology and Political Culture*, 208.

50. Wechsler, *Offerings of Jade and Silk*, 234.

51. David McMullen, "Bureaucrats and Cosmology: The Ritual Code of T'ang China," in *Rituals of Royalty: Power and Ceremonial in Traditional Societies*, ed. David Cannadine and Simon Price (Cambridge: Cambridge University Press, 1987), 186.

52. John Lagerway, *Taoist Ritual in Chinese Society and History* (New York: Macmillan, 1987), 254. For an overview on Daoism's ongoing role as an "official religion of the state" in traditional China (253), see chap. 15, "Taoism and Political Legitimacy."

53. Livia Kohn, "Lord Lao and Laojun," in *The Routledge Encyclopedia of Taoism*, ed. Fabrizio Predagio (New York: Routledge, 2011), 613–15.

54. Anna Seidel, "The Image of the Perfect Ruler in Early Taoist Messianism: Laozi and Li Hung," *History of Religions* 9 (1969–1970): 216–22. In *The Emergence of Daoism: Creation of Tradition* (New York: Routledge, 2012), qualifying this vision of Daoist kingship in the Han, Gil Raz has examined a stele erected during the reign of emperor Huandi (r. A.D. 147–67) with an inscription revealing that although the Daoist sage at that juncture enjoyed "divine status as the embodiment of the *dao*," he was not yet revered as a "cosmic god"; he was regarded as a superhuman adept, a perfect model for the ultimate practitioner, the emperor (878–79).

55. For more on Kou Qianzhi's potent Daoist influence on the Northern Wei, see Richard Mather, "K'ou Ch'ien-chih and the Taoist Theocracy of the Northern Wei," in *Facets of Taoism: Essays in Chinese Religion*, ed. Holmes Welch and Anna Seidel (New Haven: Yale University Press, 1979), 103–22; and Julia Ching, *Mysticism and Kingship in China* (Cambridge: Cambridge University Press, 1997), 222. See also Seidel, "The Image of the Perfect Ruler," 242; Lagerway, *Taoist Ritual*, 255; and Livia Kohn, "Kou Qianzhi," in Predagio, *The Routledge Encyclopedia of Taoism*, 601–02.

56. Peter Nickerson, "The Southern Celestial Masters," in *Daoism Handbook*, ed. Livia Kohn (Leiden: Brill, 2004), 258–60.

57. Livia Kohn, *Daoist Mystical Philosophy: The Scripture of Western Ascension* (Magdalena, N.Mex.: Three Pines, 2007), 164; Lagerway, *Taoist Ritual*, 256.

58. For more on the role of the divine Lord Lao in the founding and legitimation of the Tang, see Seidel, "The Image of the Perfect Ruler," 244; and Woodbridge Bingham, *Founding of the Tang Dynasty* (New York: Octagon, 1970), 118. See also chap. 9 in part III of this work.

59. Franciscus Verellen, "Liturgy and Sovereignty: The Role of Taoist Ritual and the Foundation of the Shu Kingdom (907–925)," *Asia Major*, Third Series, 2, no. 1 (1989): 59.

60. Timothy Barrett, *Taoism Under the T'ang* (London: Wellsweep, 1996), 20.

61. *Tang huiyao* [Essential Institutions of the Tang], comp. Wang Pu (Beijing: Zhonghua, 1998), 50.865 (hereafter *THY*).

62. Russell Kirkland and Livia Kohn, "Daoism in the Tang (618–907)," in Kohn, *Daoism Handbook*, 340.

63. For more on the cakravartin tradition, see Gu Zhengmei, "Wu Zetian de *Huayan jing* fowang chuantong yu Fojiao xingxiang" [Wu Zetian's *Flower Garland* Sutra Tradition of Buddhist Kingship and Buddhist Imagery], *Guoxue yanjiu* 7 (2000): 279–321; Chen Jinhua, *Monks and Monarchs, Kinship and Kingship: Tanqian in Sui Buddhism and Politics* (Kyoto: Italian School of East Asian Studies, 2002), 114–15.

64. Stanley Tambiah, "The Galactic Polity in Southeast Asia," in *Culture, Thought and Social Action*, ed. Stanley Tambiah (Cambridge: Harvard University, 1985), 255–56.

65. Scott Pearce, "A King's Two Bodies: The Northern Wei Emperor Wencheng and Representations of the Power of His Monarchy," *Frontiers of History in China* 7, no. 1 (2012): 101–02.

66. Erik Zürcher, *The Buddhist Conquest of China* (Leiden: Brill, 1972), 31.

67. Chen Jinhua, "*Pañcavārṣika* Assemblies in Liang Wudi's Buddhist Palace Chapel," *Harvard Journal of Asiatic Studies* 66, no. 1 (2006): 45 and 77. See also Max Deeg, "Origins and Development of the Buddhist Pañcavārṣika, Part II: China," *Saṃbhāṣā: Nagoya Studies in Indian Culture and Buddhism* 18 (1997): 76–79. Deeg refers to Liang Wudi as an Aśokan "imitator" (83). The festal *pañcavārṣika* is connected to ceremonies performed by the legendary King Aśoka of India, the famous Mauryan monarch who tempered his bloody conquest of a vast empire by his embrace of the Buddhist faith. In the wake of a grand tour of inspection in the third century B.C., Aśoka called for a pañcavārṣika and made a massive offering of gold and himself to the Buddhist clergy. This served the dual purpose of propagating Buddhism and celebrating his sovereignty. As John Strong contends in *The Legend of King Aśoka* (Delhi: Motilal Banarsidass, 1989), "The Pañcavārṣika was thus not only an occasion on which the king, at least symbolically, gave everything (including himself) to the sangha; it was also a time when he reaffirmed his role and position as a cakravartin. It was, moreover, something that only a cakravartin could do, since it required dominion and kingship to begin with" (95). The conjoining of the secular and sacred was mutually reinforcing. Donation and charity—extensive giving of one's self and one's possessions—was a perfect symbolic gesture of the Mahayana ideal of compassionate self-sacrifice. Material trappings were discarded, worldly manifestations were shed in an ecstatic gesture of renunciation. In essence, the ruler became a living bodhisattva yet awakened the following morning with his secular kingship intact.

68. Deeg, "Origins and Development of the Buddhist Pañcavārṣika, Part II," 78–80.

69. Kathy Cheng-mei Ku, "The Buddharāja Image of Emperor Wu of Liang," in *Philosophy and Religion in Early Medieval China*, ed. Alan K. L. Chan and Yue-kueng Lo (Albany: SUNY Press, 2010), 265–90. Ku's interpretation of Buddharājaship as "a Buddha who is also a *cakravartin*," as she points out, differs from the understanding of previous scholars like Arthur Wright and Yan Shangwen. Yan looked at Liang Wudi's kingship as a "combination of Buddhism, Confucianism, and Daoism." Wright understands "Emperor-bodhisattva" (*huangdi pusa* 皇帝菩薩) as "a fusion of the Chinese ideal kingship or 'sagely king' and the Indian ideal kingship of cakravartin," as a cultural hybrid, whereas Ku's notion of Buddharāja stems straight from the Indian/Aśokan tradition (see Ku, 265–66 and 277). While her argument is convincing, one might contend that though Liang Wudi drew heavily on the ideological sanction of Buddharājaship, he never relinquished his claim to being a Chinese emperor; he was concurrently emperor (*huangdi* 皇帝) and cakravartin.

70. Victor Cunrui Xiong, *Emperor Yang of the Sui Dynasty: His Life, His Times, His Legacy* (Albany: SUNY Press, 2006), 151–64. For a more succinct summary of Sui Wendi's patronage of Buddhism, see Hu Ji, "Sui Wendi yu Sui Yangdi de zhengzhi [The Politics of Sui Wendi and Sui Yangdi]," in *Hu Ji wencun: Sui-Tang lishi yu Dunhuang ji* [Collected Essays of Hu Ji: Volume on Sui-Tang History and Dunhuang] (Beijing: Social Sciences Press, 2004), 11.

71. Deeg, "Origins and Development of the Buddhist Pañcavārṣika, Part II," 81.

72. Translation from Arthur Wright, *The Sui Dynasty: The Unification of China, AD 581-617* (New York: Knopf, 1978), 134; cf. *Guang hongmingji*, 17.213b; *Taisho Tripitaka*, 52.2103 (hereafter *T.*).

73. Chen Jinhua, *Monks and Monarchs*; Chen Jinhua "*Pañcavārṣika* Assemblies," 97.

74. See Erik Zürcher, "Prince Moonlight: Messianism and Eschatology in Early Medieval Chinese Buddhism," *T'oung Pao* 68 (1982): 1–75; N. Harry Rothschild, "Emerging from the Cocoon: Ethnic Revival, Lunar Radiance, and the Cult of Liu Sahe in the Jihu Uprising of 682–683," *Annali* 65 (2005): 275–76; Stanley Weinstein, *Buddhism Under the T'ang* (Cambridge: Cambridge University Press, 1987), 6–7.

75. Kenneth Ch'en, *Buddhism in China* (Princeton: Princeton University Press, 1964), 172.

76. Sarah Milledge Nelson, *Gender in Archaeology: Analyzing Power and Prestige* (Walnut Creek, CA: Altamira, 1997), 19.

77. Stephen R. Bokenkamp, "A Medieval Feminist Critique of the Chinese World Order: The Case of Wu Zhao (r. 690–705)," *Religion* 28 (1998): 384.

78. Edward Schafer, *The Divine Woman: Dragon Ladies and Rain Maidens* (North Point: San Francisco, 1980), 188.

79. Ibid., 9.

80. Antonino Forte, *Political Propaganda and Ideology in China at the End of the Seventh Century: Inquiry into the Nature, Authors and Function of Dunhuang Document S. 6502 Followed by an Annotated Translation*, 2nd ed. (Kyoto: Italian School of East Asian Studies, 2005), 262.

81. There are not any comprehensive studies on the relationship between Wu Zhao and her larger pantheon of female political ancestors, but there are several essays that shed light on her relationship with specific female divinities. For more on Wu Zhao and the Luo River goddess, see Li Zhao, "Lun Wu Zetian bai Luo shoutu yu Luoshen de bianyi" [A Discussion of the Evolution of the Luo River Goddess and Wu Zetian's Worship of the Luo and Receiving the Chart], in *Wu Zetian yu Shendu Luoyang*, ed. Wang Shuanghuai and Guo Shaolin (Beijing: China Cultural History Press, 2008), 74–83; and Stephan Kory, "A Remarkably Resonant and Resilient Tang-Dynasty Augural Stone: Empress Wu's *Baotu*," *T'ang Studies* 26 (2008): 99–124. For Wu Zhao's relationship with the Mother of Qi, see Jonathan Pettit, "The Erotic Empress: Fantasy and Sovereignty in Chinese Temple Inscriptions," *T'ang Studies* 26 (2008): 125–42. Neither this list nor any of the subsequent lists is intended to be exhaustive.

82. Such studies exist: though never comprehensively, scholars have addressed many of these variables in the construction of Wu Zhao's authority. For gender politics in Tang China, see Chen Jo-shui, "Empress Wu and Proto-Feminist Sentiments in T'ang China," in *Imperial Rulership and Cultural Change in Traditional China*, ed. Frederick Brandauer and Chih-chieh Huang (Seattle: University of Washington Press, 1994), 77–114; Duan Tali, *Tangdai funü diwei yanjiu* [Research on the Position of Women in the Tang Dynasty] (Beijing: Renmin, 2000); Jowen R. Tong, *Fables for the Patriarchs: Gender Politics in Tang Discourse* (Lanham, Md.: Rowman and Littlefield, 2000); Gao Shiyu, "A Fixed State of Affairs and Mis-positioned Status: Gender Relations in Sui, Tang, and Five Dynasties," in *The Chalice and the Blade in Chinese Culture*,

ed. Min Jiayin (Beijing: Academy of Social Sciences, 1995), 270–314; Bokenkamp, "A Medieval Feminist Critique"; Diana Paul, "Empress Wu and the Historians: A Tyrant and a Saint of Classical China," in *Unspoken Worlds: Women's Religious Lives in Non-Western Cultures*, ed. Nancy Falk and Rita Gross (San Francisco: Harper Collins, 1979), 191–206; Jennifer Jay, "Imagining Matriarchy: 'Kingdoms of Women' in Tang China," *Journal of the American Oriental Society* 116 (1996): 220–29; Jay, "Vignettes of Chinese Women in Tang Xi'an (618–906): Individualism in Wu Zetian, Yang Guifei, Yu Xuanji, and Li Wa," *Chinese Culture* 31, no. 1 (1990): 77–89.

83. Without doubt, these new currents and cultural flux enabled women of seventh-century China to enjoy a more prominent social presence, greater sexual freedom, and more political influence. For the influence of Indian and Central Asian cultures on sexuality in Tang China, see Bernard Faure, *The Red Thread: Buddhist Approaches to Sexuality* (Princeton: Princeton University Press, 1998); and Robert van Gulik, *Sexual Life in Ancient China* (Leiden: Brill, 1961).

84. For more on the free-flowing and cosmopolitan nature of early Tang China, see Sen Tansen, *Buddhism, Diplomacy and Trade* (Honolulu: University of Hawaii Press, 2003); Lewis, *China's Cosmopolitan Empire*; Liu Xinru, *Silk and Religion: An Exploration of Material Life and the Thought of People, 600–1200* (New Delhi: Oxford University Press, 1996); N. Harry Rothschild, "Rhetoric, Ritual and Support Constituencies in the Political Authority of Wu Zhao, China's Only Woman Emperor" (PhD diss., Brown University, 2003), subchapter "Creating a Spiritual Capital in Keeping with the Late Seventh Century Zeitgeist: Greater Luoyang as the Hub of Wu Zhao's Cosmopolitan Empire," 66–82; Hu Ji, *Hu Ji wencun: Sui-Tang lishi yu Dunhuang ji*.

85. For two very different economic assessments of Wu Zhao's era, see Wang Shuanghuai and Zhao Wenrun, *Wu Zetian pingzhuan* [A Critical Biography of Wu Zetian] (Xi'an: Sanqin, 1993), 230–249, a chapter titled "Developing the Economy" (Fazhan jingji 發展經濟); and Jacques Gernet, *Buddhism in Chinese Society: An Economic History from the Fifth to the Tenth Centuries*, trans. Franciscus Verellen (New York: Columbia University Press, 1995). See also Denis Twitchett, *Financial Administration Under the T'ang Dynasty* (Cambridge: Cambridge University Press, 1970).

86. For the ceremony to install the Nine Tripods in Luoyang, for instance, see Ricardo Fracasso, "The Nine Tripods of Empress Wu," *Tang China and Beyond*, ed. Antonino Forte (Kyoto: Italian School of East Asian Studies, 1988), 85–96; and Rothschild, "Rhetoric, Ritual and Support Constituencies," subchapter "Wu Zhao and the Nine Tripods." For her performances of the *feng* and *shan* sacrifices, see Rothschild, "Rhetoric, Ritual and Support Constituencies," 292–309. For Wu Zhao's Buddhist *pañcavārṣika*, see Chen Jinhua, "Pañcavārṣika Assemblies"; Deeg, "Origins and Developments of the Pañcavārṣika, Part II"; Rothschild, "Zhuanlun wang, yishi, yu huozai: Wu Zhao yu 694 nian de wuzhedahui" [Cakravartin, Ceremony and Conflagration: Wu Zhao and the Pañcāvarṣika of 694], in *Qianling wenhua yanjiu* 7 (2012): 101–13. For Buddhist relic veneration ceremonies, see Chen Jinhua, *Monks and Monarchs*, 118–48; and Huang Chi-chiang, "Consecrating the Buddha: Legend, Lore, and History of the Imperial Relic-Veneration Ritual in the T'ang Dynasty," *Journal of Chung-hwa Institute of Buddhist Studies* 11 (1998): 483–533.

87. Wu Zhao's utilization of Buddhist statuary and iconography is one of the most widely researched aspects of her political and ideological authority. For an overview of her Buddhist statuary, see Patricia Karetzky, "Wu Zetian and Buddhist Art of the Tang Dynasty," *T'ang Studies* 20–21 (2002–3): 113–71. For the construction of her Bright Halls (more of an ideological hybrid than a Buddhist structure), see Antonino Forte, *Mingtang and Buddhist Utopias in the History of the Astronomical Clock: The Tower, the Statue and the Armillary Sphere Constructed by Empress Wu* (Rome: Italian Institute of East Asian Studies, 1988). For other Buddhist architecture, see Yen Chuan-ying, "The Tower of Seven Jewels and Empress Wu," *National Palace Museum Bulletin*, 22, no. 1 (March/April 1987): 1–16. For her constructions at Longmen, see Amy McNair, *Donors of Longmen: Faith, Politics, and Patronage in Medieval Chinese Buddhist Sculpture* (Honolulu: University of Hawaii Press, 2007); McNair, "Early Tang Patronage at Longmen," *Ars Orientalis* 24 (1994): 65–81; McNair, "The Fengxiansi Shrine and Longmen in the 670s," *Bulletin of Far Eastern Antiquities* 68 (1996): 325–92; Gao Junping, "Shi lun Wu Zetian shiqi Longmen shiku de Mile zaoxiang" [A Discussion of Maitreya Sculpture in the Longmen Grottoes During the Era of Wu Zetian], *Dunhuang xuejikan* no. 2 (2006): 141–44. For Dunhuang, see Roderick Whitfield, Susan Whitfield, and Neville Agnew, *Cave Temples of Mogao: Art and History on the Silk Road* (Los Angeles: Getty Conservation Institute, 2000).

Tang Daoist art has been less extensively examined. See Yang Liu, "Images for the Temple: Imperial Patronage in the Development of Tang Daoist Art," *Artibus Asiae* 61, no. 2 (2001): 189–261; and Suzanne Cahill, "The Moon Stopping in the Void: Daoism and the Literati Ideal in Mirrors of the Tang Dynasty," ed. Chou Ju-hsi and Claudia Brown, *Cleveland Studies in the History of Art*, Vol. 9: *Clarity and Luster: New Light on Bronze Mirrors in Tang and Post-Tang China, 600–1300: Papers on a Symposium on the Carter Collection of Chinese Bronze Mirrors at the Cleveland Museum of Art* (Cleveland, OH: Cleveland Museum of Art, 2005), 24–40.

There are many works on Wu Zhao's necropolis Qianling, shared with husband Gaozong; see, for instance, Chang Yuliang, *Wu Zetian yu Qianling* [Wu Zetian and Qianling] (Xi'an: Sanqin, 1986); and Fan Yingfeng and Liu Xiangyang, *Qianling wenwu shiji shucong* [A Narrative Record of the Historical Relics in the Qianling Mausoleum] (Xi'an: Shaanxi Tourism, 1987).

88. See Rothschild, "Rhetoric, Ritual and Support Constituencies," subchapter "The Calendar," 282–91.

89. See Barrett, *The Woman Who Discovered Printing* (New Haven: Yale University Press, 2008).

90. See Kuranaka Susumu, *Sokuten monji no kenkyu* [Research on the Characters of Zetian] (Tokyo: Kanrin shobo, 1995); N. Harry Rothschild, "Drawing Antiquity in Her Own Image: The New Characters of Wu Zetian," *China Yongu: The Journal of Chinese Studies of Pusan National University* 15, no. 3 (2009): 117–70; Shi Anchang, "Wu Zetian zao zi zhi ebian" [Evolution of the Characters Created by Wu Zetian], *Gugong bowuyuan yuankan* (1992), 58–62; Dong Zuobin and Wang Hengyu, "Tang Wuhou gaizi kao" [A Study of the Altered Characters of Tang Empress Wu], *Bulletin of the Institute of History and Philology of Academia Sinica* 34 (1963): 447–76; Tokiwa Daijô, "Bushû shinji no ichi kenkyû" [A Study of the New Characters of the Wu-Zhou era], *Shina bukkyô no kenkyû* 3 (1943): 395–430.

91. See Wang Yueting, "Wu Zetian yu nianhao" [Wu Zetian and Reign-era Names], in *Wu Zetian yanjiu lunwenji* [Collected Essays on Wu Zetian], ed. Zhao Wenrun and Li Yuming (Taiyuan: Shanxi guji, 1998); and N. Harry Rothschild, "An Inquiry into Reign Eras Under Wu Zhao, China's Only Female Emperor," *Early Medieval China* 12 (2006).

92. For the role that Wu Zhao's promotion of literature and poetry played in the construction of her political authority, see Wang Shuanghuai and Zhao Wenrun, *Wu Zetian pingzhuan*, 268–78; Wilt Idema and Beata Grant, *The Red Brush: Writing Women of Imperial China* (Cambridge, Mass.: Harvard University Asia Center, 2004), 60–66; Doran, "Insatiable Women"; Chen, "The Writing of Imperial Poetry"; Zhang Jian, "Wu Zetian shiwen fanying de zhengzhi sixiang zhuzhang" [The Political Thought of Wu Zetian as Reflected in Her Poetry and Writings], in *Wu Zetian yu Luoyang* [Wu Zetian and Luoyang], ed. Su Jian and Bai Xianzhang (Xi'an: Sanqin, 1993); Rothschild, "Rhetoric, Ritual and Support Constituencies," subchapters "Wu Zhao's Literary and Cultural Patronage," 86–91, and "Chen Zi'ang," 215–23; and Zhao Wenrun, "Wu Zetian yu 'wenzhang siyou'" [Wu Zetian and the Quartet of Literary Friends], *Qianling wenhua yanjiu* 6 (2011): 51–59.

93. Rothschild, "Rhetoric, Ritual and Support Constituencies," chap. 3, "Language and Power," 83–141.

94. For more on the background of the Wu clan and Wu Zhao's efforts to elevate her fellow Wus, see Chen Yinke, "Ji Tangdai zhi Li-Wu-Wei-Wang hunyin jituan" [A Record of the Marriage Bloc of the Li, Wu, Wei, and Wang Clans in the Tang Dynasty], *Lishi yanjiu* 1 (1955): 85–96; Liang Hengtang, "Tan Wu shi jiazu de qiyuan yu fanyan" [A Discussion of the Origins and Rise of the Wu Clan], in *Wu Zetian yu Yanshi*, ed. Zhao Wenrun and Liu Zhiqing (Yanshi: Lishi jiaoxue, 1997); Zhang Jie, "Wu Zetian yu tade Wushi zongqin" [Wu Zetian and Her Relatives from the Wu Clan], *Hebei shifan daxue xuebao* (1999): 114–18. On Wu Zhao's efforts as emperor to mitigate tensions between her affinal Lis and her natal Wu clan through a series of strategic marriages and the sworn oath to maintain harmonious relations in 699 at the Bright Hall, see Wang Shuanghuai and Zhao Wenrun, *Wu Zetian pingzhuan*, 294–96.

95. See Niu Laiying, "Tangdai xiangrui yu wangchao zhengzhi" [Auspicious Portents and Dynastic Politics in the Tang Dynasty], in *Tang wenhua yanjiu* [Essays on Research in Tang Culture], ed. Zheng Xuemeng and Leng Minshu (Shanghai: Shanghai People's Press, 1994), 535–44; Kory, "Tang-Dynasty Augural Stone"; Jie Yongqiang, "Wu Zetian yu xiangrui" [Wu Zetian and Auspicious Omens], in Zhao Wenrun and Li Yuming, *Wu Zetian yanjiu lunwenji*, 160–67.

96. For her uncanny ability to control the domestic uprisings against her in 684 and 688, see Wang Shuanghuai and Zhao Wenrun, *Wu Zetian pingzhuan*, 118–49; and Hu Ji, *Wu Zetian benzhuan* [Essential Biography of Wu Zetian] (Xi'an: Shaanxi Shifan daxue, 1998), 82–88 and 99–105. For Wu Zhao's management of conflicts with foreign states, see Wang Shuanghuai and Zhao Wenrun, *Wu Zetian pingzhuan*, 250–67; Jonathan Skaff, *Sui-Tang China and Its Turko-Mongol Neighbors* (New York: Oxford University Press, 2012); Pan Yihong, *Son of Heaven and the Heavenly Qaghan*; Abramson, *Ethnic Identity in Tang China*.

97. There is a great deal of material on Wu Zhao's relations with her non-Han subjects and on her foreign policy. For internationalization of Wu Zhao's empire, see Zhang Naizhu, "Wu-Zhou Zhengquan yu Zhonggu huhua xianxiang guanxi zhi tansuo" [An Exploration of the Connection Between the Political Authority of the Wu-Zhou Dynasty and Internationalization in Chinese Middle Antiquity], *Xibei shi di* no. 4 (1992): 31–39, and his article "Cong Luoyang chutu wenwu kan Wu-Zhou zhengzhi de guojiahua qingcai" [A View of the International Cultural Background of the Politics of the Wu-Zhou Dynasty from the Unearthed Relics in Luoyang], *Tang Yanjiu* 8 (2002): 205–24; see also Antonino Forte, "Iranians in China: Buddhism, Zoroastrianism, and Bureaus of Commerce," *Cahiers d'Extrême-Asie* 11 (1999–2000): 277–90; Chiu Ling-yeong, "Persians, Arabs and Other Nationals in Tang China," *Journal of the Hong Kong Royal Asiatic Society* 13 (1973): 58–72.

For Wu Zhao's non-Han generals, see Ma Chi, "Fanjiang yu Wu Zetian" [Non-Han Generals and the Political Authority of Wu Zetian], *Xuchang shizhuan xuebao* no. 4 (1991): 31–36. For foreign fund-raising to sponsor projects such as the Axis of the Sky (Tianshu), see Zhang Naizhu, "Wu-Zhou Wanguo tianshu yu Xiyu wenming" [The Wu-Zhou Axis of Sky of Myriad Nations and the Civilization of the Western Borderlands], *Xibei Shidi* no. 2 (1994): 44–45; Forte, *Mingtang and Buddhist Utopias*, 233–243; Guo Shaolin, "Da Zhou Wanguo songde tianshu kaoshi" [An Explanatory Investigation into the Axis of the Sky of Myriad Countries Exalting the Merits of the Great Zhou], *Luoyang Shifan xueyuan xuebao* no. 6 (2001): 73–77; N. Harry Rothschild, "The Koguryan Connection: The Quan (Yon) Family in the Establishment of Wu Zhao's Political Authority," *China Yongu: The Journal of Chinese Studies of Pusan National University* 14, no. 1 (2008): 199–234; Zhao Zhenhua, "Zhuchi jianzao Tianshu de waifan renwu yu 'Zilai shi'" [The "Come-as-Sons Commissioner" and Foreigners Who Supported the Construction of the Axis of the Sky], in *Wu Zetian yu Shendu Luoyang*, 294–98.

98. For a specific case study of Wu Zhao's complex relationship with prominent Confucian literati, see David McMullen, "The Real Judge Dee: Ti Jen-Chieh and the T'ang Restoration of 705," *Asia Major*, Third Series, 6, no. 1 (1993): 1–81. For a broad perspective on Wu Zhao's role in the larger transformation of the Confucian literati, see Peter Bol, *This Culture of Ours* (Stanford, Calif.: Stanford University Press, 1992), 76–107. For Wu Zhao's role in reforming the selection and assessment process, see P. A. Herbert, *Examine the Honest, Appraise the Able*, Faculty of Asian Studies Monograph, New Series, no. 10 (Canberra: Australia National University, 1988).

99. See, for instance, Andrew Eisenberg, "Emperor Gaozong, the Rise of Wu Zetian and Factional Politics in the Early Tang," *Tang Studies* 30 (2012): 45–69.

100. See Qiang Fang, "Hot Potatoes: Chinese Complaint Systems from Early Times to the Late Qing (1898)," *Journal of Asian Studies* 68, no. 4 (2009): 1105–35; Wang Shuanghuai, "Wu Zetian yu kuli de guanxi" [The Relationship Between Wu Zetian and Her Cruel Officials], in Zhao Wenrun and Li Yuming, *Wu Zetian yanjiu lunwenji*, 177–86. Hu Ji, *Wu Zetian benzhuan*, devotes two chapters to Wu Zhao's cruel officials (*ku li* 酷 吏). See also Rothschild, "Rhetoric, Ritual and Support Constituencies," subchapter "Wan Guojun," 252–59; and Ma Xiaoli, "Guanyu Wu Zetian zhongyong kuli de jidian kanfa" [Several Observations on Wu Zetian's Heavy Utilization of Cruel Officials], *Yantai daxue xuebao* no. 3 (1991): 42–44.

I. GODDESSES OF ANTIQUITY

1. William McNeill, "The Care and Repair of Public Myth," *Foreign Affairs* 61, no. 1 (Fall 1982): 5.

2. Susan Mann, "Presidential Address: Myths of Asian Womanhood," *Journal of Asian Studies* 59, no. 4 (2000): 835–37.

3. Anne Birrell, *Chinese Mythology: An Introduction* (Baltimore, Md.: Johns Hopkins University Press, 1993), 163.

4. Mann, "Myths of Asian Womanhood," 842.

5. Sir James George Frazer, *The New Golden Bough* (New Jersey: Phillips, 1965), 132.

1. WU ZHAO AS THE LATE SEVENTH-CENTURY AVATAR OF PRIMORDIAL GODDESS NÜWA

1. Mark Edward Lewis, *The Flood Myths of Early China* (Albany: State University of New York Press, 2006), 120; Schafer, *The Divine Woman*, 39.

2. Christina Miu Bing Cheng, "Matriarchy at the Edge: The Mythic Cult of Nüwa in Macau" (paper presented at the 17th Triennial Conference of the International Comparative Literature Association, Hong Kong, 8–15 August 2004).

3. Schafer, *The Divine Woman*, 37.

4. Edward Schafer, "Ritual Exposure in Ancient China," *Harvard Journal of Asiatic Studies* 14, no. 1/2 (1951): 156, referring to Chen Mengjia's 陳夢家 1936 article "Myths and Shamanism in Shang China" [Shangdai de shenhua yu wushu 商代的神話與巫術].

5. Qu Yuan, *Chuci/Ch'u Tz'u: Songs of the South*, trans. David Hawkes (Boston: Beacon, 1959), 51; and Birrell, *Chinese Mythology*, 35, from "Heavenly Questions" (Tian wen 天文).

6. Andrew Plaks, *Archetype and Allegory in Hsi yü chi and Hung lou meng* (Princeton: Princeton University Press, 1976), 30.

7. Translation from Cai Junsheng, "Myth and Reality: The Projection of Gender Relations in Pre-historic China," in Min Jiayin, *The Chalice and the Blade*, 35.

8. *Liezi*, chaps. 2 and 5, trans. Fatima Wu, in *Images of Women in Chinese Thought and Culture: Writings from the Pre-Qin Period Through the Song Dynasty*, ed. Robin Wang (Indianapolis: Hackett, 2003), 96. On the dating, in *Liezi/The Book of Lieh-tzu: A Classic of Tao* (New York: Columbia University Press, 1990), 1, A. C. Graham remarks that "the predominant opinion of scholars in China is now that it was written as late as A.D. 300." This passage also appears in *Huainanzi* [The Master of Huainan], comp. Liu An (Xi'an: *Hanji quanwen jiansuo xitong*, 2004), "Surveying Obscurities" (Lanming xun 覽冥訓), chapter 6 (hereafter *HNZ*).

9. *HNZ* 6.95. Lewis, *Flood Myths*, 111–12, translates this account of Nüwa quelling the flood.

10. *HNZ* 17.292. Translation from Cai Junsheng, "Myth and Reality," 35.

11. Cai Junsheng, "Myth and Reality," 44–45.

12. *Shanhai jing* [Classic of Mountains and Seas], trans. Anne Birrell (New York: Penguin, 1999), 173.

13. This late Eastern Han work is cited in the Northern Song *Taiping yulan* [Imperial Readings of the Taiping Era], ed. Li Fang (Beijing: Zhonghua, 1995), 78.365 (hereafter *TPYL*); translation from Derk Bodde's "Myths of Ancient China," 388.

14. Schafer, *The Divine Woman*, 38.

15. Wu Hung, *The Wu Liang Shrine* (Stanford, Calif.: Stanford University Press, 1989), 144, 156, and 161; Cheng Te-k'un, "Yin-yang Wu-hsing in Han Art," *Harvard Journal of Asiatic Studies* 20, no. 1/2 (1957): 182.

16. Denise Chao, "The Snake in Chinese Belief," *Folklore* 90, no. 2 (1979): 195.

17. Lee Irwin, "Divinity and Salvation: The Great Goddesses of China," *Asian Folklore Studies* 49, no. 1 (1990): 55.

18. Birrell, *Chinese Mythology*, 164. In *The Divine Woman*, Schafer (1980) remarks, "Orthodox belief, from Han times on, found difficulties in reconciling this zoomorphic deity with the ideal but artificial hero or heroine to which her name was finally applied, in accordance with the new 'Confucian' insistence on euhemerization. Her gradual degradation from her ancient eminence was partly due to the contempt of some eminent and educated men for animalian gods, and partly to the increasing domination of masculinity in elite social doctrine" (37).

19. Cai Junsheng, "Myth and Reality," 44.

20. Edward Schafer, *Ancient China* (New York: Time Life, 1967), 102. Justine Snow, in "The Spider's Web. Goddesses of Light and the Loom: Examining the Evidence for Indo-European Origin of Two Ancient Chinese Deities," *Sino-Platonic Papers* 118 (June 2002): 26, similarly maintains that "after the revisionist Han period this heroine was demoted and her worship was discouraged by the ruling class."

21. Edward Schafer, *Pacing the Void* (Berkeley: University of California Press, 1977), 23.

22. Robin Wang, *Yin Yang: The Way of Heaven and Earth in Chinese Thought and Culture* (New York: Cambridge University Press, 2012), 101–2.

23. *TPGJ* 304.2407; translation modified from Schafer, *The Divine Woman*, 63.

24. *QTS* 162; translation from Schafer, *The Divine Woman*, 92.

25. Li Fubu, "Gudai ming nüzi: fenfen ru Tangshi" [Celebrated Women Sprinkled in Tang Poems], *Zhishi jiushi liliang* no. 3 (2007): 72–73.

26. *HNZ*, chapter 6.

27. *XTS* 35.898, 905.

28. *XTS* 35.922.

29. For this catalog of misfortunes, see *ZZTJ* 203.6410. See also Richard Guisso, "The Reigns of the Empress Wu, Chung-tsung and Jui-tsung," in *The Cambridge History of China*, vol. 3, *Sui and T'ang China*, ed. Denis Twitchett and John Fairbank (Cambridge: Cambridge University Press, 1979), 278 (hereafter *CHC*).

30. *QTW* 218.2203.

31. Zhao Wenrun, "Wu Zetian yu 'wenzhang siyou,'" 51–52.

32. *JTS* 94.2996.

33. Zhao Wenrun, "Wu Zetian yu 'wenzhang siyou,'" 52–53.

34. *QTW* 243.2461. Li Qiao wrote this memorial on behalf of General Wei Daijia.

35. *JTS* 94.2992–93.

36. Zhao Wenrun, "Wu Zetian yu 'wenzhang siyou,'" 53. Based mostly on Li Qiao's biographies in the two Tang histories, Zhao charts the trajectory of the rhetorician's career. Li Qiao rose to chief minister during the Sage Calendar era (20 December 697 to 27 May 700).

37. Bokenkamp, "A Medieval Feminist Critique," 390; c.f. *QTW* 248.2510. In this inscription, Li Qiao mentions Wu Zhao's decision in 691 to establish a Great Cloud Monastery in every prefecture. More precisely, the inscription uses her title Maitreya, Sagely and Divine Emperor, Cakravartin of the Golden Wheel Transcending Antiquity, granted 23 November 694. As "Maitreya" was removed on 6 March 695, the inscription was likely composed during that three-and-a-half-month window.

38. *JTS* 31.1131 gives the date of the creation of the musical composition as the first year of Guangzhai (19 October 684 to 9 February 685).

39. *ZZTJ* 203.6421.

40. Guisso, *CHC*, 292.

41. *ZZTJ* chaps. 203 and 204. For summaries of this critical juncture in secondary sources, see N. Harry Rothschild, *Wu Zhao, China's Only Woman Emperor*, Longman World Biography Series (New York: Longman, 2008), 81–91; Guisso, *CHC*, 290–306.

42. Xunyu 獯鬻 is likely a reference to the Turkic tribes that resettled within the Tang borders during Gaozong's reign. It is another term for Xiongnu, the northern steppe tribes that had plagued the Central Plains since the Warring States era.

43. Juli 句驪 is an ancient name for the Korean peninsula. Gaozong conquered Koguryo in 668, the signature martial feat of his reign.

44. Gaozong and Wu Zhao jointly performed the *feng* and *shan* rites on Mount Tai in 666. See *ZZTJ* 201.6346; *JTS* 5.89–90; 23.888; see also Wechsler, *Offerings of Jade and Silk*, 184–85.

45. Rothschild, "Wu Zhao's Remarkable Aviary," *Southeast Review of Asian Studies* 27 (2005): 73. This article contains a longer section on the symbolic role of the phoenix during Wu Zhao's ascendancy and rule (72–76). *Laiyi* originally comes from a passage in the "Canon of Yao" chapter of the *Book of History*: "When the pipes and the *yong* bell are used in timely fashion, birds and beasts come rapidly; when the flute harmonizes the nine achievements, the phoenix comes and regulates (*laiyi*)"; see *Shangshu zhengyi* [Orthodox Commentary on the Book of History], ed. Kong Yingda, in *Shisan jing zhushu* [Commentaries and Notes on the Thirteen Classics], chief ed. Li Xueqin (Beijing: Beijing University Press, 1999), 5.127.

The creation of musical instruments with perfect ritual pitch and cadence was also attributed to Nüwa. See *Sui Shu* [History of the Sui Dynasty], comp. Wei Zheng (Beijing: Zhonghua, 1996), 30.375 (hereafter *SS*). For more on the connection between Wu Zhao, female divinities, the phoenix, and properly harmonious ritual instruments, see chap. 8, "The Queen Mother of the West and Wu Zhao," in this volume.

46. *Shuowen jiezi* [An Explanation and Analysis of Chinese Characters], comp. Xu Shen (Zhengzhou: Zhongyuan nongmin, 2000), 1156.

47. *ZZTJ* 171.5301. Lu Lingxuan was the influential wet nurse of young Qi emperor Gao Wei (r. 565–77).

48. *XTS* 4.87; and *ZZTJ* 204.6448.

49. See Laozi, *Tao Te Ching*, trans. D. C. Lau (London: Penguin, 1963), 57, (I.1).

50. *QTW* 217.2192.

51. Ibid.

52. Kwang-chih Chang, *Art, Myth and Ritual*, 12–13; Birrell, *Chinese Mythology*, 114–15.

53. *QTW* 217.2193

54. "Siji," *The Book of Songs* (Ji'nan: Shandong Friendship Press, 1999), 707.

55. Yang Lien-sheng, "Female Rulers in Imperial China," 52.

56. There are many variants of the Three Sovereigns. See Kwang-chih Chang, *Art, Myth and Ritual*, 2.

57. *Fengsu tongyi*, chap. 1, in *Images of Women in Chinese Thought*, trans. Fatima Wu, ed. Robin Wang, 99.

58. *QTW* 135.1362.

59. *Jin shu* [History of Jin], comp. Fang Xuanling (Beijing: Zhonghua, 1997), 35.1053 (hereafter *JS*).

60. *THY* 7.93. The Mysterious Register (*xuan lu* 玄籙) seems to have been a cryptic source of the secrets of governance.

61. *JTS* 5.111–12.

62. Like Emperor Shun of antiquity, facing south and ruling through effortless action.

63. *QTW* 13.162. This translation is drawn from a version of the edict recorded in the second chapter of Du Guangting's *Daode zhen jing guangsheng yi* 道德真經廣聖義 (recorded in the *QTW* as the *Daode shenjing guangxun* 道德真經廣訓, likely a minor mistake).

64. *QTW* 217.2193.

65. *QTW* 212.2147–48.

66. *XTS* 107.4069; *QTW* 209.2115.

67. *QTW* 209.2113.

68. *QTW* 780.8151. This text also appears in the commentary of the *Comprehensive Mirror* (*ZZTJ* 205.6502) from 695, intimating that the remonstrance of the Wife of Yidu prompted Wu Zhao to order her monk-lover Xue Huaiyi beaten to death. There is no viable evidence, however, that indicates the historicity of the Wife of Yidu, let alone that Wu Zhao followed her advice. See also Cai Junsheng, "Myth and Reality," 35.

69. This is the same sort of remonstrance a good Confucian wife, as "inner helper," might offer her husband. See Paul Rakita Goldin, *The Culture of Sex in Ancient China* (Honolulu: University of Hawaii Press, 2002), 62–65.

70. Liang Yongtao and Tang Zhigong, "Dui Guangyuan Wudai 'Da Shu Lizhou dudufy Huangzesi Zetian Huanghou Wushi xin miaoji' bei de jiaozhu ji xianguang wenti fenxi" [An Analysis and Commentary on the "New Shrine Record of Tang Empress Zetian of the Wu Family in Huangze Temple of Great Shu Commandery of Lizhou" from Five Dynasties-era Guangyuan], in *Conference Proceedings from the 11th Conference of the Wu Zetian Research Association* (Guangyuan, 2013), 431–37.

71. A version of this legend can be found in Bai Jian, "Shi xi Wu Zetian wulong ganyun shenhua de tuteng beijing jian shi Fu Xi taiyangshen shengsi xunhuan he weiyang tuteng neihan ji longshe tuteng chansheng beijing," in *Conference Proceedings from the 11th Conference of the Wu Zetian Research Association*, 442. In *Writing and Authority in Early China* (Albany: State University of New York Press, 1999), Mark Lewis notes that in one Han apocryphal tale, the mother of ancient ruler Yao, one of the ancient sage-rulers, had been impregnated by a dragon, though the dragon first presented her with a mystical chart or writing (440n43). See also Lewis, *Flood Myths*, 121.

72. Lewis, *Flood Myths*, 71.

73. *SJ* 8.341; see also, Sima Qian, *Records of the Grand Historian*, trans. Burton Watson (New York: Columbia University Press, 1993), 52.

74. This is another name for Laozi's hometown in Luyi, Henan.

75. *QTW* 259.2626–28.

76. Wu Ding was a Shang king in the late thirteenth and early twelfth century B.C. who renovated a struggling dynasty.

77. *QTW* 259.2627.

78. See Kang Weimin, "Su Anheng sanjian Wu Zetian" [Su Anheng Thrice Remonstrates with Wu Zetian], *He-Luo Chunqiu* no. 3 (2007): 50–55.

79. *QTW* 237.2391. An abbreviated version of this petition can be found in *ZZTJ* 207.6556.

80. Ibid.

81. *ZZTJ* 207.6559; *QTW* 237.2392–93.

82. *QTW* 237.2392–93.

83. Lewis, *Flood Myths*, 150.

2. SANCTIFYING LUOYANG

1. Schafer, *The Divine Woman*, 68.

2. Qu Yuan, "Li Sao," as translated by Paul Goldin in "Imagery of Copulation in Early Chinese Poetry," *Chinese Literature: Essays, Articles and Reviews* 21 (December 1999): 56. See also Goldin's translation of "Li Sao" in *Hawai'i Reader of Traditional Chinese Culture*, ed. Victor Mair, Nancy Steinhardt, and Paul Goldin (Honolulu: University of Hawaii Press, 2005), 99–100. The Wade-Giles in the translation has been changed to pinyin.

3. Goldin, "Imagery of Copulation," 56.

4. Birrell, *Chinese Mythology*, 140; cf. Tang commentator Li Shan in *Sibu congkan* edition of *Wenxuan* 19.14.

5. *The Cambridge History of Chinese Literature*, vol. 1, *To 1375*, ed. Kang-i Sun Chang and Stephen Owen (Cambridge: Cambridge University Press, 2010), 175.

6. Cao Zhi, "The Goddess of the Luo," in *Chinese Rhyme Poems*, ed. Burton Watson (New York: Columbia University Press, 1971), 56–57.

7. Robert Cutter, "The Death of Empress Zhen: Fiction and Historiography in Early Medieval China," *Journal of the American Oriental Society* 112, no. 4 (1992): 577. Cutter remarks on the consonance between the rhapsody and later *zhiguai* 志怪 (miraculous) tales featuring encounters between mortals and beautiful ghosts or divinities.

8. Schafer, *The Divine Woman*, 70.

9. Patricia Karetzky, "The Representation of Women in Medieval China: Recent Archaeological Evidence," *T'ang Studies* 17 (1999): 216, based on a copy of the painting at the Freer Gallery in Washington.

10. Susan Nelson, "Tao Yuanming's Sashes: Or, the Gendering of Immortality," *Ars Orientalis* 29 (1999): 15.

11. Zhang Mingxue, "Gu Kaizhi zhi 'Luoshen fu tu' zhong de Daojiao shenxian yiyun" [Connotations of Daoist Immortals in Gu Kaizhi's "Picture Scroll of the Luo River Nymph"], in *Shijie zongjiao wenhua* 1, no. 1 (2007): 31–32. There are four extant

Song reproductions of Gu Kaizhi's Eastern Jin masterpiece: two in the Forbidden City in Beijing (one from the Northern Song and one from the Southern Song); one in the Liaoning Museum; and one in the Freer Gallery.

12. Wu Hung, *The Double Screen: Medium and Representation in Chinese Painting* (London: Reaktion, 1996), 96–97. See also Tonia Eckfield, *Imperial Tombs in Tang China, 618–907: The Politics of Paradise* (New York: Routledge, 2005), 130.

13. *Hou Han Shu* [Later Han History], comp. Li Xián and Fan Ye (Beijing: Zhonghua, 1997), 6.259 (hereafter *HHS*).

14. *JS* 21.671.

15. *JS* 59.1591.

16. Schafer, *The Divine Woman*, 90.

17. Ibid., 113.

18. Ibid., 170–72.

19. *QTS* 474.5382.

20. Du Guangting, *Yongcheng jixian lu* [Register of the Assembled Transcendents of the Walled City], in *Yunji qiqian* [Seven Tablets from the Satchel of Clouds], comp. Zhang Junfang (Beijing: Xinhua, 1996), 717–22. For more on Du Guangting and Maoshan Daoism, see Suzanne Cahill, "Performers and Female Taoist Adepts: Hsi Wang Mu as the Patron Deity of Women in Medieval China," *Journal of the American Oriental Society* 106, no. 1 (1986): 155–56. There is no indication, however, that the Luo River goddess was considered exclusively Daoist in Wu Zhao's time.

21. For more on the traditional foundations of Luoyang, see He Guanbao, ed., *Luoyang wenwu yu guji* [Cultural Relics and Records of Sui-Tang Luoyang] (Beijing: Xinhua, 1987); and Su Jian, *Luoyang gudu shi* [A History of Ancient Capital Luoyang] (Beijing: Bowen, 1989).

22. Zhang Jian, "Wu Zetian shiwen fanying," 135. One can often find "Center of Heaven" in modern-day calligraphy samples in the Luoyang–Mount Song region.

23. *ZZTJ* 200.6308; *XTS* 3.58; *JS* 4.77.

24. See Chen Yinke, "Ji Tangdai zhi Li-Wu-Wei-Wang hunyin jituan," 85–96.

25. *ZZTJ* 204.6421; *JTS* 6.117; and *XTS* 4.83 all contain descriptions of these reforms.

26. See Forte, *Political Propaganda*, and part IV of this volume. The full name of the text is *Commentary on the Meanings of the Prophecies About the Divine Sovereign in the Great Cloud Sutra*.

27. The discovery of this augural stone (*rui shi* 瑞石) on 3 June 688 is recorded in *XTS* 4.87; *JTS* 24.925; and *ZZTJ* 204.6447. See also Forte, *Political Propaganda*, 271–72n79. This stone was found before the inscribed stone from the Luo River was presented to Wu Zhao. This is borne out by one of the ritual songs (*QTS* 5.56) written to celebrate the discovery of the latter stone: "The waters of the Si River first made manifest the mysterious image; now the kindly Luo has offered up the Eternal Diagram."

28. Forte, *Political Propaganda*, 272.

29. Ibid., 275–76. On 276n99, Forte notes that *tuzhong* 土中, "center of the territory," is a phrase used to indicate the central position of Luoyang in the *Book of History*.

30. *ZZTJ* 204.6467.

31. *XTS* 4.90, 76.3480; *JTS* 6.121; *ZZTJ* 204.6467–69.

32. *JTS* 6.122; *XTS* 4.92, 14.342; *TPGJ* 243.2453.

33. *JTS* 87.2854. Li Zhaode supervised the project, also devising a system to renovate several city gates. The date is given as 692 in both *Cefu yuangui* [Storehouse of the Original Tortoise], comp. Wang Qinruo (Beijing: Zhonghua, 1994), 504.6048 (hereafter *CFYK*); and *ZZTJ* 205.6478–79.

34. For two accounts of the development of Luoyang into a spectacular capital under Wu Zhao, see Wang Feng's essay, "Wu Zetian yu Tang Luoyang ducheng jianshe" [Wu Zetian and the Construction of Tang Capital Luoyang], *He-Luo chunqiu* no. 3 (2007): 15–20; and Guo Shaolin, *Sui-Tang Luoyang*, 34–61.

35. *JTS* 6.124; 89.2902; *XTS* 4.95; *ZZTJ* 205.6494, 6496; *TPGJ* 240.1850; 236.1816.

36. For a thorough study of this ideologically multilayered architectural marvel, see Antonino Forte, *Mingtang and Buddhist Utopias*, esp. 143–53.

37. For Wu Zhao's elaborate ceremony to install the tripods, see *ZZTJ* 206.6517; *XTS* 4.95; *THY* 11.279–80. For the original political myth of the Nine Tripods, see Kwang-chih Chang, *Art, Myth and Ritual*, 63–64 and 95–97.

38. *Tang da zhaoling ji* [Edicts and Imperial Decrees of the Tang], comp. Song Min-qiu (Shangwu, Taiwan: Huawen, 1968), 95.

39. Zhang Jian, "Wu Zetian shiwen fanying," 136.

40. See Kwang-chih Chang, *The Archaeology of Ancient China* (New Haven: Yale University Press, 1987).

41. *CFYK* 504.6048. See also later texts like Xu Song's nineteenth-century *Tang Liangjing chengfang kao* [A Study of the Walled Cities and Wards of the Two Tang Capitals] (Beijing: Zhonghua, 1985), 5.178 (hereafter *TLJCFK*).

42. *TLJCFK*, 5.178.

43. *JTS* 6.115, 119; 24.925; *XTS* 4.87; 76.3470; *ZZTJ* 204.6448. On the problematic translation of the eight-character omen that appears on the Precious Diagram, see Kory, "Tang-Dynasty Augural Stone," 101n9.

44. In *Offerings of Jade and Silk*, Howard Wechsler describes Haotian shangdi as an "all-embracing, universal Heavenly deity who belonged not to one family but to all the empire" (x).

45. *JTS* 6.115, 119; 24.925; *XTS* 4.87, 76.3470; *ZZTJ* 204.6448–54. For the most extensive and directed study of the Precious Diagram, see Kory, "Tang-Dynasty Augural Stone," 99–124. Doran, "Insatiable Women," has remarked that Wu Zhao's "great faith in a blatantly sycophantic forgery" is part of a familiar narrative construction to delegitimize female rulers, a tradition reflected in her reported "wanton acceptance" (232) of "auspicious" omens manufactured by sycophants.

46. For the role of credenda and miranda in political power, see Charles Merriam, *Political Power* (New York: Collier, 1964), 125–33.

47. Lewis, *Flood Myths*, 196n36.

48. Doran, "Insatiable Women," 224. Weinstein, in *Buddhism Under the T'ang*, similarly observed that the very name Precious Diagram suggested "the prognostication charts and books that supposedly emerged from the Yellow and Lo Rivers during the reigns of mythical sage emperors Fu-hsi and Yü" (41).

49. Robin Wang, *Yin Yang*, 208.

50. *Zhouyi zhengyi* [Correct Meanings of the Zhou Book of Changes], comp. Kong Yingda, in *Shisanjing zhushu*, ed. Li Xueqin, (Beijing University Press, 1999), 7.290.

51. Lewis, *Flood Myths*, 196n36; cf. *Mozi/Ethical and Political Works of Motse*, trans. Mei Yi-pao. (Westport, Conn.: Hyperion, 1973), 19, "Feigong xia" 非攻下.

52. Wang Shuanghuai and Zhao Wenrun, *Wu Zetian pingzhuan*, 167. For more on Fuxi as the recipient of the River Chart, see Michael Saso, "What Is the 'Ho-t'u'?" *History of Religions* 17, no. 3/4 (1978): 406–7. He cites *Han shu* [History of the Han Dynasty], comp. Ban Gu and Ban Biao (Beijing: Zhonghua, 1997), 27.315–16 (hereafter *HS*), and the Zhonghou apocryphal commentary on the *Book of Documents*. Also see Lewis, *Writing and Authority*, 200–1, who links Fuxi's association with the Yellow River Chart to his association with the origins of writing, 197–201. Fuxi is not alone in his connection with the Yellow River Chart. There is a more complex matrix of mythology surrounding the emergence and transmission of the Yellow River Chart that is linked to other culture heroes: the Yellow Emperor, Cang Jie, King Wu of Zhou.

53. *HS* 75.3189. See also Li Zhao, "Lun Wu Zetian bai Luo shoutu yu Luoshen de bianyi," 74–83.

54. Wechsler, *Offerings of Jade and Silk*, 32.

55. Lewis, *Flood Myths*, 118–19, discusses the political potency of these celebrated charts.

56. For Gaozong and Wu Zhao, "Two Sages" was not an official title, but a popular nickname that acknowledged Wu Zhao's political participation. According to the *Old Tang History* (*JTS* 6.115), "From the Xianqing reign era (656–660) on, Gaozong was often afflicted with illness. All petitions and memorials were determined by the Celestial Empress . . . for several decades, her prestige and influence was no different than that of the emperor. So people of the time called them the Two Sages." *XTS* 76.3475–76 reads, "When Shangguan Yi was executed [in 664], political power returned to behind the curtain. The Son of Heaven simply folded his hands. The officials of the four quarters who submitted memorials called emperor and empress the Two Sages." *ZZTJ* 201.6242–43 contains a similar account.

The earliest reference to the Two Sages in official histories appears in the *Later Han History*, where it is used to indicate Kings Wen and Wu of the Zhou. Mere decades before Wu Zhao's time, Sui Wendi's Empress Dugu sat on the throne with her husband and coauthored edicts. They were called "the Two Sages," a title that concealed the feminine aspect of Empress Dugu. Given this political value, it is little wonder Wu Zhao borrowed this number from Dugu's political repertoire.

57. Forte, *Political Propaganda*, 372. The Luo River Writing had tremendous resonance in Daoism as well. Catherine Despeux, in "Talismans and Sacred Diagrams," identifies the Flying Tortoise of the Yi and Luo rivers (Yi-Luo feigui 伊洛飛龜) that brought forth the Luo River Writing, as one of the talismanic cosmic diagrams, the "numinous treasures," central to the Lingbao Daoist tradition (*Daoism Handbook*, 505). In an apocryphal Daoist text of the late Han or early Period of Disunity, the tortoise-borne Luo River Writing, a talisman endowed with numinous powers that helped the practitioner connect with divine powers, is written in red and green. See Yamada Toshiaka, "The Lingbao School," in Kohn, *Daoism Handbook*, 228.

In an era in which the "three faiths" coexisted, competed, and shared many intellectual strands, Buddhism, too, appropriated some of the traditional weight of the sacrosanct Luo River Writing. Chen Jinhua, in his article "Yixing 一行 and Jiugong 九宫 ('Nine Palaces'): A Case of Chinese Redefinition of Indian Ideas," *China Report* 48 (2012): 115–16, shows that the Buddhist monk Yixing worked to integrate "the Sinitic intellectual pattern" of the Five Phases (*wuxing* 五行) encoded in the Luo River cosmogram into a mandala of his design.

58. *JTS* 24.925; *XTS* 4.87; *ZZTJ* 204.6449; *THY* 47.833. Kory ("Tang-Dynasty Augural Stone," 101–3) translates this section. He (104) points out that Wu Zhao lifted her next two reign names "Eternal Prosperity" (Yongchang 永昌) and "Heaven Bestowed" (Tianshou 天授), the first era of her Zhou dynasty, from the inscription on the augural stone. Though many rulers had honored and worshipped the Luo, Li Zhao contends that Wu Zhao's act of investing the Luo River spirit with the title "Marquise Who Reveals the Saint" was unprecedented.

59. In traditional Chinese schema of the Five Marchmounts, Mount Song was the central peak—Mount Tai to the east, Mount Hua to the west, Mount Heng 恒山 to the north, and Mount Heng 衡山 to the south are usually regarded as the other four. Mount Heng was also one of the Four Marchmounts in Buddhism, along with Mount Wutai, Mount Putuo, and Mount Emei.

60. *QTW* 209.2115. A general wishing to express his good wishes, Cheng Chubi sought a talented man of letters to convey his feelings and found Chen Zi'ang to write this memorial on his behalf. *JTS* 68.2504 contains a thumbnail biography for Cheng Chubi, appended at the end of the longer biography of his father Cheng Zhijie, who had served as a general under Taizong.

61. Kory, "Tang-Dynasty Augural Stone," 105–10.

62. Ibid., 105.

63. The first three Tang rulers: Gaozu, Taizong, and Gaozong.

64. *Yiwen leiju* [Classified Collection of the Literary Arts], comp. Ouyang Xun (Shanghai: Shanghai guji, 1982), 8.161–62.

65. *QTS* 61.723.

66. For instance, Yu is described in Kong Anguo's Western Han commentary, cited in Kong Yingda's (574–648) later commentary on the *Book of Documents*. See Timothy Wai Keung Chan, *Considering the End: Mortality in Early Medieval Chinese Poetic Representation* (Leiden: Brill, 2012), 22n52.

67. *Guben Zhushu jinian jijiao* [Comparative Annals of Ancient Bamboo Records], ed. Zhu Youzeng (Shenyang: Liaoning jiaoyu, 1997), 40.

68. *QTS* 59.706. In *Mozi*, chap. 19, the writing on the Yellow River Chart is also green. See also Lewis, *Flood Myths*, 196n36.

69. *QTW* 243.2457–58. See also Kory, "Tang-Dynasty Augural Stone," 119.

70. Kory, "Tang-Dynasty Augural Stone," translates and comments upon the entirety of Li Qiao's memorial (112–22).

71. *QTW* 217.2195.

72. *QTS* 99.1072. Niu Fengji does not appear in either of the Tang histories. This is his only poem in the *Complete Anthology of Tang Poetry*. It is accompanied by the remark that in the Protracted Longevity era (23 October 692 to 6 June 694), Wu Zhao entrusted him with the compilation of the *Tang History*.

73. *ZZTJ* 204.6454.

74. Julia Ching, "Son of Heaven: Sacral Kingship in Ancient China," *T'oung Pao* 83 (1997): 39.

75. *XTS* 76.3480; *JTS* 24.925; *ZZTJ* 204.6454. Eugene Wang, in *Shaping the Lotus Sutra: Buddhist Visual Culture in Medieval China* (Seattle: University of Washington Press, 2005); and Chen Jinhua, in *Philosopher, Practitioner, Politician: The Many Lives of Fazang (643-712)* (Leiden: Brill, 2007), both recognize this as a staged event, "part of an elaborately planned process of legitimation" (Wang, 144) in Wu Zhao's protracted campaign for emperorship.

76. *QTS* 5.55-56; *QTW* 12.107-09; *JTS* 30.1113-15. Both *JTS* and *QTW* record that there are fifteen rather than fourteen hymns. Both sources indicate that the "Harmony of Revelation" song was played twice—the first time to worship the Luo River and the second time to honor Wu Zhao receiving the diagram. As the name for the collection of songs written for the occasion, I have used the title from *JTS* 30, "Music to Honor the Luo River with Grand Sacrifice" (Da xiang bai Luo zhang 大饗拜洛章), rather than the *QTS* title, "Music for the Great Tang Sacrifice to Venerate the Luo" (Tang da xiang bai Luo yuezhang 唐大饗拜洛樂章). This ceremony to the Luo River was not the only time Wu Zhao celebrated the discovery of the Precious Diagram in song and ritual. When Wu Zhao personally composed a twelve-stanza song for the universal deity in Tang China, the Supreme Thearch of Boundless Heaven, she also alluded to the diagram. See *JTS* 30.1092; and *QTS* 5.52-53; 10.87.

77. *QTS* 5.55.

78. Doran, "Insatiable Women," 141, 143.

79. *JTS* 8.177; 24.925; *XTS* 5.126.

80. *XTS* 5.126. See also Forte, *Political Propaganda*, 207, and *Mingtang and Buddhist Utopias*, 243-45 and 267-68. Forte has remarked on the violent reaction of "the conservative wing of Confucianism" against Wu Zhao and cataloged the campaign of Xuanzong to erase her imprint upon Luoyang. Also see Tonami Mamoru, "Policy Towards the Buddhist Church in the Reign of T'ang Hsuan-tsung," *Acta Asiatica* 55 (1988): 27-47.

81. Wu Zhao took on the designation Celestial Empress in the eighth month of 674. See *JTS* 5.99; *XTS* 3.71; *ZZTJ* 202.6372-73.

82. For the dating of this memorial see Forte, *Political Propaganda*, 316n-317n. Forte remarks that "even this simple episode of the herb *zhi* shows us the connection among officials, relatives of Wu Zhao and Buddhist monks in finding and diligently interpreting the miracles and omens for the propaganda activity in favor of Wu Zhao."

83. *QTW* 218.2201.

84. Wu Hung, *The Wu Liang Shrine*, 86; cf. *Chunqiu fanlu*.

85. *QTW* 192.1944-47.

86. Wang Bo, Lu Zhaolin, and Luo Binwang are the other three.

87. A spirit or deity associated with the Yellow River.

88. *QTW* 192.1946.

89. *Xian sheng* 顯聖.

90. Forte, *Political Propaganda*, 305. Yitong (or Yi Tong, if a Daoist), Forte conjectures (305-6n235), was a Buddhist or Daoist monk whose prophetic record was compiled during Wu Zhao's regency.

91. Because of the Buddhist context of the *Record of Master Yitong*, "saint" is used here.

92. *QTW* 243.2457, translation from Kory, "Tang-Dynasty Augural Stone," 115.

93. Charles Hucker, *A Dictionary of Official Titles in Imperial China* (Stanford, Calif.: Stanford University Press, 1985), 399. Hucker is used for bureaucratic titles throughout this book.

94. *JTS* 24.914.

3. FIRST LADIES OF SERICULTURE

1. *SJ* 1.21–22. In a prototype to the *Book of Rites*, Dai De's 戴德 Western Han work *Da Dai Li Ji* 大戴禮記 [Record of Rites of Dai the Elder] (chap. 63), Nüying and Ehuang came to be considered the goddesses of the Xiang River.

2. *HS* 99.4106.

3. *Sanguo zhi* [Chronicles of the Three Kingdoms], ed. Chen Shou (Beijing: Zhonghua, 1997), 5.165 (hereafter *SGZ*). See Robert Cutter and William Crowell's translation of this chapter in *Empresses and Consorts: Selections from Chen Shou's Records of the Three States with Pei Songzhi's Commentary* (Honolulu: University of Hawaii Press, 1999), 106.

4. Bi Xiuling, "Lun Zhongguo fangzhi nüshen de jisi lisu jiqi yingxiang" [A Discussion of Sacrifices to Chinese Weaving Goddesses in Ceremony and Folk Practice], *Changjiang daxue xuebao* 30, no. 5 (2007), 14.

5. Bret Hinsch, "Textiles and Female Virtue in Early Imperial Chinese Historical Writings," *Nan nü* 5, no. 2 (2003): 182.

6. For a much more thorough account of the origins of Leizu's emergence as First Sericulturist and of other early silk deities and goddesses, see Dieter Kuhn, "Tracing a Chinese Legend: In Search of the Identity of the 'First Sericulturalist,'" *T'oung Pao*, Second Series, 70 (1984): 213–45; or Kuhn, *Science and Civilization in China*, vol. 5, *Chemistry and Chemical Technology*, part 9, *Textile Technology: Spinning and Reeling* (Cambridge: Cambridge University Press, 1988), 247–72.

7. Kuhn, "Tracing a Chinese Legend," 241.

8. Bi Xiuling, "Lun Zhongguo fangzhi nüshen," 15.

9. Francesca Bray, *Technology and Gender: Fabrics of Power in Late Imperial China* (Berkeley: University of California Press, 1997), 183.

10. Bray, *Technology and Gender*, 183, 237. In the section titled "Paired Virtues: Plowing and Weaving" (185–91), Hinsch, in "Textiles and Female Virtue," also examines the gendered pairing *geng-sang* 耕桑 (plowing and growing mulberries).

11. Hinsch, "Textiles and Female Virtue," 171–72.

12. Bret Hinsch, *Women in Early Imperial China* (Lanham, Md.: Rowman and Littlefield, 2002), 68–69.

13. Hinsch, "Textiles and Female Virtue," 182.

14. Ban Zhao, *Admonitions for Women* (Nü jie 女誡) in *Hou Han shu* 84.2789, in William De Bary and Irene Bloom, eds., *Sources of Chinese Tradition*, vol. 1, *From Earliest Times to 1600* (New York: Columbia University Press, 1999), 824. Originally translated by Nancy Swann in *Pan Chao: Foremost Woman Scholar of China* (New York: Century, 1932), 86.

Francesca Bray (*Technology and Gender*, 184) has noted that one of the variant forms of *gong* (work) included the radical signifying "silk" or "textiles." Collectively, speech, appearance, morality, and work constituted the "four virtues" (*side* 四德) of women in Confucian thought.

15. "Tianguan neizai," in *Zhouli zhushu* [Commentaries on the Zhou Book of Rites], annotated by Jia Gongyan 賈公彥 (Tang Dynasty, 7th cent.), in *Shisanjing zhushu*, ed. Li Xueqin (Beijing: Beijing University Press, 1999), 7.184. Du You's mid-Tang *Tongdian* [Comprehensive Manual of Institutions] (Beijing: Zhonghua, 1996), 46.1188 (hereafter *TD*), corroborates this record, noting that beginning in the Zhou dynasty of antiquity, empresses performed sericulture rites in the springtime, weaving silk to make ceremonial raiment.

16. Chen Jo-shui, "Empress Wu and Proto-Feminist Sentiments," 79. The sacred field ritual was often associated with First Agriculturist (*xian nong* 先農) Shennong, the Divine Farmer.

17. *HS* 4.117.

18. Hinsch, "Textiles and Female Virtue," 187–88.

19. Kuhn, "Tracing a Chinese Legend," 221.

20. *TD* 46.1188–90.

21. *JS* 19.590; 25.765.

22. Chen Jo-shui, "Empress Wu and Proto-Feminist Sentiments," 79.

23. Kuhn, *Science and Civilization in China*, vol. 5, 247.

24. *TD* 46.1190.

25. Hucker, in *A Dictionary of Official Titles*, translates *sangu* 三孤 as the "Three Solitaries," remarking that it referred to "the three posts in the topmost echelon of the central government" (398).

26. *SS* 7.145.

27. Several scholars have identified this key passage in the *Sui shu*, written in the early Tang, as clinching evidence that Leizu was indeed the First Sericulturist in Tang China. In his study on the identity of the First Sericulturist, Dieter Kuhn ("Tracing a Chinese Legend," 225) contends that by the Tang "the Chinese had no doubt as to the First Sericulturalist's identity: they simply knew that lady Hsi-ling personified the First Sericulturalist." Bi Xiuling ("Lun Zhongguo fangzhi nüshen," 14) makes a similar claim.

28. *XTS* 15.367–71.

29. *SS* 7.145. One *li* was roughly one-third of a mile; see *CHC*, xx, for weights, measurements, and distances in the Tang.

30. *XTS* 15.367–71.

31. Michael Como, "Silkworms and Consorts in Nara Japan," *Folklore Studies* 64, no. 1 (2005): 112.

32. *THY* 10.160.

33. *ZZTJ* 195.6134–35 records Wu Zhao's initial entry into Taizong's seraglio as a Talent.

34. *JTS* 4.74–75; 76.3475.

35. *JTS* 4.75; *XTS* 3.57; *TD* 46.1290; *THY* 10.260.

36. Chen Jo-shui, "Empress Wu and Proto-Feminist Sentiments," 79–80; Rothschild, "Rhetoric, Ritual and Support Constituencies," 56–57.

37. *JTS* 30.1122–23; *QTS* 12.116–17. There are several differences between the two versions. This translation adheres to the *Old Tang History* version.

38. *JTS* 4.75. In contrast to Wu Zhao's long procession, in 759, Suzong's Empress Zhang worshipped the First Sericulturist at a shrine in the imperial park just north of the imperial palace. For this rite, see *JTS* 24.935; 10.255; *THY* 10.260. The northern imperial park in Chang'an was also known as Xinei Park—see Victor Cunrui Xiong, *Sui-Tang Chang'an: A Study in the Urban History of Medieval China* (Ann Arbor: Center for Chinese Studies, University of Michigan, 2000), 57. His map of ritual centers in Chang'an (6.1) includes the location of the altar of the First Sericulturist.

39. Xiong, *Sui-Tang Chang'an*, 149.

40. *JTS* 15.370; *XTS* 12.329. In many rites and sacrifices, ceremonial jade coins were initially placed as an offering in a round basket. Corresponding in color with the direction north in Five Phases (*wuxing* 五行), the ritual coins used in the sacrifice to the First Sericulturist were black; this aligned with the ritual precinct where the rite was performed.

41. Chen Jo-shui, "Empress Wu and Proto-Feminist Sentiments," 79–80.

42. Ibid., 79, 107n12.

43. *JTS* 5.92; *XTS* 3.67; *THY* 10.260.

44. *JTS* 5.98; *XTS* 3.71; *THY* 10.260.

45. *JTS* 5.100; *XTS* 3.71; *THY* 10.260; *ZZTJ* 202.6375.

46. Chen Jo-shui, "Empress Wu and Proto-Feminist Sentiments," 107–08n13. Chen contends that Wu Zhao's repeated performance of these First Sericulturist rites was part of a wider "proto-feminist" agenda, "a larger pattern of actions (including re-designating titles for the nine ranks of women in the inner palace and mass participation of women in the *feng* and *shan* ceremonies of 666) that promoted the position and interests of women" (79–80).

47. *ZZTJ* 209.6620.

48. *QTW* 276.2805; *JTS* 51.2173; *ZZTJ* 209.6619–20.

49. *ZZTJ* 209.6620.

50. For more on the efforts of these women who followed in the wake of Wu Zhao to establish a similar set of female political ancestors, see "Appendix: Daughters of Lesser Goddesses" at the end of this chapter.

51. Doran, "Insatiable Women," 159–62.

52. Ibid., 171–72; cf. *Tangshi jishi* 唐詩紀事, comp. Ji Yougong 記有功 (Taibei: Dingwen, 1971), 3.34-35.

53. Bi Xiuling, "Lun Zhongguo fangzhi nüshen," 14.

54. *XTS* 14.357. *QTW* 189.1908 contains a memorial by courtier-official Wei Shuxia requesting that the name be changed back to the traditional "sacred field altar." This memorial was presented in Zhongzong's court in 705, shortly after Wu Zhao's ouster. Immediately after Zhongzong's restoration of the Tang, almost all of Wu Zhao's changes to ceremonial protocol and nomenclature were reversed. For more on this specific debate over the First Agriculturist altar, see *THY* 22.421–24; see also Kominami Ichiro, "Rituals for the Earth," in *Early Chinese Religion*, part 1, *Shang Through Han (1250 BC–220 AD)*, ed. John Lagerway and Mark Kalinowski (Leiden: Brill, 2009), 208–09.

55. *Chen gui* [Regulations for Ministers], comp. Wu Zhao, in *Zhongjing ji qita wuzhong*, *Congshu jicheng chubian* 0893 (Taibei: Shangwu, 1936), 60–61 (hereafter *CG*).

56. Madame Yang was not Wu Sansi's flesh-and-blood grandmother. For more on the context and background of this inscription, see Antonino Forte, in "The Chong-fusi in Chang'an: A Neglected Buddhist Monastery and Nestorianism," in his edited volume *L'inscription nestorienne de Si-ngan-fou: A Posthumous Work by Paul Pelliot* (Kyoto: Italian School of East Asian Studies, 1996), 457; and Chen Jinhua, *Monks and Monarchs*, 111–12n6. The inscription was calligraphed by Wu Zhao's son Li Dan, Ruizong.

57. *QTW* 239.2417.

58. Eliade, *Myth and Reality*, 12.

59. Hinsch, "Textiles and Female Virtue," 200.

60. Ibid., 193.

61. *QTS* 61.723 (Li Qiao); 91.987 (Wei Sili); 73.804 (Su Ting). See Doran, "Insatiable Women," subchapter "A Landscape of Immortal Women: Visiting and Imagining the Powerful Women of the Imperial Court," 143–45.

62. *QTS* 69.774.

63. *QTW* 240.2427. Translation from Doran, "Insatiable Women," 164. The Wu Girl star, like the Vermilion Bird, was associated with the south.

64. Edward Schafer, *The Vermilion Bird: T'ang Images of the South* (Berkeley: University of California Press, 1967), 124–25.

65. *QTS* 93.1004. See Doran, "Insatiable Women," 146.

66. *QTS* 106.1105. See Doran, "Insatiable Women," 151–53.

II. DYNASTIC MOTHERS, EXEMPLARY MOTHERS

1. Doran, "Insatiable Women," 38; see esp. her subchapter, "Violence and the Anti-mother: Precedents for the Unnatural Female and Her Quest for Power," 51–83.

2. Many scholars have pointed out the problematic nature of Wu Zhao's purported killing of her own children. See, for instance, Hu Ji, *Wu Zetian benzhuan*, 60–66; C. P. Fitzgerald, *The Empress Wu* (Melbourne: Cheshire, 1955), 22–23, 83–84; Richard Guisso, *Wu Tse-t'ien and the Politics of Legitimation in T'ang China* (Bellingham: Western Washington University Press, 1978), 23, 212–13n66.

3. Idema and Grant, *The Red Brush*, 17–42, contains not only commentary on and analysis of Ban Zhao's remarkable career, but translations of her poetry, several memorials that she wrote to the emperor, and *Admonitions for Women*.

4. Anne Kinney, *Representations of Childhood and Youth in Early China* (Stanford: Stanford University Press, 2004), 20–21.

5. Dorothy Ko, *Teachers of the Inner Chambers: Women and Culture in Seventeenth-Century China* (Stanford: Stanford University Press, 1994), 17.

6. Judith Butler, "Performative Acts and Gender Constitution: An Essay in Phenomenology and Feminist Theory," *Theatre Journal* 40, no. 4 (1988): 522.

7. Following Sherry Mou's numbering precedent from her translations in chap. 33, "Women in the Standard Histories," in Wang, *Images of Women*, 255–60, I indicate the chapter and entry number in Liu Xiang's *Biographies of Exemplary Women*. Here, for instance, 1.4 indicates the Woman of Tushan appears in chap. 1, entry 4.

8. The mother of Zhao general Kuo does not appear among the models of "maternal rectitude" in the opening chapter. Her account appears in the final entry of the third chapter, "Biographies of the Benign and Wise."

9. This lineage of reproduction and commentaries is discussed in detail in chap. 7 of this volume.

10. Mou ("Women in the Standard Histories," 255–64) has translated the prefaces (*xu* 序) and eulogies (*zan* 讚) for "Biographies of Exemplary Women" in three histories—*The Later Han History, The Jin History,* and the *History of the Northern Dynasties.*

11. Yu 虞 is Emperor Shun 舜. His Consort Nüying and Empress Ehuang are featured in the opening chapter of Liu Xiang's *Biographies.*

12. You Shen 有莘 of Yousong 有娀 married King Tang, the first ruler of the Shang dynasty.

13. As dowager-regent, Empress Deng presided over the Eastern Han court from A.D. 106 to A.D. 121. The famous female historian-scholar Ban Zhao served as her adviser.

14. *JS* 96.2507. Modified from Mou's translation in "Women in the Standard Histories," 257. The preface preceded accounts of thirty-five Jin-era women who Fang Xuanling, the compiler of the history, deemed worthy of inclusion.

15. Sometimes a single entry in *Biographies of Exemplary Women* contains several separate but connected women—e.g., "The Two Consorts of Yu" (1.1) or "The Three Mothers of Zhou" (1.6).

4. THE MOTHER OF QI AND WU ZHAO

1. *SJ* 2.84. There is another tradition in which Nüwa and the Woman of Tushan are conflated, so that Yu the Great and Nüwa appear as husband and wife. See Lewis, *Flood Myths,* 121, 134. This monograph treats the two women as distinct figures.

Albert O'Hara, in *The Position of Women in Early China* (Taipei: Mei Ya, 1971), 20n1, notes that Tushan was a small ancient statelet set along the Huai River in Anhui.

2. *Shu Ching,* trans. Clae Waltham (Chicago: Henry Regnery, 1971), 34.

3. *Dengfeng xianzhi* [Dengfeng County Annals] (1803; Henan: Dengfeng County Office, 1984), 81–82, (hereafter *DFXZ*). See also Birrell, *Chinese Mythology,* 122–23; Lewis, *Flood Myths,* 138. The stone of the mother of Qi is at the very foot of Mount Song, not far from modern-day Dengfeng. According to *Wuyue shihua* [Legends of the Five Marchmounts] (Beijing: Zhonghua shuju, 1982), 107, Yu's father Gun 鯀 was also known as Earl Chong (Chong bo 崇伯). Interestingly, *chong* (崇) and the *song* (嵩) of Mount Song share a common etymological origin.

4. *HS* 6.190.

5. *DFXZ,* 171–72.

6. See Paul Kroll, "The Memories of Lu Chao-lin," *Journal of the American Oriental Society* 109, no. 4 (1989): 590.

7. O'Hara, *The Position of Women,* 20–21. Translation of *Lienü zhuan* [Biographies of Exemplary Women], comp. Liu Xiang; Song woodblock edition with illustrations by Gu Kaizhi (Charlottesville, Va.: University of Virginia Library Electronic Text Center), 1.4, http://etext.virginia.edu/chinese/lienu/browse/LienuImgTOC.html (hereafter *LNZ*). Another story in the *DFXZ* (82) also illustrates the lofty character of the Tushan Girl. At one juncture, Yu the Great reputedly offered to bequeath his sovereignty not to his son Qi, but to his minister Boyi. Boyi declined and decided to

lead a reclusive life on Jishan (part of greater Mount Song; Wu Zhao and Gaozong set up a shrine here in 683; *JTS* 5.110). As a result, kingship was passed from father to son and the Xia dynasty began. When Boyi died, Qi's mother offered sacrifices on his behalf.

8. Lewis, *Flood Myths*, 79–82. He also notes that many of the offspring were, for their part, wicked and unfilial sons. Citing *Mozi* and other texts, Lewis comments that Qi, indulging in excess drink and music, "is treated as a deviant or criminal, acting as a moral inversion to his father Yu" (82).

9. "Quwu of Wei" from "Biographies of the Benign and Wise" (*LNZ* 3.14), as translated in O'Hara, *The Position of Women*. *SJ* 49.1967 contains a similar passage, which is translated in Lisa Raphals, *Sharing the Light* (Albany: State University of New York Press, 1998), 19. An anti-exemplar, Moxi is featured as the opening biography in chap. 7 of the *Lie nü zhuan*, "Biographies of Pernicious Favorites" (Niebi zhuan 孽嬖傳).

10. The "six forms of proper conduct" (*liu xing* 六行) are filial piety (*xiao* 孝), friendship (*you* 友), harmony (*mu* 睦), matrimony (*yin* 姻), a sense of duty (*ren* 任), and compassion (*xu* 恤).

11. *JS* 31.959.

12. *Nan Qi shu* [History of the Southern Qi Dynasty], comp. Xiao Zixian (Beijing: Zhonghua, 1997), 11.183 (hereafter *NQS*).

13. *Wei shu* [History of the Wei Dynasty], comp. Wei Shou (Beijing: Zhonghua, 1995), 92.1977.

14. *Zhou shu* [History of the Northern Zhou], ed. Linghu Defen (Beijing: Zhonghua, 1997), 9.147.

15. *JS* 96.2507.

16. The first ancestor of Shang, born to Jiandi after she ate the egg of a dark swallow.

17. Hou Ji, first male ancestor of the Zhou, was born to Jiang Yuan after she trod in the Supreme God's footprint. See chap. 5 in this volume.

18. *JS* 73.1936.

19. *QTW* 15.179.

20. *QTW* 192.1944.

21. *QTW* 219.2209. Cui Rong drafted this memorial for General Wei, probably Wei Daijia, who rose to eminence briefly during Wu Zhao's regency, largely due to his help in overseeing the construction of Gaozong's (and later Wu Zhao's) imperial funerary park, Qianling. He served as a prime minister from 685 to 689. This is likely when the petition was written. It is not surprising that he asked Cui Rong to draft the edict, for it is recorded in his biography (*JTS* 77.2671–72; *XTS* 98. 3904) that the general was ridiculed because of his lack of talent in the civil arts.

22. *QTW* 209.2114. This wet nurse was honored as the Lady of the State of Feng. Chen Zi'ang drafted the memorial on her behalf.

23. The 600-line inscription can be found in the *QTW* 219.2515–23. Guisso (*Politics of Legitimation*, 11–16) provides a lengthy description of the content of the inscription. The *Commentary on the Great Cloud Sutra* (see also chapter 12) expressly states that "Coiling Dragon Tower" was another name for Wu Zhao's Mingtang. See Forte, *Political Propaganda*, 269–70; Forte, *Mingtang and Buddhist Utopias*, 180, 194n.

24. This honorific was bestowed upon Wu Zhao's mother (née Yang 楊) on 20 October 690, just days after the female emperor inaugurated her Zhou dynasty. See *ZZTJ* 204.6468 and *XTS* 4.91.

25. *QTW* 249.2519.

26. *JTS* 25.951; *QTW* 281.2848.

27. *QTW* 297.3016.

28. *Shanhai jing*, 115, 177. See also *Chuci/Ch'u Tz'u: The Songs of the South*, 49–50.

29. Sarah Allen, "The Myth of the Xia Dynasty," *Journal of the Royal Asiatic Society of Great Britain and Ireland* 2 (1984): 251.

30. *Mozi/Ethical and Political Works of Motse*, 212–13.

31. *ZZTJ* 205.6499 (order) and 206.6517 (completion). See also Fracasso, "The Nine Tripods," 85–96.

32. Birrell, *Chinese Mythology*, 53.

33. Ibid., 83–84; cf. residual fragments of *The Storehouse of All Things*, a Han text that is "no longer extant except in fragments."

34. Ibid., 85; cf. *Shanhai jing*.

35. *QTW* 218.2201.

36. Forte, *Mingtang and Buddhist Utopias*, 162.

37. *TPYL* 887.3943, referring to the *Shanhai jing*.

38. Ibid., 171–72. In chap. 26 of the *Rizhilu* 日知錄, Qing scholar Gu Yanwu (1613–1682) commented that the younger sister did not originally exist and was added by later generations of historians.

39. *CFYG* 2.18. In "Relics and Flesh Bodies: The Creation of Ch'an Pilgrimage Sites," in *Pilgrims and Sacred Sites in China*, ed. Susan Naquin and Yü Chün-fang (Berkeley: University of California Press, 1992), 155–65, Bernard Faure has noted that during the early Tang, there was a Chan Buddhist "conquest" of Mount Song; these Buddhist monks suppressed local cultic centers and shrines, replacing them with monasteries and stupas. Though Wu Zhao honored Chan masters like Shenxiu and Zhishen, she also protected and patronized certain local cults connected to Mount Song, like that of the Woman of Tushan.

40. *JTS* 5.105–06.

41. *QTW* 192.1944. The precise dating for the composition of this inscription is problematic. See Pettit, "The Erotic Empress," 129n22. The most plausible guess would be between 680 and 683, during Gaozong's final years, when temples to the mother of Qi and other divinities in the vicinity of greater Mount Song were established.

42. The *Kuodizhi* 括地志 [Treatise of the Vast Earth] was a geographic manual written during Taizong's reign by his fourth son Li Tai (618–652) and Xiao Deyan (558–645).

43. *QTW* 192.1944.

44. Pettit, "The Erotic Empress," 131.

45. As with Yang Jiong's inscription for Shaoyi, the precise timing is problematic. See Pettit, "The Erotic Empress," 129n22.

46. For a biography of Cui Rong, see *JTS* 94.2996–3000 and *XTS* 114.4195–96. For a general overview of politics during Gaozong's last years and the cliques forming around the crown princes, see Denis Twitchett and Howard Wechsler, "Kao-tsung

(reign 649–83) and the Empress Wu: The Inheritor and the Usurper," in *CHC*, 269–73; and Rothschild, *Wu Zhao*, 67–80.

47. Pettit ("The Erotic Empress," 130–31) both points out the political motivation for Cui Rong's florid inscription and remarks upon the differences between Cui's inscription and Yang Jiong's.

48. Barrett, *Taoism Under the T'ang*, 41.

49. Bokenkamp, "A Medieval Feminist Critique," 387.

50. Gu Yewang (519–583) was a writer and commentator of the Northern Dynasties.

51. The commentary of *TD* 179.4737 indicates that "some people claim that capital of Yu of Xia was established in Henan's Yangdi." The "Treatise on Geography" in the *HS* 28 corroborates the claim that Yangdi was the location of the state of Yu of Xia. Following *Zhongguo lishi dituji* [Chinese Historical Atlas], ed. Tan Qixiang (Beijing: Zhongguo ditu, 1996), 2: 44–5, Yangdi, set along the Ying River, is about 35 km southeast of Mount Song. Tellingly, Yangdi is situated in Yu 禹 County—the Yu of Yu the Great.

52. Following *CFYG* 2.18, Huaxu is both the birthplace of Fuxi's mother and the name by which she is known. Nüdeng is the mother of Divine Farmer, Shennong. Youfang is the mother of Zhuanxu.

53. Guo Pu (276–324) was a Daoist erudite of the Eastern Jin.

54. Li Tong was a Jin-era scholar who wrote a work researching burials.

55. *QTW* 220.2220.

56. *QTW* 220.2222. Translation from Pettit, "The Erotic Empress," 137.

57. Pettit, "The Erotic Empress," 142.

58. *JTS* 5.110 and *THY* 7.102. A Daoist observatory was established inside Fengtian Palace in 684; see *THY* 50.878.

59. *JTS* 23.891.

60. The above-mentioned *feng* and *shan* sacrifices.

61. These titles were bestowed in the seventh lunar month of 688; see *ZZTJ* 204.6449 and chap. 2 of this volume.

62. Lesser Room was the site where Wu Zhao performed the *shan* rite in 696.

63. For more on this Daoist divinity, see chap. 8 of this volume.

64. *ZZTJ* 205.6504. See also *JTS* 6.124 and *TPYL* 110.529–30.

65. Zhao Xiaoxing, "Mogao ku di 9 ku 'Songshan shen song mingtangdian ying tu' kao" [A study of the Wall Painting in Cave Nine of the Mogao Grottoes of the God of Mount Song Sending a Pillar to the Mingtang], *Dunhuang yanjiu* no. 3 (2011), 40.

66. On Jade Capital (Yujing 玉京), see Paul Kroll, "Li Po's Transcendent Diction," *Journal of the American Oriental Society* 106, no. 1 (1986): 107; and Edward Schafer, "The Origin of an Era," *Journal of the American Oriental Society* 85, no. 4 (1965): 545.

67. Isabelle Robinet, "Shangqing—Highest Clarity," in Kohn, *Daoism Handbook*, 213.

68. *TPGJ* 1.1. The *Tang Huiyao* (50.865) records a title that Xuanzong bestowed upon Laozi in 754, Great Sage of the Exalted Great Dao, Emperor of the Primal Origin, and Golden Tower. A similar title is recorded in *XTS* 5.149 and in *ZZTJ* 217.6924.

69. *Tang liudian* [Tang Administrative and Legal Compendium of the Six Ministries], comp. Li Linfu (Beijing: Zhonghua, 1992), 7.221.

70. *QTS* 44.540. Both *XTS* 3.74 and *JTS* 5.103 indicate, for instance, that Gaozong and Wu Zhao retreated from Chang'an to the mountain palace in the fifth month of 678.

71. *THY* 50.878.

72. *QTW* 214.2166. Chen Zi'ang was directed by Zhang Changning to write the memorial. Zhang Changning's motive likely was to help elevate his brothers, Wu Zhao's favorites, Zhang Changzong and Zhang Yizhi. The timing (697) coincides neatly with the arrival of these two young men in Wu Zhao's court. For the biographies of the Zhang brothers, see *JTS* 78.3337 and *XTS* 104.3921.

73. *QTW* 98.1007.

74. *QTS* 5.53.

75. *XTS* 114.4195 and *JTS* 94.2996. The timing of the progress in question is unclear. In the *Old Tang History*, it is recorded that it was during the Sage Calendar era (20 December 697 to 28 May 700).

76. *QTS* 387.4374.

5. UR-MOTHERS BIRTHING THE ZHOU LINE

1. Lisa Raphals, "Gendered Virtue Reconsidered: Notes from the Warring States and the Han," in *The Sage and the Second Sex*, ed. Li Chenyang (Chicago: Open Court, 2000), 236.

2. *HS* 20.863–68. See Raphals, "Gendered Virtue," 228.

3. Raphals, "Gendered Virtue," 229, citing *SJ* 49.1967.

4. Ibid., 237.

5. Sarah Allen, "The Identities of Taigong Wang 太公望 in Zhou and Han Literature," *Monumenta Serica* 30 (1972–1973): 69–72.

6. Translation is from Birrell, *Chinese Mythology*, 117–18, from *Book of Songs* 245. Wade-Giles has been changed to pinyin.

7. Kinney, *Representations of Childhood*, 36.

8. Robert Campany, "The Meaning of Cuisines of Transcendence in Late Classical and Early Medieval China," *T'oung Pao*, Second Series, 91 (2005): 11–12.

9. In *Chinese Views of Childhood* (Honolulu: University of Hawaii Press, 1995), Anne Kinney observes that "great vitality" in an infant might be taken as a sign of "inborn wickedness" and might even constitute "justification to commit infanticide" (24–25).

10. Sarah Allen, in *The Shape of the Turtle: Myth, Art and the Cosmos in Early China* (Albany: State University of New York Press, 1991), remarks that the offspring of human unions with divinities are often abandoned (44).

11. *SJ* 1.3, as translated in Birrell, *Chinese Mythology*, 118. "Qi" literally means the "Discarded One" or the "Abandoned."

12. Campany, "The Meaning of Cuisines," 10.

13. Translation slightly modified from O'Hara, *The Position of Women*, 17–19. For original text, see *LNZ* 1.2.

14. *SGZ* 5.162–63. Translation Cutter and Crowell, *Empresses and Consorts*, 102.

15. Laurence E. R. Picken and Noël J. Nickson, *Music from the Tang Court 7: Some Ancient Connections Explored* (Cambridge: Cambridge University Press, 2000), 9, remark that the *yize* was considered to be one of six members of male pitch pipes in a "superior generation," while *zhonglü* were one of six members of the pitch pipes belonging to the "inferior generation."

16. According to the *Zhou Book of Rites*, the "Grand *huo*" was the music of Tang the Successful (Cheng Tang 成湯), the first ruler of the Shang.

17. *SGZ* 5.162–63. Translation from Cutter and Crowell, *Empresses and Consorts*, 102–03.

18. Ibid., 103.

19. *JS* 31.954.

20. *JS* 31.959.

21. *TD* 72.1972.

22. *XTS* 74.3136.

23. King Ling of Zhou reigned from 571 to 545 B.C.

24. My identification of King Wen as the original forefather (*yuan fu* 原夫) is also based on the fact that when Wu Zhao established her Zhou dynasty, she made the Zhou founder her Wu clan's first ancestor. This is discussed further later in this chapter.

25. King Ling reputedly was born with a mustache; see *SJ* 14.630.

26. The text of the stele inscription, "Stele for the Ascended Immortal Crown Prince," can be found in *QTW* 98.1007–08.

27. For more on the ties between Wu Zhao, Mount Goushi, the Queen Mother of the West, and Prince Jin, see chap. 8 in this volume; and Rothschild, "Wu Zhao's Remarkable Aviary," 76–79, 86–87n39.

28. *SJ* 4.121.

29. *XTS* 76.3481–82; *ZZTJ* 204.6467. For a genealogical table of the Wu family and more on Wu Zhao's family background, see Wang Shuanghuai and Zhao Wenrun, *Wu Zetian pingzhuan*, 1–7.

30. *ZZTJ* 207.6554.

31. *Chaoye jianzai* [Collected Records from Court and Country], ed. Zhang Zhuo (Beijing: Zhonghua, 1997), 3.73. The same story appears in *TPGJ* 238.1832, and the *kao yi* 考異 (examining the discrepancies) of the *ZZTJ* 207.6554. Wang Yueting, in "Wu Zetian yu nianhao," 154, mentions two meanings of Dazu—"the Buddha's great footprint" (*Fo zhi da zu* 佛之大足) or, alternatively, "the great contentment" (*da zu* 大足) that Wu Zhao's rule had brought about. Of course, these interpretations are not mutually exclusive but rather are coexisting layers. For more on the meaning of Dazu, see Rothschild, "An Inquiry into Reign Era Changes Under Wu Zhao," 140–41, and Kroll, "True Dates of Reign Periods in the Tang Dynasty," *Tang Studies* 2 (1984): 26.

32. *Shijing* [The Book of Songs], trans. Arthur Waley (New York: Grove, 1960), 241.

33. Eliade, *Myth and Reality*, 21–53, see chaps. 2 and 3, "Magic and the Prestige of 'Origins'" and "Myths and the Rites of Renewal."

34. Ishida Ei'ichiro, "Mother-Son Deities," *History of Religions* 4, no. 1 (1964): 52.

35. Michael Puett, *To Become a God: Cosmology, Sacrifice and Self-Divinization in Early China*, Harvard-Yenching Institute Monograph no. 57 (Cambridge, Mass.: Harvard University Asia Center, 2004), 74–75.

36. *TPGJ* 298.2372.

37. The "five princes" (*wu wang* 五王) who conspired to engineer the 705 coup, oust Wu Zhao, and restore the Tang, were Zhang Jianzhi, Cui Xuanwei, Jing Hui, Huan Yanfan, and Yuan Shuji. Wu Zhao's son Zhongzong invested them as princes for their role in restoring the Tang in the fifth month of 705. See *ZZTJ* 208.6591.

38. See Empress Wang's biography, *XTS* 76.3473–74.

39. *SS* 7.137. The establishment of an imperial ancestral temple to Jiang Yuan was referenced earlier: ceremonial officials (*SGZ* 5.162–63) seeking to posthumously exalt Empress Zhen pointed out that in the Zhou dynasty of old Jiang Yuan had her own ancestral temple. In this same context, the establishment of a temple for Jiang Yuan is mentioned in other sources as well (*JS* 19.602; *TD* 47.1310).

40. *JTS* 25.951; *QTW* 281.2848.

41. *QTW* 449.4598–99.

42. *SJ* 4.112.

6. WENMU AND WU ZHAO

1. *Analects*, 95, VIII.20.

2. *THY* 80.1476; *XTS* 76.3490. In both sources, Mother Wen is mentioned in terms of a ritual debate in 719 over the fitting posthumous title for Ruizong's empress Dou. See chaps. 4 and 5 in this volume.

3. The term "three mothers of the house of Zhou" is found in *LNZ* 1.6 and the *HHS* 10.426. See also Du Fangqin, "The Rise and Fall of Zhou Rites," 185–86.

4. *LNZ* 1.6.

5. Michael Nylan, *The Five Confucian Classics* (New Haven: Yale University Press, 2001), 84–85.

6. Ode 240 in "Greater Odes" (Daya 大雅), *Shijing* [The Book of Songs] (Ji'nan: Shandong Friendship, 1999), 707–09. See also Nylan, *The Five Confucian Classics*, 2001, 85.

7. *SJ* 35.1563.

8. *LNZ* 1.6, modified translation of O'Hara, *The Position of Women*, 24–25. There is a passage in the ode "Grand Illustriousness" (Daming 大明), part of the Greater Odes, that contradicts this passage (*Shijing*, 688–89). There, King Wen's first consort was a lady of "a great state" (*da bang* 大邦) whom he met on the banks of the Wei River with a bridge of boats to welcome her. Taisi appears to be his second consort, a "good lady from the state of Shen":

> The great state had a child;
> She was as if a daughter of heaven.
> [King] Wen determined an auspicious date
> and personally met her on the Wei River,
> Building rafts into a bridge;
> Illustrious was her radiance!
> By mandate from Heaven
> The throne was handed down to King Wen
> In the Zhou capital.
> The succeeding empress from Shen,
> The eldest daughter who came to marry him,
> Faithfully bore King Wu.

Famous scholar Gu Jiegang connected these verses from the *Book of Songs* to the fifth line in hexagram 54 of the *Book of Changes*, the Marrying Maiden (Gui Mei 歸妹):

"Di Yi 帝乙 marries off his daughter. The primary bride's sleeves are not as fine as the secondary bride's." Gu "guessed" that the great state in the first verse was the Shang, and that taken in tandem these above-mentioned passages from the *Book of Songs* revealed a failed union between the daughter of Di Yi, the penultimate king of the decadent Shang, and King Wen of Zhou. In *Before Confucius: Studies in the Creation of the Chinese Classics* (Albany: State University of New York Press, 1997), Edward Shaughnessy's analysis of the *Changes* corroborates and expands upon Gu's conjecture: The political marriage to Di Yi's daughter failed, and King Wu was born of Taisi, a woman of Shen, "a small state traditionally said to have been ruled by descendants of former Xia" (16).

9. Translation from *Chinese Women Poets: An Anthology of Poetry and Criticism from Ancient Times*, ed. Kang-I Sun Chang, Haun Saussy, and Charles Yim-tze Huang (Stanford: Stanford University Press, 1999), 19, originally *HS* 97.3985–86.

10. This is a reference to Nüying and Ehuang, consorts of Shun (also known as Yu 虞), not the Tushan sisters associated with Yu 禹 the Great.

11. Translation by Cutter and Crowell, *Empresses and Consorts*, 110. This imperial lament was added to Chen Shou's original in Pei Songzhi's (372–451) Liu Song–era commentary on the *SGZ* 5.167.

12. *SGZ* 5.155. See translation by Cutter and Crowell in *Empresses and Consorts*, 89.

13. *JS* 31.959.

14. Jiandi, who according to legend birthed the first male ancestor of the Shang after eating the egg of a dark swallow, does not fit the profile of these women who helped dynastic founders quite as neatly. Given this incongruity, perhaps the writer meant to record the spouse of Cheng Tang, the founder of the Shang.

15. *JS* 32.975.

16. *TD* 72.1972.

17. *NQS* 11.183. The fourth line of the poem (the entire poem is not translated here) literally means consistently keeping the compass (*gui* 軌) perfectly oriented and the square (*ju* 距) plumb.

18. *JTS* 58.2316. See Howard Wechsler, "The founding of the T'ang dynasty: Kao-tsu (reign 618–626)," in *CHC*, 159–60.

19. *ZZTJ* 201.6345–46. For more on the *feng* and *shan* rites of 666, see Rothschild, *Wu Zhao*, 59–63.

20. *QTW* 153.1568–69.

21. *ZZTJ* 199.6291; *XTS* 93.3820.

22. For more on Li Ji's role in Wu Zhao's elevation to empress, see Twitchett and Wechsler, "Kao-tsung and the Empress Wu," *CHC*, 249–51; Guisso, *Politics of Legitimation*, 17–18; and Rothschild, *Wu Zhao*, 34–35. Li Ji served as general under Gaozu, Taizong, and Gaozong, and as chief minister under Taizong and Gaozong. Guisso's work (173) contains a thumbnail biography of Li Ji.

23. *JTS* 67.2486; *XTS* 93.3820.

24. *JTS* 23.886.

25. *JTS* 23.886. *ZZTJ* 201.6344–45 contains an abridged, simpler version of Wu Zhao's persuasive speech.

26. *ZZTJ* 201.6346; *JTS* 23.887. Southwest of modern-day Taian, Sheshou is a lesser hill that is part of greater Mount Tai. Gaozong and Wu Zhao were reenacting the *shan* rite that King Cheng of Zhou had performed on the site seventeen centuries earlier.

27. *JTS* 190.5018 *QTW* 212.2147.

28. Wang Shuanghuai and Zhao Wenrun, *Wu Zetian pingzhuan*, 106–08. On another point, Wu Zhao did not heed Chen Zi'ang: Gaozong (and later Wu Zhao) was buried at Qianling, to the northwest of Chang'an, and not in the proximity of Luoyang.

29. Cited passage is *Analects* VIII.20.

30. For a more detailed overview of both text and context, see Denis Twitchett, "*Chen Gui* and Other Works Attributed to Wu Zetian," *Asia Major* 16, no. 1 (2003): 33–109; and Rothschild, "Rhetoric, Ritual and Support Constituencies," chap. 5, appendix 3. *QTW* 97.1004–05 contains the preface to the *Regulations*.

31. *CG*, preface, 1.

32. Ibid.

33. The woman who married Cheng Tang, the first ruler of the Shang, came from the Youshen 有莘 clan.

34. *QTW* 219.2209.

35. *QTW* 217.2193.

36. For more on the origin of the Wus, see Liang Hengtang, "Tan Wu shi jiazu," 49.

37. *XTS* 74.3136.

38. *XTS* 4.90.

39. *XTS* 76.3481–2; *ZZTJ* 204.6467. The elevation of the Wu clan was not a one-stage event. In the ninth month of 684, when Wu Zhao established herself as grand dowager–regent, some proposed establishing seven ancestral temples for the Wus. While she did not take that step, she did elevate and give new titles to five generations of Wus, from her great-great-great-grandfather Wu Keji to her father Wu Shiyue (see *XTS* 4.83, 76.3478; *ZZTJ* 203.6422). Spouses were included. In the second month of 689, she once again gave greater titles to the five most recently deceased generations of Wus (*XTS* 76.3480; *ZZTJ* 204.6457). After the establishment in 690 of the seven imperial temples, the lofty titles honoring her ancestors from the Ji family and further elevation of her more recent Wu ancestors, there was yet another occasion where she bestowed even gaudier posthumous honors: in the ninth month of 693, Wu Zhao again announced another titular elevation of her Wu kinsmen (*XTS* 4.93–94; *ZZTJ* 205.6492). In this last titular revision, King Wen and Mother Wen did not receive new titles.

40. *XTS* 76.3482; *ZZTJ* 204.6472.

41. *QTW* 249.2515.

42. *SJ* 8.342. See *Records of the Grand Historian*, trans. Watson, 51.

43. *QTW* 249.2515. I discuss in Chapter 3 the role of Leizu in this inscription. Guisso, *Politics of Legitimation*, translates and analyzes sections of the inscription (11–16).

44. *QTW* 239.2417.

7. FOUR EXEMPLARY WOMEN IN WU ZHAO'S
REGULATIONS FOR MINISTERS

1. *JTS* 4.74.

2. *XTS* 58.1487; *JTS* 46.2006. *Biographies of Filial Daughters* is listed only in *XTS* 58.1487. *JTS* 6.133 attributes to Wu Zhao a shorter, twenty-chapter *Biographies of Exemplary*

Women, which may, as Denis Twitchett, "Chen Gui and Other Works," 37, points out, be the result of confusion. Twitchett (35–41) lists all the works attributed to, written by, and composed by order of Wu Zhao. Keith Knapp, in *Selfless Offspring* (Honolulu: University of Hawaii Press, 2005), 63, lists Wu Zhao's twenty-chapter *Biographies of Filial Daughters* on a larger table of medieval accounts of filial offspring.

While it was by far the longest, Wu Zhao's version of *Biographies* was certainly not the only version known in the Tang or during her Zhou dynasty. Tang histories (*XTS* 58.1486–87; *JTS* 46.2006) record many editions in circulation at the time: a fifteen-chapter version of Liu Xiang's *Biographies* that included a commentary from Ban Zhao; a six-chapter edition compiled by Three Kingdoms scholar Huangfu Mi (215–282); a one-chapter version by Cao Zhi, accompanied by a poem on these celebrated women; an eight-chapter edition by Eastern Han scholar Liu Xi; and a seven-chapter edition by Mother Zhao. Jin scholar Qiwu Sui also had a seven-chapter edition; Xiang Zong compiled a ten-chapter *Later Biographies for Exemplary Women* (Lienü houzhuan 列女後傳)—presumably updating the genre (he or she also compiled a one-chapter biography of Daoist transcendent Wei Huacun); a Lady Sun also wrote a one-chapter *Preface and Eulogy for Biographies of Exemplary Women*; and Du Yu (222–285), another Three Kingdoms–era scholar-official, collated a ten-chapter *Records of Exemplary Women* (Lienü ji 列女記).

3. *XTS* 58.1486.

4. For a translation of the former, see Patricia Buckley Ebrey, "The *Book of Filial Piety for Women* Attributed to a Woman Née Zheng (ca. 730)," in *Under Confucian Eyes: Writing on Gender in Chinese History*, ed. Susan Mann and Yu-yin Cheng (Berkeley: University of California Press, 2001), 47–69. For a translation of *Analects for Women*, see Wang, *Images of Women*, 327–40. Teresa Kelleher has translated parts of both, in De Bary and Bloom, Sources of Chinese Tradition I: 824-27.

5. Twitchett, "*Chen Gui* and Other Works," 73.

6. Li Hexian, "Cong *Chen gui* kan Wu Zetian de jun-chen lunli sixiang" [Looking at the Ethics of the Ruler-Minister Relationship Through *Regulations for Ministers*], *Huazhong shifan daxue xuebao* 5 (1986): 58–62. Ji Qingyang, "Wu Zetian yu zhong-xiao guannian" [Wu Zetian and Her Concept of Loyalty and Filial Piety], Xibei daxue xuebao 39, no. 6 (2009): 138–39, also remarks upon the text's role in fostering a culture of loyalty in Wu Zhao's court.

7. *CG* 2–3.

8. *CG* 21.

9. *JTS* 87.2846.

10. *XTS* 76.3476.

11. The same sequence of texts appears in the biography of Yuan Wanqing, in *XTS* 201.5744 and *JTS* 190.5011.

12. In a subsection titled "Dynastic Crisis of the Late 670s," Twitchett, "*Chen Gui* and Other Works," 57–59, points out that amid a maelstrom of crises at this juncture, normative texts like *Regulations* helped Wu Zhao buttress her precarious political position.

13. *JTS* 86.2832; *XTS* 81.3591. The scholars of the Northern Gate were also involved in these compilations. Shaoyang 少陽—lesser *yang*—is a term referring to the imperial crown prince.

14. Twitchett, "*Chen Gui* and Other Works," 76; cf. *THY* 75.1373.

15. ZZTJ 202.6390, 6397.

16. ZZTJ 203.6409.

17. This date is given on CG 64.

18. JTS 6.116; XTS 4.82.

19. JTS 24.918; ZZTJ 205.6420.

20. Duan Tali, Tangdai funü diwei yanjiu, 57–58.

21. Josephine Chiu-Duke, "Mothers and the Well-being of the State in Tang China," Nan Nü: Women and Gender in China 8, no. 1 (2006): 59. She remarks that the "male elite narrators" in official sources depicted mothers as being "directly or indirectly involved in the preservation of state" (56).

22. Jennifer Holmgren, "Women's Biographies in the Wei Shu: A Study of Moral Attitudes and Social Background Found in Women's Biographies in the Dynastic History of the Northern Wei" (PhD diss., Australia National University, 1979), 178–81. The "learned instructresses" stand out as distinct from other categories of women such as chaste widows, devoted wives, and filial daughters, in that these women are able to exercise authority outside the domestic sphere. Raphals, Sharing the Light, 54–55, identified ten subcategories of learned instructresses, including "mothers who instruct their children" and "mothers who instruct grown sons on their conduct as officials."

23. Chiu-Duke, "Mothers and the Well-being of the State," 59. See also her subchapter "Educating Sons for Official Careers," 87–92.

24. ZZTJ 202.6372–73.

25. CG preface, 1. Both the preface and main text of the 1936 Shangwu edition of Regulations begin with page 1. Therefore, here and for all subsequent footnotes drawn from the preface the word "preface" is used. In citations from the main text, only the page number is given. This translation is slightly modified from Twitchett, "Chen Gui and Other Works," 75.

26. CG preface, 2. Twitchett, in "Chen Gui and Other Works," notes that an identical phrase was part of the memorial Wu Zhao issued in 675 to propagate her twelve-article reform (75n86).

27. Ibid.

28. Lisa Raphals, "A Woman Who Understood the Rites," in Confucius and the Analects: New Essays, ed. Bryan Van Norden (New York: Oxford University Press, 2002), 275–76. This section of the subchapter is not intended to provide an exhaustive study of Lady Ji of Lu and all the wise counsel she offered Wenbo and other members of the Ji family. Raphals shows that Jing Jiang's renown predated the Liu Xiang Biographies. Narrative of States from the early Warring States era includes eight passages on Lady Ji of Lu, many of which illustrate the moral suasion that she as a widowed mother exercised over her son Wenbo. She also instructed him on proper ceremonial deportment in hosting guests. She was well known for being a perfect Confucian daughter-in-law, revering her parents-in-law and properly mourning her deceased husband. Also see Zhou Yiqun, Festivals, Feasts, and Gender Relations in Ancient China and Greece (New York: Cambridge University Press, 2010), 245–47.

29. LNZ 1.9.

30. Zhou Yiqun, Festivals, Feasts, and Gender Relations, 258.

31. *LNZ* 1.9. O'Hara, *The Position of Women*, 30–37, translates Lady Ji of Lu's full biography.

32. Raphals, *Sharing the Light*, 30–31; see also Raphals, "A Woman Who Understood the Rites," 278.

33. Raphals, *Sharing the Light*, 31; and Raphals, "A Woman Who Understood the Rites," 277, trans. *LNZ* 1.9.

34. Bray, *Technology and Gender*, 191.

35. *LNZ* 1.9. Raphals, "A Woman Who Understood the Rites," 278–79, paraphrases this story.

36. *Liji zhengyi* [Orthodox Commentary on the Book of History], comp. Kong Yingda, in *Shisan jing zhu shu*, ed. Li Xueqin, 27.836.

37. *LNZ* 1.9. citing *Book of Songs* (Shijing). Translation from Raphals, "A Woman Who Understood the Rites," 279. This passage is not the only place Confucius praised Lady Ji of Lu. In *Narrative of States*, learning of the wise instruction she had given Wenbo's concubines after her son's death, Confucius remarked that "her wisdom is like that of a man." See translation in Goldin, "The View of Women in Early Confucianism," 141; cf. *Guoyu* 國語 [Narrative of States] (Shanghai: Shanghai guji, 1978), 5.211. For further background on the admiration of Confucius for Jing Jiang, on the debate as to the extent to which these contemporaries knew one another, on whether Wenbo was Confucius's disciple, and on the nature of Confucius's interaction with the Ji clan, see Raphals, "A Woman Who Understood the Rites."

38. Ko, *Teachers of the Inner Chambers*, 13. As Goldin, in *The Culture of Sex in Ancient China*, puts it, "the precise contours of this dichotomy are hard to reconstruct" (59).

39. Raphals, "A Woman Who Understood the Rites," 292.

40. *CG* preface, 2.

41. *LNZ* 1.11. For a full translation of the biography of the mother of Mencius, see Nancy Gibbs's translation, "The Mother of Mencius," in *Chinese Civilization: A Sourcebook*, ed. Patricia Buckley Ebrey (New York: Free Press, 1993), 72–74. O'Hara, *The Position of Women*, 39–42, and Raphals, *Sharing the Light*, 33–35, have also translated this biography. For a short biography, see Constance Cook's entry, "Mother of Mencius," in *Biographical Dictionary of Chinese Women, Antiquity Through Sui, 1600 BC–618 AD*, ed. Lily Xiao Hong Lee and A. D. Stefanowska (Armonk, N.Y.: Sharpe, 2007), 46–47.

42. Hinsch, in "Textiles and Female Virtue," remarks that "The industrious widow working at the loom to earn money for her son's education was still praised as a moral paragon even though she sold her cloth" (179). The mother of Mencius serves as the perfect illustration of the "moralistic" and "virtuous" textile weaver in Confucian tradition.

43. Robin Wang, "Ideal Womanhood in Chinese Thought and Culture," *Philosophy Compass* 5, no. 8 (2010): 637.

44. Ibid.

45. Raphals, "A Woman Who Understood the Rites," 283.

46. Chiu-Duke, "Mothers and the Well-being of the State," 59.

47. Ibid., 73. In a case of historical irony, the mother of Huan Yanfan, one of the conspirators who deposed Wu Zhao in 705, urged her son to go through with the

coup, telling him: "When loyalty and filial piety cannot coexist, it is all right that you do your duty to the state first" (*XTS* 120.4313; Chiu-Duke, 76, translates this passage). For this mother, ministerial loyalty meant the repudiation of Wu Zhao's Zhou and the restoration of the Tang. Chiu-Duke cites several other examples of Tang mothers who, as good Confucian matriarchs, conscientiously objected to their sons serving a female ruler. Her essay includes a subchapter titled "Resistance to Empress Wu," 82–85.

48. *QTW* 196.1984. With the two-character surname Erzhu 爾朱, this woman likely heralded from a Xianbei/Toba background.

49. *QTW* 257.2608. Su Ting wrote the epitaph for the Lofty and Pacific Senior Princess (Gao'an changgongzhu, 649–714), Gaozong's daughter by Pure Consort Xiao (Xiao shufei), Wu Zhao's bitter rival for the emperor's affections in the 650s.

50. *QTW* 231.2340.

51. Zhou, *Festivals, Feasts, and Gender Relations*, 246.

52. *CG* 2. Translation from Twitchett, "*Chen Gui* and Other Works," 56.

53. Ibid.

54. *CG* 54–58.

55. Twitchett, "*Chen Gui* and Other Works," 92.

56. Kam Louie, *Theorizing Chinese Masculinity: Society and Gender in China* (Cambridge: Cambridge University Press, 2002), 16, sees the Tang as a balanced era in the evolving *wen-wu* (civil-military) dyad that helped define Chinese masculinity.

57. Skaff, *Sui-Tang China and Its Turko-Mongol Neighbors*, 43–44, 308–09 (table A); cf. *ZZTJ* 202.6390–203.6443.

58. *XTS* chap. 110; *JTS* chap. 109: Wu Zhao's non-Han generals included Koguryan expat Quan Xiancheng, Li Duozuo (Mohe), Shazha Zhongyi (Tujue), Qibi Heli (Tiele), and Heichi Changzhi (Paekche). This list includes some men who served as non-Han generals under Gaozong. Also see Zhang Naizhu, "Wu-Zhou Zhengquan," 31–39. Zhang emphasizes the pivotal role of non-Han generals and the culture of the western borderlands in buttressing the political authority of female emperor Wu Zhao, further remarking that the female sovereign, in turn, utilized with great acuity the powerful influence of non-Han civilization and foreign ideologies to buttress her political might.

59. *LNZ* 1.10.

60. *CG* 54–56. See also O'Hara's translation of Liu Xiang's *LNZ* 1.10 in *The Position of Women*, 37–38.

61. Raphals, *Sharing the Light*, 40.

62. Her husband Zhao She and Lian Po were both renowned generals of the state of Zhao in the early third-century B.C.

63. The commentary in the *CG* notes that "those who face east avoid the southward gaze of the ruler" (57).

64. *CG* 56–58. See also O'Hara's translation of Liu Xiang's *LNZ* 3.15 in *The Position of Women*, 100–1. For a short biography, see Constance Cook's entry "General Zhao Kuo's Mother" in Lee and Stefanowska, *Biographical Dictionary of Chinese Women*, 26–27.

65. Twitchett, "*Chen Gui* and Other Works," 97.

66. Bokenkamp, "A Medieval Feminist Critique," 384; cf. "Gai yuan Guangzhai shewen" 改元光宅赦文, *WYYH* 463.2361.

67. *ZZTJ* 201.6343.

68. *JTS* 6.115,119, 24.925; *XTS* 4.87, 76.3480; *ZZTJ* 204.6448. See chap. 2 of this volume for the importance of this stone in connecting Wu Zhao to the Luo River goddess.

69. Twitchett, "*Chen Gui* and Other Works," 73–74.

70. *CG* 1.

71. Lü Huayu, "Wu Zetian '*Chen Gui*' pouxi," in Su Jian and Bai Xianzhang, *Wu Zetian yu Luoyang*, 90.

72. *CG* 11.

73. *CG* 4.

74. Possessing a wider, inclusive, and international vision of sovereignty, Wu Zhao extended the aegis of her motherhood to encompass not just ministers in court and generals in the field, but also her countless foreign subjects in Luoyang and Chang'an and throughout her vast realm. Wu Zhao's extended vision of motherhood included these non-Han generals as well as her court ministers. As grand dowager and empress, Wu Zhao utilized the idea "come-as-sons" (*zi lai* 子來) to describe the willing and cheerful spirit in which her subjects, her political sons, gravitated to her. Lifted from the canonical *Book of Songs*, "come-as-sons" was first featured in a verse in which subjects thronged like cheerful and willing children to build in less than a day a ceremonial tower (*lingtai* 靈臺) for the virtuous founder of the Zhou dynasty of antiquity, King Wen. In 691, as emperor, when she ordered the construction of a hundred-foot-tall monument, an Axis of the Sky (Tianshu 天樞) in the heart of her Divine Capital Luoyang, she appointed a Koguryan expatriate, son of a former king of the defunct Korean state, to an unprecedented position, Come-as-Sons Commissioner of the Axis of the Sky (Tianshu zilai shi 天樞子來使). Non-Han Chinese merchants, chieftains, and dignitaries provided money and material to fund the project. The Axis of the Sky was eventually completed in 695, requiring more than four years (rather than under a day) to complete. For primary sources on this construction, see *JTS* 6.124, 89.2902; *XTS* 4.95; *ZZTJ* 205.6496; *TPGJ* 240.1850, 236.1816.

III. DRAWING ON THE NUMINOUS ENERGIES
OF FEMALE DAOIST DIVINITIES

1. See, for instance, Lao Tzu, *Tao Te Ching*, 85 (I.28).

2. Ibid., 62 (I.6).

3. Ibid., 82 (I.25).

4. Ibid., 122 (II.61).

5. Kristofer Schipper, *The Taoist Body*, trans. Karen C. Duval (Berkeley: University of California Press, 1993), 139.

6. Schafer, *The Divine Woman*, 43.

7. *THY* 50.877. See Charles Benn, *The Cavern-Mystery Transmission: A Daoist Ordination Rite of A.D. 711* (Honolulu: University of Hawaii Press, 1991), 10–11.

8. *Shangshu zhengyi*, 295. See Rothschild, "An Inquiry into Reign Era Changes Under Wu Zhao," 130–31.

9. The *Shizi* is a twenty-chapter Warring States–era text attributed to Legalist Shi Jiao.

10. *CG* 4.

11. Barrett, *Taoism Under the T'ang*, 40–41.

12. Edward Schafer, "Hallucinations and Epiphanies in T'ang Poetry," *Journal of the American Oriental Society* 104, no. 4 (1984): 757–58.

13. Edward Schafer, "Three Divine Women of South China," *Chinese Literature: Essays, Articles, and Reviews* 1 (1979): 31.

14. For a description of the Li family background, see Wechsler, "The Founding of the T'ang Dynasty," 150–52. For more on Tang attitudes toward non-Chinese, see Abramson, *Ethnic Identity in Tang China*.

15. Barrett, *Taoism Under the T'ang*, 20.

16. Benn, *Cavern-Mystery Transmission*, 10.

8. THE QUEEN MOTHER OF THE WEST AND WU ZHAO

1. Suzanne Cahill, *Transcendence and Divine Passion: The Queen Mother of the West in Medieval China* (Stanford: Stanford University Press, 1993), 14.

2. Elfriede Knauer, "The Queen Mother of the West: A Study of the Influence of Western Prototypes on the Iconography of the Taoist Deity," in *Contact and Exchange in the Ancient World*, ed. Victor Mair (Honolulu: University of Hawaii Press, 2006), 63. Curiously, Knauer traces the Queen Mother of the West to far earlier origins (at least iconographic origins) as western Asian and greater Mediterranean deity Kybele.

3. Cahill, *Transcendence and Divine Passion*, 13–15. In the opening chapter, Cahill provides a much more comprehensive account of the evolution and development of this deity. See also Cahill, *Divine Traces of the Daoist Sisterhood* (Magdalena, N.Mex.: Three Pines, 2006), 43–69; and Michael Loewe, *Ways to Paradise: The Chinese Quest for Immortality* (Boston: Allen and Unwin, 1979), 88–97.

4. Birrell, *Chinese Mythology*, 172; cf. "Xici sanjing" 西次三經, in *Shanhai jing*, 2.19. Also see Cahill, *Transcendence and Divine Passion*, 15–16.

5. Anne Birrell, "Gendered Power: A Discourse on Female-Gendered Myth in the *Classic of Mountains and Seas*," *Sino-Platonic Papers* no. 120 (July 2002): 11, 13.

6. Ibid., 20.

7. Hinsch, *Women in Early Imperial China*, 2.

8. Birrell, *Chinese Mythology*, 144–45.

9. Loewe, *Ways to Paradise*, 95, 121.

10. Ibid., 124, 155n198.

11. Mu-chou Poo, *In Search of Personal Welfare: A View of Ancient Chinese Religion* (Albany: State University of New York Press, 1998), 155–56, cf. *HS* 27.1476–77.

12. Suzanne Cahill, "Beside the Turquoise Pond: the Shrine of the Queen Mother of the West in Medieval Chinese Poetry and Religious Practice," *Journal of Chinese Religions* 12 (1984), 25–26. See *JS* 129.3197–98; *SS* 71.1657.

13. James Hargett, "Playing Second Fiddle: The Luan-Bird in Early and Medieval Chinese Literature," *T'oung Pao*, Second Series, 75 (1989): 253.

14. Loewe, *Ways to Paradise*, 15; and Yu Yingshi, "New Evidence on the Early Chinese Conception of Afterlife—A Review Article," *Journal of Asian Studies* 41, no. 1 (1981): 81–85.

15. E. D. Edwards, *Chinese Prose Literature of the T'ang Period*, vol. 2 (London: Arthur Probsthain, 1938), 3, 97, translated from Tai Shangyin's 太上隱 Tang-era *Biographies of Immortal Officers* (Xianli zhuan 仙吏傳).

16. Birrell, *Chinese Mythology*, 174–75.

17. Loewe, *Ways to Paradise*, 116–20. Loewe includes translations from the *Bowuzhi* 博物志 (third century or later), the *Han Wu gushi* 漢武故事, and the *Han Wudi neizhuan* 漢武帝內傳 (sixth century).

18. Henri Frankfurt, *Kingship and the Gods* (Chicago: University of Chicago Press, 1948), 297.

19. Marianne Bujard, "Le culte de Wangzi Qiao ou la longue carrière d'un immortel," *Études chinoises* 19 (2000): 115–16.

20. Wu Hung, *The Wu Liang Shrine*, chap. 4, "The Gables: The World of Immortality," 108–41.

21. Nancy Thompson, "The Evolution of the T'ang Lion and Grapevine Mirror," *Artibus Asiae* 29, no. 1 (1967): 27.

22. Ibid., 19–22.

23. Ibid., 25–29.

24. Li Fubu, "Gudai ming nüzi," 72.

25. Cahill, *Transcendence and Divine Passion*, 58.

26. Cahill, "Performers and Female Daoist Adepts," 155.

27. *Shanhai jing*, book 2, chap. 3, p. 24. Apparently this is an alternate residence to Kunlun.

28. Cahill, *Transcendence and Divine Passion*, 15–16.

29. Cahill, *Divine Traces of the Daoist Sisterhood*, 57; cf. *Yunji qiqian* (Beijing: Xinhua, 1996), 114.721 (hereafter *YJQQ*).

30. Loewe, *Ways to Paradise*, 100.

31. *JTS* 37.1374; *XTS* 35.914. The date is given as 675 in the *XTS*. *TPGJ* 404.3254 indicates that the presentation of the rings did not occur during Wu Zhao's reign but at a later date. Edward Schafer, *The Golden Peaches of Samarkand* (Berkeley: University of California Press, 1963), 36, also refers to these rings. Chuzhou is in modern-day Jiangsu.

32. *TPGJ* 203.1530. The *guan* is a ritual tube akin to the *cong* 琮, an instrument shamans used to commune with spirits.

33. Forte, *Mingtang and Buddhist Utopias*, 16–18.

34. *JTS* 5.102. For further connections between the phoenix and Wu Zhao, see Rothschild, "Wu Zhao's Remarkable Aviary," 72–76. Chenzhou (near modern-day Huaiyang, Henan, about 100 miles southwest of Luoyang) was associated with Fuxi, Divine Farmer Shennong, and Emperor Shun.

35. Wu Hung, *The Wu Liang Shrine*, 111.

36. Loewe, *Ways to Paradise*, 124–25, 155n200; the passage is cited in Li Daoyuan's sixth-century *Commentary on the Classic of Waterways* (Shuijing zhu 水經注), attributed to Dongfang Shuo's *Classic on Divine Marvels* (Shenyijing 神異經). Loewe notes that it is thought to be a later production.

37. In the "Zhou yu" 周語 [Discourses of Zhou] in the *Guoyu* [Narrative of States] (chapter 1) it is the call of the *yuezhuo* 鸑鷟, a not yet fully fledged phoenix (in other sources, a purple phoenix or simply an alternative designation for a phoenix), from Mount Qishan that heralded the advent of the original Zhou dynasty.

38. *JTS* 22.862; *THY* 11.277; *ZZTJ* 204.6454. See also Forte, *Mingtang and Buddhist Utopias*, 156–58.

39. *TD* 44.254; *JTS* 22.867; *THY* 11.279; *ZZTJ* 205.6505.

40. Loewe, *Ways to Paradise*, 97.

41. Loewe, *Ways to Paradise*, 120. The Queen Mother's *sheng* headdress appears in other capacities as well. Worn on the Day of Humans (Ren ri 人日), the *sheng* appears to have been apotropaic, more closely associated with driving off demons than with sericulture. A text compiled in the Liang court in the sixth century, *Annals of the States of Jing and Chu* (Jing-Chu sui shiji 荆楚歲時記), recorded that beginning in the Jin, on the Day of Humans, the seventh day of the seventh lunar month, a date also connected to the Weaver Girl and Oxherd Boy, people in the southern reaches fashioned *sheng* headdresses for each other modeled after the Queen Mother's coronal flora.

Loewe (119) and Michael Como, in *Weaving and Binding: Immigrant Gods and Female Immortals in Ancient Japan* (Honolulu: University of Hawaii Press, 2009), 105, have both translated part of this passage. Loewe (120) has also translated a short section of the *Composition of Pearls* (Bianzhu 編珠), a Sui-era encyclopedia compiled on imperial order by Du Gongzhan, which similarly claims the *sheng* originated in the Jin. This text contained an excerpt from a third-century text that said *sheng* "were shaped like the golden *sheng* of charms. In addition they depicted the visit paid by the Queen Mother of the West, wearing her *sheng*, to [Han] Wudi."

Elfreide Knauer ("The Queen Mother of the West," 64, 75), provides a radically different understanding of the *sheng*, contending that the Chinese may have "misunderstood and interpreted" iconographic representations of the high-backed throne of western Asian and Mediterranean goddess Kybele as a loom to fit the Queen Mother of the West's role as weaver of the universe.

42. Loewe, *Ways to Paradise*, 105, citing Kominami Ichiro, *Chugoku no shinwa to monogatari* [Chinese Stories and Legends] (Tokyo: Iwanami Shoten, 1984), 47. Como, in *Weaving and Binding*, has remarked that the "Queen Mother of the West, whose main iconographic attribute was a weaving instrument that served as her headdress, was also closely associated with sericulture and the figure of the Weaver Maiden" (214). For more on the meaning of the *sheng* headdress, see Cahill, *Transcendence and Divine Passion*, 16, 249n8.

43. Ibid., 104.

44. *JTS* 4.75, 5.92, 98, 100; *XTS* 3.57, 67, 71; *TD* 46.1290. See also chap. 3 in this volume.

45. Wang, *Shaping the Lotus Sutra*, 148.

46. Wu Hung, "Bird Motifs in Eastern Yi Art," *Orientations* 16, no. 10 (1985), 30–32.

47. Loewe, *Ways to Paradise*, 52, 103. The iconography of low-relief sculpture and images on TLV mirrors often shows these symbolic creatures of the celestial bodies and sometimes, as in the case of the famous T-shaped Mawangdui funerary banner from the second century B.C., depicts both. Loewe (128) suggests that the three-legged sunbird (an iconographic motif well established by the first century B.C.) may represent an evolution (a consolidation into a single body) of the Queen Mother's trio of avian messengers from earlier tradition.

48. Ibid., 94.

49. In *Weaving and Binding*, Michael Como has illustrated that along the Korean peninsula and in the nascent Japanese state in the sixth and seventh centuries, the Queen Mother's solar crow was a recurring motif. Como (100–1) translates a passage from the *Nihon Shoki* 日本書紀, an early eighth-century history, recording a remark from a Buddhist monk in Emperor Kōtoku's 孝德 (r. 645–654) court that the Great Tang had at an early juncture sent an emissary bearing a dead three-legged sunbird. In 701, during the reign of Emperor Monmu 文武 (r. 697–707), Wu Zhao's contemporary, a three-legged peacock was presented in court and a sunbird banner was erected at the gate of the main audience hall. Como takes this to indicate that "elements of the symbolic vocabulary of the Queen Mother" had become integrated into the Japanese court (102).

50. *TPGJ* 462.3796. It is problematic to tell whether this passage, originally from *Miscellaneous Morsels from Youyang* (Youyang zazu 酉陽雜俎) refers to the same presentation of a three-legged bird or to two separate presentations. Wu Zhao assumed the title Celestial Empress in 674, but in 688 she became Sage Mother, Divine Sovereign. In 690, when she established her Zhou dynasty, she took the title Sagely and Divine Emperor. This makes the passage difficult because by 690, the date given in the *Taiping guangji* episode, she was no longer known as Celestial Empress.

51. *ZZTJ* 204.6263–64; *XTS* 76.3481; *QTW* 96.996.

52. Shi Anchang, "Cong yuanzang tuoben tanguo tan Wu Zetian zao zi" [A Discussion of the Characters Created by Wu Zetian Based on an Investigation of Rubbings in the Palace Museum Archives], *Gugong bowuyuan yuankan*, no. 4 (1983), 37.

53. Li Jingjie, "Guanyu Wu Zetian xinzi de jidian renshi" [Several Points About the New Characters of Wu Zetian], *Gugong bowuyuan yuankan* no. 4 (1997), 60.

54. See Cahill, "Performers and Female Daoist Adepts," 156.

55. For a summary of the widespread availability and use of cosmetics in Tang China, see Charles Benn, *Daily Life in Traditional China: The Tang Dynasty* (Westport, Conn.: Greenwood, 2002), 109–12.

56. *ZZTJ* 205.6487. *XTS* 76.3482 contains a similar passage, which mentions that two teeth regrew. There is no *bing-xu* day in the ninth month of 692. The purported regrowth of the tooth likely either occurred on the *bing-shen* 丙申 day (19 October 692) or the *wu-xu* 戊戌 day (22 October 692).

57. *ZZTJ* 206.6546. *JTS* 6.129 suggests that the potion was more efficacious, recording that the new reign era began because "she recovered from illness."

58. Modified from *Tao Te Ching*, 120 (II.59).

59. *XTS* 4.101.

60. See, for instance, Barrett, *Taoism Under the T'ang*, 44–45.

61. Wang, *Shaping the Lotus Sutra*, 149. He contends that another cause was her disappointment with the political capital of "ostentatious Buddhist trappings stage-managed by Xue Huaiyi."

62. *JTS* 5.110; *THY* 7.102.

63. *JTS* 6.119; *XTS* 4.87; *ZZTJ* 204.6449.

64. Translation is modified from Cahill, *Transcendence and Divine Passion*, 217; cf. *QTS* 167.

65. Cahill, *Divine Traces of the Daoist Sisterhood*, 51. Cahill's translation of *Yongcheng jixian lu* from *YJQQ* 114.721 has been slightly modified.

66. *YJQQ* 114.721; *TPGJ* 70.435–36. Both sources contain a famous episode in which a group of ten ill-intentioned monks came to harm the Immortal Maiden of the Gou clan and to burn and desecrate Wei Huacun's shrine. Though the guardian woman sat quietly on her bed, the monks were unable to see her. A deep rumbling from the earth scared the monks off. As they ran through the forest, nine of ten were devoured by tigers.

67. *HS* 1.6.

68. *JTS* 5.100.

69. Based on the textual understanding of Daoist hagiographer Du Guangting, Wang Hongjie, in *Power and Politics in Tenth Century China: The Former Shu Regime* (Amherst, N.Y.: Cambria, 2011), 165, renders this cultic Daoist immortal's name as Wang Zijin, rather than Prince Jin. In his efforts to legitimize Wang Jian (r. 907–918) and the royal house of Shu in the early tenth century, Du compiled a collection of fifty-five Daoist immortals all with the surname Wang in the aptly titled *Immortals and Gods of the Wang Clan* (Wangshi shenxian zhuan 王氏神仙傳). Du Guangting forced Prince Jin into this collection, willfully taking the wang 王 for "prince" as a surname that matched that of his patron-ruler Wang Jian.

70. Edward Schafer, "Empyreal Powers and Chthonian Edens: Two Notes on T'ang Taoist Literature," *Journal of the American Oriental Society* 106, no. 4 (1986): 667.

71. *QTW* 98.1007–08. See also *TPGJ* 4.24, taken from Liu Xiang's *Biographies of Immortals*. Prince Jin's (Qiao's) brief biography has been translated; see Franciscus Verellen, Nathan Sivin, and Kristofer Schipper's rendering in "Daoist Religion," in de Bary and Bloom, *Sources of Chinese Tradition*, 394–95.

72. *DFXZ* 1.2, 2.31.

73. Bujard, "Le culte de Wangzi Qiao," 115–55. Bujard traces the evolution of the cult of Wangzi Jin from the Han, through the North and South Dynasties, and into the Tang. While Bujard (146) notes Prince Jin "retrouvait un patronage imperial" under Wu Zhao, she only draws on two passages from the *Old Tang History* (*JTS* 6.128 and 23.891), and does not mention the Zhang brothers, who were at the center of the cult of Prince Jin's revival.

74. *ZZTJ* 206.6503–04.

75. *QTW* 98.1009.

76. *ZZTJ* 206.6539. Curiously, during this outing, courtier Yan Chaoyin prayed on Wu Zhao's behalf when she was feeling under the weather (*JTS* 78.2706). He cleansed himself and, lying on a ritual meat stand, offered his very life in her stead. When she felt better, he was richly rewarded (*ZZTJ* 206.6538).

77. The stele still exists. Kegasawa Yasunori, *Sokuten buko* [Empress Wu Zetian] (Tokyo: Hakuteisha, 1995), 318, contains an illustration of the characters. See also Wang Zhendong and Xu Yingxian, "Wu Zetian 'Shengxiantaizibei' de shufa yishu" [Calligraphy and Art on Wu Zetian's Stele of the Ascended Immortal Crown Prince], in Zhao Wenrun and Liu Zhiqing, *Wu Zetian yu Yanshi*, 240–44.

78. For a more extensive analysis of the structure of the preface to the inscription, see Wang Jingyao, *Wu Zetian yu Shengxian taizi bei* [Wu Zetian and the Stele of the Ascended Immortal Crown Prince], unpublished manuscript, Luoyang, 2003.

79. *QTW* 98.1009.

80. Van Gulik, *Sexual Life in Ancient China*, 158.

81. *JTS* 78.2706–08 (biography); *XTS* 104.4014–16 (biography); *ZZTJ* 206.6514. In the *Old Tang History*, the biography of the Zhangs disparages their literary skills, suggesting that most of the works attributed to them were in fact ghostwritten by literary masters like Song Zhiwen and Yan Chaoyin.

The Tang histories are not consistent as to whether the Zhangs both were born of the same mother (*JTS*) or two different mothers (*XTS*; *ZZTJ*).

82. *ZZTJ* 206. 6526–27, 6538. The precise timing of the establishment of the institute is not clear. In 700, the Institute of Reining Cranes was renamed the Garrison of Imperial Bodyguards (Fengchen fu 奉宸府).

83. *ZZTJ* 206.6546; *JTS* 78.2706–07; *XTS* 104.4014, 206.5840; *TPGJ* 188.1406. In *TPGJ* 240.1854, an anecdote drawn from the *Chaoye jianzai* indicates that Wu Sansi wrote a biography of Zhang Yizhi, contending that he (and not his brother, Changzong) was the incarnation of Prince Jin.

84. *TPGJ* 405.3267. This passage also contains a curious anecdote in which staunch Confucian minister Di Renjie (630–700) entered the inner palace to find Changzong clad in the gaudy, colorful cloak, engaged in a game of backgammon with Wu Zhao. The female emperor bid Di Renjie be seated and play a game with Zhang Changzong. When asked to determine the stakes, Di Renjie offered to stake his purple chief minister's robes against the flock of kingfishers cloak. When Wu Zhao pointed out the tremendous value of Changzong's robe, the stalwart minister retorted, "This robe of your humble minister is a garment one wears to court when memorializing the throne. Changzong's clothing, however, is a garment worn by favorites and flatterers. Swayed by his persuasive argument, Wu Zhao then granted the wager. Zhang Changzong, having listened to Di Renjie's argument, felt out of sorts and lost the backgammon match. Di Renjie left with the precious flock of kingfishers cloak, which, upon reaching a city gate, he gave to a slave. Also see Schafer, *Vermilion Bird*, 114, 307n87.

85. *QTS* 80.865–66.

86. Ding Lingwei was a Jin-era Daoist recluse from northeastern China, known for having transformed into an immortal crane.

87. A reference to the Nine Tripods cast for Wu Zhao's court in 697. See *ZZTJ* 206.6517.

88. Slight modification of Charles Stone's translation from The Fountainhead of Chinese Erotica (Honolulu: University of Hawaii Press, 2003), 90, c.f. *QTS* 68.767. This is not the entirety of the poem. In an abbreviated version, four stanzas of Cui Rong's poem appear in the biography of the Zhangs in the *Old Tang History* (78.2706) and also in the Ming dynasty erotic novella *The Lord of Perfect Satisfaction*. Stone sees the poem as subtly insinuating that Zhang Changzong "should enjoy his odious status as Wu Zetian's paramour while he can," because such favor, far from immortal, is transient.

In *TPGJ* 240.1854, a chapter on "sycophants and favorites," Cui Rong is mentioned as being the most shamelessly fawning of the sycophants poetically toadying to the Zhangs. In *TPGJ* 250.1935, the poem is attributed to Zhang Changling 張昌齡 (d. 705), who presented it to his brother, rather than Cui Rong.

89. *JTS* 78.2706–07; *XTS* 104.4014–15; *ZZTJ* 206.6546.

90. *ZZTJ* 206.6534.

91. Jeanne Larsen, *Willow, Wine, Mirror, Moon: Women's Poems from Tang China* (Rochester, N.Y.: BOA Editions, 2005), 25. I have slightly modified Larsen's translation from *QTS* 5.58.

92. *QTS* 80.865.

93. Franciscus Verellen, "The Beyond Within: Grotto-Heavens (*dongtian*) in Taoist Ritual and Cosmology," *Les Cahiers d'Extrême-Asie* 8 (1995): 289. Also see Miura Kunio's tables in the "dongtian and fudi" entry in Predagio, *Encyclopedia of Taoism*, 370 (table 5).

94. *QTS* 60.719.

95. Curiously, as a prime minister of Wu Zhao's grandson Xuanzong, Yao Chong would assume a very different tone, taking on a Confucian conservative voice. Despite the free-flowing Daoist airs of this verse from early in his political career, he later played a significant role in the erasure of Wu Zhao.

96. Cahill, *Transcendence and Divine Passion*, 132–33. Translation is Cahill's. I have only converted the Wade-Giles to pinyin. This is not the full poem, only the final four lines.

97. A *zhang* was about 2.46 meters during the Tang.

98. *QTS* 80.867. The commentary in the *QTS* suggests this poem should be attributed to literary master Song Zhiwen or Yan Chaoyin, rather than to Zhang Yizhi. See also Cahill's translation in *Transcendence and Divine Passion*, 133.

99. Cahill, "Performers and Female Daoist Adepts," 164.

100. Jia Jinhua, "A Study of the Jinglong Wenguan ji," *Monumenta Serica* 47 (1999): 231.

101. *QTS* 103.1090. Translation from Jia Jinhua, "Jinglong Wenguanji," 232.

9. THE MOTHER OF LAOZI AND WU ZHAO

1. *XTS* 70.1956.

2. Catherine Despeux, "Women and Daoism," in Kohn, *Daoism Handbook*, 385.

3. Peter Nickerson, "The Southern Celestial Masters," in Kohn, *Daoism Handbook*, 272. In the worldview of Celestial Masters that developed during the Southern dynasties, the dark, primordial, and inaugural *qi* emerged from the void, transforming to take the shape of the Jade Maiden of Mystery and Wonder, who begot Laozi, who in turn, being a cosmic and divine power, generated the universe.

4. These stages are drawn from Catherine Despeux and Livia Kohn, *Women in Daoism* (Cambridge, Mass.: Three Pines, 2003), 49; see also Livia Kohn, *The Taoist Experience: An Anthology* (Albany: State University of New York Press, 1993), 116. *YJQQ* 114.721 does not include a biography for the mother of Laozi, although it records that she, the Holy Mother goddess, taught the Mysterious Girl of the Nine Heavens (Jiutian xuannü 九天玄女).

5. Translation from Anna Seidel, *La divinisation de Lao-tseu sous les Han* (Paris: Ecole Francaise d'Extreme-Orient, 1969), 61.

6. Schipper, *The Taoist Body*, 117–18.

7. Anna Seidel, "Tokens of Immortality in Han Graves," *Numen* 29, no. 1 (1986): 106. I have abbreviated the title.

8. Translation from Seidel, "Tokens of Immortality," 106. I have added characters and changed the Wade-Giles to pinyin.

9. Charles Benn, "Taoism as Ideology in the Reign of Emperor Hsuan-Tsung (712–755)" (PhD diss., University of Michigan, 1977), 4. As a mortal ancestor, Laozi was not considered the first ancestor of the Li imperial family, who traced their origins back much further—to Zhuanxu of remote antiquity (*XTS* 70.1956). Beginning with the Shandong Li clan in the Western Han, various Lis had drawn kin connections to the Daoist sage.

10. Ibid., 15.

11. Ibid., 34.

12. Kirkland and Kohn, "Daoism in the Tang," 340.

13. *THY* 50.865.

14. Benn, "Taoism as Ideology," 24.

15. Ibid., 35.

16. Benn, *Cavern-Mystery Transmission*, 105. See below for more on the 662 sighting.

17. Benn, "Taoism as Ideology," 8–9. Benn (19) remarks that this divine Laozi was not only "preceptor to sage-kings and good rulers" but a messianic sage and savior capable of restoring harmony and stability.

18. *JTS* 3.48. Bozhou is in Luyi, Henan.

19. *ZZTJ* 201.6343; *XTS* 76.3475–76.

20. *ZZTJ* 201.6347; Hu Sanxing wrote his commentary on the *Comprehensive Mirror* in the early Yuan. *TD* 53.1478 records, "In Qianfeng 1 (666) of the Great Tang, Laojun was posthumously designated Grand Superior Emperor of Mysterious Origin." *THY* 50.865 records that the posthumous honorific designation was made on the twentieth day of the third lunar month.

21. *XTS* 3.65. According to *JTS* 5.90, a new temple was created in Zhenyuan County, with a director and an aide installed to properly administer the site. The change of name from Guyang to Zhenyuan is also recorded in *XTS* 38.990. See also Twitchett, "*Chen Gui* and Other Works," 81; and Victor Cunrui Xiong, "Ritual Innovation and Taoism Under Tang Xuanzong," *T'oung Pao*, Second Series, 82 (1996): 282.

22. *QTW* 933.9715. Xu Lishi was a grandson of the renowned early Tang general Xu Shao (d. 621), who befriended Tang founder Gaozu. See the Xus' joint biography in *JTS* 59.2327–30 and *XTS* 90.3770–72.

23. *Daode zhenjing guangsheng yi* 道德真經廣聖義 [Broad and Sacred Teachings of the Perfected Book on the Dao and Its Virtue], comp. Du Guangting, *Daozang* 725, 2.19a–21.

24. Benn, "Taoism as Ideology," 47. I have changed Wade-Giles to pinyin.

25. *QTW* 12.151. As mentioned, Du Guangting reported a different title, Hunyuan huangdi 混元皇帝, in contrast to Gaozong's yuanyuan huangdi 元元皇帝. *JTS* 5.90 indicates that the original title was Taishang xuanyuan huangdi 太上玄元皇帝. Du Guangting's term "Hunyuan huangdi" is curious. Two centuries after Du Guangting, Song emperor Zhenzong (r. 997–1022) did present Laozi a title that can be reduced to Hunyuan huangdi—Taishang Laojun hunyuan shangde huangdi 太上老君混元上德皇帝. This title inspired Xie Shouhao (1134–1212) to name his hagiography for Laozi "Hunyuan shengji" 混元聖紀 (Records of the Sage of Nebulous Origin). It is possible that Du Guangting originally used the title Xuanyuan huangdi 玄元皇帝, but that it

was emended to Hunyuan huangdi 混元皇帝 when his text was edited in the Song at some juncture after Zhenzong honored Laozi with the new title.

26. Benn, "Taoism as Ideology," 44–45.

27. Rothschild, *Wu Zhao*, 70, 77–78.

28. Bokenkamp, "A Medieval Feminist Critique," 387.

29. Translation of Beiji as "Northern Culmen" is drawn from Schafer, *Pacing the Void*, 44.

30. The Golden Terrace (Jintai 金臺) is associated with the Queen Mother of the West and Mount Kunlun. According to *THY* 50.869, in the third year of Chuigong (687), Wu Zhao as grand dowager changed the Longxing Observatory to Golden Terrace Observatory. According to *TPYL* 1.1 and 38.182, citing *Records of the Ten Continents* (Shizhou ji 十洲記), atop Mount Kunlun there are the "Golden Terrace and the Jade Pillars, where the primal pneumas are harmonized—this is the locale from which the Heavenly Emperor ruled." *TPYL* 811.3605 cites the *Inner Biographies of the Pass Guardian* (Guanling neizhuan 關令內傳), in which Laozi climbs Mount Kunlun and ascends the Golden Terrace.

31. The Western Mount is Mount Kunlun.

32. *QTW* 220.2220. Translation of this paragraph draws heavily on Bokenkamp's translation ("A Medieval Feminist Critique," 388).

33. Barrett, *Taoism Under the T'ang*, 38–40.

34. For a more complete account of these reforms, see *ZZTJ* 203.6421 and *QTW* 96.995; for secondary sources, see Guisso, "The Reigns of the Empress Wu, Chungtsung and Jui-tsung," 292; and Rothschild, *Wu Zhao*, 86–87.

35. Guozhou was located near the Lingbao in modern-day Henan, about 100 miles west of Luoyang.

36. After the Tang restoration, Wu Yuanchong, heralding from Hongzhou, was posthumously honored for his loyalty during Xuanzong's reign. See *QTW* 36.393.

37. *QTW* 933.9715, Du Guangting, *Lidai chongdao ji*. This "Lord Lao miracle" is also discussed briefly in Kirkland and Kohn, "Daoism in the Tang," 345.

38. Rothschild, *Wu Zhao*, 86.

39. Yang Liu, "Images for the Temple," 254.

40. Barrett, *Taoism Under the T'ang*, 39–40. On the timing of the bestowal of this title, see Forte, *Political Propaganda*, 301n214.

41. *XTS* 4.83.

42. *QTW* 96.995. Wang Pu in *THY* (50.878) records Wu Zhao's decision to honor Laozi's *wife* as Grand Dowager of the Anterior Heaven in the ninth month of 684. Curiously, Du You (*TD* 53.1478) makes the same error.

43. *XTS* 4.87; *JTS* 6.119; *ZZTJ* 204.6448.

44. Gu Zhengmei, "Wu Zetian de *Huayan jing*," 279–321.

45. *NQS* 57.990–91.

46. *THY* 50.865.

47. *ZZTJ* 204.6447.

48. *THY* 50.865.

49. Xiong, "Ritual Innovation and Taoism," 281, based on *QTW* 24.280–81. There is some debate as to the motivation behind Xuanzong's elevating the cult of Laozi. Whereas Charles Benn ("Taoism as Ideology") contends that Xuanzong's promotion

of Daoism and worship of Laozi "was intended to serve his political and ideological ends," Xiong suggests that Xuanzong's ritual innovations in the early 740s were more personal than political, related to his "quest for immortality through the help of celestial power" (305).

50. *JTS* 9.216.

51. For the turbulent years when the Taiping Princess, the Anle Princess, and Empress Wei dominated the court, see *ZZTJ*, chaps. 207–209. See also Guisso, "The Reigns of Empress Wu, Chung-tsung and Jui-tsung," 321–29.

52. Richard Kagan, "The Chinese Approach to Shamanism," *Chinese Sociology and Anthropology* 12, no. 4 (1980): 4–5.

53. Schipper, *The Taoist Body*, 125.

10. REJECTED FROM THE PANTHEON

1. See James Robson, *Power of Place: The Religious Landscape of the Southern Sacred Peak in Medieval China*, Harvard East Asian Monographs no. 316 (Cambridge, Mass.: Harvard University Press, 2009), 373–75.

2. Cahill, *Transcendence and Divine Passion*, 183–89; also "The Daoist Goddess: The Queen Mother of the West," in Wang, *Images of Women*, 348, 362–65.

3. Isabel Robinet, *Taoism: Growth of a Religion* (Stanford: Stanford University Press, 1997), 116.

4. Kirkland and Kohn, "Daoism in the Tang," 387.

5. Robson, *Power of Place*, 203. Robson examines the "elusive" and unstable nature of the term "Southern Marchmount"—a location initially defined as Huoshan in modern-day Anhui, but which later became strongly identified with Mount Hengshan 衡山 in Hunan.

6. It is beyond the scope of this chapter to provide a full biography of Lady Wei. For more biographical background, see Robson, *Power of Place*, 184–212, 373–75; Despeux and Kohn, *Women in Daoism*, 14–15; Idema and Grant, *The Red Brush*, 159–60; Despeux, "Women and Daoism," 387–88; Robinet, *Taoism*, 115–16.

7. For a succinct description of the texts, beliefs, and practices associated with the Shangqing tradition, see Isabelle Robinet, "Shangqing," in Predagio, *Encyclopedia of Taoism*, 858–66.

8. Barrett, *Taoism Under the T'ang*, 34–35.

9. *QTW* 933.9715.

10. *JTS* 5.99 for the titular change. See also Rothschild, *Wu Zhao*, 65–66; Barrett, *Taoism Under the T'ang*, 36–37; Kirkland and Kohn, "Daoism in the Tang," 343.

11. Kirkland and Kohn, "Daoism in the Tang," 340.

12. Ibid., 353.

13. Barrett, *Taoism Under the T'ang*, 35.

14. *JTS* 192.5126.

15. *QTW* 13.162.

16. *QTW* 220.2220.

17. *JTS* 5.110. Chao Fu and Xu You were celebrated Daoist renunciants mentioned in the works of Laozi, Zhuangzi, Ge Hong, and others.

18. Robson, *Power of Place*, 198–200.

19. Chen Jinhua, *Philosopher, Practitioner, Politician*, 373n26.

20. Paul Kroll, "Daoist Verse and the Quest for the Divine," in *Early Chinese Religion*, part 2, *The Period of Division (220–589)*, ed. John Lagerway and Lü Pengzhi (Leiden: Brill, 2010), 976. According to *JTS* 39.1489–90, in 627, boundaries and nomenclature were altered and Xiuwu became part of Huaizhou after Taizong pacified various rivals in the region.

21. Ibid., 977. See also Robson, *Power of Place*, 199; and Gil Raz, "Daoist Sacred Geography," in Lagerway and Lü Pengzhi, *Early Chinese Religion*, part 2, 1436. Most biographies of Wei Huacun contain the account of the visitation of the four perfected ones and Lady Wei's subsequent purification on Mount Wangwu—see *TPGJ* 58; *QTW* 259 and 340.

22. Xiong, *Emperor Yang*, 77.

23. *JTS* 4.77, 38.1424; *XTS* 38.981, 39.1010.

24. *QTS* 445.4996.

25. Cahill, *Transcendence and Divine Passion*, 60.

26. See Sima Chengzhen's *Tiandi gongfu tu* 天地宮府圖 (Chart of the Palaces and Bureaus of the Grotto-Heavens and the Blissful Lands) in *YJQQ* 27.153; and Miura Kunio, "Grotto Heavens and Blissful Lands," in Predagio, *Encyclopedia of Taoism*, 369.

27. Gil Raz, "Wangwu," in Predagio, *Encyclopedia of Taoism*, 1026.

28. Cahill, *Transcendence and Divine Passion*, 121; cf. *QTS* 282.

29. *QTW* 934.9723–24. The "Biography of the Yellow Emperor" (Xuanyuan benji 軒轅本記) in *YJQQ* 100.612 mentions that the mythic sovereign discovered a secret tract on divine elixirs and the Nine Tripods atop Mount Wangwu. Also see Charles Benn, "Du Guangting," in Predagio, *Encyclopedia of Taoism*, 387.

30. The biography of Sima Chengzhen in Li Bo's 李渤 (773–831) *Genealogies of the Perfected* (Zhenxi 真系) in the *YJQQ* 5.27 identifies him as belonging to Mount Wangwu.

31. *QTS* 3.35.

32. Kirkland and Kohn, "Daoism in the Tang," 347.

33. Slightly modified from Forte, *Political Propaganda*, 317. See part IV of this volume for a more thorough treatment and contextualization of this work.

34. Robson, *Power of Place*, 199.

35. Ibid. The preface to the inscription with this title is contained in *QTW* 259.2629, and in *Daojia jinshi lue* [A Summary of Daoist Inscriptions], comp. Chen Yuan (Beijing: Wenwu, 1988), chap. 77; and *Jinshi cuibian* [A Miscellany of Choice Inscriptions on Metal and Stone], comp. Wang Chang (Beijing: Zhongguo shudian, 1985), chap. 60.

36. *XTS* 36.937 and *TPGJ* 143.1025 note that this ill-omened sheatfish was discovered in 692—hidden in the woodwork—prophetically anticipating Lu being implicated and killed several years later.

37. Otagi Hajime, "Nangyaku Gi fujin shinko no hensen" [The Development in the Belief of Lady Wei of the Southern Marchmount], in *Rikucho dokyo no kenkyu* [Research on Daoism in the Six Dynasties Period], Research Report of the Institute for Research in Humanities, ed. Yoshikawa Tadao (Kyoto: Kyoto University, 1998), 383.

38. Otagi Hajime, "Nangyaku Gi fujin," 382–83.

39. *JTS* 189.4962; *XTS* 199.5665.

40. Kamitsuka Yoshiko, "Sokuten buko ki no dokyo" [Taoism During the Period of the Dowager-Empress Wu Zetian's Reign], in *Todai no Shukyo* [Religion in the Tang Dynasty], Research Report of the Institute for Research in Humanities, ed. Yoshikawa Tadao (Kyoto: Kyoto University, 2000), 252.

41. Otagi Hajime, "Nangyaku Gi fujin," 383–85.

42. Yoshikawa Tadao, *Sho to Dokyo no shuhen* [Texts and the Parameters of Daoism] (Tokyo: Heibonsha, 1987), 125–239; Edward Schafer, "The Restoration of the Shrine of Wei Hua-ts'un at Lin-ch'uan in the Early Eighth Century," *Journal of Oriental Studies* 15 (1977): 124–37; Russell Kirkland, "Huang Ling-wei: A Taoist Priestess in T'ang China," *Journal of Chinese Religions* 19 (1991): 47–73; Kirkland, *Taoism: The Enduring Tradition* (London: Routledge, 2004), 139–40; Suzanne Cahill, "Hua Gu," chap. 17 in *Divine Traces of the Daoist Sisterhood*, 119–26; Cahill, "Practice Makes Perfect: Paths to Transcendence for Women in Medieval China," *Taoist Resources* 2, no. 2 (1990): 23–42.

43. Amy McNair, *The Upright Brush: Yan Zhenqing's Calligraphy and Song Literati Politics* (Honolulu: University of Hawaii Press, 1998), chaps. 4–5.

44. Ibid., 83. See also Schafer, "The Restoration of the Shrine," 126, 135.

45. Schafer, "The Restoration of the Shrine," 129.

46. Yan Zhenqing, "Inscription for the Immortal Altar of Flower Maid of Well Mountain, Linchuan County in Fuzhou" (*QTW* 340.3444–45) and "Immortal Altar Stele Inscription of Lady Wei of Jin, Lady of the Southern Marchmount, Primal Mistress of Purple Tenuity, mandated Most Highly Realized Supervisor of Destinies" (*QTW* 340.3451–54). Russell Kirkland ("Huang Ling-wei," 47–73) has translated Yan Zhenqing's inscription honoring the Huang Lingwei. Yoshikawa Tadao, *Sho to Dokyo* (107–61) has also looked exhaustively at both inscriptions. Schafer ("The Restoration of the Shrine," 129–37) has translated the fifty-two four-syllable lines at the end of Yan Zhenqing's inscription for Wei Huacun, accompanying the translation with commentary drawn from Yan's much longer prefatory prose inscription.

47. Despeux and Kohn place Huang Lingwei in their chapter on "Medieval Renunciants," *Women in Daoism*, 124–25.

48. Cahill, in "Hua Gu," chap. 17 in *Divine Traces of the Daoist Sisterhood* (119–26), has translated the entirety of Du Guangting's biography of Huang Lingwei from *YJQQ* chap. 115.

49. Schafer, "Restoration of the Shrine," 135.

50. Ibid., 126.

51. Cahill, "Practice Makes Perfect," 24–25.

52. This site is west of the Linru River near Stone Well Mountain (Shijingshan 石井山). See Kirkland, "Huang Ling-wei," 48–52; Kamitsuka Yoshiko, "Sokuten buko ki no dokyo," 252; Rothschild, "Rhetoric, Ritual, and Support Constituences," chap. 5. For the primary source accounts of the discovery and repair of Wei Huacun's tomb during the Tang, see *YJQQ* 115.725 (translation in Cahill, *Divine Traces of the Daoist Sisterhood*, 124); and *QTW* 340 (Yan Zhenqing's inscription for Huang Lingwei's shrine). It may be significant and worthy of further investigation that the stone creature proximate to the revealed shrine is a turtle. Turtles, of course, play an important role in the Chinese cosmology. Steles marking temples or shrines often stand on the backs of stone turtles. One of the alternative names of Mount Kunlun, residence of

the Queen Mother of the West, was Tortoise Mountain (Guishan 龜山). According to the *TPGJ* 59.362, at the site where another Daoist divinity, the Brightstar Jade Girl (Mingxing yunü 明星玉女) rose to become an immortal, there was a giant stone turtle on the mountaintop—though it was not an animate creature.

Turtles are closely connected to longevity. Wu Zhao was fond of the turtle as an auspicious symbol. When she inaugurated the Zhou, she changed court adornments on ministerial garb from fish to turtles (*JTS* 6.121). Subjects also presented inscribed turtle shells at her court: Hu Yanqing presented a vermilion-painted turtle plastron that read "May the Son of Heaven live forever!" (*ZZTJ* 205.6484). When an auspicious stone turtle with the characters "Great Zhou" on top and the five elements and eight hexagrams on its sides was reportedly discovered at Hengshan, a site associated with Lady Wei, Li Qiao wrote a congratulatory memorial on behalf of pro-Buddhist minister Yao Shu (*QTW* 243.2457).

According to an entry titled "Natural Stones" (Ziran shi 自然石) in *TPGJ* 398.3193, "Scattered in the fields of Jianchang County in Hongzhou [Hu Chao's home region], there were natural stone steles, stone men, and stone tortoises. No one knew how many there were. They all appeared to be carved and polished, but had no inscriptions." Near to these naturally wrought stone figures was a deep, waterless stone well. Passages containing more stone figures led out from the well's interior. This would seem to indicate that stone tortoises possessed a certain numinous air and were well known in Jiangnan lore.

53. Though Wu Zhao was officially Divine and Sagely Emperor of the Golden Wheel at the time the relics were discovered in 693, Yan Zhenqing used Celestial Empress, her title from 674–683, when Gaozong was still alive.

54. *QTW* 340.3444.

55. Kirkland, "Huang Ling-wei," 52.

56. See Forte, *Political Propaganda*.

57. *ZZTJ* 204.6473.

58. *ZZTJ* 205.6490.

59. *XTS* 4.93; *ZZTJ* 205.6492.

60. *TPGJ* 288.2294; *ZZTJ* 206.6546.

61. In 1982 on Junji Peak, one of the highest peaks of Mount Song, a local found the inscribed "golden tally" that recorded the purpose of the Daoist ceremony. The inscription read:

> The ruler of the Great Zhou Wu Zhao admires the true *dao* with its long-lived immortals and spirits. Therefore, we reverently go to the Central Marchmount Mount Song to cast the Golden Tally, praying to the Three Ministers and Nine Treasures of Nature, that they might expiate the sinful name of Wu Zhao. Kowtowing repeatedly and offering obeisance as he makes this humble petition, your subject Hu Chao fills this commission.

Translation from Rothschild, "Rhetoric, Ritual and Support Constituencies," 232. Text and information about the golden tally are recorded in Su Jian, "Wu Zetian yu Shendu shiji" [Wu Zetian and Ruins in Divine Capital], in Su Jian and Bai Xianzhang, *Wu Zetian yu Luoyang*, 14. Kamitsuka Yoshiko ("Sokuten buko ki no Dokyo," 249–51) also examines the golden tally and Hu Chao's role in the "tossing the dragons" rite.

62. Cahill, *Divine Traces*, 120, 124 (translation of *Yunji qiqian*).

63. *QTS* 828.9331.

64. See, for instance, Wang Shuanghuai, "Lun Wu Zetian de gaige" [Discussing Change and Revolution Under Wu Zetian], in *Wu Zetian yu Xianyang* [Wu Zetian and Xianyang], ed. Zhao Wenrun and Xin Jialong (Xi'an: Sanqin, 2000), 117–18; and Hu Ji, *Wu Zetian benzhuan*, 85, who observes that "her appreciation of talent overrode her anger at being cursed and insulted."

65. *ZZTJ* 205.6478.

66. *ZZTJ* 203.6423–24.

67. *ZZTJ* 203.6424.

68. Benn, *Cavern-Mystery Transmission*, 10.

69. Despeux and Kohn, *Women in Daoism*, 6 and 14.

IV. BUDDHIST DEVIS AND GODDESSES

1. Weinstein, *Buddhism Under the T'ang*, 38; Wang Shuanghuai and Zhao Wenrun, *Wu Zetian pingzhuan*, 179–80; Chen Jinhua, "Śarīra and Scepter. Empress Wu's Political Use of Buddhist Relics," *Journal of the International Association of Buddhist Studies* 25 (2002): 33–150, esp. 109–12, in which Wu Zhao's relic-veneration rites are seen as being linked by both dharma (Buddhist faith) and blood (kin ties to the Yang imperial family) to the Sui line of rulers. Both Wu Zhao and Sui Yangdi instrumentally used Buddhism for validation, to fend off the label of usurper, and to mute questions surrounding political legitimation. Both cast themselves as "restorers of Buddhism" following periods of repression, beings incarnated as living bodhisattvas taking the shape of an earthly sovereign to become "divine saviors of the Dharma." Both also cast themselves as cakravartin kings.

2. Wang Shuanghuai and Zhao Wenrun, "Leaving the Palace to Become a Buddhist Nun" (Chujia dang nigu 出家當尼姑), chap. 3 in *Wu Zetian pingzhuan*, 21–24. Also see Forte, "Wu Zhao, A Buddhist Novice in Her Youth," appendix C in *Political Propaganda*, 365–68.

3. Gernet, *Buddhism in Chinese Society*, 7–8.

4. *ZZTJ* 204.6473; *QTW* 95.981.

5. *JTS* 6.122.

6. Ch'en, *Buddhism in China*, 255.

7. Chen Jinhua, "Tang Buddhist Palace Chapels," *Journal of Chinese Religions* 32 (2004): 101.

8. For a summary of Wu Zhao's many political and ideological activities involving Buddhist art and architecture, see Karetzky, "Wu Zetian and Buddhist Art," 113–71. Among the many works on Dunhuang and Longmen, see Ning Qiang, "Gender Politics in Medieval Chinese Buddhist Art: Images of Empress Wu at Longmen and Dunhuang," *Oriental Art* 49, no. 2 (2003): 28–39; MacNair, *Donors of Longmen: Faith, Politics, and Patronage in Medieval Chinese Buddhist Sculpture* (Honolulu: University of Hawaii Press, 2007); and Zhang Naizhu, "Wu Zetian yu Longmen shiku fojiao zaoxiang" [Wu Zetian and the Buddhist Statuary of the Longmen Grottoes], in Su Jian and Bai Xianzhang, *Wu Zetian yu Luoyang*, 17–31.

9. Karetzky, "Wu Zetian and Buddhist Art," 131.

10. For more on the ideological and political significance of Wu Zhao's several *mingtangs*, see Forte, *Mingtang and Buddhist Utopias*.

11. See Dorothy Wong, "The Case of Amoghapāśa," *Journal of Inner Asian Art and Archaeology* 2 (2007): 151–52; and Sherman Lee and Wai-kam Ho, "The Colossal Eleven-Faced Kuan-yin of the T'ang Dynasty," *Artibus Asiae* 22, nos. 1/2 (1959): 121–37. Though Guanyin took on a feminine aspect in subsequent eras, Yü Chün-fang, *Kuan-yin: The Chinese Transformation of Avalokiteśvara* (New York: Columbia University Press, 2001), convincingly illustrates that "Kuan-yin was perceived as masculine and was so depicted in art prior to and during the Tang" (6). Though Guanyin, "like all great bodhisattvas . . . cannot be said to possess any gender characteristics," the deity is usually represented as a princely and handsome young man (294). Wu Zhao did not bring about the feminization of Guanyin.

12. Zhiru Ng, *The Making of a Savior Bodhisattva*, Kuroda Institute Studies in East Asian Buddhism 21 (Honolulu: University of Hawaii Press, 2007), 118–20.

13. *XTS* 4.94, 76.3483; *JTS* 6.123; *ZZTJ* 205.6492.

14. *XTS* 4.95. Alternatively, this could be rendered "Compassionate One." See chap. 11 in this volume; and Forte, *Political Propaganda*, 225–31.

15. See *ZZTJ* 205.6522 for Wu Zhao's *pañcāvarṣika* of 694. See Rothschild, "Zhuan-lunwang, yishi, ji huozai," 101–13.

16. Chen Jinhua, "Śarīra and Scepter," 127–45.

17. Jamie Hubbard, *Absolute Delusion, Perfect Buddhahood: The Rise and Fall of a Chinese Heresy* (Honolulu: University of Hawaii Press, 2001), 203–8. Hubbard notes that neither of her two inexhaustible storehouses, one established in Luoyang in 692 and the other in Chang'an between 701 and 705, was successful. Also see Gernet, *Buddhism in Chinese Society*, 211–12.

18. Chen Jinhua, "The Tang Buddhist Palace Chapels," 102, shows that Wu Zhao had at least four palace chapels during her regency and reign and that her most important Buddhist propagandists worked in them, including the framers of the *Commentary on the Great Cloud Sutra*. Kenneth Ch'en, *The Chinese Transformation of Buddhism* (Princeton: Princeton University Press, 1973), 106, provides a thumbnail institutional history of palace chapels and also mentions Wu Zhao's role in expanding their importance.

19. Gernet, *Buddhism in Chinese Society*, 24, 281.

20. Chen Yinke, "Wu Zhao yu Fojiao" [Wu Zhao and Buddhism], *Chen Yinke xiansheng quanji* [The Complete Collected Works of Professor Chen Yinke] (Taipei: Jiusi, 1971), 421–36.

21. Rita Gross, *Buddhism After Patriarchy: A Feminist History, Analysis and Reconstruction of Buddhism* (Albany: State University of New York Press, 1993), 10.

22. Hu Ji, *Wu Zetian benzhuan*, 165.

23. Weinstein, *Buddhism Under the T'ang*, 41.

24. Guisso, "The Reigns of Empress Wu, Chung-tsung and Jui-tsung," 305. In his monograph *Wu Ts'e-t'ien and the Politics of Legitimation in T'ang China*, Guisso is more measured in his assessment of Buddhism's role in Wu Zhao's legitimation, remarking that it "was not negligible but neither was it predominant" (68).

25. Sen Tansen, *Buddhism, Diplomacy and Trade*, 95.

26. For a brief summary of Wu Zhao's long, involved relationship with Buddhism, see Rothschild, *Wu Zhao*, 137–56.

27. Wang Shuanghuai and Zhao Wenrun, *Wu Zetian pingzhuan*, 205.

28. Bernard Faure, *The Power of Denial: Buddhism, Purity and Gender* (Princeton: Princeton University Press, 2003), 24–27.

29. This queen (or devi) was, in fact, known in China. Central Indian monk Guṇabhadra (Chinese: Qiunabatouluo 求那跋陀羅, 394–468) translated the second-century A.D. Indian text in which the Buddha grants a woman the ability to teach the dharma, the *Sutra of the Lion's Roar of Queen Śrīmālā* (Shengman shizi hou jing 勝鬘師子吼經; Sanskrit: Śrīmālādevī Simhanāda Sūtra).

30. One might argue that there is another Buddhist mother. In 686, during Wu Zhao's tenure as grand dowager, Indian Buddhist monk Divākara translated several brief sutras centered on Cundī (Chinese: Zhunti 准提), also known as the Buddhist mother goddess of the 70 million (Chinese: Qijuzhi fomu 七俱胝佛母; Sanskrit: Saptakoṭi Buddhabhagavatī). See *Foshuo Qijuzhi fomu xinda Zhunti tuoluoni jing* [Dhāraṇī Sutra of the Buddha's Words on Saptakoṭi Buddhabhagavatī], trans. Divākara, *T.* 20.1077. Those who recited the sutra might slough off evil karma, receive protection from illness and harm, and encounter benevolent Buddhas and bodhisattvas. See Richard McBride, "Popular Esoteric Deities and the Spread of Their Cults," in *Esoteric Buddhism and the Tantras in East Asia*, ed. Charles Orzech, Henrik Sorensen, and Richard Payne (Leiden: Brill, 2011), 219, who shows this divinity's connections to the Hindu goddess Chandi. For additional information on Divākara's importance as a Buddhist propagandist, see Forte, *Political Propaganda*, 50, 163–67. In "Icon and Incantation: The Goddess Zhunti and the Role of Images in the Occult Buddhism of China," in *Images in Asian Religions*, ed. Phyllis Graff and Koichi Shinohara (Vancouver: University of British Columbia, 2004), Robert Gimello describes Cundī as an "unheralded" Buddhist goddess, a complex and "mysterious" being whom the faithful invoked with *dhāraṇī* recitations or vividly rendered in paintings. The "object of special or discrete veneration, the central focus of her own self-contained and self-sufficient cult," she existed well outside the sphere of orthodox Buddhism (225–26). There is not sufficient material on Cundī to warrant a separate chapter.

11. DHARMA ECHOES OF MOTHER MĀYĀ IN WU ZHAO

1. Victor Mair, "The Narrative Revolution in Chinese Literature: Ontological Presumptions," *Chinese Literature: Essays, Articles, Reviews* 5, nos. 1/2 (1983): 10 and 21.

2. This story is frequently retold with some variations in both primary and secondary sources. For instance, see Warren Matthews, *World Religions*, 6th ed. (Belmont, Calif.: Wadsworth, 2010), 105.

3. *Mohe Moye jing* [Sutra of Great Māyā], trans. Tanjing, chap. 2, in *T.* 17.815. In his article "Wang Chin's Dhōta Temple Stele Inscription," *Journal of the American Oriental Society* 83, no. 3 (1963): 346n63, Richard Mather translates a section of the sutra in which, centuries after the extinction of Buddhist law, several *bhikṣus* appear, promising to revive the faith and destroy heretical views.

4. See Sonya Lee, *Surviving Nirvana: The Death of Buddha in Chinese Visual Culture* (Hong Kong: Hong Kong University Press, 2010), 94–98. Ch'en, *Chinese Transformation*, 34–35, notes that in this sutra the Buddha, to refute the oft-repeated Confucian charge of unfiliality, plays the role of a dutiful and filial son.

5. Māyā appears in this capacity in both the sixty-chapter Eastern Jin translation by Buddhabhadra, *Dafangguang Fo Huayan jing* [Flower Garland Sutra], chap. 57, in *T.* 9.278, and in Śikṣānanda's *Dafangguang Fo Huayan jing* [Flower Garland Sutra], chap. 76, in *T.* 10.279, from Wu Zhao's reign as emperor. See translation in annotations of the *Samguk Yusa* [Omitted Events of the Three Kingdoms Period], comp. Iryeon, 4.15, in *Collected Works of Korean Buddhism, Volume 10: Korean Buddhist Culture— Accounts of a Pilgrimage, Monuments and Eminent Monks*, ed. Roderick Whitfield, trans. and annotated Matty Wegehaupt, Michael Finch, and Sem Vermeersch (Seoul: Jogye Order of Korean Buddhism, 2012), 343n524.

6. Serinity Young, *Courtesans and Tantric Consorts: Sexualities in Buddhist Narrative, Iconography and Ritual* (New York: Routledge, 2004), 23–24.

7. Wu Hung, "Buddhist Elements in Early Chinese Art (2nd and 3rd Century AD)," *Artibus Asiae* 47, nos. 3/4 (1986): 271.

8. Sherman Lee, "The Golden Image of the New-Born Buddha," *Artibus Asiae* 18, nos. 3/4 (1955): 225.

9. Dorothy Wong, *Pre-Buddhist and Buddhist Use of Symbolic Form* (Honolulu: University of Hawaii Press, 2004), 99.

10. Wang, *Shaping the Lotus Sutra*, 47–50.

11. Katherine Tsiang, "Monumentalization of Buddhist Texts in the Northern Qi Dynasty: The Engravings of Sūtras in Stone at the Xiangtangshan and Other Sites in the Sixth Century," *Artibus Asiae* 56, nos. 3/4 (1996): 236.

12. *Da Tang Neidian lu* [Great Tang Catalog of Scriptures], comp. Daoxuan, in *T.* 55.2149. Chap. 4 mentions a two-chapter *Sutra of Great Māyā*, remarking that it was also known simply as the *Sutra of Māyā*; chap. 8 also mentions a *Sutra of Great Māyā*; chaps. 6 and 9 give the same name, adding that it was the translation of Southern Qi monk Tanjing; chap. 10 notes that there was a three-chapter copy of the sutra.

13. *Da Zhou kanding zhongjing mulu* [Great Zhou Catalog of Buddhist Scriptures], comp. Mingquan and others, chap. 13, in *T.* 55.2153. Here, the *Sutra of the Great Māyā* is recorded as a two-chapter or twenty-five-page text.

14. *TPGJ* 441.3599.

15. Livia Kohn and Michael LaFargue, eds., *Lao Tzu and the Tao-te-ching* (Albany: State University of New York Press, 1998), 53. The early sixth-century *History of the Southern Qi* (*NQS* 54.931) contains a version of the story in which Māyā's name Jingmiao is given.

16. Kristof Schipper, "Purity and Strangers: Shifting Boundaries in Medieval Taoism," *T'oung Pao* 80 (1994): 72.

17. *Samguk Yusa*, 211n107 and 215n117. Clearly Seondok herself was heir to a longer Buddhist lineage. Kang Woobang, in *Korean Buddhist Sculpture*, trans. Choo Yoonjung (Chicago: Art Media Resources; Gyeong-gi: Yeolhwadang, 2005), 209, mentions that the convention of Buddhist terms appearing in the names of Sillan kings dates back to King Jabi (Compassionate King; Chinese: *cibei wang* 慈悲王) in the mid-fifth century.

18. *Samguk Yusa*, 4.6, "The Nine-Story Pagoda at Hwangnyongsa," 219. For more on the vital role that the idea of "receiving the prophecy" (*shouji*) played in Wu Zhao's

ideological campaign to establish the Zhou dynasty, see Forte, *Political Propaganda;* and chap. 12 in this volume.

19. Whitfield, *Collected Works of Korean Buddhism,* 219n128.

20. Pan Yihong, *Son of Heaven and the Heavenly Qaghan,* 209–17.

21. *QTW* 908.9477.

22. Wang Shuanghuai and Zhao Wenrun, *Wu Zetian pingzhuan,* 180.

23. See, for instance, *Da Tang Da Ci'ensi Sanzang Fashi zhuan* [Biography of Dharma Master Sanzang of the Great Ci'en Temple of the Great Tang], written by Yan Cong in 688 (chap. 9 in *T.* 50.2053). The single-chapter *Si shamen Xuanzhuang shang biao ji* [A Record of Petitions Presented by the Buddhist Monk Xuanzhuang] (*T.* 52.2119) contains Sanzang's petition inviting the newly born future emperor to enter the Buddhist orders as his disciple.

24. *CFYK* 21.227.

25. Wang Yongping, "Tang Gaozong, Wu Zetian shiqi yu Linyi de guanxi" [Foreign Relations with Champa During the Reigns of Tang Gaozong and Wu Zetian], in *Conference Proceedings from the 11th Conference of the Wu Zetian Research Association* (Guangyuan, Sept. 2013), supplemental essay, 4–5.

26. Nanditha Krishna, *Sacred Animals of India* (New Delhi: Penguin, 2010), 119–28.

27. Wang Yongping, "Tang Gaozong, Wu Zetian shiqi yu Linyi,", 3.

28. *TPYL* 890.3955. This was possibly an incarnation of rain god Indra's famous mount Airavata. In *Sacred Animals of India,* Nanditha Krishna notes that the Iravati (Irrawaddy) River in Burma means "produced from water" and echoes the name of Indra's sacred mount. Associated with water, this divine white elephant is symbolized by huge rain clouds that might anoint the populace with their salubrious precipitation (127).

29. *XTS* 47.1217.

30. *ZZTJ* 205.6492. For more on Wu Zhao's identification as a cakravartin, see Forte, subchapter titled "Wu Zhao, Cakravartin of the Golden Wheel," in *Political Propaganda,* 204–14.

31. *XTS* 4.95, 76.3482–83; *ZZTJ* 205.6492; *JTS* 6.123.

32. *T.* 55.2153, preface. Translation from Forte, *Political Propaganda,* 219 (parenthetical notations omitted).

33. For the origins of the Nine Tripods as symbols of virtue and legitimacy, see Kwang-chih Chang, *Art, Myth and Ritual,* 95–97.

34. For the completion of Communing with Heaven Palace, the *mingtang* complex finished in 696, see *ZZTJ* 205.6505. For the grand ceremony to install the tripods, see *ZZTJ* 206.6517; *XTS* 4.95; *TD* 44.254; *THY* 11.279–80. For detail on the manufacture and design, see *JTS* 22.867–68.

35. *QTS* 5.51.

36. Forte, "The Two Mingtang Compared," in *Mingtang and Buddhist Utopias,* chap. 3.

37. Rothschild, subchapter "The Nine Tripods," in "Rhetoric, Ritual and Support Constituencies," 309–23. In contrast, Ricardo Fracasso, in his essay "The Nine Tripods of Empress Wu," contends that Wu Zhao had tripods manufactured to placate an anti-Buddhist faction while buttressing her political authority with a traditional symbol of legitimacy.

38. *Tang liudian,* 4.114–15.

39. *JTS* 198.5312; *XTS* 222.6308.

40. *XTS* 222.6308. These white elephants must have been considered sacred in this region of Southeast Asia, for according to the *New Tang History*, they were thought to be highly intelligent and awe-inspiring. When a person had a legal complaint he or she would kneel before the massive white pachyderm of judgment and burn incense. The elephant would render a verdict and then leave.

41. See Chen Jinhua, *Philosopher, Practitioner and Politician*, esp. appendix C, "Biankongsi and Śikṣānanda's Translation Bureau," 367–76.

42. *QTW* 97.1001–02.

43. *T.* 10.279, chap. 74. Wu Zhao's propagandists expanded upon a shorter, sixty-chapter version of the *Flower Garland Sutra* composed in the Eastern Jin (*T.* 9.278).

44. Ann Heirman, "Yijing's View on the *Bhikṣunīs'* Standard Robes," *Chung-Hwa Buddhist Journal* 21 (2008): 150–54.

45. Yijing refers to Māyā in the opening chapter of *Genben shuo yiqie youbu Binaiye chujia shi* [Matters of Renunciation in the Mūlasarvāstivāda Vinaya], in *T.* 23.1444.

46. *Genben shuo yiqie youbu Binaiye* [Mūlasarvāstivāda Vinaya], trans. Yijing, preface, in *T.* 23.1442.

47. *T.* 23.1444, chap. 1.

48. *Genben shuo yiqie youbu Binaiye zashi* [Miscellany from the Mūlasarvāstivāda Vinaya], trans. Yijing, chap. 20, in *T.* 24.1451.

49. See *ZZTJ* 205.6442; *XTS* 4.85, 76.3479, 35.910, 37.962–63; *TPGJ* 397.3176–77.

50. *XTS* 35.910.

51. See Forte, *Political Propaganda*, 197, 269, 318. Both of these texts will be discussed in more detail in chap. 12.

52. *QTW* 249.2515.

53. *ZZTJ* 204.6462; *XTS* 76.3481.

54. Yijing not only mentions "Divine Mother" in the opening chapter of *Matters of Renunciation in the Mūlasarvāstivāda Vinaya* (*T.* 23.1444), as mentioned above, but he also uses the term in the *Mūlasarvāstivāda Vinaya* (*T.* 23.1442, chap. 39) and in *Miscellany from the Mūlasarvāstivāda Vinaya* (*T.* 24.1451, chap. 37).

55. *T.* 10.279, chaps. 47, 58.

56. *T.* 50.2053, chap. 3.

57. Chen Jinhua, *Śarīra and Scepter*, 113.

58. *Fo benxing ji jing*, comp. Jñāngupta, chap. 7, in *T.* 3.190.

59. *Fayuan zhulin*, comp. Daoshi, chap. 9, in *T.* 53.2122.

60. *Fangguang da zhuangyan jing*, trans. Divakara, chap. 3, in *T.* 3.187.

61. Patricia Karetzky, *Early Buddhist Art: Illustrations from the Life of the Buddha* (Lanham, Md.: University Press of America, 2000), 140–41.

62. Ibid., 138. See *ZZTJ* 167–68 for more on Li Zu'e's rise to become Emperor Qi Wenxuan's (r. 550–559) empress and empress dowager, followed by her demise after her son, bearing the apt and depressing posthumous name Emperor Fei (r. 559–60), the Deposed Emperor, was killed. She was forced into a sexual relationship with her brother-in-law Emperor Wucheng (r. 561–65) and eventually became a Buddhist nun.

63. See Alexander Soper, "A T'ang Parinirvāṇa Stele," *Artibus Asiae* 22, nos. 1/2 (1959): 159–60; Karetzky, "The Representation of Women," 226; Karetzky, "Wu Zetian and Buddhist Art," 117–20.

64. *ZZTJ* 204.6449. For more on the pivotal role that these Great Cloud temples played in the establishment of Wu Zhao's Zhou dynasty and their ideological significance, see chap. 12 in this volume.

65. Soper, "A T'ang Parinirvāṇa Stele," 160.

66. Ibid., 163.

67. Mary Anne Cartelli, "On a Five-Colored Cloud: The Songs of Mount Wutai," *Journal of the American Oriental Society* 124, no. 4 (2004): 737. Cartelli maintains that, reflected in the poetry of the era, a full-fledged cult of Mañjuśrī developed on Mount Wutai.

68. Weinstein, *Buddhism Under the T'ang*, 37; Ch'en, *Buddhism in China*, 276–77; Ch'en, *Chinese Transformation*, 172. Forte, *Political Propaganda*, 129–36, has made some preliminary observations about Wu Zhao's patronage of the Mañjuśrī cult on Wutai as emperor. Degan, one of the monks who presented the *Commentary* to Wu Zhao in 690, heralded from Bingzhou and helped elevate the Wutai cult of Mañjuśrī during the female emperor's final years on the throne.

69. *XTS* 4.80.

70. Chen Jinhua, "Śarīra and Scepter," 106–07. Chen maintains that "the geographical proximity between Wutaishan and the Wu family's ancestral homeland (i.e., Wenshui in present-day Shanxi) suggests that the Buddhapālita legend was probably a strategy on the part of the empress and her ideologues to tout her family's divine origin by establishing its intrinsic ties to this sacred mountain and the principal Buddhist deity dwelling there, Mañjuśrī" (109–10). Also see Forte, *Political Propaganda*, 126; and James Benn, *Burning for the Buddha: Self-Immolation in Chinese Buddhism* (Honolulu: University of Hawaii Press, 2007), 135. The Dhāraṇī Sutra of the Buddha's Crowning Victory is contained in T. 19.967.

71. Isabelle Charleux, "Padmasambhava's Travel to the North," *Central Asian Journal* 46, no. 2 (2002): 187. This grotto was sacred in Mongolian and Tibetan Buddhism.

72. *QTS* 265.2944.

73. *JTS* 8.165.

74. For more on Xuanzong's adversarial posture toward the Buddhist establishment, especially early in his reign, see Tonami Mamoru, "Policy Towards the Buddhist Church," 29–32. Xuanzong issued a series of imperial pronouncements that forced monks to pay obeisance to parents and ruler, drastically reduced fashioning of Buddhist statuary, prevented Buddhist monks from mingling with officials and nobles, laicized irregularly ordained Buddhist clergy, abolished supernumerary temple offices, forbid excessive propagation of sutras, prohibited construction of new temples, and brought requests for repairs and improvements to existing temples under close state scrutiny.

12. BODHISATTVA WITH A FEMALE BODY

1. Forte, *Political Propaganda*, based on his reading of Dunhuang document S.6502.

2. Gernet, *Buddhism in Chinese Society*, 288.

3. Forte, *Political Propaganda*, chap. 1, appendix A, has shown that there is ongoing confusion as to the translator—it might be either Dharmakṣema (also Tanwuchen 曇無讖, 385–433) or Zhu Fonian 竺佛念. Both translated the sutra independently,

but it is unclear whose version survived. From the late seventh century forward, Dharmakṣema is credited as the translator of the extant rendition of the sutra. For a more extensive study on Dharmakṣema, see Chen Jinhua, "The Indian Buddhist Missionary Dharmakṣema (385–433): A New Dating of His Arrival in Guzang and of His Translations," *T'oung Pao* 90 (2004): 215–63.

4. Forte, *Political Propaganda*, 48, 321.

5. Ibid., 342–43; cf. *T.* 12.387.

6. Forte, *Political Propaganda*, 215.

7. Ibid., 342–43, 348.

8. Ibid., 51.

9. *THY* 48.847; and *Henan zhi* [Treatise on Henan], comp. Xu Song (Beijing: Zhonghua, 1994), 1.34.

10. Forte, *Political Propaganda*, 50.

11. Dunhuang document S.6502, "Commentary on the Meaning of the Prophecy About Shenhuang in the Great Cloud Sutra," translated in Forte, *Political Propaganda*, 260.

12. Ibid., 301. In "Daojiao tu Ma Yuanzhen yu Wu-Zhou geming" [Daoist Ma Yuanzhen and the Wu-Zhou Revolution], *Zhongguo shi yanjiu* (2004): 73–80, contemporary scholar Lei Wen has shown that Master Ma was likely Ma Yuanzhen, head of a Daoist abbey in Chang'an and that the prophecy was composed after Gaozong's death.

13. Ibid., 308–09. Though Ziwei 紫薇, often rendered "Purple Tenuity," is part of one of Wei Huacun's titles on one of Yan Zhenqing's stele inscriptions, this is not a reference to her. Rather, this is likely Divine Lady Wang of Ziwei whom Robert Campany, in To Live as Long as Heaven and Earth: A Translation and Study of Ge Hong's Traditions of Divine Transcendents (Berkeley: University of California Press, 2002), 134n4, describes as "a colleague of Lady Wei Huacun of the Southern Peak."

14. Translation from Forte, *Political Propaganda*, 276.

15. Ibid., 270.

16. Forte, *Political Propaganda*, 265, 271–72n79. The discovery of the stone is mentioned in *XTS* 4.87 and *ZZTJ* 204.6449.

17. Translation from Forte, *Political Propaganda*, 271, 273.

18. Ibid., 274. According to Wu Zhao's biography in the *New Tang History* (*XTS* 76.3474), Taizong bestowed the name Enchanting Wu upon her when she was his concubine. In *New Tang History* (35.918) and the *TPGJ* 163.1182, it is noted that during the Yonghui era (650–656) at the beginning of Gaozong's reign, when Wu Zhao was brought back into the palace and rose to become empress, everyone sang "Enchanting Miss Wu." The song was composed earlier, by courtier Tang Lingze 唐令則 in the late Kaihuang 開皇 era (581–600) of the Sui, likely to the accompaniment of the *pipa* 琵琶. The song "Tangtang" was often written as homophone 堂堂.

19. Though Jambudvīpa, the southern continent of the four lands in Buddhist cosmology, was more closely associated with India than China, Wu Zhao's propagandists blurred the distinction—for a cakravartin governed all four continents.

20. Forte, *Political Propaganda*, 271.

21. Forte, "The Maitreyist Huaiyi and Taoism," *Tang yanjiu* 4 (1998): 22.

22. Forte, *Political Propaganda*, 216 and 281–83.

23. Diana Paul, *Women in Buddhism: Images of the Feminine in the Mahayana Tradition* (Berkeley: University of California Press, 1985), 186; Gross, *Buddhism After Patriarchy*, 62.

24. Patricia Karetzky, *Guanyin* (New York: Oxford University Press, 2004), 24. This process may just, as Suzanne Cahill suggests, "represent the dual nature of Guanyin in China" (epistolary correspondence, 1 July 2013).

25. Forte, *Political Propaganda*, 279–80. For more on the five bodhisattva precepts (*pusajie* 菩薩戒), prohibitions against killing, theft, harming living beings, and bad conduct, see the two-fascicle *Fanwang jing* [Sutra on Brahma's Net], trans. Kumāravjiva, T. 24.1484. For secondary sources on the precepts, see Martine Batchelor, *The Path of Compassion: The Bodhisattva Precepts* (Walnut Creek, Calif.: Altamira, 2004), 19.

26. See chap. 2 in this volume.

27. Forte, *Political Propaganda*, 285–87.

28. Ibid., 287.

29. Ibid., 296–97. The *Illustrations of Opposing Backs* was likely written by astronomer and horological specialist Li Chunfeng (602–670); see 295n192.

30. Ibid., 351.

31. *JTS* 6.121; *XTS* 4.90; *ZZTJ* 204.6466. All of these Confucian sources mistakenly refer to the source as either the *Great Cloud Sutra*, or, alternatively, a "falsely compiled" (*wei xuan* 偽選) or "apocryphal" (*wei zao* 偽造) version of the sutra.

32. *XTS* 4.91; *ZZTJ* 204.6469.

33. *T* 19.1024, 717–21. Timothy Barrett has studied this text extensively, with special attention to its role in the development of printing technology. He shows that the text built on the earlier "Indian practice of combining text and stupa" (*The Woman Who Discovered Printing*, 26) to create a mass-produced stand-in for Buddhist relics. This gave these texts a talismanic force. See *The Woman Who Discovered Printing*; and Barrett, "Stūpa, Sūtra and Śarīra in China, c. 656–706 CE," *Buddhist Studies Review* 18, no. 1 (2001): 1–64.

34. Chen Jinhua, "Śarīra and Scepter," 111–12. Mitraśānta likely worked with brilliant Sogdian ideologue-thaumaturge Fazang and Khotanese Śikṣānanda to complete this work in 704 or 705. See also Barrett, *The Woman Who Discovered Printing*, 93–94, 99.

35. Barrett, "Stūpa, Sūtra and Śarīra, 53.

36. Chen Jinhua, "Śarīra and Scepter," 132.

37. Barrett, *The Woman Who Discovered Printing*, 94–95. For a more detailed account of the content of the spell, see Chen Jinhua, "Śarīra and Scepter," 112–14.

38. Michael Welch, "Fa-tsang, Pure Light and Printing: An Inquiry Into the Origins of Textual Xylography" (Master's thesis, Library Sciences, University of Minnesota, 1981), 101–02.

39. *Song gaoseng zhuan* [Biographies of Eminent Monks, Compiled in the Song Dynasty], comp. Zanning, chaps. 2, 34, in *T*. 50.2061.

40. Du Doucheng, "Guanyu Wu Zetian yu fojiao de jige wenti" [Several Issues Concerning Wu Zetian and Buddhism], *Zongjiao xue yanjiu* (1994): 31.

41. Forte's interpretation (*Political Propaganda*, 357) of Wu Zhao's name is illuminating:

> I believe that the form of Zhao 曌 was actually inspired by this text of Maitreyan millennialism [the *Sutra of Primal Causes* (Benyin jing 本因經)], where Kongwang 空王 (King of Space) is the first of the Seven Buddhas, and Mingwang 明王 (Luminous or Illuminated King) is the one who historically will actualize the prophecy. *Kong* 空 and *ming* 明 symbolize the union of the two powers in

the person of Wu Zhao or merely represent the visual evocative symbol of the second sutra of the *Zhengming jing* and the ideas contained therein.

42. Hu Ji, *Wu Zetian benzhuan*, 170.

43. *THY* 48.848.

44. *QTS* 155.1600.

45. Ibid. Cui Shu was a native of Songzhou (modern-day Dengfeng, at the foot of Mount Song) who never rose very high in bureaucratic rank.

46. The Duke of Zhou.

47. *QTW* 192.1936. Paoxi is another term for Fuxi.

48. *T.* 52.2118, chap. 5. This was a way of attempting to subordinate Daoism to Buddhism in the ideological rivalry of the time. The Dajiaye bodhisattva was Mahākāśyapa, one of the Buddha's great disciples. If Laozi were merely the Buddha's disciple, then the Daoist faith would be nothing more than a derivative subset of Buddhism.

49. *ZZTJ* 205.6494, 6499–6500. Zhang Naizhu, "Luoyang xinji shike suojian Tangdai zhongyuan zhi fojiao" [Tang Buddhism of the Central Plains as Reflected in Recently Compiled Stone Carvings from Luoyang], *Zhongyuan wenwu* no. 5 (2008): 81, observed that as in 663 the discovery of the hoofprint of a *qilin* in front of the newly constructed Hanyuan Basilica in Chang'an prompting Gaozong and Empress Wu to change the name of the reign era to Unicorn Virtue, the same auspicious event prompted construction of the Unicorn's Hoof Buddhist temple.

50. *ZZTJ* 205.6494.

51. Ibid.

52. Ibid., 205.6499–6500.

53. Forte, *Political Propaganda*, chap. 3, esp. the appendix, "The Translators of the *Ratnamegha Sutrā* in 693," 246–53.

54. *Baoyu jing*, *T.* 16.660. Translation from Forte, *Political Propaganda*, 196. Lunar Radiance likely appeared in a Buddhist-related title ten years earlier. Inspired by popular millenarian Buddhism, a charismatic local leader may have taken the title Yueguang (Candraprabha) in a revolt of his Jihu people in Shaanbei in the early 680s. Also see Rothschild, "Emerging from the Cocoon," 257–82.

55. Forte, *Political Propaganda*, 196n30.

56. Ibid., 196–97; Chen Jinhua, *Monks and Monarchs*, 117.

57. *ZZTJ* 205.6492.

58. Chen Jinhua, *Monks and Monarchs*, 114–15. See also Tambiah, "The Galactic Polity in Southeast Asia," 252–86. Though this work focuses on kingship in a different region in a later era, the idea of a Buddhist (or Hindu-Buddhist), "galactic polity" with a ruler—cakravartin, dharma wielder, and living bodhisattva—situated at the cosmological, topographical, and political center that he describes was not unconnected to developing notions of Buddhist sovereignty in early medieval and medieval China.

59. Forte, *Political Propaganda*, 287.

60. *QTS* 80.867.

61. Doran, "Insatiable Women," 197–98. The *Vimalakirti Sutra* (Weimojie jing 維摩詰經, *T.* 14.475) was translated into Chinese by Kumarajiva in 406.

62. *The Vimalakirti Sutra*, trans. Burton Watson (New York: Columbia University Press, 1997), 90–91. This translation is based on Kumarajiva's.

63. Ibid.

64. Doran, "Insatiable Women," 198.

65. Forte, *Political Propaganda*, 264.

66. Ibid., 230. Forte provides a summary of the *Sutra of Attestation* (358–64), with a partial translation including boldface print of every section that was used as evidence in the *Commentary*.

67. Ibid., 263–64. Forte notes that in 594 Buddhist compiler Fajing had placed the one-chapter *Attestation Sutra* on a list of false works.

68. Ibid., 265. Xue Huaiyi was the architect of the *mingtang* complex and the *Attestation Sutra* likely served as a loose ideological architectural blueprint for Wu Zhao's Divine Palace of Myriad Images (Wanxiang shengong 萬象神宮), completed in 689—see 234–35.

69. Ibid., 362, translation of *Zhengming jing*, *T.85.2879*.

70. Ibid., 228.

71. *ZZTJ* 205.6497.

72. Forte, *Mingtang and Buddhist Utopias*, 114–15.

73. Ibid., 205.6502.

74. Forte, "Wu Zhao de mingtang yu tianwen zhong" [The *Mingtang* of Wu Zhao and Her Armillary Sphere], in Zhao Wenrun and Li Yuming, *Wu Zetian yanjiu lunwenji*, 142.

75. Gao Junping, "Shi lun Wu Zetian shiqi Longmen shiku," 141.

76. Amy McNair, in *Donors of Longmen*, devotes an entire chapter (111–22) to the Vairocana image at Longmen. She has translated the inscription (115–16, 177).

77. For instance, Gong Dazhong, *Longmen shiku yishu* [The Art in the Longmen Grottoes] (Shanghai: Shanghai Renmin chuban she, 1981), 141–42.

78. Gong Dazhong, *Longmen shiku yishu*, 142. Also see Ning Qiang, "Gender Politics in Medieval Chinese Buddhist Art," 29.

79. Karetzky, "Wu Zetian and Buddhist Art," 121.

80. McNair, *Donors of Longmen*, 117.

81. Guo Shaolin, "Longmen Lushena fo diaoxiang zaoxing yiju Wu Zetian shuo jiumiu" [Correcting Misconceptions That the Longmen Vairocana Is Modeled on Wu Zetian], in *Sui-Tang lishi wenhua* [Culture and History of the Sui and Tang] (Beijing: Zhongguo Wenshi, 2005), 162–63.

82. Zeng Qian, "Wu Zetian zaoqi de zongjiao qingxiang yu Lushena dafo de xiujian" [Religious Tendencies in the Early Period of Wu Zetian and the Construction of the Giant Rushana Buddha], *Qianyan* no. 8 (2009): 182–83.

83. McNair, *Donors of Longmen*, 118.

84. Forte, *Political Propaganda*, translation of Dunhuang S.6502, 260. Translation is slightly modified.

85. Doran, "Insatiable Women," 353–54.

CONCLUSIONS

1. For an examination of the coexistence of the "three faiths" and a brief overview of some of the ideological shifts during Wu Zhao's regency and reign, see Chen Meilin, "Zhou-Tang zhengquan de gengdie yu Ru-Dao-Shi xingshuai" [Shifts in Political

Authority of the Zhou-Tang and the Rise and Fall of Confucianism, Daoism, and Buddhism], *Hebei shiyuan xuebao* no. 3 (1997): 38–43; and Kou Jianghou, "Wu Zetian yu Zhongzong de sanjiao gongcun yu foxian daohou zhengce" [The Policies of "Coexistence of the Three Faiths" and "Buddhism before Daoism" Under Wu Zetian and Zhongzong], *Shaanxi shifan daxue xuebao* (1999): 19–22.

2. Forte, *Mingtang and Buddhist Utopias*.

3. *JTS* 22.864.

4. *JTS* 47.2046, 78.2707, 97.3050, 104.4014; *XTS* 59.1563.

5. Birrell, "Gendered Power," 1.

6. Ibid., 5–18.

7. Ibid., 25.

8. Ibid., 28.

9. Chen Jo-shui, "Empress Wu and Proto-Feminist Sentiments," 90.

10. Karetzky, "The Representation of Women," 227–28, 243.

11. Gao Shiyu, "A Fixed State of Affairs and Mis-positioned Status," 292–93. Most famously, in the early seventh century, the Turkish empress of Emperor Sui Yangdi refused to allow him to have any concubines. When he commented upon the exquisite hands of a palace maid, the empress had the girl's hands cut off and served at his next meal.

12. James T. C. Liu, "Polo and Cultural Change: From T'ang to Sung China," *Harvard Journal of Asiatic Studies* 45, no. 1 (1985): 203–24; Rong Xinjiang, "Nüban nanzhuang: Sheng Tang funü xingbie yishi" [Donning Male Attire: Gender Consciousness of Women in the High Tang], in *Abstracts and Papers from the Tang Women's Studies Conference* (Beijing University, 2001), 320–44.

13. Gao Shiyu, "A Fixed State of Affairs and Mis-positioned Status," 311.

14. Benn, *Daily Life in Traditional China*, 107–13.

15. Alexander Soper, "*T'ang Ch'ao Ming Hua Lu*: Celebrated Painters of the T'ang Dynasty by Chu Ching-hsüan of T'ang," *Artibus Asiae* 21, nos. 3/4 (1958): 215n64; Duan Wenjie, *Dunhuang Art: Through the Eyes of Duan Wenjie* (New Delhi: Indira Gandhi Centre for the Arts, 1994), 151.

16. Yang Lien-sheng, "Female Rulers in Imperial China," 55–59.

17. Richard Guisso, *Women in China: Current Directions in Historical Scholarship* (Youngstown, N.Y.: Philo Press, 1981), 60.

18. Mann, "Myths of Asian Womanhood," 842.

19. Hall and Ames, "Sexism, with Chinese Characteristics," in *The Sage and the Second Sex: Confucianism, Ethics, and Gender*, ed. Li Chenyang (Chicago: Open Court, 2000), 84.

20. *ZZTJ* 215.6877.

21. Translation from Patricia Ebrey, *Illustrated History of China* (Cambridge: Cambridge University Press, 1999), 34. See also *Shijing*, trans. Arthur Waley, 235. While the *Book of Songs* is attributed to Confucius, most of the verses are generally dated from several centuries earlier.

22. *Liji zhengyi*, 27.836.

23. Bray, *Technology and Gender*, 191.

24. Chen, "The Writing of Imperial Poetry," 97–98.

Bibliography

ABBREVIATIONS

BS Beishi 北史
CFYK Cefu yuangui 冊府元龜
CHC Denis Twitchett and John Fairbank, eds., *Cambridge History of China*, Vol. 3, *Sui and Tang China*
CG Chen gui 臣軌
DFXZ Dengfeng xianzhi 登封縣志
HS Han shu 漢書
HHS Hou Han shu 後漢書
HNZ Huainanzi 淮南子
JS Jin shu 晉書
JTS Jiu Tang shu 舊唐書
LNZ Lienü zhuan 列女傳
NQS Nan Qi shu 南齊書
QTS Quan Tang shi 全唐詩
QTW Quan Tangwen 全唐文
SGZ Sanguo zhi 三國誌
SJ Shi ji 史記
SS Sui shu 隨書
T. Taisho Tripitika 大藏經
TD Tongdian 通典
THY Tang huiyao 唐會要
TPGJ Taiping guangji 太平廣記
TPYL Taiping yulan 太平御覽
TLJCFK Tang liangjing chengfang kao 唐兩京城坊考
WYYH Wenyuan yinghua 文苑英華
XTS Xin Tang shu 新唐書
YJQQ Yunji qiqian 雲笈七籤
ZZTJ Zizhi tongjian 資治通鑒

PREMODERN SOURCES

Baoyu jing 寶雨經 [Ratnamegha Sutra; Sutra of the Rain of Jewels], 10 chaps., Bodhiruci (Chinese: Putiliuzhi 菩提流支, d. 727) in 693. *T.* 16.660.

Beishi 北史 [History of the Northern Dynasties], 100 chaps., comp. Li Yanshou 李延壽 (7th cent.). Beijing: Zhonghua 中華書局, 1997.

Cefu yuangui 冊府元龜 [Storehouse of the Original Tortoise], 1,000 chaps., comp. Wang Qinruo 王欽若 and others between 1005 and 1013. Beijing: Zhonghua, 1994.

Chaoye jianzai 朝野僉載 [Collected Records from Court and Country], 6 chaps., ed. Zhang Zhuo 張鷟 (667–731). In *Tang-Song shiliao biji congkan* 唐宋史料筆記叢刊 [Collection of Tang and Song Historical Materials and Brush Notes]. Beijing: Zhonghua, 1997.

Chen gui 臣軌 [Regulations for Ministers], comp. Wu Zetian 武則天 (624–705), 2 chaps. In *Zhongjing ji qita wuzhong* 忠經及其他五種 [The Canon of Loyalty and Five Other Works], *Congshu jicheng chubian* 叢書集成初編 [Collected Collecteana, First Series] 0893. Taibei: Shangwu, 1936.

Chuci 楚辭. *Ch'u Tz'u: Songs of the South*, Qu Yuan, trans. David Hawkes. Boston: Beacon, 1959.

Da fangguang Fo Huayan jing 大方廣佛華嚴經 [Flower Garland Sutra], 60 chaps., trans. Buddhabhadra (Fotuobatuoluo 佛馱跋陀羅) in Eastern Jin. *T.* 9.278.

Da fangguang Fo Huayan jing 大方廣佛華嚴經 [Flower Garland Sutra], 80 chaps., trans. Śikṣānanda between 695 and 699. *T.* 10.279.

Da Tang Da Ci'ensi Sanzang Fashi zhuan 大唐大慈恩寺三藏法師傳 [Biography of Dharma Master Sanzang of the Great Ci'en Temple of the Great Tang], 10 chaps., Yan Cong 彥悰 in 688, based on Huili 慧立 draft. *T.* 50.2053.

Da Tang Neidian lu 大唐內典錄 [Great Tang Catalog of Scriptures], comp. Daoxuan 道宣, 10 chaps., *T.* 55.2149.

Da Tang Xinyu 大唐新語 [New Words from the Great Tang], 12 chaps., Liu Su 劉肅 (fl. 806–820). In *Tang-Song shiliao biji congkan* 唐宋史料筆記叢刊 [Collection of Tang and Song Historical Materials and Brush Notes]. Beijing: Zhonghua, 1997.

Da Zhou kanding zhongjing mulu 大周刊定眾經目錄 [Great Zhou Catalog of Buddhist Scriptures], 15 chaps., comp. Mingquan 明佺 (fl. late seventh century) and others. *T.* 55.2153.

(*Daodejing* 道德經). *Tao Te Ching*, 2 chaps., Laozi, trans. D. C. Lau. London: Penguin, 1963.

Daode zhenjing guangsheng yi 道德真經廣聖義 [Broad and Sacred Teachings of the Perfected Book on the Dao and Its Virtue], comp. Du Guangting 杜光庭 (850–933), *Daozang* 道藏 725.

Daojia jinshi lue 道家金石略 [A Summary of Daoist Inscriptions], Chen Yuan 陳垣 (1880–1971). Beijing: Wenwu, 1988.

Dayunjing shenhuang shouji yishu 大雲經神皇授記義疏 [*Commentary on the Meanings of the Prophecies About the Divine Sovereign in the Great Cloud Sutra*], written by Xue Huaiyi 薛懷義, Faming 法明 et al. in 690. Annotated translation (259–319) and plates of original Dunhuang document S6502 (542–74) in Antonino Forte, *Political Propaganda and Ideology in China at the End of the Seventh Century*.

Dengfeng xianzhi 登封縣志 [Dengfeng County Annals], 1803. Henan: Dengfeng County Office, 1984.

Fangguang da zhuangyan jing 方廣大莊嚴經 [Lalitavistara Sutra], 12 chaps., trans. Divākara (Dipoheluo 地婆訶羅). *T.* 3.187.

Foshuo Qijuzhi fomu xinda Zhuntituoluoni jing 佛說七俱胝佛母心大准提陀羅尼經 [Dhāraṇī Sutra of the Buddha's Words on Saptakoṭi Buddhabhagavatī], 1 chap., trans. Divākara in 686. *T.* 20.1077.

Foshuo Qijuzhi fomu Zhunti damingtuoluoni jing 佛說七俱胝佛母准提大明陀羅尼經 [Greatly Illumined *Dhāraṇī* Sutra of the Buddha's Words on Saptakoṭi Buddhabhagavatī], 1 chap., trans. Divākara. *T.* 20.1075.

Fanwang jing 梵網經 [Sutra on Brahma's Net], 2 chaps., trans. Kuchan monk Kumāravjiva (Chinese: Jiumoluoshi 鳩摩羅什, 344–413). *T.* 24.1484.

Fayuan zhulin 法苑珠林 [Pearl Forests of the Dharma Garden], 100 chaps., completed by Daoshi 道世 in 668. *T.* 53.2122.

Fo benxing ji jing 佛本行集经 [Sutra on the Collection of the Buddha's Original Practices], 60 chaps., comp. Jñāngupta c. 590. *T.* 3.190.

Gaoseng zhuan 高僧傳 [Biographies of Eminent Monks], 14 chaps., Huijiao 慧皎 (497–554). *T.* 50.2059.

Genben shuo yiqie youbu Binaiye 根本說一切有部毗奈耶 [Mūlasarvāstivāda Vinaya], 50 chaps., trans. Yijing 義淨 in 703. *T.* 23.1442.

Genben shuo yiqie youbu Binaiye chujia shi 根本說一切有部毗奈耶出家事 [Matters of Renunciation in the Mūlasarvāstivāda Vinaya], 4 chaps., trans. Yijing in 703. *T.* 23.1444.

Genben shuo yiqie youbu Binaiye zashi 根本說一切有部毘奈耶雜事 [Miscellany from the Mūlasarvāstivāda Vinaya], 40 chaps., trans. Yijing in 703. *T.* 24.1451.

Guben Zhushu jinian jijiao 古本竹書紀年輯校 [Comparative Annals of Ancient Bamboo Records], ed. Zhu Youzeng 朱右曾 (fl. 1838). Shenyang: Liaoning jiaoyu, 1997.

Guang hongmingji 廣弘明集 [An Expansion of the Collection for Glorifying and Elucidating Buddhism], 30 chaps., comp. Daoxuan 道宣 and completed in 666. *T.* 52.2103.

Guoyu 國語 [Narrative of States], 21 chaps., comp. Zuo Qiuming 左丘明 (fl. 5th century B.C.) Shanghai: Shanghai guji, 1978.

Han shu 漢書 [History of the Han Dynasty], 100 chaps., Ban Gu 班固 (32–92) and Ban Biao 班彪 (3–54). Beijing: Zhonghua, 1996.

Henan zhi 河南志 [Treatise on Henan], 4 chaps., comp. Xu Song 徐松 (1781–1848). Beijing: Zhonghua, 1994.

Hou Han shu 後漢書 [Later Han History], 120 chaps., comp. Li Xián 李賢 and Fan Ye 范曄. Beijing: Zhonghua, 1997.

Huainanzi 淮南子 [The Master of Huainan], Liu An 刘安, from *Hanji quanwen jiansuo xitong* 汉籍全文检索系统 (繁体本), Xi'an, 2004, electronic 4th edition. See also *The Essential Huainanzi*, ed. John S. Major, Sarah Queen, Andrew Meyer, and Harold Roth. New York: Columbia University Press, 2012.

Jin shu 晉書 [History of Jin], 130 chaps., comp. Fang Xuanling 房玄齡 (578–648). Beijing: Zhonghua, 1997.

Jinshi cuibian 金石萃編 [A Miscellany of Choice Inscriptions on Metal and Stone], 160 chaps., comp. Wang Chang 王昶 (1725–1806). Beijing: Zhongguo shudian, 1985.

Jiu Tang shu 舊唐書 [Old Tang History], 200 chaps., comp. Liu Xu 劉昫 (887–946). Beijing: Zhonghua, 1997.

"Li Sao," by Qu Yuan (343–278 B.C.), trans. by Paul Goldin in "Imagery of Copulation in Early Chinese Poetry," *Chinese Literature: Essays, Articles and Reviews* 21 (December 1999): 56; also in *Hawai'i Reader of Traditional Chinese Culture*. Honolulu: University of Hawaii Press, 2005: 99–100.

Liang shu 梁書 [History of the Liang Dynasty], 56 chaps., comp. Yao Cha 姚察 (533–606). Beijing: Zhonghua, 1997.

Lienü zhuan 列女傳 [Biographies of Exemplary Women], 8 chaps., comp. Liu Xiang 劉向 (79–8 B.C.). Song woodblock edition with illustrations by Gu Kaizhi 顧凱之 (345–409). Charlottesville, Va.: University of Virginia Library Electronic Text Center. http://etext.virginia.edu/chinese/lienu/browse/LienuImgTOC.html.

Liezi 列子. The *Book of Lieh-tzu: A Classic of Tao*, trans. and introduction by A. C. Graham. New York: Columbia University Press, 1990.

Liji zhengyi 禮記正義 [Orthodox Commentary on the Book of History], comp. Kong Yingda 孔穎達 (574–648), in *Shisan jing zhu shu* [Commentaries and Notes on the Thirteen Classics], ed. Li Xueqin (Beijing: Beijing University Press, 1999).

Lun yu 論語. The *Analects*, Confucius, trans. D. C. Lau. New York: Penguin, 1979.

Lysistrata and Other Plays. Aristophanes, trans. Alan Summerstein. New York: Penguin Classics, 1973.

Mohe Moye jing 摩訶摩耶經 [Sutra of Great Māyā], 30 chaps., trans. Tanjing 曇景. T. 17.815.

Mozi 墨子. *Ethical and Political Works of Motse*, trans. Mei Yi-pao. Westport, Conn.: Hyperion, 1973.

Nan Qi shu 南齊書 [History of the Southern Qi Dynasty], 60 chaps., comp. Xiao Zixian 蕭子顯 (489–537). Beijing: Zhonghua, 1997.

Quan Tang shi 全唐詩 [Complete Anthology of Tang Poetry], 900 chaps., comp. Peng Dingqiu 彭定求 in 1705. Beijing: Zhonghua, 1995.

Quan Tangwen 全唐文 [Complete Anthology of Tang Prose], 1,000 chaps., comp. Dong Gao 董誥 (1740–1818) in 1814. Beijing: Zhonghua, 1996.

Samguk Yusa 三國遺事 [Omitted Events of the Three Kingdoms Period], comp. Iryeon 一然 (1206–1289). In Roderick Whitfield, ed., *Collected Works of Korean Buddhism*, vol. 10, *Korean Buddhist Culture—Accounts of a Pilgrimage, Monuments and Eminent Monks*, trans. and annotated Matty Wegehaupt, Michael Finch, and Sem Vermeersch. Seoul: Jogye Order of Korean Buddhism, 2012.

Sanguo zhi 三國誌 [Chronicles of the Three Kingdoms], 65 chaps., comp. Chen Shou 陳壽 (233–297). Beijing: Zhonghua, 1997.

Shangshu zhengyi 尚書正義 [Orthodox Commentary on the Book of History], comp. Kong Yingda 孔穎達 (574–648). In *Shisan jing zhu shu*, ed. Li Xueqin. Beijing: Beijing University Press, 1999.

Shanhai jing 山海經 [Classic of Mountains and Seas], trans. Anne Birrell. New York: Penguin, 1999.

Shisan jing zhu shu 十三經注疏 [The Thirteen Classics with Annotations and Commentaries], 13 vols., ed. Li Xueqin 李學勤. Beijing: Beijing University Press, 1999.

Shi ji 史記 [Records of the Grand Historian], 130 chaps., comp. Sima Qian 司馬遷 (145–86 B.C.). Beijing: Zhonghua, 1995. See also *Records of the Grand Historian*, trans. Burton Watson. New York: Columbia University Press, 1993.

Shijing 詩經 [The Book of Songs] [in Chinese and English]. Ji'nan: Shandong Friendship, 1999.

Shijing [The Book of Songs], trans. Arthur Waley. New York: Grove, 1960.

Shu Ching, trans. Clae Waltham. Chicago: Henry Regnery, 1971.

Shuowen jiezi 說文解字 [An Explanation and Analysis of Chinese Characters], comp. Xu Shen 許慎 in early second century. Zhengzhou: Zhongyuan nongmin, 2000.

Si shamen Xuanzhuang shang biao ji 寺沙門玄奘上表記 [A Record of Petitions Presented by the Buddhist Monk Xuanzhuang], 1 chap., *T.* 52.2119.

Song gaoseng zhuan 宋高僧傳 [Biographies of Eminent Monks, Compiled in the Song Dynasty], 30 chaps., comp. Zanning 贊寧 (919–1001). *T.* 50.2061.

Sui shu 隨書 [History of the Sui Dynasty], 85 chaps., comp. Wei Zheng 魏徵 (580–643). Beijing: Zhonghua, 1996.

Taiping guangji 太平廣記 [Miscellaneous Records of the Taiping Era], 500 chaps., comp. Li Fang 李昉 (925–996). Beijing: Zhonghua, 1996.

Taiping yulan 太平御覽 [Imperial Readings of the Taiping Era], 1,000 chaps., comp. Li Fang. Beijing: Zhonghua, 1995.

Tangdai muzhiming huibian fukao 唐代墓誌銘彙編附考 [A Collection of Tang Epitaphs], comp. Mao Hanguang 毛漢光, 18 vols. Taibei: Academia Sinica Research Institute and Taiwan Shangwu, 1984–1994.

Tang da zhaoling ji 唐大詔令集 [Edicts and Imperial Decrees of the Tang], 130 chaps., completed in 1070 by Song Minqiu 宋敏求 (1019–1079). Taiwan: Huawen, 1968.

Tang huiyao 唐會要 [Essential Institutions of the Tang], 100 chaps., comp. Wang Pu 王溥 (922–982). Beijing: Zhonghua, 1998.

Tang liangjing chengfang kao 唐兩京城坊考 [A Study of the Walled Cities and Wards of the Two Tang Capitals], 5 chaps., comp. Xu Song. Beijing: Zhonghua, 1985.

Tang liudian 唐六典 [Tang Administrative and Legal Compendium of the Six Ministries], 30 chaps., comp. Li Linfu 李林甫 (d. 753). Beijing: Zhonghua, 1992.

Tangshi jishi 唐詩紀事 [Accounts of Matters Concerning Tang Poetry], comp. Ji Yougong 記有功 (fl. 12th cent.). Taibei: Dingwen, 1971.

Tongdian 通典 [Comprehensive Manual of Institutions], 200 chaps., comp. Du You 杜佑 (735–812). Beijing: Zhonghua, 1996.

Weimojie jing 維摩詰經 [The Vimalakirti Sutra], 3 chaps., trans. Burton Watson from Kumarajiva's 406 translation. New York: Columbia University Press, 1997. *T.* 14.475.

Wei shu 魏書 [History of the Wei Dynasty], 114 chaps., comp. Wei Shou 魏收 in 554. Beijing: Zhonghua, 1995.

Wenyuan yinghua 文苑英華 [Flowers and Blossoms of the Garden of Literature], 1,000 chaps., comp. Li Fang. Beijing: Zhonghua, 1982.

Xin Tang shu 新唐書 [New History of the Tang], 225 chaps., comp. Ouyang Xiu 歐陽修 (1007–1072). Beijing: Zhonghua, 1997.

Xu Gaoseng zhuan 續高僧傳 [Continued Biographies of Eminent Monks], 30 chaps., comp. Daoxuan 道宣 c. 645. *T.* 50.2060.

Yiwen leiju 藝文類聚 [Classified Collection of the Literary Arts], 100 chaps., comp. Ouyang Xun 歐陽詢 (557–641). Shanghai: Shanghai guji, 1982.

Yongcheng jixian lu 墉城集仙錄 [Register of the Assembled Transcendents of the Walled City], Du Guangting 杜光庭 (850–933). *YJQQ* 717–722.

Yunji qiqian 雲笈七籤 [Seven Tablets from the Satchel of Clouds], 122 chaps., comp. Zhang Junfang 張君房 (d. 1001). Beijing: Xinhua, 1996.

Zhang Yangong ji 張燕公集 [Collections from Zhang, Duke of Yan], 25 chaps., Zhang Yue 張說 (667–731). Taibei: Taiwan Shangwu yinshuguan, 1983.

Zhenxi 真系 [*Genealogies of the Perfected*], Li Bo 李渤 (773–831), in *Yunji qiqian*, chapter 5.

Zheyi lun 折疑論 [Discourses on Solving Puzzles], 5 chaps., comp. Zicheng 子成 in 1351. *T.* 52.2118.

Zhou shu 周書 [History of the Northern Zhou], 50 chaps., ed. Linghu Defen 令狐德棻 (583–666). Beijing: Zhonghua, 1997.

Zhouli zhushu 周禮註疏 [Commentaries on the Zhou Book of Rites], annotated by Jia Gongyan 賈公彥 (Tang Dynasty, 7th cent.), in *Shisanjing zhushu*, ed. Li Xueqin. Beijing: Beijing University Press, 1999.

Zhouyi zhengyi 周易正義 [Correct Meanings of the Zhou Book of Changes], comp. Kong Yingda, in *Shisanjing zhushu*, ed. Li Xueqin. Beijing: Beijing University Press, 1999.

Zhuan nüshen jing 轉女身經 [Sutra of Transforming a Woman's Body], 1 chap., trans. Dharmamitra (Tanmomiduo 曇摩蜜多, 355–442). *T.* 14.564.

Zizhi tongjian 資治通鑒 [Comprehensive Mirror for the Advancement of Governance], 294 chaps., comp. Sima Guang 司馬光 (1019–1086); commentary by Hu Sanxing 胡三省 (1230–1302) from the Yuan edition. Beijing: Zhonghua, 1995.

MODERN SOURCES

Abramson, Marc. *Ethnic Identity in Tang China*. Philadelphia: University of Pennsylvania Press, 2008.

Adamek, Wendi Leigh. *The Mystique of Transmission: On Early Chan History and Its Contexts*. New York: Columbia University Press, 2007.

——. "Robes of Purple and Gold: Transmission of the Robe in the Lidai fabao ji (Record of the Dharma-Jewel Through the Ages)." *History of Religions* 40, no. 1 (2000): 58–81.

Allen, Sarah. "The Identities of Taigong Wang 太公望 in Zhou and Han Literature." *Monumenta Serica* 30 (1972–1973): 57–99.

——. "The Myth of the Xia Dynasty." *Journal of the Royal Asiatic Society of Great Britain and Ireland* 2 (1984): 242–56.

——. *The Shape of the Turtle: Myth, Art and the Cosmos in Early China*. Albany: State University of New York Press, 1991.

Ames, Roger. *The Art of Rulership: A Study in Ancient Chinese Political Thought*. Honolulu: University of Hawaii Press, 1983.

——. "Taoism and the Androgynous Ideal." In Richard Guisso and Stanley Johansen, *Women in China: Current Directions in Historical Scholarship*, 21–45. Youngstown, N.Y.: Philo, 1981.

Ames, Roger, and David Hall. "Sexism, with Chinese Characteristics." In Li Chenyang, *The Sage and the Second Sex*, 75–95.

Anonymous. *Wu yue shihu* 五嶽史話 [Legends of the Five Marchmounts]. Beijing: Zhonghua, 1982.

Bai Jian 白劍. "Shi xi Wu Zetian wulong ganyun shenhua de tuteng beijing jian shi Fu Xi taiyangshen shengsi xunhuan he weiyang tuteng neihan ji longshe tuteng chansheng beijing" 試析武則天烏龍感孕神話的圖騰背景兼釋伏羲太陽神生死循環和未羊圖騰內涵及龍蛇的產生背景 [An Attempt to Analyze the

Background of the Dark Dragon Totem and the Miraculous Birth of Wu Zetian, and an Explanation of the Cycle of Life and Death of Sun God Fu Xi and the Connotations of the "Wei-yang" Totem for the Genesis of Snakes and Dragons]. In *Conference Proceedings from the 11th Conference of the Wu Zetian Research Association*, 442–49. Guangyuan, 2013.

Barrett, Timothy. "The Emergence of the Taoist Papacy in the T'ang Dynasty." *Asia Major*, Third Series, 7, no. 1 (1994): 89–106.

—. "Stūpa, Sūtra and Śarīra in China, c. 656–706 CE." *Buddhist Studies Review* 18, no. 1 (2001): 1–64.

—. *Taoism Under the T'ang*. London: Wellsweep, 1996.

—. *The Woman Who Discovered Printing*. New Haven, Conn.: Yale University Press, 2008.

Batchelor, Martine. *The Path of Compassion: The Bodhisattva Precepts*. Walnut Creek, Calif.: Altamira, 2004.

Bendix, Richard. *Kings or People: Power and the Mandate to Rule*. Berkeley: University of California Press, 1978.

Benn, Charles. *The Cavern-Mystery Transmission: A Daoist Ordination Rite of A.D. 711*. Honolulu: University of Hawaii Press, 1991.

—. *Daily Life in Traditional China: The Tang Dynasty*. Westport, Conn.: Greenwood, 2002.

—. "Taoism as Ideology in the Reign of Emperor Hsuan-Tsung (712–755)." PhD dissertation, University of Michigan, 1977.

Benn, James. *Burning for the Buddha: Self-Immolation in Chinese Buddhism*. Honolulu: University of Hawaii Press, 2007.

Bi Xiuling 畢旭玲. "Lun Zhongguo fangzhi nüshen de jisi lisu jiqi yingxiang" 論中國紡織女神的祭祀禮俗及其影響 [A Discussion of Sacrifices to Chinese Weaving Goddesses in Ceremony and Folk Practice]. *Changjiang daxue xuebao* 長江大學學報 [Journal of Yangzi University] 30, no. 5 (2007), 14–18.

Bingham, Woodbridge. *Founding of the Tang Dynasty*. New York: Octagon, 1970.

Birrell, Anne. *Chinese Mythology: An Introduction*. Baltimore, Md.: Johns Hopkins University Press, 1993.

—. "Gendered Power: A Discourse on Female-Gendered Myth in the *Classic of Mountains and Seas*." *Sino-Platonic Papers*, no. 120 (July 2002): 1–52.

Bodde, Derk. "Myths of Ancient China." In *Mythologies of the Ancient World*, ed. Samuel Noah Kramer, 367–408. Garden City, N.Y.: Anchor, 1961.

Bokenkamp, Stephen R. "A Medieval Feminist Critique of the Chinese World Order: The Case of Wu Zhao." *Religion* 28 (1998): 378–90.

Bol, Peter. *This Culture of Ours*. Stanford, Calif.: Stanford University Press, 1992.

Bray, Francesca. *Technology and Gender: Fabrics of Power in Late Imperial China*. Berkeley: University of California Press, 1997.

Bujard, Marianne. "Le culte de Wangzi Qiao ou la longue carrière d'un immortel." *Études chinoises* 19 (2002): 115–55.

Butler, Judith. "Performative Acts and Gender Constitution: An Essay in Phenomenology and Feminist Theory." *Theatre Journal* 40, no. 4 (1988): 519–31.

Cahill, Suzanne, "Beside the Turquoise Pond: the Shrine of the Queen Mother of the West in Medieval Chinese Poetry and Religious Practice." *Journal of Chinese Religions* 12 (1984): 19–32.

——. "The Daoist Goddess: The Queen Mother of the West." In Wang, *Images of Women*, 346–365.

——. *Divine Traces of the Daoist Sisterhood.* Magdalena, N.Mex.: Three Pines, 2006.

——. "The Moon Stopping in the Void: Daoism and the Literati Ideal in Mirrors of the Tang Dynasty." In *Cleveland Studies in the History of Art.* Vol. 9, *Clarity and Luster: New Light on Bronze Mirrors in Tang and Post-Tang China, 600–1300: Papers from a Symposium on the Carter Collection of Chinese Bronze Mirrors at the Cleveland Museum of Art.* Cleveland, Ohio: Cleveland Museum of Art, 2005, 24–40.

——. "Performers and Female Daoist Adepts: Hsi Wang Mu as the Patron Deity of Women in Medieval China." *Journal of the American Oriental Society* 106, no. 1 (1986): 155–68.

——. "Practice Makes Perfect: Paths to Transcendence for Women in Medieval China." *Taoist Resources* 2, no. 2 (1990): 23–42.

——. *Transcendence and Divine Passion: The Queen Mother of the West in Medieval China.* Stanford, Calif.: Stanford University Press, 1993.

Cai Junsheng. "Myth and Reality: The Projection of Gender Relations in Pre-historic China." In *The Chalice and the Blade*, ed. Min Jiayin, 34–90.

Campany, Robert. "The Meaning of Cuisines of Transcendence in Late Classical and Early Medieval China." *T'oung Pao*, Second Series, 91 (2005): 1–57.

——. *To Live as Long as Heaven and Earth: A Translation and Study of Ge Hong's Traditions of Divine Transcendents.* Berkeley: University of California Press, 2002.

Canetti, Elias. *Crowds and Power*, trans. Carol Stewart. New York: Seabury, 1978.

Cartelli, Mary Anne. "On a Five-Colored Cloud: The Songs of Mount Wutai." *Journal of the American Oriental Society* 124, no. 4 (2004): 735–57.

Chan, Alan K. L., and Yue-Kueng Lo, eds. *Philosophy and Religion in Early Medieval China.* Albany: State University of New York Press, 2010.

Chan, Timothy Wai Keung. *Considering the End: Mortality in Early Medieval Chinese Poetic Representation.* Leiden: Brill, 2012.

Chao, Denise. "The Snake in Chinese Belief." *Folklore* 90, no. 2 (1979): 193–203.

Chang Kang-I Sun, Haun Saussy, and Charles Yim Huang, eds. *Chinese Women Poets: An Anthology of Poetry and Criticism from Ancient Times.* Stanford, Calif.: Stanford University Press, 1999.

Chang Kang-I Sun and Stephen Owen, eds. *The Cambridge History of Chinese Literature*, vol. 1, *To 1375.* Cambridge: Cambridge University Press, 2010.

Chang, Ruth H. "Understanding Di and Tian: Deity and Heaven from Shang to Tang Dynasties." *Sino-Platonic Papers* 108 (September 2000): 1–65.

Chang Yuliang 昌玉良. *Wu Zetian yu Qianling* 武則天與乾陵 [Wu Zetian and Qianling]. Xi'an: Sanqin, 1986.

Charleux, Isabel. "Padmasambhava's Travel to the North." *Central Asian Journal* 46, no. 2 (2002): 168–232.

Chen, Jack. "The Writing of Imperial Poetry in Medieval China." *Harvard Journal of Asiatic Studies* 65, no. 1 (2005): 57–98.

Chen Jinhua. "Images, Legends, Politics and the Origin of the Great Xiangguo Monastery in Kaifeng: A Case Study of the Formation and Transformation of Buddhist Sites in Medieval China." *Journal of the American Oriental Society* 125, no. 3 (2005): 353–78.

——. "The Indian Buddhist Missionary Dharmakṣema (385–433): A New Dating of His Arrival in Guzang and of His Translations." *T'oung Pao* 90 (2004): 215–63.

——. *Monks and Monarchs, Kinship and Kingship: Tanqian in Sui Buddhism and Politics.* Kyoto: Italian School of East Asian Studies, 2002.

——. "More Than a Philosopher: Fazang as a Politician and Miracle Worker." *History of Religions* 42, no. 4 (May 2003): 320–58.

——. "Pañcavārṣika Assemblies in Liang Wudi's Buddhist Palace Chapel." *Harvard Journal of Asiatic Studies* 66, no. 1 (2006): 43–103.

——. *Philosopher, Practitioner, Politician: The Many Lives of Fazang (643–712).* Leiden: Brill, 2007.

——. "Śarīra and Scepter. Empress Wu's Political Use of Buddhist Relics." *Journal of the International Association of Buddhist Studies* 25 (2002): 33–150.

——. "Tang Buddhist Palace Chapels." *Journal of Chinese Religions* 32 (2004): 101–73.

——. "Yixing 一行 and Jiugong 九宮 ('Nine Palaces'): A Case of Chinese Redefinition of Indian Ideas." *China Report* 48 (2012): 115–24.

Chen Jo-shui. "Empress Wu and Proto-feminist Sentiments in T'ang China." In *Imperial Rulership and Cultural Change in Traditional China,* ed. Frederick Brandauer and Chih-chieh Huang, 77–114. Seattle: University of Washington Press, 1994.

Chen Meilin 陳美林. "Zhou-Tang zhengquan de gengdie yu Ru-Dao-Shi xingshuai" [Shifts in Political Authority of the Zhou-Tang and the Rise and Fall of Confucianism, Daoism and Buddhism] 周唐政權的更迭與儒道釋興衰. *Hebei shiyuan xuebao* 河北師院學報 [Journal of Hebei Normal University] no. 3 (1997): 38–43.

Chen Yinke 陳寅恪. "Ji Tangdai shi Li-Wu-Wei-Wang hunyin jituan" 記唐代之李武韋王婚姻集團 [A Record of the Marriage Bloc of the Li, Wu, Wei, and Wang Clans in the Tang Dynasty]. *Lishi yanjiu* 歷史研究 [Historical Research] 1 (1955): 85–96.

——. "Wu Zhao yu Fojiao" 武曌與佛教 [Wu Zhao and Buddhism]. In *Chen Yinke xiansheng quanji* 陳寅恪先生全集 [The Complete Collected Works of Professor Chen Yinke], 421–36. Taipei: Jiusi, 1971.

Ch'en, Kenneth. *Buddhism in China.* Princeton: Princeton University Press, 1964.

——. *The Chinese Transformation of Buddhism.* Princeton: Princeton University Press, 1973.

Cheng, Christina Miu Bing. "Matriarchy at the Edge: The Mythic Cult of Nüwa in Macau." Paper presented at the 17th Triennial Conference of the International Comparative Literature Association, Hong Kong, 8–15 August 2004.

Cheng Te-k'un. "Yin-yang Wu-hsing in Han Art." *Harvard Journal of Asiatic Studies* 20, nos. 1/2 (1957): 162–86.

Ching, Julia. *Mysticism and Kingship in China.* Cambridge: Cambridge University Press, 1997.

——. "Son of Heaven: Sacral Kingship in Ancient China." *T'oung Pao* 83 (1997): 3–41.

Chiu Ling-yeong. "Persians, Arabs and Other Nationals in Tang China." *Journal of the Hong Kong Royal Asiatic Society* 13 (1973): 58–72.

Chiu-Duke, Josephine. "Mothers and the Well-being of the State in Tang China." *Nan Nü: Women and Gender in China* 8, no. 1 (2006): 55–114.

Como, Michael. "Silkworms and Consorts in Nara Japan." *Folklore Studies* 64, no. 1 (2005): 111–31.

——. *Weaving and Binding: Immigrant Gods and Female Immortals in Ancient Japan*. Honolulu: University of Hawaii Press, 2009.

Cook, Constance. "Ancestor Worship During the Eastern Zhou." In Lagerway and Kalinowski, *Early Chinese Religion*, part 1, 237–80.

Creel, Herlee. *The Birth of China*. New York: Frederick Ungar, 1961.

Cutter, Robert Joe. "The Death of Empress Zhen: Fiction and Historiography in Early Medieval China." *Journal of the American Oriental Society* 112, no. 4 (1992): 577–83.

Cutter, Robert Joe, and William Gordon Crowell. *Empresses and Consorts: Selections from Chen Shou's Records of the Three States with Pei Songzhi's Commentary*. Honolulu: University of Hawaii Press, 1999.

De Bary, William, and Irene Bloom, eds. *Sources of Chinese Tradition*. Vol. 1, *From Earliest Times to 1600*. New York: Columbia University Press, 1999.

Deeg, Max. "Origins and Development of the Pañcavārṣika. Part I: India and Central Asia." *Saṃbhāṣā: Nagoya Studies in Indian Culture and Buddhism* 16 (1995): 67–90.

——. "Origins and Development of the Buddhist Pañcavārṣika. Part II: China." *Saṃbhāṣā: Nagoya Studies in Indian Culture and Buddhism* 18 (1997): 63–96.

DeRauw, Tom. "Beyond Buddhist Apology: The Political Use of Buddhism by Emperor Wu of the Liang Dynasty (r. 502–549)." PhD dissertation, Ghent University, 2008.

Despeux, Catherine. "Talismans and Sacred Diagrams." In Kohn, *Daoism Handbook*, 498–540.

——. "Women and Daoism." In Kohn, *Daoism Handbook*, 384–412.

Despeux, Catherine, and Livia Kohn. *Women in Daoism*. Cambridge, Mass.: Three Pines, 2003.

Dong Zuobin 董作賓 and Wang Hengyu 王恆餘. "Tang Wuhou gaizi kao" 唐武后改字考 [A Study of the Altered Characters of Tang Empress Wu]. *Bulletin of the Institute of History and Philology of Academia Sinica* 34 (1963): 447–76.

Doran, Rebecca. "Insatiable Women and Transgressive Authority: Constructions of Gender and Power in Early Tang China." PhD dissertation, Harvard University, 2011.

Du Doucheng 杜斗城. "Guanyu Wu Zetian yu fojiao de jige wenti" 關於武則天與佛教的幾個問題 [Several Issues Concerning Wu Zetian and Buddhism]. *Zongjiao xue yanjiu* 宗教學研究 [Research in Religious Studies] (1994): 26–33.

Du Fangqin, "The Rise and Fall of Zhou Rites: A Rational Foundation for the Gender Relationship Model." In Min Jiayin, *The Chalice and the Blade*, 169–225.

Duan Tali 段塔麗. *Tangdai funü diwei yanjiu* 唐代婦女地位研究 [Research on the Position of Women in the Tang Dynasty]. Beijing: Renmin, 2000.

Duan Wenjie, *Dunhuang Art: Through the Eyes of Duan Wenjie*. New Delhi: Indira Gandhi Centre for the Arts, 1994.

Ebrey, Patricia. *Illustrated History of China*. Cambridge: Cambridge University Press, 1999.

Ebrey, Patricia Buckley. "The *Book of Filial Piety for Women* Attributed to a Woman Née Zheng (ca. 730)." In Susan Mann and Yu-yin Cheng, *Under Confucian Eyes: Writing on Gender in Chinese History*, 47–69.

Ebrey, Patricia Buckley, ed. *Chinese Civilization: A Sourcebook*. 2d ed. New York: Free Press, 1993.

Eckfield, Tonia. *Imperial Tombs in Tang China, 618-907: The Politics of Paradise*. New York: Routledge, 2005.

Edwards, E. D. *Chinese Prose Literature of the T'ang Period*, vol. 2. London: Arthur Probsthain, 1938.

Eisenberg, Andrew. "Emperor Gaozong, the Rise of Wu Zetian and Factional Politics in the Early Tang." *Tang Studies* 30 (2012): 45–69.

——. *Kingship in Early Medieval China*. Leiden: Brill, 2008.

——. "Kingship, Power and the Hsuan-wu Men Incident of the T'ang." *T'oung Pao* 80 (1994): 223–59.

Eliade, Mircea. *Myth and Reality*. New York: Harper and Row, 1963.

Etzioni, Amitai. *A Comparative Analysis of Complex Organizations*. New York: Free Press, 1975.

Fan Yingfeng 樊英峰 and Liu Xiangyang 劉向陽. *Qianling wenwu shiji shucong* 乾陵文物史跡述叢 [A Narrative Record of the Historical Relics in the Qianling Mausoleum]. Xi'an: Shaanxi Tourism, 1987.

Faure, Bernard. *The Power of Denial: Buddhism, Purity and Gender*. Princeton: Princeton University Press, 2003.

——. *The Red Thread: Buddhist Approaches to Sexuality*. Princeton: Princeton University Press, 1998.

——. "Relics and Flesh Bodies: The Creation of Ch'an Pilgrimage Sites." In *Pilgrims and Sacred Sites in China*, ed. Susan Naquin and Yü Chün-fang, 150–89. Berkeley: University of California Press, 1992.

Fitzgerald, C. P. *The Empress Wu*. Melbourne: Cheshire, 1955.

Forte, Antonino. "The Chongfusi in Chang'an: A Neglected Buddhist Monastery and Nestorianism." In *L'inscription nestorienne de Si-ngan-fou: A Posthumous Work by Paul Pelliot*, ed. Antonino Forte, 429–72. Kyoto: Italian School of East Asian Studies, 1996.

——. "Iranians in China: Buddhism, Zoroastrianism, and Bureaus of Commerce." *Cahiers d'Extrême-Asie* 11 (1999–2000): 277–90.

——. "The Maitreyist Huaiyi and Taoism." *Tang yanjiu* 唐研究 [Tang Research] 4 (1998): 15–29.

——. *Mingtang and Buddhist Utopias in the History of the Astronomical Clock: The Tower, the Statue and the Armillary Sphere Constructed by Empress Wu*. Rome: Italian School of East Asian Studies, 1988.

——. *Political Propaganda and Ideology in China at the End of the Seventh Century: Inquiry into the Nature, Authors and Function of Dunhuang Document S.6502 Followed by an Annotated Translation*. 2nd ed. Kyoto: Italian School of East Asian Studies, 2005.

——. "Wu Zhao de mingtang yu tianwen zhong" 武曌的明堂與天文鐘 [The *Mingtang* of Wu Zhao and Her Armillary Sphere]. In Zhao Wenrun and Li Yuming, *Wu Zetian yanjiu lunwenji*, 140–47.

Fracasso, Ricardo. "The Nine Tripods of Empress Wu." In *Tang China and Beyond*, ed. Antonino Forte, 85–96. Kyoto: Italian School of East Asian Studies, 1988.

Frankfurt, Henri. *Kingship and the Gods*. Chicago: University of Chicago Press, 1948.

Frazer, Sir James George. *The New Golden Bough*. Great Meadows, New Jersey: Phillips, 1965.

Gao Junping 高俊苹. "Shi lun Wu Zetian shiqi Longmen shiku de Mile zaoxiang" 試論武則天時期龍門石窟的彌勒造像 [A Discussion of Maitreya Sculpture in the Longmen Grottoes During the Era of Wu Zetian]. *Dunhuang xuejikan* 敦煌学辑刊 [Journal of Dunhuang Studies] no. 2 (2006): 141–44.

Gao Shiyu. "A Fixed State of Affairs and Mis-positioned Status: Gender Relations During the Sui, Tang and Five Dynasties." In Min Jiayin, *The Chalice and the Blade*, 270–314.

Gernet, Jacques. *Buddhism in Chinese Society: An Economic History from the Fifth to the Tenth Centuries*, trans. Franciscus Verellen. New York: Columbia University Press, 1995.

Gimello, Robert. "Icon and Incantation: The Goddess Zhunti and the Role of Images in the Occult Buddhism of China." In *Images in Asian Religions*, ed. Phyllis Graff and Koichi Shinohara, 225–56. Vancouver: University of British Columbia, 2004.

Goldin, Paul Rakita. *The Culture of Sex in Ancient China*. Honolulu: University of Hawaii Press, 2002.

——. "Imagery of Copulation in Early Chinese Poetry." *Chinese Literature: Essays, Articles and Reviews* 21 (December 1999), 35–66.

——. "On the Meaning of Xiwangmu, Spirit-Mother of the West." *Journal of the American Oriental Society* 122, no. 1 (January–March 2002): 83–85.

——. "The View of Women in Early Confucianism." In Li Chenyang, *The Sage and the Second Sex*, 133–61.

Gong Dazhong 宮大中. "Cong Luoyang Tangdai shike kan Wu Zetian zai Dongdu" 從洛陽唐代建築刻石看武則天在東都 [Examining Wu Zetian in Her Eastern Capital from the Tang Dynasty Stone Carvings in Luoyang]. In Zhao Wenrun and Liu Zhiqing, *Wu Zetian yu Yanshi*, 181–90.

——. *Longmen shiku yishu* 龍門石窟藝術 [The Art in the Longmen Grottoes]. Shanghai: Shanghai Renmin, 1981.

Gross, Nancy. *Buddhism After Patriarchy: A Feminist History, Analysis and Reconstruction of Buddhism*. Albany: State University of New York Press, 1993.

Gu Zhengmei 古正美 (Kathy Cheng-mei Ku). "The Buddharāja Image of Emperor Wu of Liang." In *Philosophy and Religion in Early Medieval China*, ed. Alan K. L. Chan and Yue-Kueng Lo, 265–90. Albany: State University of New York Press, 2010.

——. "Wu Zetian de *Huayan jing* fowang chuantong yu Fojiao xingxiang" 武則天的華嚴經佛王傳統與佛教形像 [Wu Zetian's *Flower Garland* Sutra Tradition of Buddhist Kingship and Buddhist Imagery]. *Guoxue yanjiu* 國學研究 7 (2000): 279–321.

Guisso, Richard. "The Reigns of the Empress Wu, Chung-tsung and Jui-tsung." *CHC* 279–320.

——. Review of Howard Wechsler's *Offerings of Jade and Silk: Ritual and Symbol in the Legitimization of the T'ang*. *Pacific Affairs* 59, no. 2 (Summer 1986): 302–3.

——. *Wu Tse-t'ien and the Politics of Legitimation in T'ang China*. Bellingham: Western Washington University Press, 1978.

Guisso, Richard and Stanley Johansen. *Women in China: Current Directions in Historical Scholarship*. Youngstown, N.Y.: Philo, 1981.

Guo Shaolin 郭紹林. "Da Zhou Wanguo songde tianshu kaoshi" 大周萬國天樞大周萬國頌德天樞考釋 [An Explanatory Investigation into the Axis of the Sky of Myriad Countries Exalting the Merits of the Great Zhou]. *Luoyang shifan xueyuan xuebao* 洛陽師範學院學報 [Academic Journal of Luoyang Normal University] no. 6 (2001): 73–77.

——. "Longmen Lushena fo diaoxiang zaoxing yiju Wu Zetian shuo jiumiu" 龍門盧舍那佛雕像造型依据武則天說糾謬 [Correcting Misconceptions That the Longmen Vairocana Is Modeled on Wu Zetian]. In *Sui-Tang lishi wenhua* 隋唐歷史文化 [Culture and History of the Sui and Tang], 162–70. Beijing: Zhongguo Wenshi, 2005.

——. *Sui-Tang Luoyang* 隋唐洛陽 [Sui and Tang Luoyang]. Xi'an: Sanqin, 2006.

Hargett, James. "Playing Second Fiddle: The Luan-Bird in Early and Medieval Chinese Literature." *T'oung Pao*, Second Series, 75 (1989): 235–62.

He Guanbao 賀官保, ed. *Luoyang wenwu yu guji* 隋唐洛陽文物與古跡 [Cultural Relics and Records of Sui-Tang Luoyang]. Beijing: Xinhua, 1987.

Heirman, Ann, "Yijing's View on the *Bhikṣuṇīs*' Standard Robes." *Chung-Hwa Buddhist Journal* 21 (2008): 145–58.

Henderson, Jeffrey. *Aristophanes: Lysistrata*. Oxord: Clarendon, 1987.

Henricks, Robert. "On the Whereabouts and Identity of a Place Called K'ung-sang (Hollow Mulberry) in Early Chinese Mythology." *Bulletin of the School of Oriental and African Studies* 58 (1995): 69–90.

Herbert, P. A. *Examine the Honest, Appraise the Able*. Faculty of Asian Studies Monograph, New Series, no. 10. Canberra: Australia National University, 1988.

Hinsch, Bret. "Textiles and Female Virtue in Early Imperial Chinese Historical Writings." *Nan nü* 5, no. 2 (2003): 170–202.

——. *Women in Early Imperial China*. Lanham, Md.: Rowman and Littlefield, 2002.

Hiraoka Takeo 平岡武夫. *Todai no koyomi* 唐代の曆 [The Tang Calendar]. Shanghai: Shanghai guji, 1990.

Hobsbaum, Eric, and Terence Ranger, eds. *The Invention of Tradition*. Cambridge: Cambridge University Press, 2010.

Holmgren, Jennifer. "Women's Biographies in the *Wei Shu*: A Study of Moral Attitudes and Social Background Found in Women's Biographies in the Dynastic History of the Northern Wei." PhD diss., Australia National University, 1979.

Holzman, Donald, "Immortality-Seeking in Early Chinese Poetry." In *The Power of Culture: Studies in Chinese Cultural History*, eds. W. J. Peterson and A. H. Plaks, 103–18. Hong Kong: Institute of Chinese Studies, University of Hong Kong, 1993.

——. *Immortals, Festivals and Poetry in Medieval China*. Aldershot, UK: Ashgate, 1998.

——. "The Wang Ziqiao Stele." *Rocznik Orientalistyczny* 47, no. 2 (1991): 77–83.

Hu Ji 胡戟. *Hu Ji wencun: Sui-Tang lishi yu Dunhuang ji* 胡戟文存: 隋唐歷史與敦煌卷 [Collected Essays of Hu Ji: Volume on Sui-Tang History and Dunhuang]. Beijing: Social Sciences Press, 2004.

——. *Wu Zetian benzhuan* 武則天本傳 [Essential Biography of Wu Zetian]. Xi'an: Shaanxi Shifan daxue, 1998.

Huang Chi-chiang. "Consecrating the Buddha: Legend, Lore, and History of the Imperial Relic-Veneration Ritual in the T'ang Dynasty." *Journal of Chung-hwa Institute of Buddhist Studies* 11 (1998): 483–533.

Hubbard, Jamie. *Absolute Delusion, Perfect Buddhahood: The Rise and Fall of a Chinese Heresy*. Honolulu: University of Hawaii Press, 2001.

Hucker, Charles. *A Dictionary of Official Titles in Imperial China*. Stanford, Calif.: Stanford University Press, 1985.

—. Review of Howard Wechsler's *Offerings of Jade and Silk: Ritual and Symbol in the Legitimization of the T'ang. American Historical Review* 91, no. 2 (April 1986): 444.

Idema, Wilt, and Beata Grant. *The Red Brush: Writing Women of Imperial China.* Cambridge, Mass.: Harvard University Asia Center, 2004.

Irwin, Lee. "Divinity and Salvation: The Great Goddesses of China." *Asian Folklore Studies* 49, no. 1 (1990): 53–68.

Ishida Ei'ichiro. "Mother-Son Deities." *History of Religions* 4, no. 1 (1964): 30–52.

Janousch, Andreas. "The Emperor as Bodhisattva: The Bodhisattva Ordination and Ritual Assemblies of Emperor Wu of the Liang Dynasty." In *State and Court Ritual in China*, ed. J. P. Mc Dermott, 112–49. Cambridge: University of Cambridge Press, 1999.

—. "The Reform of Imperial Ritual During the Reign of Emperor Wu of the Liang Dynasty (502–549)." PhD dissertation, University of Cambridge, 1998.

Jay, Jennifer. "Imagining Matriarchy: 'Kingdoms of Women' in Tang China." *Journal of the American Oriental Society* 116 (1996): 220–29.

—. "Vignettes of Chinese Women in Tang Xi'an (618–906): Individualism in Wu Zetian, Yang Guifei, Yu Xuanji, and Li Wa." *Chinese Culture* 31, no. 1 (1990): 77–89.

Ji Qingyang 季慶陽. "Wu Zetian yu zhong-xiao guannian" 武則天與忠孝觀念 [Wu Zetian and Her Concept of Loyalty and Filial Piety]. *Xibei daxue xuebao* 西北大學學報 [Journal of Northwest University] 39, no. 6 (2009): 138–40.

Jia Jinhua. "A Study of the Jinglong Wenguan ji." *Monumenta Serica* 47 (1999): 209–36.

Jiang Yonglin. *The Mandate of Heaven and the Great Ming Code.* Seattle: University of Washington Press, 2011.

Jie Yongqiang 介永強. "Wu Zetian yu xiangrui" 武則天與祥瑞 [Wu Zetian and Auspicious Omens]. In Zhao Wenrun and Li Yuming, *Wu Zetian yanjiu lunwenji*, 160–67.

Johnson, Wallace. *The T'ang Code.* Vol. 1, *General Principles.* Princeton: Princeton University Press, 1979.

Kagan, Richard. "The Chinese Approach to Shamanism." *Chinese Sociology and Anthropology* 12, no. 4 (1980): 1–135.

Kamitsuka Yoshiko 神塚淑子. "Sokuten buko ki no dokyo" 則天武后期の道教 [Taoism During the Period of the Dowager-Empress Wu Zetian's Reign]. In *Todai no Shukyo* 唐代の宗教 [Religion in the Tang Dynasty], Research Report of the Institute for Research in Humanities, ed. Yoshikawa Tadao 吉川忠夫. Kyoto: Kyoto University, 2000.

Kang Weimin 康為民. "Su Anheng sanjian Wu Zetian" 蘇安恆三諫武則天 [Su Anheng Thrice Remonstrates with Wu Zetian]. *He-Luo Chunqiu* 河洛春秋 [Springs and Autumns of the Luo and Yellow River] no. 3 (2007): 50–55.

—. "Wu Zetian yuanhe xing Goushan" 武則天緣何幸緱山 [Why Wu Zetian Went to Mount Gou]. In Zhao Wenrun and Liu Zhiqing, *Wu Zetian yu Yanshi*, 219–27.

Kang Woobang. *Korean Buddhist Sculpture,* trans. Choo Yoonjung. Chicago: Art Media Resources; Gyeong-gi: Yeolhwadang, 2005.

Karetzky, Patricia. *Early Buddhist Art: Illustrations from the Life of the Buddha.* Lanham, Md.: University Press of America, 2000.

—. *Guanyin.* New York: Oxford University Press, 2004.

—. "The Representation of Women in Medieval China: Recent Archaeological Evidence." *T'ang Studies* 17 (1999): 213–51.

——. "Wu Zetian and Buddhist Art of the Tang Dynasty." *T'ang Studies* 20–21 (2002–2003): 113–171.

Kantorowicz, Ernst. *The King's Two Bodies: A Study in Mediaeval Political Theology.* Princeton: Princeton University Press, 1957.

Kegasawa Yasunori 氣賀澤保規. *Sokuten buko* 則天武后 [Empress Wu Zetian]. Tokyo: Hakuteisha, 1995.

Keightley, David. "The Making of Ancestors: Late Shang Religion and Its Legacy." In *Religion and Chinese Society.* Vol. 1: *Ancient and Medieval China,* ed. John Lagerway. Hong Kong: Chinese University Press, 2004.

Kern, Martin. "Announcements from Mountains: The Stele Inscriptions of the First Emperor." In *Conceiving the Empire: China and Rome Compared,* ed. Fritz Heimer-Muschler and Achim Mittag, 217–40. New York: Oxford University Press, 2008.

Kinney, Anne. *Chinese Views of Childhood.* Honolulu: University of Hawaii Press, 1995.

——. *Representations of Childhood and Youth in Early China.* Stanford, Calif.: Stanford University Press, 2004.

Kirkland, Russell. "Huang Ling-wei: A Taoist Priestess in T'ang China." *Journal of Chinese Religions* 19 (1991): 47–73.

——. *Taoism: The Enduring Tradition.* London: Routledge, 2004.

Kirkland, Russell, and Livia Kohn. "Daoism in the Tang (618–907)." In Kohn, *Daoism Handbook,* 339–83.

Klöpsch, Volker. "Lo Pin-wang's Survival: Traces of a Legend." *T'ang Studies* 6 (1988): 77–97.

Knapp, Keith. *Selfless Offspring.* Honolulu: University of Hawaii Press, 2005.

Knauer, Elfriede. "The Queen Mother of the West: A Study of the Influence of Western Prototypes on the Iconography of the Taoist Deity." In *Contact and Exchange in the Ancient World,* ed. Victor Mair, 62–115. Honolulu: University of Hawaii Press, 2006.

Ko, Dorothy. *Teachers of the Inner Chambers: Women and Culture in Seventeenth-Century China.* Stanford, Calif.: Stanford University Press, 1994.

Kohn, Livia. *Daoist Mystical Philosophy: The Scripture of Western Ascension.* Magdalena, N.Mex.: Three Pines, 2007.

Kohn, Livia. "Lord Lao and Laojun." In Predagio, *Encyclopedia of Taoism,* 613–15.

——. *The Taoist Experience: An Anthology.* Albany: State University of New York Press, 1993.

Kohn, Livia, ed. *Daoism Handbook.* Leiden: Brill, 2004.

Kohn, Livia, and Michael LaFargue, eds. *Lao Tzu and the Tao-te-ching.* Albany: State University of New York Press, 1998.

Kominami Ichiro 小南一郎. *Chugoku no shinwa to monogatari* 中國の神話傳說と古小說 [Chinese Stories and Legends]. Tokyo: Iwanami Shoten, 1984.

——. "Rituals for the Earth." In Lagerway and Kalinowski, *Early Chinese Religion,* part 1, 201–35.

Koposov, Nikolay. "The Armored Train of Memory: The Politics of History in Post-Soviet Russia." *Perspectives on History* 49 (January 2011): 23–26.

Kory, Stephan. "A Remarkably Resonant and Resilient Tang-Dynasty Augural Stone: Empress Wu's *Baotu.*" *T'ang Studies* 26 (2008): 99–124.

Kou Jianghou 寇疆候. "Wu Zetian yu Zhongzong de sanjiao gongcun yu foxian daohou zhengce" 武則天與中宗的三教共存與佛先道后政策 [The Policies of

"Coexistence of the Three Faiths" and "Buddhism before Daoism" Under Wu Zetian and Zhongzong]. *Shaanxi shifan daxue xuebao* 陝西師範大學學報 [Journal of Shaanxi Normal University] (1999): 19–22.

Krishna, Nanditha. *Sacred Animals of India*. New Delhi: Penguin, 2010.

Kroll, Paul. "Daoist Verse and the Quest of the Divine." In John Lagerway and Lü Pengzhi, *Early Chinese Religion*, part 2, 953–88.

——. "Li Po's Transcendent Diction." *Journal of the American Oriental Society* 106, no. 1 (1986): 99–117.

——. "The Memories of Lu Chao-lin." *Journal of the American Oriental Society* 109, no. 4 (1989): 581–92.

——. "True Dates of Reign Periods in the Tang Dynasty." *T'ang Studies* 2 (1984): 25–32.

Kuhn, Dieter. *Science and Civilization in China*. Vol. 5, *Chemistry and Chemical Technology*, part 9, *Textile Technology: Spinning and Reeling*. Cambridge: Cambridge University Press, 1988.

——. "Tracing a Chinese Legend: In Search of the Identity of the 'First Sericulturalist.'" *T'oung Pao*, Second Series, 70 (1984): 213–45.

Kuranaka Susumu 蔵中進. *Sokuten monji no kenkyu* 則天文字の研究 [Research on the Characters of Zetian]. Tokyo: Kanrin shobo, 1995.

Kwang-chih Chang. *The Archaeology of Ancient China*. New Haven, Conn.: Yale University Press, 1987.

——. *Art, Myth and Ritual*. Cambridge, Mass.: Harvard University Press, 1983.

Larsen, Jeanne. *Willow, Wine, Mirror, Moon: Women's Poems from Tang China*. Rochester, N.Y.: BOA Editions, 2005.

Lagerway, John. *Daoist Ritual in Chinese Society and History*. New York: Macmillan, 1987.

Lagerway, John, and Mark Kalinowski, eds. *Early Chinese Religion*. Part 1, *Shang Through Han (1250 BC–220 AD)*. Leiden: Brill, 2009.

Lagerway, John, and Lü Pengzhi, eds. *Early Chinese Religion*. Part 2, *The Period of Division (220–589)*. Leiden: Brill, 2010.

Lee, Lily Xiao Hong, and A. D. Stefanowska, eds. *Biographical Dictionary of Chinese Women, Antiquity Through Sui, 1600 BC–618 AD*. Armonk N.Y.: Sharpe, 2007.

Lee, Sherman. "The Golden Image of the New-Born Buddha." *Artibus Asiae* 18, nos. 3/4 (1955): 225–37.

Lee, Sherman E., and Wai-kam Ho. "The Colossal Eleven-Faced Kuan-yin of the T'ang Dynasty." *Artibus Asiae* 22, nos. 1/2 (1959): 121–37.

Lee, Sonya. *Surviving Nirvana: The Death of Buddha in Chinese Visual Culture*. Hong Kong: Hong Kong University Press, 2010.

Lei Wen 雷聞. "Daojiao tu Ma Yuanzhen yu Wu-Zhou geming" 道教徒馬元貞與武周革命 [Daoist Ma Yuanzhen and the Wu-Zhou Revolution]. *Zhongguo shi yanjiu* 中國史研究 [Journal of Chinese Historical Studies] (2004): 73–80.

Lewis, Mark Edward. *China's Cosmopolitan Empire: The Tang Dynasty*. Cambridge, Mass.: Harvard University Press, 2009.

——. *The Flood Myths of Early China*. Albany: State University of New York Press, 2006.

——. *Writing and Authority in Early China*. Albany: State University of New York Press, 1999.

Li Chenyang, ed. *The Sage and the Second Sex: Confucianism, Ethics, and Gender*. Chicago: Open Court, 2000.

Li Fubu 李弗不. "Gudai ming nüzi: fenfen ru Tangshi" 古代名女子:紛紛入唐詩 [Celebrated Women of Antiquity Sprinkled in Tang Poems]. *Zhishi jiushi liliang* 知識就是力量 [Knowledge Is Power] no. 3 (2007): 72–74.

Li Hexian 李荷先. "Cong *Chen gui* kan Wu Zetian de jun-chen lunli sixiang" 從臣軌看武則天的君臣倫理思想 [Looking at the Ethics of the Ruler-Minister Relationship Through *Regulations for Ministers*]. *Huazhong shifan daxue xuebao* 華中師范大學學報 [Scholarly Journal of Huazhong Normal University] 5 (1986): 58–62.

Li Jingjie 李静杰. "Guanyu Wu Zetian xinzi de jidian renshi" 關於武則天新字的幾點認識 [Several Points About the New Characters of Wu Zetian]. *Gugong bowuyuan yuankan* 故宮博物院院刊 [Bulletin of the Palace Museum] no. 4 (1997): 60–64.

Li Zhao 李昭. "Lun Wu Zetian bai Luo shoutu yu Luoshen de bianyi" 論武則天拜洛受圖與洛水神的變异 [A Discussion of the Evolution of the Luo River Goddess and Wu Zetian's Worship of the Luo and Receiving the Chart]. In Wang Shuanghuai and Guo Shaolin, *Wu Zetian yu Shendu Luoyang*, 74–83.

Liang Hengtang 梁恒唐. "Tan Wu shi jiazu de qiyuan yu fanyan" 談武氏家族的起源與繁衍 [A Discussion of the Origins and Rise of the Wu Clan]. In Zhao Wenrun and Liu Zhiqing, *Wu Zetian yu Yanshi*, 49–58.

Liang Yongtao 梁詠濤 and Tang Zhigong 唐志工. "Dui Guangyuan Wudai 'Da Shu Lizhou dudufu Huangzesi Zetian Huanghou Wushi xin miaoji' bei de jiaozhu ji xianguang wenti fenxi" 對廣元五代《大屬利州都督府皇澤寺唐則天皇后武氏新廟記》碑的校注及相關問題分析 [An Analysis and Commentary on the "New Shrine Record of Tang Empress Zetian of the Wu Family in Huangze Temple of Great Shu Commandery of Lizhou" from Five Dynasties-era Guangyuan]. In *Conference Proceedings from the 11th Conference of the Wu Zetian Research Association*, 431–37. Guangyuan, 2013.

Liebenthal, Walter. "Chinese Buddhism during the 4th and 5th Centuries." *Monumenta Nipponica* 11, no. 1 (1955): 44–83.

Link, Arthur (1960) "Shih Seng-yu and His Writings." *Journal of the American Oriental Society* 80, no. 1 (1960): 17–43.

Liu, James T. C., "Polo and Cultural Change: From T'ang to Sung China." *Harvard Journal of Asiatic Studies* 45, no. 1 (1985): 203–24.

Liu Jinglong 劉景龍. *Longmen shiku* 龍門石窟 [The Longmen Grottoes]. Beijing: Zhishi, 1996.

Liu Xinru. *Ancient India and China*. Delhi: Oxford University Press, 1997.

——. *Silk and Religion: An Exploration of Material Life and the Thought of People, 600–1200*. New Delhi: Oxford University Press, 1996.

Liu Zezhang. *Zhongguo lishi changzhi* 中國歷史常知 [Common Knowledge in Chinese History]. Beijing: Higher Education, 2007.

Loewe, Michael. *Ways to Paradise: The Chinese Quest for Immortality*. London: Allen and Unwin, 1979.

Louie, Kam. *Theorizing Chinese Masculinity: Society and Gender in China*. Cambridge: Cambridge University Press, 2002.

Lü Huayu 盧華語. "Wu Zetian 'Chen Gui' pouxi" 武則天臣軌剖析 [Dissecting Wu Zetian's *Regulations for Ministers*]. In Su Jian and Bai Xianzhang, *Wu Zetian yu Luoyang*, 85–95.

Ma Chi 馬馳. "Fanjiang yu Wu Zetian" 番將与武則天政權 [Non-Han Generals and the Political Authority of Wu Zetian]. *Xuchang shizhuan xuebao* 許昌史專學報 [Xuchang Academic Journal] no. 4 (1991): 31–36.

Ma Xiaoli 馬曉麗. "Guanyu Wu Zetian zhongyong kuli de jidian kanfa" 關於武則天重用酷吏的幾點看法 [Several Observations on Wu Zetian's Heavy Utilization of Cruel Officials]. *Yantai daxue xuebao* 煙臺大學學報 [Journal of Yantai University] no. 3 (1991): 42–44.

Mair, Denis. "The Dance of Qian and Kun in the Zhouyi." *Sino-Platonic Papers* 152 (2005): 1–18.

Mair, Victor. "The Narrative Revolution in Chinese Literature: Ontological Presumptions." *Chinese Literature: Essays, Articles, Reviews* 5, nos. 1/2 (1983): 1–27.

Mair, Victor, Nancy Steinhardt, and Paul Goldin, eds. *Hawai'i Reader of Traditional Chinese Culture*. Honolulu: University of Hawaii Press, 2005.

Mann, Susan. "Presidential Address: Myths of Asian Womanhood." *Journal of Asian Studies* 59, no. 4 (2000): 835–62.

Mann, Susan, and Yu-yin Cheng, eds. *Under Confucian Eyes: Writing on Gender in Chinese History*. Berkeley: University of California Press, 2001.

Mather, Richard. "K'ou Ch'ien-chih and the Taoist Theocracy of the Northern Wei." In Welch and Seidel, *Facets of Taoism*, 103–22.

——. "Wang Chin's Dhōta Temple Stele Inscription." *Journal of the American Oriental Society* 83, no. 3 (1963): 338–59.

Matthews, Warren. *World Religions*. 6 ed. Belmont, Calif.: Wadsworth, 2010.

McBride II, Richard. "Popular Esoteric Deities and the Spread of Their Cults." In *Esoteric Buddhism and the Tantras in East Asia*, ed. Charles Orzech, Henrik Sorensen, and Richard Payne, 215–19. Leiden: Brill, 2011.

McDermott, Joseph, ed. *State and Court Ritual in China*. Cambridge: Cambridge University Press, 1999.

McMullen, David. "Bureaucrats and Cosmology: The Ritual Code of T'ang China." In *Rituals of Royalty: Power and Ceremonial in Traditional Societies*, eds. David Cannadine and Simon Price, 181–237. Cambridge: Cambridge University Press, 1987.

——. "The Real Judge Dee: Ti Jen-Chieh and the T'ang Restoration of 705." *Asia Major*, Third Series, 6, no. 1 (1993): 1–81.

——. *State and Scholars in T'ang China*. New York: Cambridge University Press, 1988.

McNair, Amy. *Donors of Longmen: Faith, Politics, and Patronage in Medieval Chinese Buddhist Sculpture*. Honolulu: University of Hawaii Press, 2007.

——. "Early Tang Patronage at Longmen." *Ars Orientalis* 24 (1994): 65–81.

——. "The Fengxiansi Shrine and Longmen in the 670s." *Bulletin of Far Eastern Antiquities* 68 (1996): 325–92.

——. *The Upright Brush: Yan Zhenqing's Calligraphy and Song Literati Politics*. Honolulu: University of Hawaii Press, 1998.

McNeill, William. "The Care and Repair of Public Myth." *Foreign Affairs* 61, no. 1 (Fall 1982): 1–13.

Merriam, Charles. *Political Power*. New York: Collier, 1964.

Min Jiayin, ed. *The Chalice and the Blade in Chinese Culture*. Beijing: Academy of Social Sciences, 1995.

Moule, A. C. *The Rulers of China, 221 BC to AD 1949*. New York: Praeger, 1957.

Nelson, Sarah Milledge. *Gender in Archaeology: Analyzing Power and Prestige.* Walnut Creek, Calif.: Altamira, 1997.

——. "The Queens of Silla: Power and Connections to the Spirit World." In *Ancient Queens: Archaeological Explorations,* ed. Sarah Nelson, 77–92. Walnut Creek, Calif.: Altamira Press, 2003.

Nelson, Susan. "Tao Yuanming's Sashes: Or, the Gendering of Immortality." *Ars Orientalis* 29 (1999): 1–27.

Ng, Zhiru. *The Making of a Savior Bodhisattva.* Kuroda Institute Studies in East Asian Buddhism 21. Honolulu: University of Hawaii Press, 2007.

Nickerson, Peter. "The Southern Celestial Masters." In Kohn, *Daoism Handbook,* 256–82.

Nietzsche, Friedrich. *Basic Writings of Neitzsche.* New York: Random House, 2000.

Ning Qiang. "Gender Politics in Medieval Chinese Buddhist Art: Images of Empress Wu at Longmen and Dunhuang." *Oriental Art* 49, no. 2 (2003): 28–39.

Niu Laiying 牛來穎. "Tangdai xiangrui yu wangchao zhengzhi" 唐代祥瑞與王朝政治 [Auspicious Portents and Dynastic Politics in the Tang Dynasty]. In *Tang wenhua yanjiu* 唐代文化研究論文集 [Essays on Research in Tang Culture], eds. Zheng Xuemeng 鄭學檬 and Leng Minshu 冷敏述, 535–44. Shanghai: Shanghai People's Press, 1994.

Nylan, Michael. *The Five Confucian Classics.* New Haven, Conn.: Yale University Press, 2001.

O'Hara, Albert. *The Position of Women in Early China.* Taipei: Mei Ya, 1971.

Otagi Hajime 愛宕元. "Nangyaku Gi fujin shinko no hensen" 南嶽魏夫人信仰變遷 [The Development in the Belief of Lady Wei of the Southern Marchmount]. In *Rikucho dokyo no kenkyu* 六朝道教の研究 [Research on Daoism in the Six Dynasties Period], Research Report of the Institute for Research in Humanities, ed. Yoshikawa Tadao. Kyoto: Kyoto University, 1998.

Pan Yihong. *Son of Heaven and the Heavenly Qaghan: Sui-Tang China and Its Neighbors.* Bellingham: Western Washington University Press, 1997.

Pang Sunjoo. "The Consorts of King Wu and King Wen in the Bronze Inscriptions of Early Chou." *Monumenta Serica* 33 (1977): 124–35.

Paper, Jordan. "The Persistence of Female Deities in Patriarchal China." *Journal of Feminist Studies in Religion* 6, no. 1 (1990): 25–40.

Paul, Diana. "Empress Wu and the Historians: A Tyrant and a Saint of Classical China." In *Unspoken Worlds: Women's Religious Lives in Non-Western Cultures,* ed. Nancy Falk and Rita Gross, 191–206. San Francisco: Harper Collins, 1979.

——. *Women in Buddhism: Images of the Feminine in the Mahayana Tradition.* Berkeley: University of California Press, 1985.

Pearce, Scott. "A King's Two Bodies: The Northern Wei Emperor Wencheng and Representations of the Power of His Monarchy." *Frontiers of History in China* 7, no. 1 (2012): 90–104.

Pettit, J. E. E. "The Erotic Empress: Fantasy and Sovereignty in Chinese Temple Inscriptions." *T'ang Studies* 26 (2008): 125–142.

Picken, Laurence E. R., and Noël J. Nickson, *Music from the Tang Court 7: Some Ancient Connections Explored.* Cambridge: Cambridge University Press, 2000.

Piggott, Joan. *The Emergence of Japanese Kingship.* Stanford, Calif.: Stanford University Press, 1997.

Plaks, Andrew. *Archetype and Allegory in Hsi yü chi and Hung lou meng*. Princeton: Princeton University Press, 1976.

Poceski, Mario. *Introducing Chinese Religions*. New York: Routledge, 2009.

Poo Mu-chou. *In Search of Personal Welfare: A View of Ancient Chinese Religion*. Albany: State University of New York Press, 1998.

Predagio, Fabrizio, ed. *The Routledge Encyclopedia of Taoism*. New York: Routledge, 2011.

Puett, Michael. *To Become a God: Cosmology, Sacrifice and Self-Divinization in Early China*. Harvard-Yenching Institute Monograph no. 57. Cambridge, Mass.: Harvard University Asia Center, 2004.

Pulleyblank, Edwin G. "Jihu: Indigenous Inhabitants of Shaanbei and Western Shanxi." In *Opuscula Altaica: Essays Presented in Honor of Henry Schwarz*, ed. Edward Kaplan and Donald Whisenant, 498–530. Seattle: University of Washington Press, 1994.

Qiang Fang, "Hot Potatoes: Chinese Complaint Systems from Early Times to the Late Qing (1898)." *Journal of Asian Studies* 68, no. 4 (2009): 1105–35.

Raphals, Lisa. "Gendered Virtue Reconsidered: Notes from the Warring States and the Han." In Li Chenyang, *The Sage and the Second Sex*, 223–247.

——. *Sharing the Light: Representations of Women and Virtue in Early China*. Albany: State University of New York Press, 1998.

——. "A Woman Who Understood the Rites." In *Confucius and the Analects: New Essays*, ed. Bryan Van Norden, 275–302. New York: Oxford University Press, 2002.

Raz, Gil. "Daoist Sacred Geography." In John Lagerway and Lü Pengzhi, *Early Chinese Religion*, part 2, 1399–1442.

——. *The Emergence of Daoism: Creation of Tradition*. New York: Routledge, 2012.

Robinet, Isabel. "Shangqing." In Predagio, *Encylopedia of Taoism*, 858–66.

——. *Taoism: Growth of a Religion*. Stanford, Calif.: Stanford University Press, 1997.

Robson, James. "Buddhism and the Chinese Marchmount (Wuyue 五嶽) System: A Case Study of the Southern Marchmount (Mt. Nanyue 南嶽)." In *Religion and Chinese Society, Vol. 1: Ancient and Medieval China*, ed. Lagerway, 341–83. Hong Kong: Chinese University Press, 2004.

——. *Power of Place: The Religious Landscape of the Southern Sacred Peak in Medieval China*. Harvard East Asian Monographs no. 316. Cambridge, Mass.: Harvard University Press, 2009.

Rong Xinjiang 榮新江. "Nüban nanzhuang: Sheng Tang funü xingbie yishi" 女扮男 裝: 盛唐婦女性別意識 [Donning Male Attire: Gender Consciousness of Women in the High Tang]. In *Abstracts and Papers from the Tang Women's Studies Conference*, 320–44. Beijing University, 2001.

Rothschild, N. Harry. "Beyond Filial Piety: *Biographies of Exemplary Women* and Wu Zhao's New Paradigm of Political Authority." *T'ang Studies* 23-4 (2005–2006): 149–68.

——. "Drawing Antiquity in Her Own Image: The New Characters of Wu Zetian." *China Yongu: The Journal of Chinese Studies of Pusan National University* 15, no. 3 (2009): 117–70.

——. "Emerging from the Cocoon: Ethnic Revival, Lunar Radiance, and the Cult of Liu Sahe in the Jihu Uprising of 682–683." *Annali* 65 (2005): 257–82.

——. "An Inquiry into Reign Era Changes Under Wu Zhao, China's Only Female Emperor." *Early Medieval China* 12 (2006): 123–49.

——. "The Koguryan Connection: The Quan (Yon) Family in the Establishment of Wu Zhao's Political Authority." *China Yongu: The Journal of Chinese Studies of Pusan National University* 14, no. 1 (2008): 199–234.

——. "Rhetoric, Ritual and Support Constituencies in the Political Authority of Wu Zhao, China's Only Woman Emperor." PhD dissertation, Brown University, 2003.

——. "Story of a Stone: Wu Zhao and the Mother of Qi." In Wang Shuanghuai and Guo Shaolin, *Wu Zetian yu Shendu Luoyang*, 110–29.

——. "Wu Zhao and the Queen Mother of the West." *Journal of Daoist Studies* 3 (2010): 29–56.

——. *Wu Zhao: China's Only Woman Emperor*. Longman World Biography Series. New York: Longman, 2008.

——. "Wu Zhao's Remarkable Aviary." *Southeast Review of Asian Studies* 27 (2005): 71–88.

——. "Zhuanlun wang, yishi, yu huozai: Wu Zhao yu 694 nian de wuzhedahui" 轉輪王、儀式、及火災：武曌與 694 年的無遮大會 [Cakravartin, Ceremony and Conflagration: Wu Zhao and the Pañcāvarṣika of 694]. *Qianling wenhua yanjiu* 乾陵文化研究 [Journal of Research on the Culture of Qianling Tomb] 7 (2012): 101–13.

Saso, Michael. "What Is the 'Ho-t'u'?" *History of Religions* 17, nos. 3/4 (1978): 406–7.

Schafer, Edward. *Ancient China*. New York: Time Life, 1967.

——. *The Divine Woman: Dragon Ladies and Rain Maidens*. North Point: San Francisco, 1980.

——. "Empyreal Powers and Chthonian Edens: Two Notes on T'ang Taoist Literature." *Journal of the American Oriental Society* 106, no. 4 (1986): 667–77.

——. *The Golden Peaches of Samarkand*. Berkeley: University of California Press, 1963.

——. "Hallucinations and Epiphanies in T'ang Poetry." *Journal of the American Oriental Society* 104, no. 4 (1984): 757–60.

——. "The Origin of an Era." *Journal of the American Oriental Society* 85, no. 4 (1965): 553–60.

——. *Pacing the Void*. Berkeley: University of California Press, 1977.

——. "The Restoration of the Shrine of Wei Hua-ts'un at Lin-ch'uan in the Early Eighth Century." *Journal of Oriental Studies* 15 (1977): 124–37.

——. "Ritual Exposure in Ancient China." *Harvard Journal of Asiatic Studies* 14, nos. 1/2 (1951): 130–84.

——. "Three Divine Women of South China." *Chinese Literature: Essays, Articles, and Reviews* 1 (1979): 31–42.

——. *The Vermilion Bird: T'ang Images of the South*. Berkeley: University of California Press, 1967.

——. "Ways of Looking at the Moon Palace." *Asia Major*, Third Series, 1, no. 1 (1988): 1–13.

Schimmel, Solomon. *Wounds Not Healed by Time: The Power of Repentance and Forgiveness*. New York: Oxford University Press, 2004.

Schipper, Kristofer. "Purity and Strangers: Shifting Boundaries in Medieval Taoism." *T'oung Pao* 80 (1994): 61–81.

——. *The Taoist Body*, trans. Karen C. Duval. Berkeley: University of California Press, 1993.

Seidel, Anna. *La divinisation de Lao-tseu sous les Han*. Paris: Ecole Francaise d'Extreme-Orient, 1969.

——. "The Image of the Perfect Ruler in Early Taoist Messianism: Laozi and Li Hung." *History of Religions* 9 (1969–1970): 216–47.

——. "Tokens of Immortality in Han Graves." *Numen* 29, no. 1 (1986): 79–122.

Sen Tansen. *Buddhism, Diplomacy and Trade*. Honolulu: University of Hawaii Press, 2003.

Shaughnessy, Edward. *Before Confucius: Studies in the Creation of the Chinese Classics*. Albany: State University of New York Press, 1997.

Shi Anchang 施安昌. "Cong yuanzang tuoben tanguo tan Wu Zetian zao zi" 從院藏拓本探過談武則天造字 [A Discussion of the Characters Created by Wu Zetian Based on an Investigation of Rubbings in the Palace Museum Archives]. *Gugong bowuyuan yuankan* (1983): 34–38.

——. "Wu Zetian zao zi zhi ebian" 武則天造字之訛變 [Evolution of the Characters Created by Wu Zetian]. *Gugong bowuyuan yuankan* (1992): 58–62.

Shinohara, Koichi. "Stories of Miraculous Images and Paying Respect to the Three Jewels: A Discourse on Image Worship in Seventh-Century China." In *Images in Asian Religions*, ed. Phyllis Graff and Koichi Shinohara, 180–222. Vancouver: University of British Columbia, 2004.

Shryock, John. *The Origin and Development of the State Cult of Confucius*. New York: Paragon, 1966.

Skaff, Jonathan. *Sui-Tang China and Its Turko-Mongol Neighbors*. New York: Oxford University Press, 2012.

Snow, Justine. "The Spider's Web. Goddesses of Light and the Loom: Examining the Evidence for the Indo-European Origin of Two Ancient Chinese Deities." *Sino-Platonic Papers* 118 (June 2002): 1–82.

Soothill, William, and Lewis Hodous, comp. *A Dictionary of Chinese Buddhist Terms*. London: Kegan Paul, 1937.

Soper, Alexander. "*T'ang Ch'ao Ming Hua Lu*: Celebrated Painters of the T'ang Dynasty by Chu Ching-hsüan of T'ang." *Artibus Asiae* 21, nos. 3/4 (1958): 204–30.

——. "A T'ang Parinirvāṇa Stele." *Artibus Asiae* 22, nos. 1/2 (1959): 159–69.

Spring, Madeline. *Animal Allegories in T'ang China*. New Haven, Conn.: American Oriental Series, Vol. 76, 1993.

Stone, Charles. *The Fountainhead of Chinese Erotica*. Honolulu: University of Hawaii Press, 2003.

Strong, John. *The Legend of King Asoka*. Delhi: Motilal Banarsidass, 1989.

Su Jian 蘇健. *Luoyang gudu shi* 洛陽古都史 [A History of the Ancient Capital Luoyang]. Beijing: Bowen, 1989.

——. "Wu Zetian yu Shendu shiji" 武則天與神都史跡洛陽 [Wu Zetian and Ruins in the Divine Capital]. In Su Jian and Bai Xianzhang, *Wu Zetian yu Luoyang*, 1–16.

Su Jian and Bai Xianzhang 白獻章, eds. *Wu Zetian yu Luoyang* 武則天與洛陽 [Wu Zetian and Luoyang]. Xi'an: Sanqin, 1993.

Swann, Nancy. *Pan Chao: Foremost Woman Scholar of China*. New York: Century, 1932.

Tambiah, Stanley, "The Galactic Polity in Southeast Asia." In *Culture, Thought and Social Action*, ed. Stanley Tambiah, 252–86. Cambridge: Harvard University Press, 1985.

Tan Qixiang 譚其驤, ed. *Zhongguo lishi dituji* 中國歷史地圖集 [Chinese Historical Atlas], 8 vols. Beijing: Zhongguo ditu, 1996.

Tang Changdong 唐昌東. *Da Tang bihua* 大唐壁畫 [Magnificent Frescos from the Great Tang Dynasty]. Xi'an: Shaanxi Tourism, 1996.

Thompson, Nancy. "The Evolution of the T'ang Lion and Grapevine Mirror." *Artibus Asiae* 29, no. 1 (1967): 25–54.

Tokiwa Daijô 常盤大定. "Bushû shinji no ichi kenkyû" 武周新字の一研究 [A Study of the New Characters of the Wu-Zhou era]. *Shina bukkyô no kenkyû* 支那仏教 の 一研究 3 (1943): 395–430.

Tonami Mamoru. "Policy Towards the Buddhist Church in the Reign of T'ang Hsuan-tsung." *Acta Asiatica* 55 (1988): 27–47.

Tong, Jowen R. *Fables for the Patriarchs: Gender Politics in Tang Discourse*. Lanham, Md.: Rowman and Littlefield, 2000.

Tsiang, Katherine. "Monumentalization of Buddhist Texts in the Northern Qi Dynasty: The Engravings of Sūtras in Stone at the Xiangtangshan and Other Sites in the Sixth Century." *Artibus Asiae* 56, nos. 3/4 (1996): 233–61.

Twitchett, Denis. "*Chen Gui* and Other Works Attributed to Wu Zetian." *Asia Major* 16, no. 1 (2003): 33–109.

——. *Financial Administration Under the T'ang Dynasty*. Cambridge: Cambridge University Press, 1970.

——. "How to Be an Emperor: T'ang T'ai-tsung's Vision of His Role." *Asia Major*, Third Series, 9, no. 1/2 (1996): 1–103.

——. *The Writing of Official History Under the T'ang*. New York: Cambridge University Press, 1992.

Twitchett, Denis, and John Fairbank, eds. *Cambridge History of China*. Vol. 3, *Sui and Tang China, 589–906, part I*. Cambridge: Cambridge University Press, 1979.

Twitchett, Denis, and Howard Wechsler. "Kao-tsung (reign 649–83) and the Empress Wu: The Inheritor and the Usurper." *CHC* 242–89.

van Gulik, Robert. *Sexual Life in Ancient China*. Leiden: Brill, 1961.

Verellen, Franciscus. "The Beyond Within: Grotto-Heavens (*dongtian*) in Taoist Ritual and Cosmology." *Les Cahiers d'Extrême-Asie* 8 (1995): 265–90.

——. "Liturgy and Sovereignty: The Role of Taoist Ritual and the Foundation of the Shu Kingdom (907–925)." *Asia Major*, Third Series, 2, no. 1 (1989): 59–78.

Vetter, Lisa Pace. "*Women's Work*" *as Political Art: Weaving and Dialectical Politics in Homer, Aristophanes, and Plato*. Oxford, UK: Lexington, 2005.

Wang Aihe. *Cosmology and Political Culture in Early China*. Cambridge: Cambridge University Press, 2000.

Wang, Eugene. *Shaping the Lotus Sutra: Buddhist Visual Culture in Medieval China*. Seattle: University of Washington Press, 2005.

Wang Feng 王鋒. "Wu Zetian yu Tang Luoyang ducheng jianshe" 武則天與唐洛陽都城建築 [Wu Zetian and the Construction of Tang Capital Luoyang]. *He-Luo chunqiu* 河洛春秋 [Seasons of the Yellow and Luo Rivers] no. 3 (2007), 15–20.

Wang Hongjie. *Power and Politics in Tenth Century China: The Former Shu Regime*. Amherst, N.Y.: Cambria, 2011.

Wang Jing. *The Story of Stone: Intertextuality, Ancient Chinese Stone Lore, and the Stone Symbolism in Dream of the Red Chamber, Water Margin and Journey to the West*. Durham, N.C.: Duke University Press, 1992.

Wang Jingyao 王景堯. "Wu Zetian yu Shengxiantaizibei" 武則天與升仙太子碑 [Wu Zetian and the Stele of the Ascended Immortal Crown Prince]. Unpublished manuscript, Luoyang, 2003.

Wang, Robin. "Ideal Womanhood in Chinese Thought and Culture." *Philosophy Compass* 5, no. 8 (2010): 635–44.

——. *Yin Yang: The Way of Heaven and Earth in Chinese Thought and Culture.* New York: Cambridge University Press, 2012.

Wang, Robin, ed. *Images of Women in Chinese Thought and Culture: Writings from the Pre-Qin Period Through the Song Dynasty.* Indianapolis: Hackett, 2003.

Wang Ruichen 王瑞臣 and Han Gang 韓剛. "Cong 'Shengxian taizi bei' ji qi beiwen kan Wu-Zhou shengshi" 從'升仙太子碑'及其碑文看武周盛世 [Looking at Flourishing Era of Wu Zetian and the Zhou Dynasty Through the Stele of the Ascended Immortal Crown Prince and Other Inscriptions]. In Zhao Wenrun and Liu Zhiqing, *Wu Zetian yu Yanshi*, 237–39.

Wang Shuanghuai. "Lun Wu Zetian de gaige" 論武則天改革 [Discussing Change and Revolution Under Wu Zetian]. In Zhao Wenrun and Xin Jialong, *Wu Zetian yu Xianyang*, 110–22.

——. "Wu Zetian yu kuli de guanxi" 武則天與酷吏的關係 [The Relationship Between Wu Zetian and Her Cruel Officials]. In Zhao Wenrun and Li Yuming, *Wu Zetian yanjiu lunwenji*, 177–86.

——. "Wu-Zhou zaixiang shumu" 武周宰相數目考 [An Examination of the Count of Chief Ministers During Wu Zhao's Zhou Dynasty]. *Tangshi luncong* 唐史論叢 [Collections of Essays on Tang History] 5 (1990): 97–105.

Wang Shuanghuai and Guo Shaolin, eds. *Wu Zetian yu Shendu Luoyang* 武則天與神都洛陽 [Wu Zetian and Her Divine Capital Luoyang]. Beijing: China Cultural History Press, 2008.

Wang Shuanghuai and Zhao Wenrun. *Wu Zetian pingzhuan* 武則天評傳 [A Critical Biography of Wu Zetian]. Xi'an: Sanqin, 1993.

Wang Yueting 王月珽. "Wu Zetian yu nianhao" 武則天與年號 [Wu Zetian and Reign-Era Names]. In Zhao Wenrun and Li Yuming, *Wu Zetian yanjiu lunwenji*, 148–59.

Wang Yongping 王永平. "Tang Gaozong, Wu Zetian shiqi yu Linyi de Guanxi" 唐高宗、武則天時期与林邑的關系 [Foreign Relations with Champa During the Reigns of Tang Gaozong and Wu Zetian]. In *Conference Proceedings from the 11th Conference of the Wu Zetian Research Association, supplemental essay* (Guangyuan, 2013).

Wang Zhendong 王振東 and Xu Yingxian 徐英賢. "Wu Zetian 'Shengxiantaizibei' de shufa yishu" 武則天'升仙太子碑'的書法藝術 [Calligraphy and Art on Wu Zetian's Stele of the Ascended Immortal Crown Prince]. In Zhao Wenrun and Liu Zhiqing, *Wu Zetian yu Yanshi*, 240–44.

Watson, Burton. *Chinese Rhyme Poems.* New York: Columbia University Press, 1971.

Weber, Max. *Economy and Society.* Berkeley: University of California Press, 1978.

Webster, Thomas. *Athenian Culture and Society.* Berkeley: University of California Press, 1973.

Wechsler, Howard. "The Founding of the T'ang Dynasty: Kao-tsu (reign 618–626)." In *CHC*, 150–87. Cambridge: Cambridge University Press, 1979.

——. *Offerings of Jade and Silk: Ritual and Symbol in the Legitimization of the T'ang.* New Haven, Conn.: Yale University Press, 1985.

Welch, Holmes, and Anna Seidel, eds. *Facets of Taoism: Essays in Chinese Religion*. New Haven, Conn.: Yale University Press, 1979.

Welch, Michael. "Fa-tsang, Pure Light and Printing: An Inquiry into the Origins of Textual Xylography." Master's thesis, Library Sciences, University of Minnesota, 1981.

Weinstein, Stanley. *Buddhism Under the T'ang*. Cambridge: Cambridge University Press, 1987.

Whitfield, Roderick, Susan Whitfield, and Neville Agnew. *Cave Temples of Mogao: Art and History on the Silk Road*. Los Angeles: Getty Conservation Institute, 2000.

Witherspoon, Gary. "Cultural Motifs in Navajo Weaving." In *North American Indian Anthropology: Essays on Society and Culture*, ed. Raymond DeMallie, 355–76. Norman: University of Oklahoma Press, 1994.

Wong, Dorothy. "The Case of Amoghapāśa." *Journal of Inner Asian Art and Archaeology* 2 (2007): 151–58.

——. *Pre-Buddhist and Buddhist Use of Symbolic Form*. Honolulu: University of Hawaii Press, 2004.

Wright, Arthur. *The Sui Dynasty: The Unification of China, AD 581–617*. New York: Knopf, 1978.

Wu Hung. "Bird Motifs in Eastern Yi Art." *Orientations* 16, no. 10 (1985): 30–41.

——. "Buddhist Elements in Early Chinese Art (2nd and 3rd Century AD)." *Artibus Asiae* 47, nos. 3/4 (1986): 263–352.

——. *The Double Screen: Medium and Representation in Chinese Painting*. London: Reaktion, 1996.

——. *The Wu Liang Shrine*. Stanford, Calif.: Stanford University Press, 1989.

Wu Zetian yanjiuhui 武則天研究會 [Wu Zetian Research Association]. "Di 11 jie Wu Zetian yanjiuhui, huiyi taolun lunwenji" 第 11 屆武則天研究會, 會議討論論文集 [Conference Proceedings from the 11th Conference of the Wu Zetian Research Association]. Guangyuan, 2013.

Xiong, Victor Cunrui. *Emperor Yang of the Sui Dynasty: His Life, His Times, His Legacy*. Albany: State University of New York Press, 2006.

——. *Historical Dictionary of Medieval China*. Lanham, Md.: Scarecrow, 2009.

——. "Ritual Innovation and Taoism Under Tang Xuanzong." *T'oung Pao*, Second Series, 82 (1996): 258–316.

——. *Sui-Tang Chang'an: A Study in the Urban History of Medieval China*. Ann Arbor: Center for Chinese Studies, University of Michigan, 2000.

Xu Jinxing 徐金星 and Huang Minglan 黃明蘭, eds. *Luoyang shi wenwu zhi* 洛陽市文物志 [Treatise on the Relics and Antiquities of Luoyang]. Luoyang: Luoyang Cultural Press, 1985.

Xu Jinxing and Xu Guisheng 許桂聲, eds. *He-Luo shihua* 河洛史話 [Tales of the Luo and Yellow Rivers]. Zhengzhou: Zhongzhou guji, 1995.

Yamada Toshiaki. "The Lingbao School." In Kohn, *Daoism Handbook*, 225–55.

Yan Hui 延慧. "Nüwa shenhua yu nüxing" 女媧神話與女性 [The Myth of Nüwa and Womanhood]. *Wenxue yanjiu* 文學研究 no. 3 (2011): 120–21.

Yang, C. K. *Religion in Chinese Society*. Berkeley: University of California Press, 1967.

Yang Lien-sheng. "Female Rulers in Imperial China." *Harvard Journal of Asian Studies* 23 (1960–1961): 47–61.

Yang Lihui 楊利慧. *Nüwa suyuan: Nüwa xinyang qiyuandi de zai tuice* 女媧溯源：女媧信仰起源地的再推測 [The Origin of Nüwa: Another Conjecture on the Nüwa Cult's Place of Origin]. Beijing: Beijing Normal University Press, 1999.

Yang Liu. "Images for the Temple: Imperial Patronage in the Development of Tang Daoist Art." *Artibus Asiae* 61, no. 2 (2001): 189–261.

Yen Chuan-ying, "The Tower of Seven Jewels and Empress Wu." *National Palace Museum Bulletin* 22, no. 1 (March–April 1987): 1–18.

Yoshikawa Tadao 吉川忠夫. *Sho to Dokyo no shuhen* 書と道教の周辺 [Texts and the Parameters of Daoism]. Tokyo: Heibonsha, 1987.

Yoshiko Kamitsuka. "Sokuten buko ki no dokyo" 則天武后期の道教 [Daoism in the Era of Empress Wu]. In *Todai no Shukyo* 唐代の宗教 [Religion in the Tang Dynasty], Research Report of the Institute for Research in Humanities, ed. Yoshikawa Tadao. Kyoto: Kyoto University, 2000.

Young, Serinity. *Courtesans and Tantric Consorts: Sexualities in Buddhist Narrative, Iconography and Ritual.* New York: Routledge, 2004.

Yü Chün-fang. *Kuan-yin: The Chinese Transformation of Avalokiteśvara.* New York: Columbia University Press, 2001.

Yu Yingshi. "New Evidence on the Early Chinese Conception of Afterlife—A Review Article." *Journal of Asian Studies* 41, no. 1 (1981): 81–85.

Zeng Qian 曾謙. "Wu Zetian zaoqi de zongjiao qingxiang yu Lushena dafo de xiujian" 武則天早期的宗教傾向與盧舍那大佛的修建 [Religious Tendencies in the Early Period of Wu Zetian and the Construction of the Giant Rushana Buddha]. *Qianyan* 前沿 [Forward Position] no. 8 (2009): 180–83.

Zhang Jian 張劍. "Wu Zetian shiwen fanying de zhengzhi sixiang zhuzhang" 武則天詩文反映的政治思想主張 [The Political Thought of Wu Zetian as Reflected in Her Poetry and Writings]. In Su Jian and Bai Xianzhang, *Wu Zetian yu Luoyang*, 131–47.

Zhang Jie 張杰. "Wu Zetian yu tade Wushi zongqin" 武則天與她的武氏宗親 [Wu Zetian and Her Relatives from the Wu Clan]. *Hebei shifan daxue xuebao* 河北師範大學學報 [Academic Journal of Hebei Normal University] (1999): 114–18.

Zhang Mingxue 張明學. "Gu Kaizhi zhi 'Luoshen fu tu' zhong de Daojiao shenxian yiyun" 顧愷之洛神賦圖中的道教神仙意蘊 [Connotations of Daoist immortals in Gu Kaizhi's "Picture Scroll of the Luo River Nymph"]. *Shijie zongjiao wenhua* 世界宗教文化 [Religious Cultures of the World] 1, no. 1 (2007): 30–33.

Zhang Naizhu 張乃翥. "Cong Luoyang chutu wenwu kan Wu-Zhou zhengzhi de guojiahua qingcai" 從洛陽出 土文物看武周政治的國際文化情采 [A View of the International Cultural Background of the Politics of the Wu-Zhou Dynasty from the Unearthed Relics in Luoyang]. *Tang Yanjiu* 8 (2002): 205–24.

——. "Luoyang xinji shike suojian Tangdai zhongyuan zhi fojiao" 洛陽新輯石刻所見唐代中原之佛教 [Tang Buddhism of the Central Plains as Reflected in Recently Compiled Stone Carvings from Luoyang]. *Zhongyuan wenwu* 中原文物 [Cultural Relics of the Central Plains] no. 5 (2008): 81–93.

——. "Wu Zetian yu Longmen shiku fojiao zaoxiang" 武則天與龍門石窟佛教造像 [Wu Zetian and the Buddhist Statuary of the Longmen Grottoes]. In Su Jian and Bai Xianzhang, *Wu Zetian yu Luoyang*, 17–31.

——. "Wu-Zhou Wanguo tianshu yu Xiyu wenming" 武周萬國天樞與西域文明 [The Wu-Zhou Axis of Sky of Myriad Nations and the Civilization of the Western

Borderlands]. *Xibei Shidi* 西北史地 [Historical and Geographical Review of Northwest China] no. 2 (1994): 44–45.

——. "Wu-Zhou Zhengquan yu Zhonggu huhua xianxiang guanxi zhi tansuo" 武周政權與中華胡化現象關係之探索 [An Exploration of the Connection Between the Political Authority of the Wu-Zhou Dynasty and Internationalization of Chinese Middle Antiquity]. *Xibei shi di* no. 4 (1992): 31–39.

Zhao Wenrun 趙文潤. "Wu Zetian yu 'wenzhang siyou'" 武則天與文章四友 [Wu Zetian and the Quartet of Literary Friends]. *Qianling wenhua yanjiu* 6 (2011): 51–58.

Zhao Wenrun and Li Yuming 李玉明, eds. *Wu Zetian yanjiu lunwenji* 武則天研究論文集 [Collected Essays on Wu Zetian]. Taiyuan: Shanxi guji, 1998.

Zhao Wenrun and Liu Zhiqing 劉志清, eds. *Wu Zetian yu Yanshi* 武則天與偃師 [Wu Zetian and Yanshi]. Tianjin: Lishi jiaoxue, 1997.

Zhao Wenrun and Xin Jialong 辛加龍, eds. *Wu Zetian yu Xianyang* 武則天與咸陽 [Wu Zetian and Xianyang]. Xi'an: Sanqin, 2000.

Zhao Xiaoxing 趙曉星. "Mogao ku di 9 ku 'Songshan shen song mingtangdian ying tu' kao" 莫高窟第九窟 "嵩山神送明堂殿應圖" 考 [A Study of the Wall Painting in Cave Nine of the Mogao Grottoes of the God of Mount Song Sending a Pillar to the Mingtang]. *Dunhuang yanjiu* 敦煌研究 [Dunhuang Research] no. 3 (2011): 40–43.

Zhao Zhenhua 赵振华. "Zhuchi jianzao Tianshu de waifan renwu yu 'Zilai shi,'" 主持建造天樞的外蕃人物與 '子来使' [The "Come-as-Sons Commissioner" and Foreigners Who Supported the Construction of the Axis of the Sky]. In Wang Shuanghuai and Guo Shaolin, *Wu Zetian yu Shendu Luoyang*, 294–98.

Zhou Yiqun. *Festivals, Feasts, and Gender Relations in Ancient China and Greece*. New York: Cambridge University Press, 2010.

Zürcher, Erik. *The Buddhist Conquest of China*. Leiden: Brill, 1972.

——. "Prince Moonlight: Messianism and Eschatology in Early Medieval Chinese Buddhism." *T'oung Pao* 68 (1982): 1–75.

Index

Page numbers in *italics* indicate illustrations.

abandonment, 276n10
abdication, 41–42
"Absolute Loyalty" (fascicle in *Chen Gui*), 142–43
Admonitions for Women (Nüjie), 62, 75–76, 268n14, 271n3. *See also* Ban Zhao
agelessness, 156–57
agriculture, 97, 99, 100, *100*
Allen, Sarah, 85, 96, 276n10
Altair, 73
altar, 55, 64–65, 71, 186, 270n38
Altar of Audiences (Chaojin), 92
Ames, Roger, 233
Amoghapāśa, 192
Amplifying the Dao (Hongdao reign era) 35–36, 173, 181
Analects (Lunyu), 109, 119, 248n8
ancestors, 277n24; blood, 102–5, 120–22; in pluralistic society, 12–15; political, 1–22, 102, 113, 210, 227–35, *232*; worship of, 5–9
ancestral temples, 100–102, 104, 107–8, 278n39, 280n39
ancestress (*xian bi*), 107, 116
Ancient China (Schafer), 27–28
Anle Princess, 73–74
An Lushan, 234
An Lushan Rebellion, 28
Annals of Dengfeng, 86
Annals of the States of Jing and Chu (Jing-Chu sui shiji), 288n41

Annals of Revelations of Diverse States (Bieguo dongming ji), 153
"Annals of Zhou" (in *Records of the Grand Historian*), 98, 103–4
apocryphal texts, 48, 222, 265n52, 265n57, 307n31
apotheosis, 86
apotropaic purification, 45
apsara, *216*
Ascended Immortal Crown Prince, 91. *See also* Wang Zijin; Zijin
Ascended Immortal Observatory, 159
Aśoka (king), 14–15, 252n67
Atargatis, 26
Attestation Sutra. See Sutra of Attestation
augural stones, 141–42, 214, 263n27. *See also* Precious Diagram
August Heaven Plateau, 173–74
auspicious omens 85, 103, 105, 155, 197, 202, 264n45. *See also* phoenix; white elephant; three-legged bird
avaivartika, 220
Avalokiteśvara cult, 192. *See* Guanyin
Axis of Sky, 48, 285n74
axle. *See* loom

A Bag of Pearls from the Three Caverns (Sandong zhunang), 181
Ban (Han Lady of Handsome Fairness), 112
Ban Zhao, 62, 75–76, 272n12. *See Admonitions for Women*

Barrett, Timothy, 13, 88, 147, 215, 307n33

Bendix, Richard, 5

"Benefiting the People" (fascicle in Regulations for Ministers), 71

"Benevolent Persons" (category of women in History of the Han Dynasty), 95

Benn, Charles, 148, 169, 171–72, 189, 294n49

Bingzhou, 206, 305n68

"Biographies of Empresses and Consorts" (in Chronicles of the Three Kingdoms) 113

Biographies of Exemplary Women (Liu Xiang's Han ed.), 76–78, 98–100, 102, 109, 272n11; paragons in, 125, 136, 228, 233, 272n15; on Woman of Tushan, 80. See also Kuo of Zhao; Wen (mother); Zifa of Chu

Biographies of Exemplary Women (Wu Zhao's ed.), 125, 126, 127, 133–35, 134, 280n2

"Biographies of Exemplary Women" (in History of Jin), 77–78, 82–83

"Biographies of Exemplary Women" (in History of the Wei Dynasty), 82

Biographies of Filial Daughters, 280n2

Biographies of Filial Sons, 127

Biographies of Immortals, 150

"Biographies of the Benign and Wise" (in Liu Xiang's ed. of Biographies of Exemplary Women), 81, 272n8

Biography of King Mu, 150

bird, three-legged, 155, 288n47, 289nn49–50. See also solar crow; sunbird

Birrell, Anne, 23, 26, 85, 149, 229–30

"The Birth of a People" ("Shengmin" in Book of Songs), 96–97, 105

Bi Xiuling, 61, 71, 269n27

Black Spirit, 89

blood ancestor, 102–5, 120–22

Bodhiruci, 202

bodhisattvas (Buddhas-to-be), 186, 192, 219–21, 252n69; feminization of, 213; mother of all, 197

Bo Juyi, 182

Bokenkamp, Stephen, 16, 88, 172

Book of Changes, 50, 113, 278n8

Book of History, 47, 146, 249n11, 263n29

Book of Rites, 132, 234

Book of Songs, 99, 101, 110, 234, 278n8; in connection to "Come-as-sons," 285n74. See also "The Birth of a People"

Book of the Inner Exegesis of the Three Heavens (Santian neijie jing) 198

Book of Transformations of Laozi (Laozi bianhua jing), 168

Boyi, 272n7

Bozhou, 170

Bray, Francesca, 61, 234, 268n14

Bright Hall complexes, 54–55, 153, 229

Brightstar Jade Girl, 297n52

Buddha, 195–97, 196, 199–200, 203–4, 205–6, 210, 211–15, 302n4. See also Laozi; Sutra of the Rain of Jewels; white elephants

Buddha mother, 19, 207. See also Māyā

Buddhapālita, 206, 305n70

Buddharāja (fowang), 252n69

Buddhism, 191, 192–93, 218–19, 228–29, 265n57, 305n74; Daoism and, 169, 191, 308n48; political authority legitimized by, 13–15, 192–93, 299n1, 300n24

Buddhist festival (pañcavārṣika), 14, 224, 252n67

Buddhist goddesses, 193–94. See also Māyā and Vimalaprabhā

Buddhist monks, 202–3, 274n39, 289n49. See also Yijing; Fazang; Xue Huaiyi; Śikṣānanda; Bodhiruci

Buddhist motherhood, 199–200

Buddhist nuns, 203–4, 219

Buddhist propagandists, 20, 300n18. See also Xue Huaiyi; Commentary on the Meanings of the Prophecies About the Divine Sovereign in the Great Cloud Sutra

Buddhist relics (stūpas), 14–15, 307n33

Buddhist rites, 191
Buddhist sovereignty, 308n58. *See also*
    Aśoka; cakravartin; Golden Wheel
Buddhist treasures, 200–202. *See also*
    Daoist relics
butchering, 191
Butler, Judith, 76

Cahill, Suzanne, 151, 164, 165, 185–86,
    306n24
Cai Junsheng, 26–27, 28
Cai Mo, 114
cakravartin, 13–15, 186–87, 211, 220,
    252n69, 306n19
calendar 10, 11, 21, 65, 156
Campany, Robert, 97
Candraprabha (Yueguang), 15, 220,
    308n54
Canetti, Elias, 10–11
can mu. See silkworm mothers
cannibalism, 29
Canon of Filial Piety (Xiaojing), 229
"Canon of Yao" (in *Book of History*),
    260n45
can shen. See silkworm goddess
Cao Pi, 44, 60
Cao Rui, 100, 113
Cao Zhi, 44, 45, 53
cavern heavens (*dongtian*), 182
Celestial Altar, 182
Celestial Emperor. *See* Gaozong
Celestial Empress (title of Wu Zhao) 69,
    267n81, 298n53
celestial light, 154–56
Celestial Masters, 292n3
celestial world, poets and, 147
central Asian steppe cultures, 234
Central Marchmount (Zhongyue),
    79, 80
Central Peak of Five Marchmounts.
    See Mount Song
ceremonial dance, 31–32
Chang, K. C., 5
Chang'an, 231, 270n38, 275n70
Chang E, 73, 74, 150, 155
Chao Fu, 295n17

chapels (*neidaochang*), 192, 300n18
characters (invented in 689), 11, 21,
    155–56, 217
charity, 252n67
Charleux, Isabelle, 207
chastity, cult of, 231
Chen, Jack, 7–8, 235
Cheng (Han emperor), 112
Cheng Chubi, 266n60
Chengdu, 81
Chen gui. See Regulations for Ministers
Cheng of Zhou (king), 279n26
Cheng Tang, 279n14, 280n33
Cheng Zhijie, 266n60
Chen Jinhua, 191, 205, 215, 300n18,
    305n70
Chen Jo-shui, 62–63, 69, 231, 270n46
Chen Shou, 113
Chen Yinke, 192
Chen Zhenjie, 85, 107
Chenzhou, 152
Chen Zi'ang, 118–19, 123, 229, 266n60,
    273n22; on Laozi, 92; memorial of, 52,
    276n72; vocabulary created by, 36–37
chickens, 3, 249n11
children, 75, 271n2
Chinese Buddhism. *See* Buddhism
Chiu-Duke, Josephine, 128, 134–35,
    282n21, 283n47
Chong (earl), 272n3
Chronicle of Dragon Ladies
    (Longnüzhuan), 46
Chronicles of the Three Kingdoms (Sanguo
    zhi) 113
Chu (Warring States era state), 77
Chuigong (reign era), 146
Chu Suanzi, 114
Chuzhou, 287n31
cinnabar, 183, 188
civic duty, 126
Classic of Filial Piety (Xiaojing), 127
Classic of Mountains and Seas (Shanhai
    jing), 26, 86, 149, 152, 229–30
Clear Purity. *See* Jinpyeong
"Climbing the Celestial Altar to View
    the Sea at Night" (Li Yi), 182

cloak, 161, 291n84

Coiling Dragon Terrace stele inscription, 84, 121–22

coins, 270n40

Collected Records of Court and Country (Chaoye jianzai), 105

come-as-sons (zi lai) idea, 285n74

Commentary on the Meanings of the Prophecies About the Divine Sovereign in the Great Cloud Sutra (Dayunjing shenhuang shouji yishu), 48, 57, 183, 186–87, 204, 209–26

Communing with Heaven Palace (Tongtian gong), 201

Como, Michael, 288nn41–42, 289n49

compass (gui), 26, 279n17

Complete Anthology of Tang Poetry (Quan Tangshi), 92, 266n72

Complete Anthology of Tang Prose (Quan Tangwen),185

Composition of Pearls (Bianzhu), 288n41

Comprehensive Commentary on Popular Customs (Fengsu tongyi), 26, 35

Comprehensive Mirror for the Advancement of Governance (Zizhi tongjian), 32, 105, 170, 219

concubines, 310n11

Confucian authority, of widowhood, 128–29

Confucianism, 9–11, 228–29, 230, 248n8; Buddhism's subordination of, 218–19; Daoism placed above, 169; women influenced by, 75–76

Confucian mothers, 18–19, 128–29

Confucian values, 124–25, 128–29. See also weaving-government analogy

Confucius, 6, 218–19, 248n8, 249n25, 283n37; investment of, 11; on Ji of Lu, 132. See also Analects

Consort Fu. See Luo River Goddess

consorts, 113

Convent of Devi (Tiannü nisi), 211

Cook, Constance, 5–6

coup, 107, 277n37

courtesans, 231

Court of State Ceremonial, 191

crane, 159, 291n86

"Crane" (Li Qiao), 164

Cui Rong, 29–31; edict drafted by, 273n21; effusion of, 161, 163; inscription of, 87–90, 92, 172–73, 181; memorials of, 33–34, 36, 53, 56, 84, 85–86, 92, 120; poem of, 291n88

Cui Shen, 152

Cui Shu, 218, 308n45

Cui Xuanwei, 277n37

Cundī, 301n30

Daizong (Tang emperor), 185

damming, 159

dance, 31–32

dao, 145–46, 147

Daodejing (Laozi), 145–46, 186

Daoism, 191, 228–29, 265n57, 308n48; Tang, 169–70; Tushan women elevated by, 90–92

Daoist canon, 181

Daoist convent, 91

Daoist divinities, 147, 182, 237

Daoist emperorship, 12–13, 149–51

Daoist establishment, 92, 145, 173–75, 180–81

Daoist governance, 145,

Daoist monasteries, 86

Daoist nuns, 91

Daoist observatory, 275n58

Daoist paradise, 157–66, 162

Daoist relics, 186–87. See also Buddhist treasures; white elephants

Daoists, 90–92, 212

Daoxuan, 197

Dark Tortoise plateau, 186

daughters, 73–74, 75

Day of Humans, 288n41

Dazu (reign era), 277n31

Declarations of the Perfected, 180

Degan, 305n68

deities. See divinities

demiurge, 168–69

demiurgic energy, 195

Deng (Han empress), 78, 272n12

Despeux, Catherine, 167–68, 265n57

devas, 223

Devi of Pure Radiance. See Jingguang

devis, 194, 209–10, 219, 230, 301n29; identification with, 221; prophecies and, 211–15

Dhāraṇī Sūtra of the Buddha's Crowning Victory, 206

Dharmakṣema, 305n3

"Diagram Regurgitated by the Dragon" (Longtu tu) 214

Di Ku, 34

Di Renjie, 291n84

Distant Vision (Jiushi reign era), 157

Divākara, 301n30

Divine Capital (Shendu). See Luoyang

divine footprint, 105–6

divine mother (shenmu), 204–5. See also Māyā

Divine Palace of Myriad Images, 309n68

Divine Peak. See Mount Song

divine wife, 180

The Divine Woman (Schafer), 16–17, 46, 259n18

divinities, 67, 182, 197, 229–30, 235, 276n10; female, 23–24, 147, 172–73, 229–30; of three faiths, 13–15. See also Daoist divinities; Four Divinities

Di Yi, 279n8

Dizang, 192

"Domestic Rules" ("Neize" in Book of Rites), 132

Dongfang Shuo, 150, 153, 166

Dong Zhongshu, 56

Doran, Rebecca, 50, 55, 226, 247n2, 264n45

Dou (Ruizong's consort, posthumously named empress), 85, 107, 116, 117–18, 207–8, 278n2

dowager, 31–32, 136

dragonspawn, 38–39, 261n71

dream conception, 203–4

drought, 45, 184

Duan Tali, 128

Du Doucheng, 217

Du Gongzhan, 288n41

Dugu (Sui empress), 265n56

Duke of Zhou, 2, 11, 47, 103, 249n25

Du Guangting, 46, 156, 158–59, 179–80, 290n69, 293n25; on Li (mother), 168, 171; on Nine Tripods, 182–83

Du Mu, 46

Dunhuang grottoes, 191, 206, 216

Du You, 269n15

dynastic mothers, 98–102, 100, 237

earth god, sacrifice to, 157

Eastern Capital, 182. See also Luoyang

Ehuang, 60, 71, 81, 82, 83, 122, 268n1, 272n11, 279n10

Elegies of Chu (Chuci), 25. See also Qu Yuan

elephants, 200–205. See also white elephants

Eliade, Mircea, 9, 72, 105

emperor, 1–5, 4, 6, 12–13, 87, 175–76

Emperor of Central Heaven, 90

empire, 5–9

Empress Day, 38

empresses, 31–32, 114, 116, 117–18, 310n11

Empress of Central Heaven, 90

"Enchanting Miss Wu," 212, 306n18

"Examining the fire pearl atop the Bright Hall" (Cui Shu), 218

extended self, 24

extraordinary woman (feichang furen), 115

faiths, 228–29

Fajing, 309n67

family, 5–9, 128–29, 142–43

"Family Genealogies" (in Records of the Grand Historian), 110

famine, 29

Fang Xuanling, 35, 62, 77–78, 82–83, 272n12

Fan Ye, 77, 265n56

fathers, 80–81, 176–77

Fazang, 202, 307n34

Fei (Northern Qi emperor), 304n62

female adepts, 184

female body, 219–21

female divinities, 23–24, 147, 172–73, 229–30
female exemplars, 125–28
female political ancestors, 1–22, 102, 113, 210, 227–35, *232*
female potency, 229–30
female sovereign, 231–32, *232*
Feng (Wei empress), 175
Feng (Zhou capital), 8
feng and *shan* rites, 115–16, 117–18, 153, 260n44, 275n62, 279n26
fenghuang. See phoenix
Fengxian Observatory, 40–41
Fengxian Temple, 225
Fifth Master. *See* Zhang Yizhi
filial piety (*xiao*), 126, 134–35, 142–43
filicide, 75
finial, 218
First Agriculturalist altar (*xiannong tan*), 71
First Sericulturist (*xian can*), 60–72, *64*, *67*, 153–54, 231, 270n38, 270n46. *See also* Leizu
Five Classics, 233, 248n8
Five Impediments (*wuzhang*), 213
Five Marchmounts, 266n59
Five Phases (*wuxing*), 60, 183, 204, 265n57, 270n40
Five Precepts, 213
five princes (*wu wang*), 107, 277n37
flock of kingfishers, cloak, 161
flood, 26, 80, 159, 258n9. *See also* Yu the Great
The Flood Myths of Early China (Lewis), • 80–81, 273n8
Flower Garland Sutra (Huayan jing), 197, 202–3, 205, 304n40
Flower Maid. *See* Huang Lingwei
footprint (*lü di*), 104, 105–6
Foremost Sage (*xian sheng*), 249n25
Forte, Antonino, 51, 186–87, 202, 204, 209, 211, 220, 222, 223, 224, 267n82, 267n90, 305n3, 307n41
The Fountainhead of Chinese Erotica, 291n88
Four Marchmounts, 266n59
four virtues (*side*), 268n14

fowang. See Buddharāja
Frankfort, Henri, 150–51
Frazer, James George, 24
Fu. *See* Luo River Goddess
Fuqiu (duke), 159, 161
Future Pure Radiance, 219
Fuxi, 26, *27*, 32, 33, 34, 275n52. *See also* Nüwa; Yellow River Chart
Fuzhou, 184–88

galactic polity, 308n58
Gandhāra, 198
Gao Pu, 89
Gao Shiyu, 231
Gao Ying, 107–8
Gaozong (Tang emperor), 2, 47, 90, 106, 129, 225, 260n43; death of, 29–30, 31–32, 40–41, 119, 174–75; edict promulgated by, 35–36; illness of, 126–27; inscription of, 40–41, 83; petition to, 115–16, 117. *See also* Li Zhi, Two Sages
Gaozu (Tang emperor), 13, 39, 122, 169
Garrison of Imperial Bodyguards. *See* Institute for Reining Cranes
Gate of Solemn Righteousness, 65
gender, 95–96, 143, 221, 226; Buddhism and, 14, 178, 193, 213, 221–22, 226, 300n11; Chinese and Western differences in, 233; labor and 60–61, 72
"Genealogies of Prime Ministers" (in *New Tang History*), 102–3
Genealogies of the Perfected (Zhenxi), 296n30
generals, 137–40, 284n58. *See also* "Good Generals"; Mother of Kuo of Zhao; Mother of Zifa of Chu
generalship, 137–41
Gernet, Jacques, 209–10
ghostbuster (*yiguizhe*), 106–7
goddesses, 23, 73–74, 88, 193–94, 237. *See also* female divinities
gold, 14
Golden Age, 9–11; and Mother Wen, 120, 122, 123

golden age, rite and, 10–11
The Golden Bough (Frazer), 24
golden sparrow, 152
golden tally, 298n61
Golden Tower, 91–92,172, 275n68, 294n30
Golden Wheel, 192, 220
Goldtower (lady), 91
Goldtower Gate, 91
Goldtower Pavilion, 91
Gongliu, 107–8
"Good Generals" (fascicle in *Regulations for Ministers*), 136–41, *140*
Goujian of Yue (king), 138
Goushi County, 159
Grand Canal, 47
Grand Dowager of Anterior Heaven, 171, 174–75, 183, 228
Grand Dowager of Jade Capital, 90–91
grand dowagers, 173–75, 233
"Grand *huo*," 277n16
great cloud, 225–26
Great Cloud (bodhisattva), 210,
Great Cloud (monastery), 214–15, 260n37
Great Cloud Sutra, 209–10, 211–15, *216*, 217. *See also Commentary on the Meanings of the Prophecies About the Divine Sovereign in the Great Cloud Sutra*
Greater Room (Taishi), 80, 86, 93, 159. *See also* Mount Song
Great Footprint (reign era), 105–6. *See also* Dazu
Great Spell of Unsullied Pure Radiance (Wugou jingguang tuoluonijing), 215, 217
Great Zhou Catalog of Buddhist Scriptures (Da Zhou kanding zhongjing mulu) 198, 200–201
Green Fields (Qingtian), 164
grottoes, 191, 206–7, *216*, 305n71
guan. *See* ritual tube; white jade
Guangwu inscription, 212
Guangyuan 38–39
Guangzhai (reign era), 174–75
Guanxiu, 188
Guanyin, 300n11, 306n24

Guanzhong 47
Guanzhong families, 47
Guidance City (Huacheng), 223
Guishui River, 78, 83, 102, 122
Guisso, Richard, 31, 193, 233, 300n24
Gu Kaizhi, 44–45, *45*, 262n11
Gu Kuang, 207
Guṇabhadra, 301n29
Guo Pu, 275n53
Guo Xian, 150
Guozhou, 173–74, 294n35
Guyang County. *See* Zhenyuan County
Gu Yanwu, 274n38
Gu Yewang, 88
Gu Zhengmei, 175–76

Hall, David, 233
Han court, 78
Han Gan, 231
Han Wendi, 62
Han Wudi, 79, 150, 154, 159, 165
Hanyuan Basilica, 308n49
Haotian shangdi, 264n44
headdress, 44, 150, 235, 288nn41–42. *See also sheng*
heaven, 30, 85–86
"Heaven-bestowed Diagram of the Sage." *See* Precious Diagram
Heaven Bestowed (Tianshou reign era), 215, 217
Heaven's Ford Bridge, 49
Henei, 40, 183, 188, 219
Highest Clarity Palace, 180
Hinsch, Bret, 60, 61, 72, 283n42
Historical Records Exalting Daoism (Lidai chongdao ji), 173–74
History of the Han Dynasty (Han shu), 50, 79, 87
History of Jin (Jin shu), 35, 62, 77–78, 82–83
History of the Sui Dynasty (Sui shu), 63, 260n45
History of the Wei Dynasty (Wei shu), 82
Holmgren, Jennifer, 128
homage to stone, 79, 80
hometown, 206, 262n74

hoofprint, 308n49

Hou Ji, 8, 77, 83, 96–98, *100*, 108, 273n17. *See also* Qi, Lord Millet

households, 250n48

Hsi-ling, 269n27

Hu (Wei empress), 198

Huainan, 163

Huainanzi, 26, 28–29, 79, 150

Huaizhou, 181–84

Huandi (Han emperor), 251n54

Huang Lingwei, 184–88

Huangze Temple, 38, *39*

Huan Yanfan, 277n37, 283n47

Huanyuan Pass, 86

Huaxu, 88, 275n52

Huazhu, 89

Hu Chao, 157, 186, 187, 188, 189

Hufa. *See* Jingguang

Hui (Han emperor), 41

Hu Ji, 193, 217

Hu Sanxing, 32–33, 170

Hu Yanqing, 297n52

Illustration of Opposing Backs (Tuibeitu), 214

immortality, 156–66, *162*, 294n49

Immortal Maiden, 290n66

Immortals and Gods of the Wang Clan (Wangshi shenxian zhuan), 290n69

imperial crown prince (*shaoyang*), 281n13

inaugural address, 174–75

Indra, 303n28

inexhaustible storehouse (*wujin cang*), 192, 300n17

infanticide, 276n9

Inner Chapters of Mystery and Wonder (Xuanmiao neipian), 198

Institute of Reining Cranes (Konghejian), 161, 163, 229, 291n82

Iravati River, 303n38

Irwin, Lee, 26

Iryeon, 199

Jabi (king), 302n17

jade, 152–54, 270n40

Jade Capital (Yujing), 90–91

Jade Verity, 158

Jajang, 199

Jambudvipa, 212, 306n19

Japan, 215, 250n34, 289n49

Jia Jinhua, 166

Jiandi, 34, 96, 114, 273n16, 279n14

Jiang Yonglin, 9

Jiang Yuan, 95, 96–108, *100*, 118, 273n17, 278n39

Jiaye Zhizhong, 70

Ji clan, 78, 102–3, 108, 121, 282n28

Jihu people, 308n54

Jin (Zhou prince), 91, 157–66, *162*, 290n69, 290n73, 291n83

Jingguang, 210, 211–15, *216*, 228, 237; gender and, 226; name of, 217; reincarnation and, 226, 234. *See also Commentary on the Meanings of the Prophecies About the Divine Sovereign in the Great Cloud Sutra*; Pure Radiance

Jing Jiang. *See* Ji of Lu

Jin Hui, 277n37

Jinpyeong, 198–99

Jin Wudi, 45–46

Ji of Lu (lady), 130–36, *131*, *134*, 235, 237, 282n28

Ji Shanxing, 169

Jiu Tangshu. See Old Tang History

Jñāngupta, 205

Kagan, Richard, 177

Karetzky, Patricia, 44–45, 191, 205, 213, 225

Kasyapa, 196

Khitan, 137

King Father of East, 151

kingfishers cloak, 291n84

King of Central Heaven, 90

kingship, 12–15, 211

Kinney, Anne, 76, 97, 276n9

Kirkland, Russell, 180, 186

Knauer, Elfriede, 149, 286n2, 288n41

Ko, Dorothy, 76

Koguryo, 199, 260n43

Kohn, Livia, 180

Kongwang, 307n41
Kory, Stephan, 52
Kōtoku (emperor), 289n49
Kou Qianzhi, 13
Ku (emperor), 96, 102
Ku, Kathy Cheng-mei, 14
Kuhn, Dieter, 60–61, 62, 269n27
Kunlun (mountain) 150, 153
Kuodizhii. See Treatise of the Vast Earth
Kuo of Zhao (general). *See* mother of
    Kuo of Zhao
Kybele, 286n2, 288n41
Kyoto Museum, 153

Lady of Southern Marchmount.
    See Wei Huacun
Lagerway, John, 12
Lao (lord). *See* Laozi
Laojun, 293n20
Laojun Temples, 170, 174–75
Lao-tzu Goddess, 146
Laozi (Lao Tzu), 12–13, 40, 145–46,
    147, 157, 161, 163, 168, 169–70,
    173–74, 178, 180, 186, 198, 293n25; as
    ancestor, 293n9; as Buddha's disciple,
    308n48; cult of, 294n49; father of,
    176–77; hometown of, 262n74; as
    sage, 293n17; tomb of, 92. *See also*
    Laojun; Li (mother); Li Er; Li Hong;
Later Han History, 77, 265n56
learned instructresses, 128–29, 282n22
Leizu, 17, *64*, *67*, 122–23, 227, 235, 237,
    269n27; aura surrounding, 72; cults
    of, 61; overview of, 60–62; sacrifices
    to, 62–72
Lesser Clear Barrens Grotto (Xiaoyou
    qingxu), 182
lesser goddesses, 73–74
Lesser Room (Xiaoshi), 56, 86–87, 93,
    158, 275n62
Lewis, Mark, 9, 42, 50, 80–81
Li (mother), 167–70, 173–78, 232, 237,
    292n4. *See also* Grand Dowager of
    Anterior Heaven
Liang Wudi, 14, 252n69
Lian Po, 139, 140

Li Bo, 28, 158, 296n30
Li clan, 145, 176. *See also* Li family, House
    of Tang
Li Dan, 173, 200, 271n56. *See also* Ruizong
Li Deyi, 40
Li Er, 13, 167
Liezi, 26
Li family, 13, 40–41, 147–48, 173–75,
    293n9
Li Gongxie, 40
Li Hexian, 126
Li Hong, 75, 91, 199–200
Li Ji, 115–16, *117*, 117–18, 123, 279n22
Li Jing, 176–77
Li Lingxuan, 32
Li Longji, 84
Ling (Zhou king), 103, 277n23
Lingwei (duke), 161
Linyi, 200
Li princes, 40–41
Li Qiao, 30–31, 164, 204, 259n36, 297n52;
    inscription of, 84; on Precious
    Diagram, 52–53, 57
Li Ruyi, 40
"Li Sao," 43–44
Li Shan, 44
Li Shangyin, 37–38, 151
Li Shenji, 40, 41
Li Tai, 274
literary masters. *See* propagandists
Li Tong, 89, 275n54
Little Auntie. *See* Shaoyi
Liu (Tang empress), 85
Liu An, 26, 150, 163
liu shang. See Six Matrons
Liu Sung, 14
Liu Xiang, 150. *See also Biographies of
    Exemplary Women*
Liu Yizhi, 91, 126
Liu Yu, 13
*Lives of Eminent Monks (Song Gaoseng
    zhuan)*, 215
Li Xián, 75, 87–88, 127
Li Xiǎn, 31, 40–41, 56, 87, 88, 163, 173.
    See also Zhongzong
Li Yi, 182

Li Zhaode, 264n33
Li Zhi, 8
Li Zu'e, 205, 304n62
Loewe, Michael, 150, 288n41
Lofty and Pacific Senior Princess
   (Gao'an changgognzhu), 284n49
longevity potion, 157, 187
Longlife Hill, 8
Longmen grottoes, 191, 224–25
Longtai, 173–74
Longxing Observatory, 294n31
loom, 130–36, 131, 134, 153–54, 283n42
Lord on High, 97
Lord Millet 8, 18
loyalty (zhong), 134–36, 142–43, 283n47.
   See also Regulations for Ministers
Lü (Han empress), 41
Lu Cangyong, 73
lü di. See footprint
Lü Huayu, 142
Lu Jingchun, 183–84, 188, 296n36
Lunar Pure-radiance, 219–21
Lunar Radiance, 220, 308n54
Luo Binwang, 2–3, 189, 248n7
Luo River, 23, 49–55, 214. See also
   Consort Fu
Luo River goddess, 229, 237, 262n20,
   266n58; inscription and, 56–57;
   overview of, 43–46, 57–59; picture of,
   44–45, 45; in rhetoric, 56–57; stele,
   56–57; in text, 56–57; trysts with, 46
Luo River Writing, 50–51, 53, 227,
   265n57. See also Precious Diagram
Luoyang, 163, 174, 182, 218, 219, 263n29;
   elevation of, 47–49; sanctification of,
   43, 47–49
Lu Tong, 93
Lu Yuanming, 88
Lu Zhaolin, 79

Ma (Han empress), 72, 78
Ma (master), 306n12
magpie bridge, 73
Mahācīna, 206
Mahāmegha, 210
maid, 310n11

Mair, Victor, 195
Maitreya, 192, 219, 221–24, 226, 260n37
Mañjuśrī, 199, 206, 305n68, 305n70
Mann, Susan, 23–24, 233
Maoshan, 179–80
Mao Ying, 180
Marquise Who Reveals the Sage. See
   Consort Fu
matriarchs, as martial, 136–41, 139, 140,
   233–34
Matters of Renunciation in the
   Mūlasarvāstivāda Vinaya (Genben
   shuo yiqie youbu Binaiye zashi),
   203–4
Māyā, 195–98, 196, 199, 200–208
Māyā (lady), 198–99
Ma Yuanzhen, 306n12
McMullen, David, 12
McNair, Amy, 225
McNeill, William, 23
memorial, 34, 52, 57, 276n72, 282n26. See
   also Cui Rong
Mencius, 18, 77, 130, 133–35, 134
metaphor of axle, 130–36, 131, 134
Mingdi (Han emperor), 62
Ming (Jin emperor), 44–45, 45
Mingwang, 307n41
ministers, 100–102, 109, 116, 118–20,
   135–36
Ministry of Rites, 184, 191
Miscellaneous Morsels from Youyang
   (Youyang zazu), 289n50
Miscellaneous Records of the Taiping Era
   (Taiping guangji),106–7, 152, 155
Miscellany from the Mūlasarvāstivāda
   Vinaya (Yijing), 204
Mitraśānta, 215, 307n34
"Models of Maternal Rectitude" ("Muyi,"
   opening chapter in Biographies of
   Exemplary Women), 76–78, 98–100,
   130, 136–37
Mogao grottoes. See Dunhuang grottoes
monasteries, 86, 191, 214–15, 260n37
monks, 202–3, 207, 274n39, 289n49,
   290n66
moon, 154, 155–56

mortality, 156–57
Mother and Sagely Thearch, 214
motherhood, 134–35, 141–43, 199–200,
    232–34, 285n74
mother of Kuo of Zhao, 136–37, 139–41,
    140, 233–34, 237, 272n8
Mother of Mencius, 133–35, 134, 136,
    237, 283n42
Mother Meng. See Mother of Mencius
Mother of Qi. See Woman of Tushan
Mother Wen 83, 104, 109, 111, 115–23,
    117, 176, 228, 237, 278n2, 278n8;
    in memorial, 34; as paragon of
    womanhood, 110–15
mother of Zifa of Chu, 78, 136–39, 139,
    140–41, 233–34, 237
mothers, 128–29, 134–41, 139, 140,
    196–97, 232–34; demiurge, 168–69;
    dynastic, 98–102, 100, 237; goddess,
    88; overview of, 75–78; sons
    influenced by, 76, 80–81; state
    preserved by, 282n21; three, 112–13;
    twinned, 173–75; as virtuous, 95.
    See also Buddha mother; Confucian
    mothers; Kuo of Zhao; Mother of
    Mencius; Zifa of Chu
mountains, 3, 86, 150, 181. See also
    Mount Goushi; Mount Song
Mount Beimang, 169
Mount Felicity (Qingshan), 204
Mount Goushi, 103–4, 158–59, 160
Mount Kunlun, 294nn30–31, 297n52
Mount Mang, 69, 170–71, 180
Mount Song, 51, 157–58, 159–60, 189,
    274n39. See also Woman of Tushan
Mount Tai, 260n44, 279n26
Mount Tiantai, 183
Mount Wangwu, 182–83, 296n29
Mount Wutai, 199, 206–7
Mount Yan, 150, 152
Mozi, 50, 85
mu. See tomb
Mu (Southern Qi empress), 82, 114
Mu (Zhou king), 150, 152, 165
Mujian inscription, 183–84
Mūlasarvāstivāda Vinaya, 203–5

mulberries, 69–70
"Mulberry Branch Song" (sangtiao ge),
    69–70
mulberry leaves, 153
Mu of Qin (duke), 73
murder, 75, 224
mushroom (zhi), 56, 85–86, 267n82
music, of heaven, 85–86
musical instruments, 260n45
"Music to Honor the Luo River with a
    Grand Sacrifice," 54–55
Mysterious Girl of Nine Heavens (Jiutian
    xuannü), 292n4
Mysterious Woman (Xuannü), 183, 188
Myth and Reality (Eliade), 72, 105

Narendrayaśas, 15
Narrative of States (Guoyu), 282n28,
    283n37, 287n37
neidaochang. See chapel
Nelson, Sarah Milledge, 15, 45
New Tang History (Xin Tangshu), 63,
    102–3, 126–27, 183–84, 204, 304n40,
    306n18
Nihon Shoki, 289n49
Nine Tripods, 48, 85, 183, 201, 291n87,
    296n29, 303n37
Ning Qiang, 225
nirvana, after death (paranirvāṇa), 205–6
Niu Fengji, 54, 266n72
noblewomen, 64; ritual involvement of
    62–65, 117
Nongyu, 73, 74Nüdeng, 88–89, 275n52
nuns, 91, 184, 203–4, 219
Nüwa, 25–38, 27, 40–42, 237, 260n45,
    272n1
Nüying, 272n11, 279n10
Nylan, Michael, 110

Offerings of Jade and Silk (Wechsler), 12
Old Tang History (Jiu Tangshu), 31–32,
    90–91, 176–77, 265n56, 276n75,
    291n81, 291n88
omens, 56, 155
Omitted Events of the Three Kingdoms
    Period (Samguk yusa), 199

oracle bones, 5, 149
original forefather (*yuan fu*), 277n24
Origin of Records (Zaichu reign era),
    10–11
Orthodox Patterns for Princes (Shaoyang
    zheng fan), 127
Otagi Hajime, 184
Ouyang Xiu, 204
Oxherd Boy, 73

Paekche, 199
Palace of Nine Perfections, 91
pañcavārṣika. See Buddhist festival
Pan Shizheng, 86, 181
paranirvāṇa. See nirvana, after death
patriarchal authority, 130
Pearce, Scott, 13–14
Pearls and Blossoms of the Three Faiths
    (Sanjiao zhuying), 163, 229
Pei (Southern Qi imperial consort), 114
Pei Yaoqing, 85
Penetrating Heaven Palace
    (Tongtiangong), 153
Penetrating Heaven Terrace
    (Tongtiantai), 153
peony (as symbol of Luoyang), 46
Perpetual and Eternal Luo. *See* Luo River
Persia, 202
petition, 33–34, 41–42, 115–16, 117
Pettit, Jonathan, 87
phoenix, 52–53, 152–54, 287n37
Phoenix Regulator (Yifeng reign era),
    152
Piao, 202
pillar, 153, 197
Ping (Zhou king), 103–4
Pingyang Princess, 115
pitch pipes, 276n15
Plaks, Andrew, 25
Plan for an Emperor (Difan), 8, 250n34
plot, 127
pluralistic society, 12–15
poetry, 7–9, 70
poets, 147, 151
political ancestors, 1–22, 102, 113, 210,
    227–35, 232

political authority, 13–15, 20–21, 122,
    192–93, 299n1, 300n24
*Political Propaganda and Ideology in China
    at the End of the Seventh Century*
    (Forte), 209, 267n82, 305n3
political sons, 75, 127–28. *See also
    Biographies of Exemplary Women;
    Regulations for Ministers*
polo, 231
potion, 157, 187, 289n57
power blocs, 47
Precious Diagram (Bao tu), 49–54, 58,
    264n48, 267n76
precious elephant, 201
*Preface to the Former Collection of
    Miraculous Records of the Forest of Zen*
    (Chanlin miaoji qianji xu), 199
priestesses, 165
primitive spirit, 149–51
primordial entity. *See* dao
Prince of Buddha Light. *See* Xuanzang
Prince Jin, 91, 104; Zhang Changzong
    and 157–66. *See also* Ascended
    Immortal Prince; Wang Zijin
princes, 40–41, 103, 107, 120–21, 277n37
propagandists, 20, 28–31, 300n18,
    304n40, 306n19
prophecy (*shouji*), 199, 211–15. *See also
    Commentary on the Meanings of the
    Prophecies About the Divine Sovereign in
    the Great Cloud Sutra
Prophecy of Master Ma of the Central Peak,*
    211
proto-feminist agenda, 270n46
Protracted Longevity era, 156–57
public-mindedness, 126, 144
"Public-mindedness and Rectitude"
    (fascicle in *Regulations for Ministers*),
    126
Puett, Michael, 105–6
Pure Radiance, 215–17, *216,* 219, 222–23
purification, 45–46

Qaghan, Ilterish, 137
Qin (first emperor Qinshihuang), 6, 87
Qin (as one of Warring States), 137–39

Qingmiao, 198
Qi of Xia (emperor), 85–86, 90, 103, 272n7, 273n8, 276n11; birth of, 79, 98–100; overview of, 79–81. *See also* Woman of Tushan
Queen Mother of West, 156–66, *162*, 228, 229, 237, 286n2. *See also* bird, three-legged; headdress; Mount Wangwu; solar crow; sunbird
Qu Yuan, 25, 43–44

Rain of Jewels. See Sutra of Rain of Jewels
Ram's Horn Peak (Yangjiaoshan), 169
Raphals, Lisa, 95, 131, 134, 138, 282n22, 282n28
Realities and Categories of Highest Clarity (Shangqing daolei shixiang), 181
recluse, 152, 291n86
Record of Heaven-bestowed Diagram of the Sage, 55
Record of Master Yitong, 57
Record of Penetrating Mysteries (Dongming ji), 150
Records of Mount Songgao, 88
Records of the Grand Historian (Shiji), 79, 103–4, 110, 111
Records of Traces of Saints on Celestial Altar Peak of Mount Wangwu (Du Guangting), 182–83
Red Emperor, 88–89
reform, 282n26
Register of the Assembled Transcendents of the Walled City (Tiantan Wangwushan shengji ji), 46, 168
Regulations for Ministers (Chen Gui), 71, 119–20, 125–28, 143–44, 146; loom lessons, 130–36, *131*, *134*; maternal rectitude models in, 130–36, *131*, *134*; political position buttressed by, 281n12
regulator (*yi*), 152
reincarnation, 226, 234
relics, 14–15, 186–87, 307n33
resurrection, 44. *See also* reincarnation
retirement, 41–42
revolt, 40–41, 308n54

"Rhapsody of a Great Man" (Sima Xiangru), 154
"Rhapsody of the Luo Goddess" (Cao Zhi), 44
rhetoric, 56–57, 154–56
rhetoricians. *See* propagandists
rice cakes, 138
rings, 152, 287n31
rites, golden age and, 10–11
Rites of Zhou, 6, 11, 47, 101
ritual, 45–46, 176–77, 270n40
ritual tube (*guan*), 287n32
River Chart (Hetu), 53
River Guishui. *See* Guishui River
Robinet, Isabel, 179, 180
Robson, James, 179
Ru Chun, 44
Ruizong (Tang emperor), 31, 85, 128, 175, 187, 278n2. *See* Li Dan
ruler-minister dynamic, 146–47. *See also Regulations for Ministers*
rulers, 80–81, 126, 200–205, 248n5. *See also Commentary on the Meanings of the Prophecies About the Divine Sovereign in the Great Cloud Sutra; Great Cloud Sutra*
Runzhou 184
Ruzhou hot springs, 86

sacred field altar, 270n54
sacred topography, 51, 86, 93
sacrifices, 53, 90, 100–102, 172, 176–77, 250n48; creation of, 97; to earth god, 157; to Leizu, 62–72; Two Sages influenced by, 58. *See also feng* and *shan* rites; Leizu
sage (*sheng*), 12–15, 175–76, 197, 293n17. *See also* Two Sages
sage-kings, 51, 57, 82, 201–2
Sagely and Divine Emperor (Shengshen huangdi), 176
Sage Mother (Shengmu), 17, 141–42, 175–76
sage mother (*shengmu*), 205
sage-rulers, 51–52, 80–81, 82
saintly mother (*shengmu*), 175–76
Śākya clan, 199

Śākyamuni, 206
Samanthabhadra, 223
"The Same Organism" (fascicle in
    Regulations for Minsiters), 126, 146
sanctification, of Luo River, 49–55
sangtiao ge. See "Mulberry Branch Song"
sangu. See Three Solitaries
Sanzang, 200, 205, 303n23
Śāriputra, 221
Schafer, Edward, 26, 27–28, 43, 46, 73,
    146, 147, 259n18
Schimmel, Solomon, 1
Schipper, Kristofer, 146, 168, 178
scholar-recluse, 152
Scholars of the Northern Gate (Beimen
    xueshi), 91, 126–27, 143, 281n13
Secret Jade Tally Record (Yuzhang bi
    jue), 168
Seidel, Anna, 12–13, 168
Selections of Refined Literature
    (Wenxuan), 44
self-fashioning, 235
Sen Tansen, 193
Seondok (Sillan queen), 198–99, 302n17
sericulture, 60–61, 269n15. See also Leizu
sericulturist. See First Sericulturist
sexism, 233
Shaanbei, 308n54
Shaanxi, 117
Shandong, 47
Shang dynasty, 5, 96–97, 103
Shang gods, 249n14
Shangguan Wan'er, 70, 73–74
Shangguan Yi, 265n56
Shangqing Abbey, 170–71
Shangqing Daoism, 91–92. See also Daoist
    establishment; Wei Huacun
Shangyang Palace, 91, 107
shan rites. See feng and shan rites
Shao Sheng, 73
shaoyang. See imperial crown prince
Shaoyi, 86–87
Shaping the Lotus Sutra, 157
sheatfish, 183–84, 296n36
Shen (ancient state), 278n8
sheng. See crown; sage

sheng headdress 152–53; golden victory
    headdress (jin sheng), 153–54
shengmu. See sage mother; saintly
    mother
shenmu. See Māyā
Shennong, 35, 71, 201, 269n16, 275n52,
    287n34
Sheshou, 279n26
Shi Anchang, 155
Shi Jiao, 285n9
Shizi, 285n9
"Shizong" (Wu Zhao), 164
shouji. See prophecy
shrines, 87–90, 159, 183–84, 187
Shun (emperor), 108, 272n11
Shuowen jiezi, 32, 33
side. See four virtues
Śikṣānanda, 197, 202–3, 205, 302n5,
    304n40, 307n34
silk, 70, 152–54, 269n15. See also First
    Sericulturist
silk divinities, 67
Silk Road, 20, 192, 208
silkworm goddess (can shen), 62
silkworm mothers (can mu), 62
Silla, 198–99, 302n17
Sima Chengzhen, 183, 296n30
Sima Guang, 32, 105, 170, 188–89, 219
Sima Qian, 79, 103–4, 110, 111
Sima Xiangru, 154
Sima Zhen, 32–33
sisters, 86, 274n38
six forms of proper conduct, 273n10
Six Matrons (liu shang), 63
Sixth Master. See Zhang Changzong
sky-mending, 28–31, 40–41
slave, 219
smothering, 75
solar crow, 155, 156, 289n49
solar disk, 154
Song dynasty, 137
"Song for the Fifth Day of the Eighth
    Month" (Gu Kuang), 207
Songyang Monastery, 86
Song Yingxing, 131–32
Song Zhiwen, 73

sons, 75, 76, 80–81, 127–28
Soper, Alexander, 206
Southern Marchmount, 295n5
Southland, 122, 123
sovereignty, 34–37, 201, 222–23, 308n58.
    See also cakravartin
"Speech at Mu" (in Book of History),
    249n11
spells. See Great Spell of Unsullied Pure
    Radiance
Spirit of Lesser Room, 86–87
spouse, 81–83
Śrīmālā (queen), 194
Star Ford Bridge, 49
state, 126, 128–29, 142–43, 282n21
statecraft. See weaving-government
    analogy
state cultic sacrifices, 172
statue, 174, 224–25
"Stele Inscription for Little Auntie
    Temple of the Lesser Room" (Yang
    Jiong), 56–57
steles, 55, 86, 87–90, 92, 121–23, 181; at
    Mount Goushi, 160; on turtles, 297n52
steppe cultures, 234
stones, 79–80, 141–42, 204, 214, 263n27,
    272n3. See also Precious Diagram
stone tortoises, 297n52
Stony Torrents, 164, 165, 166
"Stony Torrents." See "Shizong"
stupa pillar, 197
stūpas. See Buddhist relics
Su Anheng, 41, 42
"Successes of Wu" ("Wucheng" in Book
    of History), 146
Śuddhodana, 195, 199
Sudhana, 197
suicide, 75
Suiren, 35
Sui Wendi, 14–15, 265n56
Sui Yangdi, 47, 107, 182, 299n1, 310n11
sun, 155–56
sunbird (yang niao), 154, 155, 288n47,
    289nn49–50
Supreme Thearch of Boundless Heaven,
    49–50. See also Haotian shangdi

Su Ting, 135, 284n49
Sutra of Attestation (Zhengming jing),
    222–23, 309n67
Sutra of Great Māyā, 197–98
Sutra of Primal Causes (Benyin jing), 222
Sutra of the Lion's Roar of Queen Śrīmālā,
    301n29
Sutra of the Rain of Jewels (Baoyu jing),
    204, 219–21, 223
Sutra on the Collection of the Buddha's
    Original Practices, 205
sutras, 197–98, 301n30
Su Weidao, 52

"Table of Persons Ancient and Modern"
    (in History of the Han Dynasty), 95
Taijiang, 109
Taiping Princess, 73–74, 84, 146
Taiqing Palace, 176–77
Tairen, 78, 109, 111, 113
Taishang. See Laozi
Taisi. See Mother Wen
Taiwu, 13
Taizong (Tang emperor), 2, 7–9, 169, 170,
    250n34, 296n20, 306n18; on Nüwa,
    35; self-fashioning of, 235; Seondok
    contacting, 199
Tambiah, Stanley, 13
Tang (dynasty), 121, 163–64, 231;
    Buddhism influencing, 193; court,
    169; Daoism, 169–70; dynasty, 6–7,
    28, 127, 137, 176; emperor, 12–13;
    imperial family, 40; mirror, 153;
    mothers, 128–29; poets, 151
Tang (Shang king), 272n12
Tang Administrative and Legal Compendium
    of the Six Ministries (Tang liudian), 202
Tang Lingze, 306n18
"Tangtang" (song), 306n18
Tang the Successful, 277n16. See also
    Cheng Tang
Tang Tongtai, 49
Tanjing, 197–98
Tanling, 202
Tao Hongjing, 180
Tathāgata, 13–14, 211

teeth, 289n56
Temple of Mysterious Origin, 176–77
Temple of the Ascended Immortal
Prince, 160
Temple of Western Light (Ximing si),
200
Temple of Worship of the Immortals
(Fengxian guan), 174
temples, 86, 169, 197, 293n21; ancestral,
100–102, 104, 107–8, 278n39, 280n39;
sacrifice, 172
Ten Thousand Years Peak (Wansui feng),
79, 80
textiles. See weaving
texts, 56–57, 124–25, 307n33
textual amplification, 202–5
Three Consorts, 63
Three Dukes, 63
Three Dynasties, 17–18
three faiths, 4–5, 13–15, 228–29. See also
political ancestors
three-legged bird, 155, 288n47,
289nn49–50
three mothers, 112–13
Three Mothers of Zhou, 110, 111. See also
Taijiang, Tairen, Taisi
Three Solitaries (sangu), 269n25
Three Sovereigns (Sanhuang), 34–36
Tiancheng Weft of the Jade Plan of the Lady
Ziwei, 211
Tibetans, 137
timelessness, 156–57
toad, 154, 155
tokens, 152, 155
tomb (mu), 28, 92, 117, 121, 197
tonsure, 91, 212
topography, 51, 86, 93
Tortoise Mountain (Guishan). See
Mount Kunlun
tortoises, 297n52
tower, 70, 223, 285n74
tradition, 3, 10, 122
treasures of state, 152
"Treatise of Music" (in Old Tang History)
31–32
Treatise of the Vast Earth, 87, 274n42

"Treatise on Rites and Ceremonies" (in
Old Tang History), 90–91
"Treatise on Rites and Music" (in New
Tang History), 63
"Treatise on the Five Phases" (in New
Tang History), 183–84
"Tripod-Dragging Anthem" (Wu Zhao),
201–2
tripods, political authority buttressed
by, 300n24. See also Nine Tripods
Tumulus of Nüwa, 28
Turner, Victor, 1
turtles, 297n52
Tushan, 83. See also Woman of Tushan
Tushan, Woman of, 18, 77, 79–86, 80,
87–90, 114, 227–8, 272n1; overview
of, 93–94; stone of, 79–80, 272n3. See
also Shaoyi
Tushan sisters, Daoist elevation of,
90–92
Twitchett, Denis, 7, 126, 137, 140, 280n2,
281n12, 282n26
Two Sages (Ersheng), 115–16,
170–72, 177, 188, 211, 275n70;
Buddha prayed to by, 199–200;
Daoist establishment supported
by, 180–81; elephants presented
to, 200; Luoyang appended to
by, 182; as nickname, 265n56;
sacrifice influencing, 158; temples
refurbished by, 206. See also feng and
shan rites; Precious Diagram

Unicorn's Hoof Temple (Linzhi si), 219,
308n49

Vairocana, 221, 224–25, 226
vanity industry, 231
Vega, 73
Verellen, Franciscus, 13
"Verse of Immortal Cranes" (Wu Sansi),
161
Vimalakirti Sutra, 221
Vimalaprabhā. See Jingguang
virtue ethics, 95–96
vitality, 276n9

wandering bard, 218
Wang (Tang empress), 106–7
Wang, Eugene, 154, 157
Wang, Robin, 134
Wang Aihe, 5, 6, 12
Wang Bao, 182
Wang Ji, 109
Wang Jian, 290n69
Wang Mang, 60
Wang Shuanghuai, 193
Wang Wanche, 106–7
Wang Xuanhe, 180–81
Wang Yi, 25–26
Wang Zijin, 290n69
water, women as, 17
watermill, 183–84
Weaver Maiden, 288n42
weaving, as womanhood, 61–62
weaving-government analogy, 130–36,
    131, 134, 234–35
Weaving Maid, 73
Wechsler, Howard, 6–7, 12, 264n44
Wei (family), 184
Wei (Tang empress), 69–70, 73–74, 166
Wei (lady). See Wei Huacun
Wei Daijia, 273n21
Wei dynasty, 78
Wei Huacun, 19, 158–59, 179–90, 237,
    290n66
Weinstein, Stanley, 193, 264n48
Wei Shuxia, 270n54
Welch, Michael, 215
Wen (king), 11, 103, 111, 277n24, 278n8;
    capital established by, 8; titular
    elevation to emperor, 121; in Two
    Sages, 265n56. See also come-as-sons
    idea; Taisi; Wu princeling
Wen, Mother. See Mother Wen
Wenbo, 78, 130–36, 131, 134, 282n28
Wencheng (Wei emperor), 13–14
Wenmu. See Mother Wen
Wenxiang County, 173–74
Wen Yucheng, 225
wet nurse, 84, 273n22
white elephants, 198, 199, 200–205,
    304n40

White Elephant Ward, 198
White Emperor, 89
white jade, 152
widow, 129, 136, 283n42
widowhood, 128–29
"Wife of Yidu," 37–38, 261n68
wine vat, 107
wives, 86, 113, 180, 261n69
womanhood, 61–62, 110–15, 234–35
womb, 86
women, 229–31, 232, 234–35, 272n12,
    272n15, 284n48; Buddhism's
    limitations for, 192–93; Confucianism
    influencing, 75–76; Daoists elevating,
    90–92; as emperor, 1–5, 4; as
    extraordinary, 115; four virtues of,
    268n14; as minister, 109, 118–20;
    proto-feminist agenda for, 270n46;
    texts for, 124–25; as water, 17. See
    also Biographies of Exemplary Women;
    motherhood; mothers
work (gong), 268n14
Wounds Not Healed By Time (Schimmel), 1
Wu (Liu Song emperor), 102, 114
Wu (Northern Zhou emperor), 13
Wu (Southern Qi emperor), 82, 102
Wu (Zhou king), 103–4, 109, 110, 111,
    111, 118,119, 121, 146, 265n52; birth
    of, 278n8; rule of, 146; place among
    political ancestors, 11, 29–30, 36, 58,
    103, 248n8; and Yellow River Chart,
    50; and Two Sages, 265n56
Wucheng (emperor), 304n62
Wu Chengsi, 49, 200
Wu clan, 277n24, 280n39
Wu Ding (Shang king), 41, 262n76
wu feng guan. See crown
Wugong, 8
Wu Hung, 45, 151
wujin cang. See inexhaustible storehouse
Wu Liang shrine, 152–53
Wu princeling (in Zhou, King Ping's
    youngest son), 103, 120–21
Wu Sansi, 122–23, 161, 164, 291n83;
    and inscription composed for
    grandmother Madame Yang, 71

Wu Shiyue, 38, 121–22, 204
Wu Tse-t'ien. *See* Wu Zetian
wuxing. See Five Phases
Wu Yuanchong, 173–74, 294n36
Wu Zetian, 38–39, *39*, 193, 210, 247n1,
    291n88
Wu Zetian (Zheng Zhenduo), *4*
wuzhang. See Five Impediments
Wu Zhao, *39*, *232*; birth of, 38, 39;
    name of, 217, 307n41; overview of,
    1–22; retirement of, 41–42. *See also*
    Biographies of Exemplary Women;
    Biographies of Filial Daughters;
    Regulations for Ministers; texts; Two
    Sages; Wu Zetian; Zetian

Xia, 17–18, 47, 78, 81, 84, 272n7; and
    Woman of Tushan, 81, 82, 83. *See
    also* Yu the Great
xian bi. See ancestress
xian can. See First Sericulturist
xiannong tan. See First Agriculturalist
    altar
xian sheng. See Foremost Sage
xiao. See filial piety
Xiao Deyan, 274
Xiao Kuang, 46
Xia Tower, 84
Xie, 34, 83, 96, 273n16
Xiling, 63, 122–23. *See also* Leizu
Xiong, Victor, 176–77, 270n38
Xiongnu, 260n42
Xiuwu, 296n20
Xuan (Wei empress), 78
Xuanzong (emperor), 28, 55, 84, 85, 183,
    187, 202, 207–8; Buddhism restricted
    by, 305n74; Laozi worshipped by,
    294n49; ritual innovation of, 176–77.
    See also Li Longji
Xue Huaiyi, 209–26, *216*, 219, 289n61,
    309n68. *See also Commentary on the
    Meanings of the Prophecies About the
    Divine Sovereign in the Great Cloud Sutra*
Xu Lishi, 170–71, 293n22
Xu Ning, 46
Xunyu, 260n42

Xunzi, 149
Xu Shao, 293n22
Xu You, 295n17

Yan Chaoyin, 290n76
Yang, 84, 191, 274n24
Yang (Jin empress), 81, 102, 113
Yang (Madame), 71, 122–23, 271n56
Yang, C. K., 5
Yangdi, 275n51
Yang Jian, 205
Yang Jiong, 56–57, 83–84, 86–87, 90, 135,
    218–19
Yang Lien-sheng, 34, 233
yang niao. See sunbird
Yang Xi, 180
Yan Shangwen, 252n69
Yan Shigu, 50, 79, 87
Yan Zhenqing, 185–86, 188
Yao (one of Five Emperors), 99, 261n71
Yao Chong, 164–65, 292n95
Yao Shu, 297n52
Ye Fashan, 187
Yellow Emperor, 26, 39, 53, 60–61, 183,
    296n29
Yellow Path Bridge, 49
Yellow River, 29
Yellow River Chart, 50, 87, 265n52. *See
    also* River Chart
yi. See regulator
yiguizhe. See ghostbuster
Yijing, 203–5
Yin, 78, 114. *See also* Shang (dynasty)
Yingfu. *See* Li (mother)
Ying Shao, 16, 35
Yin Wencao, 181
Yin Xi, 198
Yi River, 158
Yishi, 205–6
Yi the Archer, 150
Yitong, 267n90
Yixing, 265n57
yize. See pitch pipes
Yoshiko Kamitsuka, 184
Youfang, 89, 275n52
Youshen, 272n12, 280n33

Yu the Great, 78, 113, 272n11
yuan fu. See original forefather
Yuan Shuji, 277n37
Yuanze, 199
Yü Chün-fang, 300n11
Yudizhi, 88
Yueguang, 308n54
yuezhuo. See phoenix
Yu the Great, 2, 6, 7, 50, 55, 77, 79, *80*,
    111–12, 272n1, 272n7; Luo River
    Writing revealed to, 53; Spirit of
    Lesser Room connected to, 86–87
Yuwen, 11
Yuwen Tai, 6
Yuwen Yu, 6

Zanning, 215
Zeng Qian, 225
Zengzhang, 210, 220. *See also* Jingguang
Zetian, 90–91
Zetian Gate, 48
Zhang (Tang empress), 270n38
Zhang Changling, 291n88
Zhang Changning, 276n72
Zhang Changzong, 157–66, 160–61, *162*,
    276n72, 291n84, 291n88
Zhang Jianzhi, 277n37
Zhang Mingxue, 45
Zhangsun (Tang empress), 65, 83, 116,
    117–18
Zhang Yizhi, 160–61, 165, 276n72,
    291n81, 291n83
Zhang Yue, 135
Zhan Qian, 60
Zhao (Wei empress), 78
Zhao Fengjie, 1
Zhao Kuo. *See* Kuo of Zhao
Zhao Wenrun, 193, 259n36
Zhao Yanzhao, 166
Zhen (Cao Wei empress), 44, 100–102,
    278n39

Zheng Xuan, 120
Zheng Yin, 73
Zheng Zhenduo, *4*
Zhenyuan County, 170, 171, 293n21
Zhenzong, 293n25
zhi fungus, 85–86. *See also* mushroom
Zhixian, 205
zhong. See loyalty
zhonglü. See pitch pipes
Zhongzong (Tang emperor), 40–41,
    127–28, 166, 176, 270n54, 277n37; five
    princes helping, 107; removal of, 31
Zhou (Shang king), 167
Zhou Book of Rites, 62, 277n16
Zhou dynasty (of antiquity), 17–18, 41,
    77, 96–100, 107–8, 113, 228, 277n24;
    idealization of, 18–20, 110–12
Zhou dynasty (of Wu Zhao, 690–705), 3,
    20, 37, 58. 84, 163, 178; and Buddhist
    propaganda, 204, 214; and Daoism
    186, 189; end of, 107; inauguration of,
    10, 36–37, 48, 58, 92, 148, 229; linked
    to Zhou of antiquity, 18, 31, 102–5,
    120–23, 124, 173
"Zhou yu" (in *Narrative of States*), 287n37
Zhuangzi, 149
Zhuanxu, 275n52
Zhu Fonian, 305n3
zhu pusa mu. See Buddhas-to-be
Zhu Zizhu, 35
Zifa of Chu (general). *See* mother of Zifa
    of Chu
Zijin. *See* Prince Jin
zi lai idea. *See* come-as-sons idea
Ziqiao (crown prince), 103. *See also*
    Prince Jin
Zi Si, 133
Ziwei (lady), 211
*Zizhi tongjian. See Comprehensive Mirror
    for the Advancement of Governance*
Zürcher, Erik, 14